FAILED AMBITIONS

FAILED AMBITIONS
KEW COTTAGES AND CHANGING IDEAS OF INTELLECTUAL DISABILITIES

LEE-ANN MONK AND DAVID HENDERSON
WITH CHRISTINE BIGBY, RICHARD BROOME AND KATIE HOLMES

Published by Monash University Publishing
Matheson Library Annexe
40 Exhibition Walk
Monash University
Clayton, Victoria 3800, Australia
publishing.monash.edu/

Monash University Publishing: the discussion starts here

© Copyright 2023 Lee-Ann Monk, David Henderson, Christine Bigby, Richard Broome and Katie Holmes
Lee-Ann Monk, David Henderson, Christine Bigby, Richard Broome and Katie Holmes assert their right to be known as the authors of this work.

All rights reserved. Apart from any uses permitted by Australia's *Copyright Act 1968*, no part of this book may be reproduced by any process without prior written permission from the copyright owners. Enquiries should be directed to the publisher.

Failed Ambitions: Kew Cottages and Changing Ideas of Intellectual Disabilities

ISBN: 9781922633781 (paperback)
ISBN: 9781922633798 (pdf)
ISBN: 9781922633804 (epub)

 A catalogue record for this book is available from the National Library of Australia

Design: Les Thomas
Typesetting: Jo Mullins
Cover photographs: Top: 'Working Girls', *c.* late 1960s. Photographer unknown; courtesy Kew Cottages Historical Society Collection. Bottom: The Cottages, *c.* 1900, with the Asylum in the background. Nicholas Caire, photographer; courtesy Wellcome Collection, Public Domain Mark.

Printed in Australia by Griffin Press

Contents

Foreword by Ronald Sackville vii

Introduction xiii

Part One: Unfulfilled Promise

1   In the 'City of the Insane' (1867–87) 3

2   'Always a Curious Boy' (1887–1908) 19

3   'For the Care and Training of Feeble-minded Children'
(1887–1907) 34

4   'Mental Defectives: A Serious Social Problem' (1907–24) 56

5   'A New Deal for Mental Defectives' (1924–39) 86

6   'A Hillside of Sadness' (1939–50) 113

Part Two: A Passion for Reform

7   Eric Cunningham Dax and the Reform of the
Kew Children's Cottages (1951–60) 133

8   The Tipping Campaign and Public Support (1961–65) 155

9   The Kew Cottages Parents' Association (1958–70) 180

10 Normalisation Emerges (from 1970) 204

11 A Disastrous Fire (1996) 230

12 Deinstitutionalisation (1985–2008) 251

Epilogue: Connecting Past and Present 278

Appendix of Institutions in Victoria for those with
    Intellectual Disabilities 287

Acknowledgments 289

Project Outcomes (2006–23) 292

Notes 297

Select Bibliography 336

Index 345

About the Authors 359

Foreword

When Professor Christine Bigby kindly invited me to write the Foreword to *Failed Ambitions: Kew Cottages and Changing Ideas of Intellectual Disabilities*, I accepted the invitation despite at that stage not having read the book. I had four reasons for happily accepting the invitation.

First, the Royal Commission into Violence, Abuse, Neglect and Exploitation of People with Disability, which I chair, had the very great benefit of Professor Bigby's evidence at an important early public hearing on 'The Experience of Living in a Group Home for People with Disability'.[1] Professor Bigby's statement and oral evidence prompted me to read some—admittedly a small portion—of her extraordinarily impressive and influential body of scholarly work examining the quality of support in group homes and the measures needed to improve the lives of residents of those homes. I therefore had every reason to think that a project overseen by Professor Bigby (in this case with Professors Richard Broome and Katie Holmes) and written primarily by Dr Lee-Ann Monk and Dr David Henderson would be of very high quality.

Second, I gathered from the title of the volume that it would trace the chequered history of an important Victorian institution (in both senses) that affected the lives of so many children with intellectual disabilities for over 135 years. Growing up in Melbourne, I was familiar with the name 'Kew Cottages'. Like most people at that time, I imagined the institution, located not very far from where I lived, to be a 'Hillside of Sadness',[2] occupied by very unfortunate children destined to be confined to an institution for a very long time, if not forever. It was a place to be avoided. I was even aware of Dr Eric Cunningham Dax, a central figure in *Failed Ambition*'s narrative. My recollection is that Dr Dax seemed to relish his role as a prominent and occasionally controversial public figure in the fairly insular world of 1950s Melbourne.

vii

Third, the title of the volume also suggested that, although this was a study of one particular institution, it would shed light on the broader changes in our understanding of intellectual disability since Kew Cottages was established in the late nineteenth century. As *Failed Ambitions* points out in the Epilogue:

> Public policy's perception of people with intellectual disabilities changed dramatically over the course of Kew Cottages' history. Attitudes cycled through regarding people with intellectual disabilities as: objects of pity in need of care; people who might contribute to society if only they were trained well; a menace to be feared from whom society should be protected; a vulnerable group in need of care; and, finally, equal citizens with rights to inclusion.

As we approach the end of the first quarter of the twenty-first century, we are experiencing the early stages of fundamental changes in community attitudes towards people with disability, particularly people with intellectual disability. Yet in many ways the long shadow of entrenched prejudice and fear towards people with intellectual disability remains with us.

The fourth reason is personal. For the first four decades or so of my life, my sister and I believed that our mother had only one sibling, an older brother. More or less by accident we discovered that our mother in fact had two siblings. The second was an older sister, Suzie, who had been placed in an institution in her late teens following what appears to have been a serious mental illness. My mother and grandmother never spoke to us of Suzie, although we now know they visited her. By the time my sister and I learned of Suzie's existence she had died, never having left the institution. Suzie had been laid to rest without a headstone marking her grave. Years after her death this very small acknowledgment of her life was erected. I thought it was very likely that Suzie's story would be mirrored in the experiences of generations of children placed by parents, families or the state in Kew Cottages. Those children deserve to be remembered.

FOREWORD

The expectations aroused by Professor Bigby's invitation were more than fulfilled when I read *Failed Ambitions*. This is a meticulously researched, clear-eyed and profoundly humane study, made more compelling by the judicious use of contemporaneous photographs. The authors lay bare the egregious errors of the past—many of which had dreadful consequences for the children confined within Kew Cottages. Yet the authors are wise enough to acknowledge the good intentions of many people responsible for creating and operating the institution, even if those intentions were often not realised.

Failed Ambitions can be seen as an example of microhistory, in the sense that it examines the history of a single institution central to the lives of generations of children with disability. Elisabeth Bredberg has explained the value of microhistory in disability studies:

> microhistory, by drawing on small, closely prescribed detail, can produce a much more personalised historical narrative than the no less important overview. In so doing it can begin to represent the activity of disabled people in history rather than institutional attempts to solve social problems ... [T]he restricted scale and precisely identified location in time and place of microhistory can serve as a foil for the over-generalisation and anachronism that has pervaded so much of disability history to date.[3]

One lesson from the history of Kew Cottages is that societal attitudes do not necessarily progress towards enlightenment in a linear fashion. We know from the lamentable history of the first half of the twentieth century (and, for that matter, the first quarter of the twenty-first century) that the Whig or progressive version of history is deeply flawed. But it is tempting to think that contemporary attitudes and beliefs concerning social issues must always be more enlightened than the attitudes and beliefs of earlier generations. For example, Chapter 3 ('For the Care and Training of Feeble-minded Children' 1887–1907) shows that in the early days of Kew Cottages the staff, under the leadership of Dr James McCreery,

ix

made strenuous efforts to maximise the potential of the children through education, industrial training and physical exercise. These endeavours may have been of limited value from the perspective of the social model of disability or a human rights framework. But it is undeniable that the designers of the educational and training programs aspired to achieve a better quality of life for the children resident in the institutions.

By way of contrast, Chapters 4 and 5 detail the descent of Kew Cottages in the early twentieth century, as training dwindled into 'practical nothingness' and the residents were 'disgracefully neglected'. The descent reflected widespread (but not universal) social attitudes that the 'feeble minded' were productive of crime and misery. Since the 'mental defectives' constituted an evil in the midst of the community, the children in Kew Cottages were to be segregated and, according to some, subjected to eugenic controls.[4] The supporters of eugenics in Australia did not achieve the success of their counterparts in the United States, but the extreme hostility exhibited towards children with intellectual disability, documented in *Failed Ambitions*, represented a retreat into the depths of fear and prejudice.

It is undoubtedly true, as the authors point out, that public policies relating to people with disability are now generally influenced by human rights principles, particularly those articulated in the United Nations *Convention on the Rights of Persons with Disabilities*. But societal attitudes are always a work in progress and can regress. Care must also be taken to ensure that reforms do not have unintended consequences that can work against the interests of people with disability. For example, while *Failed Ambitions* suggests that deinstitutionalisation in Victoria seems generally to have been successful, that has not been the universal experience in Australia.

The introduction to *Failed Ambitions* makes a further point about the importance of engaging the disabled in telling their own stories, explaining that recent histories of disability 'seek to redress previous omission of the intellectually disabled from their own history as a result of their voiceless-ness and consequent disempowerment'. The authors of *Failed Ambitions* have thus diligently sought to bring to light the stories and experiences of the children institutionalised in Kew Cottages. It is very sad that the absence of records has precluded the possibility of more of their stories being told in their own words. But the accounts that are included in *Failed Ambitions* honour not only the children who can be identified, but the other voiceless and disempowered children who shared their experiences.

Failed Ambitions provides insights into many other issues through the authors' careful examination of institutional practices, personal experiences and community attitudes. We read, for example, of: the anguish of parents forced to yield care of their children to an institution; the persistent advocacy of parents on behalf of their children, including by some parents who vigorously resisted the closure of Kew Cottages in the first decade of the twentieth century;[5] the efforts of determined reformers to influence policies towards children with intellectual disability; the equally determined resistance of community groups and their elected representatives to reforms; and the role frequently played by the media in pre-internet days in exposing institutional cruelty and neglect inflicted on children with intellectual disability and in demanding reforms.

Understanding the history of Kew Cottages is important because this institution shaped and circumscribed the lives of thousands of Victorian children with intellectual disability. But the authors have also produced a study of significance that transcends the particular circumstances of a single institution. It is an outstanding example of microhistory.

Ronald Sackville AO KC

Introduction

The creation of the National Disability Insurance Scheme (NDIS) by the Gillard government in 2012 provided a 'transformational' change in disability services that cracked the mould of past practices. When introducing the new ground-breaking legislation, Julia Gillard declared: 'Rather than attempt to patch and mend the existing system through further incremental change, we will build a new system from the ground up'.[1] This book explores the history of Kew Cottages, Australia's first purpose-built institution for people with intellectual disabilities, in the era of patching and mending. The stories told within this history do not always make for easy reading, although some are uplifting and hopeful. But grim or not, they must be told.

The establishment of Kew Cottages in 1887, was a pivotal moment in the history of intellectual disability in Australia. It was the first significant acknowledgment by government of responsibility for the care of people with intellectual disabilities. Following overseas models of care, it challenged the prevailing view that intellectual disability was an incurable malady beyond any hope of amelioration. Kew Cottages offered residential care, but also education, in an idyllic setting on the Yarra River, about eight kilometres from central Melbourne.

The cottages were established in a rural setting in the grounds of the existing Kew Asylum, and this choice of site became crucial in their history. Suburban development soon surrounded the institution, triggering opposition from some Kew citizens. They were backed by the Kew Council, which received no rates from this large area of state government land. The government succumbed to pressure and deemed the cottages temporary, a decision that underpinned their continued underfunding. However, their prime suburban location kept Kew Cottages in the sight and awareness of Melburnians. And they never housed a closed community because family, official visitors, benefactors, tradesmen and others came and went.

More importantly, journalists also came from time to time, sometimes at the invitation of officials keen to show progress. But, when conditions lagged, they were quick to publicise the problems and thus alert the public.

Within a few years of the cottages' creation, some visitors praised their facilities as the most progressive of their kind in Australia. But in subsequent decades hope faded, to be replaced by pessimism, fear and government neglect; a brief burst of optimism in the 1950s seemed to promise renewal, but hope soon withered again. By the time the institution closed in 2008, it was considered a relic of a time when many people with intellectual disabilities were locked away, neither seen nor heard, and excluded from participating in society.

This book traces the history of Australia's oldest institution for people with intellectual disabilities from its establishment in 1887 to its closure in 2008. It reveals the larger story of how a society manages (or mismanages) human difference, and cares for (or ignores) its least powerful and most marginalised members. By locating Kew Cottages in wider social, cultural and policy contexts, it reveals how shifting attitudes and policies towards intellectual disability shaped the lives of the cottages' residents. These contexts extend to changes in international thinking about intellectual disability, often carried to Australia and Kew Cottages by a succession of medical staff hired from the United Kingdom to work in Victoria. This approach enables us to trace the ways the Australian disability service system has, over more than a century, perceived, accommodated and responded to people with intellectual disabilities.

Kew Cottages was part of a system that developed institutions as solutions to a range of social problems, including mental illness and intellectual disability. This institutional approach persisted for over a century during which the number of such institutions increased. Initially referred to as asylums, over time their names changed to reflect changing/newer understandings about how mental illness and intellectual disabilities should be treated. For instance, Kew Cottages began as the Kew Idiot Asylum, then became the Kew Children's Cottages, Kew Cottages, Kew Cottages

INTRODUCTION

Training Centre and finally, Kew Residential Services. The resulting plethora of institutions and name changes are outlined in the Appendix.

Despite growing awareness among policy makers and professionals in the field, historians' understandings of disability, and specifically intellectual disabilities in Australia, have lagged. The first moves to write the history of intellectual disability before the mid-1970s were made by educators, medical professionals and policy makers. They largely wrote in a 'progressivist' framework, focusing on the evolution of ideas about intellectual disability and the 'pioneers' in its treatment.[2] Understandably, these writers conceptualised intellectual disabilities within a medical model and overlooked the lived experience of people with intellectual disabilities.

By the 1980s, historians had moved beyond the medical model, arguing that it failed to acknowledge or adequately explain the social and cultural marginalisation of so many people with disabilities. Inspired by the change of mindset fostered by the civil rights era in the United States, these historians explored the lives of people with disabilities and the factors that shaped the social meanings of disability. For them, disability was a social construction, meaning disability was less about physical or mental impairment than about how society responds to such impairment.[3]

Some historians realised the absence of people with disabilities from history reflected their marginalisation and disempowerment within the larger society. This instigated a second-wave disability history that focused on the myriad patterns of abuse, discrimination and oppression that had silenced the victims and rendered them invisible in earlier accounts. This new generation of historians began to produce nuanced cultural and social analyses concerned with unravelling the origins and complex nature of institutional care.

Our history builds on this body of work about institutional care, exploring the trajectory of ideas, both global and local, that underpinned the history of Kew Cottages. These ideas range across the humanitarian impulse behind its opening, the eugenic assumptions that underpinned its darkest days, the thinking about normalisation and human rights that shaped its reform, and the neo-liberal push for deinstitutionalisation that drove the cottages' closure.

A third wave of histories of disability seeks to redress previous omission of the intellectually disabled from their own history as a result of their voicelessness and consequent disempowerment. Historians in this third wave stress the cultures, values, and activism of people with disabilities. At the heart of this new wave of research is a focus on the agency of people with intellectual disabilities, which has produced histories of the self-advocacy movement, of disability activism, and of people with intellectual disabilities who resisted the definitions and 'cures' imposed on them.[4]

This focus on agency has also led to important methodological innovations and the increasing inclusion of people with intellectual disabilities in the research process.[5] Because this approach took hold faster internationally than in Australia, the voices of people with intellectual disabilities have remained sparse in our recent histories of intellectual disability. However, new research is encouraging such voices to rupture the long silence.[6]

This history is one of many outcomes from an Australian Research Council (ARC) funded project (2005–08) between La Trobe University and Kew Residential Services—formerly Kew Cottages (see the appendix 'Project Outcomes'). Also among the outcomes were several short films featuring the artworks of people from Kew Cottages. Most prominently, their voices were captured in Corinne Manning's *Bye Bye Charlie: Stories from the Vanishing World of Kew Cottages* (2008). For her oral history, Corinne Manning conducted more than twenty interviews with former residents of the cottages, in order to 'give voice to some of Australia's most silenced and forgotten people'.[7] Following on from this ARC-funded project, David Henderson and Christine Bigby have used inclusive methods of research to explore the history of Reinforce, the oldest self-advocacy organisation for people with intellectual disabilities in Victoria.[8]

This book, wherever possible, attempts to give voice to the experiences of residents. However, the archival basis of this history stretching back to 1887, which is its strength in telling this long story in its political and institutional context, nevertheless obscures the experiences of residents.

INTRODUCTION

This is to a large extent unavoidable because their voices were generally ignored by the medical men who dominated Kew Cottages' institutional structure and produced the archive. Almost no first-person accounts of life in Kew Cottages survive. In this context, the experiences of the institution's residents can only be approached through the observations and reportage of others, whether visitors to the institution or the officers responsible for their management.

A brief consideration of the cottages' surviving patient case histories, created and maintained by medical men, reveals the difficulties of approaching patients' subjective experiences through such mediated sources.[9] The law required the institution's medical officers to create and maintain a case history for every patient admitted to the institution.[10] As a result, case histories form the most extensive source in the archive of Kew Cottages. However, as with case histories more generally, the content of those from the cottages reflects the purposes and preoccupations of their authors, tending to be long on accounts of the treatment of physical illness, for example.[11] In contrast, they rarely record the direct speech of patients and seldom their actions for us to read and analyse for meaning. Moreover, patient case histories privilege 'episodes of behaviour which staff found disruptive', such as escapes or instances of self-harm, but often without providing the context that might allow deeper understanding of these 'disruptive' actions.[12] Doctors' assumptions about their 'patients', and about mental disorders, shaped their recorded explanations about why the 'objects' of their gaze behaved as they did.[13]

There are further silences in the records. While other institutions' histories and accounts from survivors confirm that abuse was commonplace, remaining sources from Kew say almost nothing about the abuse of cottage residents. Yet, given how marginalised and powerless these people were, it is almost certain to have occurred. While we can argue that the very system that managed and controlled people with intellectual disabilities, and which often lapsed into indifference and neglect, was a form of abuse, we also occasionally glimpse some evidence of deliberate and overt cruelty. But, in general, the case files throw little light on patient abuse or its extent, for doctors may have been blind to it, and even if they did have their suspicions it was not in their interests to highlight such behaviour.

The cottages' archive also provides very little information about other important aspects of the lives of those incarcerated for their intellectual disabilities. The day-to-day lives of patients are rarely recorded, and much remains opaque to us about their experiences, both particular and overall. Perhaps most tragic of all is the fact that, in writing this history, we have had to obscure even the names of patients by pseudonyms for those who appear in the records after 1912. Their very identities have thus been erased, not by us but by the demands of modern privacy law. People obscured and ignored by history are forced further into the shadows by historians not being able to voice or write their names. However, careful analysis of case notes can provide some glimpses of how residents, 'patients' as they were called back then, experienced their institutionalisation.[14]

To write about people of the past with intellectual disabilities is akin to trying to gain impressions of peopling walking past on a dark night. So often our knowledge remains shadowy glimpses. Fortunately, annual reports, royal commissions, journalists' investigations, oral histories and disparate other sources record at least something of the residents' material lives. Indeed, articles written by journalists were often vital to the public's knowledge of conditions at Kew Cottages and are important sources for historians as well. And photographs sometimes bring us a little closer to understanding the experiences of those at Kew Cottages.

Records from the cottages, created, shaped and controlled by medical men, tell us very little about the other people who were important in the lives of residents: their families and the staff who managed/cared for them. Again, we have unearthed other records and recorded oral histories that reveal something of their role and influence in the lives of residents. Parents, for instance, became a force in the politics of intellectual disability after the 1940s.

Without an archives-based history of Kew Cottages, however, we cannot know the shifts in policy and ideas, the hopes and failures of governments, and the budgetary problems and other contexts that shaped the changing fortunes of Kew Cottages' residents and their families. Along the way we have attempted where possible to give the residents and their families voice, to discover *their* experience, and to recognise *their* agency, constrained as it might have been. In this way, we join the challenge to lift the silence history has imposed on them.[15] This approach acknowledges that residents (not 'patients') were people with thoughts and feelings about their lives under confinement, and attempts to glimpse a range of experiences now mostly lost to us. Our attempt validates their humanity.[16]

For this reason, too, we use 'people-first language' in this book.[17] Much of the language used in the past to refer to what we now call 'intellectual disabilities' is grossly offensive and indeed uncomfortable even to read. Given the hurt it can cause, the question of whether to use it at all in a historical work is a difficult one for historians to answer easily.

There are, however, important reasons to use such language, though only in the right manner and context. Ideas about what constituted a lack of intellectual capacity have changed over time, shaped by their social, cultural, political and economic contexts. These shifting definitions expanded and contracted to include different people at different stages of our history. Consequently, people now considered to have intellectually disabilities may not have been so labelled in the past, and *vice versa*.[18] The contingent nature of 'intellectual disability' this suggests is reflected in the many different names used to refer to differences in intellectual capacity over time. The shifting language also reflects the changing understandings of, and attitudes to, such differences and the people to whom they were applied. Histories need to track these shifting meanings, for this process reveals the social construction of intellectual disability over time. Historian James Trent argues that, while they are offensive, older terms such as 'idiocy' or 'mental deficiency' make manifest the various meanings attached to such differences. For that reason, their use has purpose.[19]

We have, however, tried to steer a middle way between the terms of the past and those of the present. In Part One, that is before 1950, we have often used 'patients' to remind our readers of the dominance of the medical model of intellectual disabilities in that era. Yet, we have also used 'residents' at times in Part One to remind us also of the common humanity we all share with people with intellectual disabilities. Throughout the book, when quoting directly from historical documents, we have maintained the language of the day, but *only* within quotation marks. These small punctuation signifiers are designed to show we do not share the ideas that underpin these outdated terms. In this way, readers are alerted to what people in the past thought, why they acted as they did, and how far our attitudes have shifted over time. However, we share our disdain for these terms and the values they connote through inverted commas.

So, with theses exceptions, we use 'people-first language' to focus on the person, rather than the perceived disability, as the primary subject.[20] With this in mind, together with the limitations as well as the new approaches set out above, we invite you to explore this history of intellectual disability at Kew Cottages, and to reflect on the changing ideas that shaped this and other similar institutions. Such grim truth-telling and reflection will make for a more compassionate and inclusive Australia.

PART ONE

UNFULFILLED PROMISE

Chapter 1

In the 'City of the Insane' (1867–87)

On a spring morning in 1868, some four kilometres from Melbourne, an anonymous journalist took the turn from the Heidelberg road that led to Yarra Bend Lunatic Asylum. Once through the white gates marking the institution's entrance, he found himself in a veritable 'city of the insane', home to more than eight hundred patients (Figure 1.1). Situated on the Yarra River, it was, he thought, a 'pretty' place with

> the river winding round the base of the hill on which the asylum stands, the green trees below and, just now, greener grass, the many flowers here and there in the gardens, the red-bricked cottages peeping out from among the trees.

It was in two or three such cottages that he came upon 'the child idiots'. He found this encounter the most distressing of his visit, confiding to his readers that 'one can better bear to see, or hear of, insanity in adults, than these children doomed to what may be a long life of mental darkness'. While he found being with them 'inexpressibly painful', still there was cause for optimism, for among the children there were 'one or two interesting faces … and in some cases hope of partial recovery'.[1]

Yarra Bend Asylum was the first institution in Victoria dedicated to the care and confinement of those deemed 'insane'. It opened in October 1848 in response to concerns about the intellectually disabled and mentally disturbed individuals then wandering Melbourne's streets or confined to its gaols.[2] In its first years the asylum was home to less than a hundred patients, but with the discovery of gold in 1851 Victoria's population exploded. While some found riches, for many the quest for gold caused only disappointment and despair. Patient numbers rose dramatically, to 300 in 1857 and 683 by 1860.[3]

Figure 1.1: Frederick Grosse, engraver, 'The Yarra Bend Asylum for the Insane', wood engraving, *Illustrated Australian News*, 23 May 1868
(Courtesy State Library Victoria)
Children with intellectual disabilities lived among the more than eight hundred patients in this 'city of the insane'. The propriety of caring for 'idiot children' in asylums was increasingly questioned in following years.

Children with intellectual disabilities were among the hundreds of patients admitted in the 1850s and 1860s.[4] In 1861 the 'official visitors', formally appointed by government to regularly inspect and report on the asylum, praised the 'great kindness and care' they received from their female attendant.[5] However, they and others increasingly questioned whether 'idiot children' belonged in asylums. Elsewhere, experiments demonstrating that 'idiot children' were in fact capable of improvement had encouraged the establishment of institutions dedicated to their education. There was, however, little chance of improvement while they remained in general asylums for the insane.

In 1863 Victoria appointed its first inspector of asylums. Recruited from England, Dr Edward Paley was familiar with the new thinking about the educability of 'idiot children'. Over the next two decades, he pushed for the establishment of a separate asylum for these children, arguing that it would help ease the chronic overcrowding, provide for the training of the children and remove them from the dangers to which living among the adult insane exposed them. In 1887, twenty-five years after his arrival, Victoria established Australia's first purpose-built institution for people with intellectual disabilities.

'The Maddest Place in the World'

From the late 1850s the management of the Yarra Bend Asylum was the subject of several official inquiries and much public comment, its surgeon-superintendent, Dr Robert Bowie, criticised for his outmoded treatments. In June 1862 the O'Shanassy government decided to replace him and sent to England 'for a first class man of energetic habits, and who would come with the latest lights on the treatment of insanity'.[6] It commissioned Hugh Childers, an eminent member of the Victorian Legislative Council (and after 1860 a member of the House of Commons), to conduct the search. Initial approaches to England's foremost 'alienists' (as psychiatrists were then called) proved unsuccessful. Childers then sought help from the Lunacy Commission, which oversaw the English asylums, and Dr John Conolly, the most famous 'mad-doctor' of the age. They advised placing an advertisement in the medical journals, which aroused considerable interest. Childers, with the unanimous agreement of both Conolly and the commissioners, appointed Dr Edward Paley to the position. Paley came well recommended. The elaborate 'testimonial brochure' that accompanied his application included seventeen references from professional colleagues and the superintendents of asylums in which he had worked.[7]

Britain's *Journal of Mental Science*, the leading publication in the field, hailed his appointment: 'No better man could have been found to represent English Psychology in this distant colony. Dr Paley combines experience, temper, and judgement, and he has invariably gained the respect and esteem of all those with whom he has worked'.[8] Accompanied by his new wife, Harriet, Paley sailed for the colony on Christmas Eve 1862. Seven weeks later he was in Melbourne.

By 1862 the Yarra Bend Asylum was extremely overcrowded; many of those waiting on admission languished in the colony's gaols. Several months after Paley's arrival, a commission appointed to consider the problem recommended building a second metropolitan asylum and two district asylums in the colony's interior.[9] The new superintendent spent the first years of his administration overseeing this expansion. In 1867 two asylums opened in the country towns of Ararat and Beechworth. The new metropolitan asylum, built on the bank of the river opposite Yarra Bend in Kew, followed. Occupying a high slope above the water and set in five hundred acres of reserved land, it presented a striking contrast to the older institution. Monumental in construction, its long white façade dominated by two high towers, it was visible for many miles. One of the grandest public buildings in the colony, it reflected the confidence and wealth of Victoria in the wake of the gold rushes and a desire to appear benevolent and modern (Figure 1.2).[10]

The new asylums provided only a temporary respite from the unremitting demand for admission.[11] By the close of 1870, three years after the two country asylums opened their doors, more than a thousand patients crammed the wards of Yarra Bend.[12] The resulting overcrowding forced the opening of a section of the new asylum at Kew even before the building was complete, and within only a few years it, too, overflowed with patients.[13] In 1879, the government opened a fifth asylum at Sunbury to the north-west of Melbourne. The apparent prevalence of insanity these numbers implied created considerable disquiet. In 1884 they caused Ephraim Zox, chairman of a royal commission investigating the asylums, to exclaim that Victoria was in 'the most unenviable position of being the maddest place in the world'.[14]

Contemporaries advanced various explanations for this worrying state of affairs. In 1885, Dr J.W. Springthorpe told the royal commission that Victoria's history was a 'very important cause' of the prevalence of insanity:

In the 'City of the Insane' (1867–87)

Figure 1.2: 'Studley Park. Lunatic Asylum. Kew', 1875
(Courtesy State Library Victoria)
Set on a high slope above the Yarra River, the new Kew Lunatic Asylum dominated the skyline, its monumental scale in marked contrast to the older Yarra Bend in the foreground.

'You may call it our fevered past—the time of the goldfields—the distinct nervous tendency inherited from those times, the excited natures that came out, and which have been transmitted to their descendants'.[15] Yet it was more than gold mania, for the great majority of the population were immigrants, including a high proportion of single men far from home and lacking extended family. The psychological challenges of making a new life in the colony proved overwhelming for some.[16]

Others believed the cause lay elsewhere. Addressing the impression that the prevalence of insanity in Victoria in 1871 outstripped that of the United Kingdom, Paley suggested that the explanation lay in the 'different modes' by which each provided for their insane: 'In Victoria, the whole of the insane population, with very trifling exceptions, has been poured into the lunatic asylums'.[17] Fifteen years later the chief secretary, Graham Berry, blamed the broad legal definition of insanity in use, which caused

Victoria to cast its 'net' wide. The Lunacy Statute of 1867 defined a lunatic as 'any person idiot lunatic or of unsound mind and incapable of managing himself or his affairs'. The consequence, Berry believed, was to allow the admission of people who were elsewhere excluded from asylum treatment, thus increasing the percentage of those deemed insane in Victoria.[18] The conviction that Victoria's asylums were crowded with people who could not benefit from asylum treatment was an important reason for the eventual establishment of a separate institution for 'idiot children' (Figure 1.3).

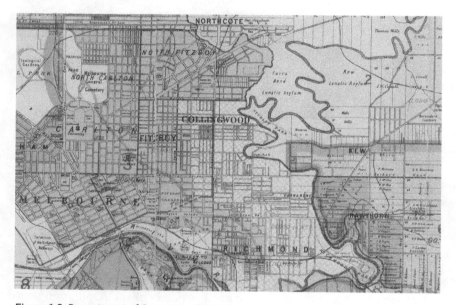

Figure 1.3: Department of Crown Lands and Survey, *Melbourne and Suburbs*, 1876, detail
(Courtesy State Library Victoria)
This map of Melbourne shows the location of Yarra Bend and Kew Lunatic Asylums in 1876, their substantial reserves of land clearly evident.

'The Imbecile Class of the Insane'

The problem of overcrowding focused attention on the composition of the asylum population. Did all the patients who crowded the wards of Victoria's asylums belong there or could they be cared for elsewhere? In 1871 Paley explained that the purpose of 'asylums and hospitals for the insane' was to care for and treat those patients 'who could not be properly managed without them'. Among such patients he counted, first, 'curable cases of all kinds', and second, 'those who are suicidal, destructive, or dangerous, whether curable or not'. For these patients, admission should be prompt and all resources marshalled in their treatment. However, once their number was subtracted from the total asylum population, a large class of so-called 'harmless imbeciles' remained. These patients he characterised as 'marked by mental deficiency rather than mental aberration; the mind being partially extinguished rather than deranged'. He counted among them:

> semi-idiotic adults; the paralysed or infirm, in whom weakness of mind has followed weakness of body; old men and women in their dotage; confirmed epileptics who are not violent; vagrants worn out in body and mind; and the simply imbecile who have not sufficient sense to look after themselves and earn their own livelihood.[19]

Included in this category were 'idiotic children' like those living at Yarra Bend. Together they constituted 'the imbecile class of the insane'.

The admission of 'imbeciles' had posed no real difficulty in the early years of the colony, given the small number of the insane overall. When patient numbers exceeded the capacity of Yarra Bend, the construction of the new asylums overcame the 'embarrassment'. By 1871, however, Paley believed their continued presence threatened the proper working of the asylums. Their admission contributed significantly to the accumulation of chronic incurable cases that were gradually overwhelming the asylums. If this continued unchecked, he feared their numbers must eventually bar the admission of potentially curable patients, unless the government committed to the considerable expense of building additional asylums. Paley argued that there was no reason to do so because, while accommodating 'imbeciles' in the asylums did them no harm, neither did it provide any 'commensurate advantage', as the incurable nature of their condition prevented any hope of recovery.[20]

But where should 'imbecile' patients be accommodated, and what care did they need if asylum treatment provided them with no benefit? Paley considered a number of alternatives, beginning with the payment of a small allowance to families whose financial means otherwise prevented them caring for their relatives at home. He was less confident about the practice of 'boarding out' patients to strangers, in use elsewhere, believing that individuals seeking to profit by accommodating patients in their homes would be reluctant to take in those of the 'imbecile' class, most of whom needed 'help instead of giving any'. The commercial nature of the arrangement, in which profit was the only tie, also left patients vulnerable to ill-treatment. Close supervision was consequently required, significantly increasing the cost of the scheme. However, if boarding out could be made to work, Paley believed it would greatly relieve the asylums, saving the expense of building extra accommodation.[21]

Separate cottages in or near the grounds of the existing asylums were another possibility, cottages being 'much more homelike and comfortable than large wards' and more economical to build. Nevertheless, he was initially unconvinced of the economic merits of separate institutions reserved exclusively for the 'imbecile class'. These did not share the advantage of home care, where the family's unpaid labour reduced the cost to the state, or of the workhouse, where sane inmates took the place of paid staff. Consequently, they offered little economic advantage over the asylum proper. However, the establishment of such institutions in England subsequently persuaded him that they might be cheaper than curative asylums.[22]

By the early 1870s, then, children (and adults) with intellectual disabilities were considered part of a larger category of 'inherently problematic' patients—the 'imbecile class' of the insane. Contemporaries believed these patents were 'silting up' the asylum and undermining its curative purpose. Differentiating 'imbecile' patients in this way was the first step toward establishing specialised institutions for them.[23] In subsequent years, as the asylums became ever more crowded, Paley returned repeatedly to the presence of 'imbecile' patients and the need to provide them with alternative care outside the asylum. However, the 'problem' of 'imbecile' patients was not itself sufficient to prompt the establishment of a specialised institution for 'idiot children'.

'Susceptible of Instruction'

Paley's musings on the need for a separate institution intersected with, and were shaped by, a new optimism overseas about the potential of 'idiot children'. Attempts by French physician Dr Jean-Marc-Gaspard Itard to teach Victor, the so-called 'Wild Boy of Aveyron', and the subsequent work of his pupil Édouard Séguin demonstrated that 'idiot children' were capable of individual mental improvement through training, thus overturning the traditional belief that 'idiots' were ineducable. These experiments encouraged the establishment of institutions in Europe dedicated to the care and training of 'idiot children'. Their apparent success inspired a campaign to establish a similar institution in England.[24]

The first British 'idiot asylum' opened in North London in 1848, moving in 1855 to new premises on Earlswood Common.[25] Four regional asylums established on the Earlswood model followed. Their collective purpose was the training of so-called 'educable idiots'.[26] Through the inculcation of socially acceptable behaviour, classroom lessons, physical exercises, and industrial training and occupation, they aimed to encourage self-control and independence. Pupils would return to their families and communities more self-reliant and better able to contribute to their own support.[27]

After a visit to England in 1873, Paley recommended that an attempt should be made to teach the children in Victoria's asylums. While some among them seemed 'so destitute of intellect as to preclude all hope of their being taught', others he considered 'susceptible of instruction'.[28] In 1875 he suggested that the need to create extra space in the asylums for 'recent and curable cases' might 'be best met by building a separate small asylum exclusively for idiot children'. This proposal would separate the children from adult patients and free up space for new admissions, forestalling the need to extend the asylums, at least for a time. Nor did the new building need to be expensive. While these reasons were addressed to the problem of overcrowding and the mixing of the children with the adult insane, Paley's knowledge of the developments in the treatment of 'idiot children' in England clearly influenced his recommendation. A separate institution for children would, he argued, provide an opportunity to 'initiate a system of industrial training and occupation, like that carried on at some of the home asylums, notably at the Royal Albert Asylum, Lancaster, and at the Earlswood Asylum, Redhill'.[29]

No similarly specialised institution then existed in the Australian colonies. Tasmania had separated 'idiot' boys from the adult insane by building a cottage for them in the grounds of the New Norfolk Asylum, but, in the other colonies, children (and adults) with intellectual disabilities lived in the general wards.[30] In 1872, the NSW government established an Asylum for Imbeciles and Idiots in an old military barracks in Newcastle. While this institution also initially accommodated elderly and demented patients, their number was slowly falling by 1876, and the inspector of the insane, Dr Frederick Norton Manning, expected the Newcastle Asylum would shortly accommodate only 'the imbecile and idiotic'.[31] Manning shared the contemporary optimism about the capacity of 'idiot children', which in his opinion was 'thoroughly demonstrated in the English and Scottish institutions and in the American Schools for the feeble minded', many of which he had visited. However, want of facilities at Newcastle had so far prevented any 'systematic teaching'. Staff directed their attention to 'the physical needs of the patients, the induction of habits of cleanliness and order, and to the employment of those among them who are more intelligent in such avocations as their strength will allow'.[32]

Journalists and other observers also argued the need to train the children in the asylums. In 1874 a visitor to Yarra Bend criticised the lack of any effort to instruct them. While conceding that some were undoubtedly 'totally destitute of intellect', the many who suffered 'from a mere defect of the mental faculties could not fail' to benefit.[33] Two years later, Julian Thomas, the well-known journalist who wrote under the *nom de plume* 'A Vagabond', worked for several weeks as an attendant at Kew and Yarra Bend asylums. The presence of the children was, he declared to his *Argus* readers, 'a great evil, as they are liable to be corrupted by their seniors' and the failure to educate them was 'a great mistake, as by patience these boys could be taught something, and their minds opened to a certain extent'. He added that 'one of the lads seemed brighter than many a dull boy I have seen in public schools'.[34] Referring to the Newcastle Asylum, he declared Victoria 'should not be behind her sister colony in respect of its provision for idiot children'.[35]

By 1877 Paley had persuaded the Berry government to establish an institution for 'imbeciles and idiot children'. Located in a former industrial school in Ballarat, it proved a short-lived experiment, closing two years later when the government decided to return the buildings to the Industrial Schools Department.[36] When the Ballarat Asylum opened, Paley had intended to transfer all the children then living in the asylums to it and, having separated them from the adults, to make 'an effort to ameliorate their condition'. The closure derailed his plans.[37]

Despite this setback, Paley remained determined to implement his plans, repeatedly urging the government to provide separate buildings for the children. The official visitors also expressed their concern, pressing particularly for the segregation of boys from men.[38] In June 1882 their persistent lobbying finally bore fruit when the chief secretary, James Grant, approved construction of separate cottages for the children at Yarra Bend. By August 1883 the site for the new Idiot Asylum had moved from Yarra Bend to Kew.[39] Two years later, work had progressed no further than the clearing and fencing of the site, despite appeals from the inspector and chief secretary to the Public Works Department (PWD) to expedite the work.[40] In 1884 the appointment of a royal commission brought work to a complete halt. Delays and abandoned plans were to be a recurring feature of attempts to improve conditions for people with intellectual disabilities at Kew.

After two decades as the head of Victoria's asylums, Edward Paley had been forced into retirement by declining health the previous year. He and Mrs Paley sailed for England in March. He died of heart disease in 1886.[41] By then the institution he had long advocated was finally under construction.

An Asylum for 'Idiot Children'

The late 1870s saw increasing concern about the state of the Victoria's asylums. Having spent lavishly on their construction, governments had expended very little to maintain the buildings in the decade since.[42] In 1879 an inspection of the Kew Asylum by the Victorian branch of the British Medical Association revealed how dilapidated it had become. Accusing past governments of neglect, the association lobbied the Berry government to improve the condition and management of the asylums.[43] Newspapers also expressed alarm, reporting the association's investigations in considerable detail.[44] In parliament Ephraim L. Zox, MLA for East Melbourne, repeatedly voiced concern about the 'shocking' state of the asylums and pressed for a royal commission.[45] Finally, in 1884, Graham Berry, now chief secretary, bowed to pressure and appointed a royal commission to investigate the asylums.

Chaired by Zox, the commission conducted a broad-ranging investigation into the state and management of the asylums, including the question of how best to care for the 'idiot children' living among the insane. Witnesses unanimously condemned the 'indiscriminate mixing' of the children with adult patients.[46] Dr Solomon Iffla, one of the official visitors, spoke for many when he asserted that it was 'a great cruelty to place those children amongst confirmed lunatics'.[47] They should instead be educated, as there was 'scarcely a child in that condition but is susceptible of an amount of instruction and improvement'.[48] Dr John Fishbourne, formerly an asylum medical officer, testified that confinement in asylums was 'utterly fatal to the improvement of idiots'. Overseas experience proved, he said, that it was 'far cheaper and better to keep them in proper training schools, where the imitative faculty can be developed and the intellect brightened'.[49]

The commission showed considerable interest in the educability of 'idiot children', asking witnesses about their capacities and whether overseas methods would yield similar improvements in Victoria. Would they be able to leave the asylum, perhaps even earn their own livelihoods?

Was the necessary expertise available in the colony, or should an expert be imported from England?[50] Zox was clearly convinced. After hearing about the impressive results achieved at the Illinois Asylum, he asked whether it was not the duty of 'the Australian colonies to get, if possible, a similar amount of training for our idiot children?'[51] While other witnesses were more circumspect about how much progress could be expected, all agreed some improvement was possible.[52] The assumption that an institution was the most appropriate environment in which to train 'idiot children' went completely unquestioned.

In its report the commission declared that 'idiot' children 'were capable of great improvement by training'. It lamented that Victoria had 'no proper refuge' for them, despite the need for their better treatment having been 'abundantly established', particularly in regard to their mixing with adult patients.[53] This and future royal commissions played a significant role in the history of Kew, providing forums in which important questions about the treatment of people with intellectual disabilities were asked.

The government did not wait for the commission's final report, however. In October 1885, after consulting with the commissioners, it authorised the establishment of a separate 'Asylum for Idiot Children' on the Kew Asylum reserve. Located only five hundred yards south of the existing asylum, the new buildings would stand literally in the shadow of the old. But their design was in marked contrast to the main buildings' monumental bulk (Figure 1.4). International opinion had turned against such 'barrack' asylums and favoured the 'cottage system'. The plans for the new 'Idiot Asylum' provided for six cottages, each with accommodation for twenty children, surrounding 'central buildings comprising a large schoolroom, a recreation-room, quarters for the head nurse and kitchens and bathhouses' (Figure 1.5).[54]

The central schoolhouse symbolised the educative purpose of the enterprise, consistent with Paley's earliest recommendation. As the *Argus* explained, the new asylum would 'give to the imbecile children of the colony that regular elementary education which is imparted with a gratifying measure of success in England and other countries'.[55]

Figure 1.4: Charles Nettleton, photographer, 'Kew Lunatic Asylum Australia', c. 1885–87
(Courtesy State Library Victoria)
The sheer size of the Kew Asylum is evident in this photograph of its central administration block. By the mid-1880s, when this photograph was taken, international opinion had turned against such 'barrack' asylums, a shift that shaped the design for the new 'Asylum for Idiot Children'.

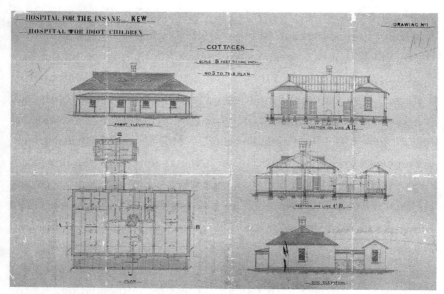

Figure 1.5: Kew Hospital for the Insane Hospital for Idiot Children. Drawing No. 1
(Courtesy Public Record Office Victoria, VPRS 3686/P0017, MHK 1.7, PROV)
This plan shows the design for the original cottages, each intended to accommodate twenty children and their attendants. Built around a central schoolhouse on the asylum reserve, they would gift the institution the name by which it was later known, Kew Cottages.

The *Herald* reported that Dr James McCreery, superintendent of the Kew Asylum, believed 'that by accustoming these poor little creatures to pleasant surroundings some of them may recover', adding that, if a cure proved impossible, it remained incumbent on 'society to see that their lives are made as comfortable as possible'.[56]

Several long-term themes in the history of the cottages were present at their foundation. The economising that would plague the institution began immediately, with the government's decision to begin by building only three of the six planned cottages, providing space to accommodate only the number of children then living in the asylums.[57] Patient numbers would quickly outrun the existing accommodation, beginning the pattern of overcrowding and expansion that occurred repeatedly in the following decades.[58]

Construction of the new asylum proceeded at a glacial pace. In November 1885 the Public Works Department awarded the tender to Kyneton builder Richard Grant, at a cost of £8599 16s—a far cry from the nearly £200,000 spent on the nearby Kew Asylum.[59] Almost a year later the buildings remained unfinished, whereas the building of Melbourne's massive 1880 Exhibition Building was completed in a little over a year.[60] The *Argus* reported that the PWD had 'been asked to push forward the work, with a view to its early completion ... the Minister of Public Works has received assurances that it will be ready for occupation by the end of the present year'.[61] By January 1887 the buildings were at last approaching completion.[62] However, furnishing and drainage works occupied a further four months![63] In May 1887 the new inspector of asylums, Thomas Dick, was finally able to report that the new 'idiot ward' would 'shortly be fit for occupation'.[64]

Not everyone welcomed the new Idiot Asylum. Many Kew residents had objected to the establishment of an asylum in their suburb from the outset.[65] By 1886 Kew Council was petitioning the government to remove the asylum to some other site, declaring its presence 'a great drawback to the district'.[66] The chief secretary, Alfred Deakin, promised to make 'no further additions ... to the present buildings'. The new cottages appeared to break that promise.[67] In October 1887 a deputation from Kew Council waited on Deakin to protest, declaring that more permanent buildings would 'hinder the ultimate removal of the institution from that locality'. Deakin replied that the cottages were not permanent and 'would offer no additional impediment to the removal of the asylum'.[68] In was in these circumstances of uncertainty that the new Idiot Asylum opened in May 1887.

Chapter 2

'Always a Curious Boy' (1887–1908)

In July 1897 the Peacock family of Forest Hill, eighteen kilometres east of Melbourne, sought the advice of the doctors at the Kew Asylum. Writing on the family's behalf, local justice of the peace, Mr E. Bishop, explained that they were 'in great distress, owing to one of their children (a twin) 5 years of age, having been afflicted with insanity from its birth'. No improvement had resulted from the advice of local medical men, and the family was now anxious to have the child examined by experts. Significantly, however, they did not seek advice with the intention of admitting their child to the asylum 'but rather for their guidance in its future treatment'.[1]

Family decisions such as this were central to the history of Kew Cottages. Official asylum statistics show that families initiated just under half of all admissions in the first two decades after their establishment. Indeed, from 1887 children admitted directly from home outnumbered children committed from any other source, including transfers from other institutions.[2] Even so, like the Peacocks, most families were not admitting their children at the first opportunity. Quite the reverse. Institutionalisation was in fact a last resort in this period. The median age of patients at admission in these decades was twelve, revealing that many families sought admission only after caring for their children at home for considerable periods.[3] Thereafter, many strove to sustain the bonds of parental and family love.

Letters like the one sent on behalf of the Peacock family are rare in the cottages' archive. Admission documents can, however, provide a window into the lives of families caring for children with intellectual disabilities and their reasons for seeking admission in the first two decades of the cottages' history.[4] By law, admission to the asylums required two doctors to certify independently to the 'insanity' of the person for whom admission was sought, a provision intended to protect against 'wrongful confinement', whether malicious or mistaken.[5] In their certificates, doctors recorded both 'facts indicating insanity' observed by themselves and, separately, 'other facts (if any) indicating insanity' communicated to them 'by others'. In admissions to the Idiot Asylum, these 'others' were most often the child's parents, sometimes siblings or occasionally other relatives. Historian David Wright argues these 'other facts' constituted family testimonies revealing 'precipitating factors which led to institutional confinement as well as general attitudes of what constituted idiocy for poor families'.[6]

The law also required those seeking to admit another person to an asylum to complete a formal order requesting their admission. Because applicants had to provide information about themselves as well as those they sought to admit, including their occupation, place of abode and relationship to the future patient, orders can reveal the social background of families seeking to admit their children.[7] The asylum, in its turn, was legally obliged to keep a 'case book' in which the superintendent recorded 'the mental state and bodily condition of every patient' at admission and kept a 'history' of the patient during their stay.[8] Information from certificates and orders was often transcribed into these case books.

These documents and a handful of surviving letters allow us to answer important questions. What were the lives of families caring for children with intellectual disabilities at home like? What influenced parents' decisions to admit their children, and what did that decision mean for the bond between parent and child? There are, however, limits to what admission documents can reveal. By their nature, they represent only those families who admitted their children and are silent about those who did not. The experiences of the very many families—probably the majority—who kept their children at home are absent from the cottages' archive.[9] Thus the rewards families gained from caring for their child at home are also invisible in these documents.

'Incessant Attention'

The testimony of parents in admission documents reveals what caring could entail. The impression is one of constant work and worry. In 1891, Amelia Burrell probably spoke to the experience of many families when she told the certifying doctor that her six-year-old son required 'incessant attention'.[10] In the same year, Mrs Gregory explained that her five-year-old boy would 'never eat like an ordinary child but always has to be fed with a spoon'. Annie Sullivan had to wash and dress her nine-year-old son like a baby. Some children were entirely 'helpless'. Many were incontinent, creating much heavy labour in an era before washing machines.

Some children were perpetually restless or agitated. Mrs Sullivan described her son 'continuously moving about all the day pulling open doors and slamming them, and constantly shifting about from place to place anything moveable; that he talks incoherently and incessantly all day'. Others were destructive, tearing their clothes, breaking dishes or smashing windows. In 1891 Rachel Posner told the doctor that her sixteen-year-old son bit 'the buttons off everything he sees'.

The behaviour of some children risked harming themselves or others. Mary Manger's twelve-year-old daughter was 'subject to outbursts of passion' during which she would 'take up anything to strike other children'. Several parents testified to their children's fascination with fire, a great danger in an era reliant on candles, wood stoves and open fireplaces.[11] Sixteen-year-old Joseph Posner was, his mother said, 'always getting lost' if allowed out of the house, while five-year-old Myrtle Wilson was prone to 'run away from her parents and rush amongst horses and carts', the nineteenth-century equivalent of running into traffic. Managing such behaviour required constant vigilance. Many parents testified that their children could 'not be trusted alone for a moment' or had 'always to be watched'.

Sometimes, families resorted to restraint of one kind or another. In 1896 Sarah McNeilly told the doctor that she had to keep her fourteen-year-old brother 'closed up in a room', and a relative slept with him at night. Ten-year-old John Finlayson was locked into his room at night.

Others employed more drastic measures. In 1890 Mrs Woolley told the doctor that her ten-year-old daughter had to be 'bound down at night in a straight [*sic*] jacket otherwise she tears her clothes to pieces; breaks the windows & wanders about the street in her night dress'.

Responsibility for care fell mostly on mothers, and so it was usually mothers who described their children's disabilities and the difficulties of caring for them to certifying doctors.[12] However, fathers also played a role in caring for their children, as their occasional testimony reveals. In 1906 Walter Harrison, a compositor from Kensington, told the doctor that his three-year-old son was 'quite unable to understand anything or recognise objects' and was unable to 'speak or feed himself'. His wife Minnie corroborated his testimony, adding that their son did not recognise them. Fathers no doubt intervened when children were beyond the control or strength of female relatives.[13]

It is unclear how much other family members helped with care. Other researchers speculate that siblings, especially elder sisters, played a key role. When Elsie Neilson was committed to the Idiot Asylum in 1901, it was her sister Annie who signed the request for admission and brought her to Kew. Young unmarried women like Annie, who did not work outside the family home, were often seen as available carers for a disabled brother or sister.[14]

The introduction of compulsory education in 1872, which saw children absent from home for much of the day, must have reduced their ability to contribute to the care of their siblings. So, too, did their eventual departure to seek work or marry, as Annie Neilson did eight months after she admitted Elsie to the asylum.[15] However, evidence from admission documents suggests that adulthood did not necessarily end their contribution to care of their disabled brother or sister. In some instances, care passed from one generation to the next, from parents to adult sons and daughters, perhaps as parents aged, became incapacitated or died. When fourteen-year-old Robert McNeilly was admitted in 1896, both his parents were deceased, his mother most recently three years earlier. His admission warrant suggests that, following their deaths, his elder siblings stepped into the breach. His sister, Sarah, spoke with the certifying doctors while his brother, William, signed the request for admission. His admission history listed both as next of kin. Sarah and an aunt brought him to the asylum.[16]

How much support extended families provided is difficult to determine, the archive providing few clues. Admission documents only rarely noted the presence of anyone other than immediate family, but there are exceptions. When Mrs Kilby described the behaviour of her three-year-old son to the doctors at the Children's Hospital in 1894, for example, the boy's aunt confirmed her statements. The presence of other relatives at certification suggests some involvement in care.

Few of the families who admitted children to the Idiot Asylum could afford to employ help to care for their children. Most were working class: fathers predominantly employed as labourers or tradesmen; and mothers, where they worked outside the home, in domestic service. Frank Travers, owner of a Gippsland butter factory, was a rare exception. When he took his four-year-old daughter to the doctor in 1902 he was accompanied by her nurse, Miss Ryan, the doctor recording testimony from both.[17]

'In Great Distress'

Many parents recognised their children's disability from an early age. Asked to indicate the 'age at first attack' in the request for admission (a question devised with insanity in mind), many wrote 'from birth'.[18] In 1890, Joseph Stott told the doctor that his thirteen-year-old son had 'always been an idiot'. A year later, Mary Manger similarly declared that her twelve-year-old daughter 'had always been silly'. Yet, in neither of these cases, nor in many others, did this recognition result in immediate resort to institutionalisation. What then brought families finally to seek certification, after caring so long for their children at home?

The testimony in the medical certificates discussed above suggests that for many parents the decision resulted from sheer exhaustion of their physical, financial and emotional reserves.[19] As children grew older, they became potentially more difficult to care for and sometimes to control. In 1907, Mrs Carroll explained that her fourteen-year-old son, 'an idiot since birth', was 'becoming violent and destructive: that he uses obscene language freely and that she finds that she can no longer control him'. Other parents admitted that their children's behaviour threatened the safety of other family members. In 1899 Mrs Trainor sought the admission of her 23-year-old sister, by then in her care for 'about five years'. While her sister 'had always been an imbecile' and experienced epileptic seizures, she had lately 'threatened to use violence to Mrs Trainor's children'.

Many families had to cope with the seizures their children experienced, sometimes very frequently. Mark Nyeman's five-year-old daughter had 'fits every day, sometimes four or five to twelve ... [with] great screaming in them'. Faced with increasing frequency or severity of seizures, and the fear and disruption these could cause families, some parents may have decided to relinquish their children. In 1897, Mrs Mays told the doctor that her fifteen-year-old stepdaughter had 'been subject to epileptic fits for six years. Lately more frequent. Has become violent. Threatens to kill her brothers and sisters'.

The absence of one or both parents could precipitate admission. In a significant minority of cases one, or very occasionally both, parents were deceased. In these cases, the deceased parent was much more likely to be the father.[20] If they did not work, widows like Mrs Vigor had to depend on their male relatives, or perhaps charity, for support. In the absence of that support, mothers had little choice but to seek work, making care more difficult. For fathers, the difficulty was to find someone to care for their child while they worked. In the case of John Nattrass, who was living apart from his wife when his son was admitted in 1901, that person had been his sister. His seventeen-year-old son, 'always a curious boy since his birth' according to his father, had lived with her in Beechworth for thirteen years before returning to John's farm block in Bunyip South three years earlier. John faced hard times in the Federation Drought, testifying that he had earned '£4 during the last four months altogether'; his other son was already in the Department for Neglected Children.

The decision to seek institutional admission, as Wright observes, resulted from the paucity of other available options.[21] In nineteenth-century Victoria, there were few alternatives. Little in the way of community care existed. The boarding-out system, which Inspector Paley had first proposed as a means to relieve the overcrowding in the asylums, proved mostly a failure. Few people were willing to care for asylum patients in their own homes.[22] In any case, boarding-out was intended to relieve the asylums of patients already accommodated in them. Nor was the alternative Paley suggested, that poorer families receive a small allowance to enable them to care for their 'imbecile' relatives at home, adopted.[23] The establishment of hostels and day centres was still decades away, as were organised parent groups.[24]

So too was state provision for special education. Addressing the Victorian branch of the British Medical Association in 1890, Dr Fishbourne remarked on the 'many children' in Melbourne 'who, although not strictly speaking idiotic, were so feeble-minded as to require instruction for which the state schools made no provision'.[25] In 1876 the government had exempted children with intellectual disabilities from compulsory education.[26] Some families sent their children to school regardless. Others, like Elsie Neilson, did not attend. In 1897 Fishbourne stepped into the gap he had identified, opening a private school for 'backward' children in his Moonee Ponds home, St Aiden's. At least two patients admitted to the Idiot Asylum were pupils there in the early 1900s, but St Aiden's small size—it provided for between thirty and forty pupils at any one time—and fees (for resident pupils £16 16s per quarter, laundry an additional £1) made it an option for very few.[27]

The lack of community care left only institutions of various kinds. Official asylum statistics indicate that about a third of the patients admitted to the Idiot Asylum came from other public institutions (including transfers from the general asylums).[28] Case histories similarly show patients arriving at Kew from a range of state and charitable institutions for neglected and orphaned children. Evidence from the asylum archive suggests that families initiated at least some of these admissions. In 1908, for example, Sebastopol mother Annie McCarthy attempted to admit her twelve-year-old daughter, Rita, to Nazareth House, a local Catholic home for girls between the ages of six and sixteen. The Sisters refused to accept her, as did other local institutions. Perhaps other families were luckier.

Mrs McCarthy's case also suggests that poverty forced some families to surrender their children to the asylum. According to local police constable John Hooley, Rita was 'simple in her ways and manner since birth' and could not 'be trusted out of her mother's sight'. But the family were 'in poor financial circumstances' and Mrs McCarthy was 'unable to take care of' her daughter, having 'to go out to work'. After the local institutions refused to admit her, the family priest sought advice on their behalf. Rita, he was told, 'would have to be brought before the court as a lunatic' to be admitted. The family agreed, a hearing quickly followed, and Rita was committed to the asylum.

While children with intellectual disabilities certainly found their way into other public and private institutions, Mrs McCarthy's example and the transfers from other institutions to the Idiot Asylum also suggest that those institutions were not always willing to admit or continue to care for them. These refusals left families with even fewer alternatives. However, given the optimism about the Idiot Asylum, some parents must have hoped that admission would improve, perhaps even cure, their children's condition. Three months after the cottages opened, the inspector of asylums reported that he had already received 'several inquiries' from parents 'anxious to take advantage of the means of education offered by this institution'.[29] Parents had reason to be hopeful, given the reports of successes achieved in similar institutions elsewhere. In April 1886, journalist Catherine Hay Thomson followed the Vagabond's example, going 'under cover' as an asylum attendant and reporting her observations. Recounting her visit to Yarra Bend, she lamented 'the absence of any school for the children' confined there. Declaring that the Earlswood Asylum in England had 'triumphantly answered the question, "What can we do with our idiots?"' she described its achievements at some length:

> One inmate had become nurse in a family, another was becoming an expert shoemaker, a former female inmate was employed as teacher in an elementary school. All the inmates are employed doing something, and even in the case of those so deficient in intellect that they could

never be brought the length of entirely supporting themselves, it is found possible to teach many of them handicrafts, by means of which they can partially contribute to their maintenance, and in every instance they are made happier by the awakened sense of usefulness.[30]

After the Idiot Asylum opened in May 1887, the newspapers published encouraging reports on the strides it was making. In 1897 the *Age* attended a Christmas entertainment in which 207 of the children performed, proof that the 'course of instruction at the asylum' was producing 'very gratifying results'. Two years earlier, the *Leader* had been equally impressed (Figures 2.1 to 2.3). The fact that 'several children' had 'already been discharged and are now living with their parents' proved what could be achieved.[31] Case histories are also revealing of this expectation; a handful of families removed their son or daughter when the hoped-for improvement did not materialise.[32]

Significantly, while families initiated almost half of all admissions, there were cases in which the admission proceeded against the parent's wishes. James Clarke certainly opposed the committal of his 25-year-old son, William. In January 1897 a resident in Clunes alerted local authorities 'to the fact that an idiot man named Clarke was in the habit of wandering about the streets to the fright and danger of women and children' and suggested he should be institutionalised.[33] The magistrates agreed that William was 'a proper case for the Asylum' but refrained from committing him after his father pledged to lock him up. Whether James Clarke was unable or unwilling to confine William is unclear, but further complaints revealed that William continued to 'wander about' the town 'pretty frequently'. In early March 1897, he was committed to the Idiot Asylum.[34]

William Clarke's case reveals that both compassion and intolerance informed public attitudes toward people with intellectual disabilities in the first generation of Kew Cottages' existence. The attitudes these complaints reflect raise questions about how willing neighbours may have been to tolerate children or adults with intellectual disabilities or to contribute to their care and why some families chose to keep their children confined at home.[35]

Figure 2.1: Kew Cottages, Nicholas Caire, photographer, c. 1900
(Courtesy Royal Melbourne Hospital Health Sciences Library incorporating the
Victorian Mental Health Library and Photograph Collection)
A decade after the new Idiot Asylum opened in 1887, prominent Melbourne photographer Nicholas Caire took a series of photographs illustrating the institution. By the turn of the century, several additional cottages had been added to accommodate the ever-increasing number of patients.

Figures 2.2 and 2.3: Kew Cottages communal dining room and male
dormitory, Nicholas Caire, photographer, c. 1900
(Courtesy Royal Melbourne Hospital Health Sciences Library, incorporating the
Victorian Mental Health Library and Photograph Collection)
Caire's photographs, such as these of the communal dining room and the male dormitory, show how different this new institutional world was from the family homes from which many residents were admitted.

Some historians have argued that intolerant attitudes and a refusal to accept behaviour outside the norm pressured families into institutionalising their children.[36] Some children did behave in ways that could embarrass their families publicly. In 1902 one father told the certifying doctor that his nineteen-year-old son preferred 'the company of children younger than himself who make a butt of him and ask him to expose himself which he readily does'. In 1890 Mrs Appleton told the doctor that her thirteen-year-old son's 'habits in public' were 'not those of a sane boy'. Other parents seemed disturbed by their children's behaviour. One mother remarked that her ten-year-old son acted 'in many ways quite unnaturally and differently from other children of the same age'.

After the heartbreaking decision was finally made, only the journey to Kew remained. For some families a short tram ride brought them to the asylum. For others, the journey was more difficult. Annie and Elsie Neilson took the coach from their home in the village of Whroo to nearby Rushworth, 180 kilometres north of Melbourne, where they boarded a train to the city via Murchison East. Elsie's admission to the Idiot Asylum marked the end of her family's responsibility for her day-to-day care. But the letter requesting her admission, written on their behalf by a local doctor, included the assurance that should Elsie be admitted, the family would continue to 'show her such care as your rules will permit'. Could families sustain their bond with their institutionalised children? Could they find ways to continue caring for their children, as the Neilsons hoped?

'Please Let Me Know How My Little Boy is Keeping'

In December 1898 Mrs Thompson travelled from the family farm in the Mallee region in Victoria's north west to Kew, where she surrendered her eight-year-old son William to the Idiot Asylum. Seven years later she wrote to the senior medical officer, Dr MacFarlane, asking how William was 'keeping'. Was he contented and enjoying himself? Did the 'fits' he experienced still trouble him and how did he sleep? In 1906 she wrote again to inquire 'how her little boy was keeping?' Did he 'seem to be failing any', and did MacFarlane think he could 'live though so much suffering from the fits'? She had, she confided, 'just buried his little sister that was suffering much the same as he is'. Believing her daughter had 'been relieved of all her suffering', she hoped William might be also: 'It would be such a relief to the dear child if he was taken from this world of suffering'. She pleaded to know what Macfarlane 'really' thought.[37]

Mrs Thompson's letters are a powerful expression of her continuing love for her son and the anguish his disability caused her. Unfortunately, few such letters survive. Mrs Thompson's letters, which ceased only when William died aged eighteen in May 1909, remain pinned to the patient case book, and it is in these case books that the evidence of family contact now survives. Dr MacFarlane, who assumed control of Kew in August 1905, recorded family visits and letters in the patient case notes whereas his predecessor, Dr James McCreery, did not.[38] These notes and a handful of surviving letters provide the only evidence of how families experienced the cottages and managed to sustain their relationship with their children in the early twentieth century.

McFarlane noted the receipt of letters from other parents, mostly mothers, though their contents now have to be inferred from the record of his replies. Between 1906 and 1908, Mrs Armstrong wrote several times from Glen Park in country Victoria asking after 'the Health and Welfare' of her sons Thomas and Morgan.[39] South Melbourne mother Margaret Goldby admitted her six-year-old daughter Alison in early April 1906. She visited in May, wrote in June and then again in August, enquiring if her daughter's condition had improved. Noting his reply in the case history, MacFarlane added: 'There is no change for the better nor is there ever likely to be'. Such assessments must have been heartbreaking for parents hoping for improvement.[40] Undaunted, Mrs Goldby continued to write until 1916, three years before Alison's death in January 1919.[41] Many patient histories noted changes to family addresses, reflecting their desire to keep in touch with the institution. Sometimes a new relative was added, as other family members assumed responsibility after the death of parents.

Some relatives visited, sometimes so often that MacFarlane remarked on their 'constant' attendance.[42] Others came occasionally, or in response to news their children were gravely ill. In 1906, when Annie Campbell's temperature rose to 105F (40.5C), MacFarlane wrote to her mother in Traralgon, in Victoria's east. Annie recovered, and her case history records her mother visiting on consecutive days.[43] However, it seems from the surviving notes that many families never came. A failure to visit is not necessarily an indication of a lack of feeling, however, as surviving letters from parents show. Geographical distance or the availability or cost of transport created insurmountable obstacles for some. In October 1904 Karl Schmidt replied to a letter from Kew, expressing the family's sadness at news their daughter Mary was ill. But visiting was impossible. Since her admission, the family had moved to Western Australia and found themselves stranded. Schmidt closed his letter by remarking on how bad 'things were' there; they would be glad when they could get their 'passage money back to Victoria'. The longer patients remained in the asylum, the more likely it became that age and illness would prevent parents seeing their children. For some parents the emotional pain of visiting may have been simply too much to bear.

Institutional timetables could present obstacles to attempts by parents to sustain their bond with their children. In November 1906 MacFarlane noted the visits of Edward Grant with some exasperation. Grant, he wrote, had been visiting his sons William and Clarence 'every Sunday morning lately. Arriving at most irregular hours'. Sunday visiting hours were 9.30 – 11.00 am, but Grant arrived 'sometimes at 12' and stayed 'until 1.30 & 2 p.m., keeping his children away from their dinner, until he has been requested to leave'.[44] Why Grant visited at these times is unclear, but MacFarlane's exasperated remarks suggest that the asylum's rules and routines might have posed a problem to parents.

Some families continued to include their children in family celebrations. In December 1905, and again the following year, Violet Brown's family took her home for Christmas, against the advice of the medical officer.[45] Others sent parcels to their children.[46] Some assistance seemed to follow a request from the cottages. In February 1906 MacFarlane wrote to Mrs Craig, whose daughter Mary had been in the asylum four months, informing 'her that her daughter was going on allright' [*sic*]. He added that he had 'sent a list of clothing from the Matron for her to send down to her child'. Three months later he acknowledged receipt of a 'parcel of clothing'.[47] How families understood these requests for support is hard to gauge. Once again the responsibility fell to mothers. When Karl Schmidt responded to the news that his daughter was unwell, he also promised to 'forward her some cloathing [*sic*] as soon as her Mother can get them made'. Making clothes may have been an unwelcome chore for some mothers. But for others it provided a chance to express their love and care in a tangible way, in an object their child would wear—the time taken in the making also allowing a space to remember.

Photographs could provide another form of remembrance (Figures 2.4 and 2.5). In October 1907, Dr MacFarlane wrote several times to Mary Ellen Garrett's father after she experienced an epileptic seizure, the third time enclosing a photograph of seven-year-old Mary.[48] By this time, photographing patients was a routine part of admission, but it was not the custom to send copies to parents, suggesting that Mr Garrett had particularly requested it. His desire to have it with him is telling of the love he and other parents continued to feel for their institutionalised children. Perhaps other families arranged to have photographs taken before admitting their children, as keepsakes. How many, we will never know.

It is clear that institutionalisation, a step taken in many cases when there seemed no alternative, did not sever the bonds of affection many parents felt for their children. Admission to the Idiot Asylum did, however, separate parent and child. Many parents fought hard to close the gap, continuing to express their love for their children by writing and visiting, keeping them close in their thoughts and memories. Even so, their decision to commit their children to the asylum saw their sons and daughters enter a new world. That world (later known as Kew Cottages), and the experiences of the people within it, are the subject of the following chapters.

Figure 2.4: Patients and their nurses pose for the camera in the girl's playground, Nicholas Caire, photographer, c. 1900
(Courtesy Royal Melbourne Hospital Health Sciences Library, incorporating the Victorian Mental Health Library and Photograph Collection)

Figure 2.5: Some of youngest of the cottages' residents, a group of infants and their nurses, Nicholas Caire, photographer, c. 1900
(Courtesy Mrs Norma Sutherland)

Chapter 3

'For the Care and Training of Feeble-minded Children' (1887–1907)

In April 1886 police found eight-year-old Edmund Legge wandering the streets of Benalla, 212 kilometres north-east of Melbourne. Their subsequent inquiries revealed that Edmund's father was deceased and his mother, Emily, in dire circumstances. Deserted by her present husband, 'weak in mind and body' and 'very poor', Emily was also attempting to support a second child. Edmund was committed by the local court to the care of the Department for Neglected Children and taken to Melbourne, where he was admitted to the Boys Depot in Parkville. His stay there proved brief. Judged to be an 'idiot', perhaps because of his inability to speak, he was transferred to Yarra Bend Asylum eight days later.[1]

In Kew, the new Idiot Asylum (later known as Kew Cottages) was already under construction. In May 1887, a year after his admission to Yarra Bend, Edmund was among the first patients transferred to the new institution.[2] The inspector of asylums was so anxious to segregate the boys from the adult male patients that Edmund and the others arrived at an institution still under construction.[3] Three months later, the central buildings, comprising the schoolhouse, kitchen and teacher's house, and three cottages were finally completed and the grounds enclosed by a picket fence.[4] The first female patients arrived from Yarra Bend at the beginning of October,[5] and, by the end of 1887, the new cottages were home to fifty-four patients, two-thirds of whom were male.[6]

The establishment of the new Idiot Asylum finally provided the opportunity to establish the type of institution Edward Paley had imagined, one dedicated to 'the care and training of feebleminded children'. Its realisation confronted considerable obstacles, not least the dire economic depression of the 1890s. But by 1900 contemporaries believed it to be at the forefront of the treatment of 'idiot' children in Australia. Its public achievements certainly seemed to confirm that impression, but other evidence, including the few voices of residents and families that survive, suggest that not all was as positive as that image suggested. By the early twentieth century, government was beginning to question whether the results the institution had achieved justified its cost, foreshadowing a new era of pessimism.

'An Institution for the Care and Training of Feeble-minded Children'

Oversight of the new Idiot Asylum fell to the superintendent of the nearby Kew Asylum, Dr James McCreery. Born and educated in Ireland, McCreery immigrated to Victoria as a young man. After time in Tasmania and later practising on the New Zealand goldfields, he returned to Victoria. In 1868 he joined the Lunacy Department, appointed assistant medical officer at the Ararat Asylum. By 1883, he was superintendent of the Kew Asylum.[7]

According to journalist Alice Henry, who visited the Idiot Asylum in January 1898, McCreery was 'a quiet, reserved man, with a shy, hesitating manner'. He reminded her 'at first sight of one of Melbourne's most learned canons'.[8] Despite his manner, McCreery was a determined reformer.[9] He was convinced of the potential of 'idiot' children and took a keen interest in the management of the Idiot Asylum. Appointed inspector of lunatic asylums in 1894, McCreery also continued to act as superintendent of the Kew Asylum until 1899, when the government finally relieved him of his dual roles. While the appointment of a new superintendent freed him from the responsibility to manage the main Kew Asylum, he retained oversight of the Idiot Asylum at his own request, reflecting his personal commitment to its development.[10]

Five years after the Idiot Asylum opened, McCreery explained the guiding principles of its management to the Intercolonial Medical Congress of Australasia. As the establishment of a separate institution for 'feeble-minded children' was a new venture for Victoria, McCreery decided to model it as far as possible on the English idiot asylums. Consequently, the first principle of its management was 'to admit only idiots and imbeciles, and not to receive any adult insane. The second, to work it as a training school, in which the physical, mental and moral powers of the inmates would be developed'.[11]

McCreery acknowledged that the start the institution had made in this direction owed much to its head teacher, Theophilus J. Eastham (Figure 3.1).

Figure 3.1: A portrait of Theophilus Eastham, head teacher of the asylum, on his wedding day
(Courtesy Mrs Norma Sutherland)
With his experience at the Royal Albert Asylum, Eastham played a significant part in establishing an institution for 'feeble-minded' children based on the English model.

Eastham was particularly well qualified for the position, having worked for seven years at the Royal Albert Asylum for Idiots and Imbeciles in Lancashire. The Royal Albert was world-renowned and its medical superintendent, Dr George Shuttleworth, one of the leading experts in the training of 'idiot' children. Initially employed as an 'ordinary attendant', Eastham quickly advanced to the position of school attendant and was 'second in charge of the School' when he resigned in 1879. References from Shuttleworth and the Albert's schoolmaster, Edward Woods, attested to his ability. Eastham immigrated to New Zealand, where he worked as an attendant at the Sunnyside Hospital for the Insane in Christchurch. By October 1885 he was in Victoria where he found employment as a temporary attendant at Sunbury and Yarra Bend asylums. In August 1886 he applied for the position of head teacher. His application demonstrated both considerable knowledge of and vocation for the work of training of 'idiot' children. He included with it a detailed description of the Royal Albert's methods and closed by expressing his 'great desire to be amongst idiot children again'.[12]

Both McCreery and the inspector of asylums, Thomas Dick, considered Eastham eminently qualified. But at thirty-six he was older than the maximum age allowable for permanent appointment to the Victorian public service. While the chief secretary, Alfred Deakin, seemed willing to appoint someone less qualified from the existing staff, Dick urged the government to exempt Eastham from the age requirement, arguing that '[h]is experience in the Royal Albert would be of great value and an opportunity like the present is not likely soon again to arise'. The Public Service Board eventually solved the problem by reclassifying the position.[13] Dick and McCreery's insistence on Eastham's appointment reflected their intention to establish an institution specifically designed for the care and training of feeble-minded children, and Eastham had considerable influence on the development and management of the asylum in the following years.[14] Consciously modelling the training at Kew on the regime at the Royal Albert,[15] he constructed a system of educating children with intellectual disabilities consisting of several interconnected elements.

Moral training emphasised self-control and proper social behaviour. McCreery's remarks to the Intercolonial Medical Congress about the progress achieved give a sense of what moral training encompassed. The boys had learned to 'come into the dining-room in an orderly manner, take their places; stand up till grace is said and then eat their food with knives and forks or spoons'. Escapes had initially caused considerable trouble but, with the development of their 'self-control', residents could be safely allowed outside the institution's fences. Use of 'bad language' was rare and 'sexual vices ... kept within a very limited compass'. Many of the children could recite the Lord's Prayer and most attended 'simple religious services'.[16] The continence of many of the children had improved.

Figure 3.2: Writing classes in the schoolroom,
Nicholas Caire, photographer, c. 1900
(Courtesy Mrs Norma Sutherland)
Other teaching appliances—a large clock face and abacus—are visible and, in the background, the instruction 'try to be tidy' reflects the moral training that constituted another element in the training of 'idiot' children.

Schooling aimed to develop the children's 'mental faculties'.[17] When Alice Henry visited in 1898 she observed the school room equipped:

with all sorts of appliances of the kindergarten type—coloured balls for counting, models and diagrams to teach form, peg-boards with which to train slow and clumsy fingers to accuracy of touch. The alphabets and simple reading lessons are illustrated with striking pictures of animals, toys, chairs, and other common objects, all on a bigger and more pronounced scale than is necessary for the normal child.[18]

In addition to instruction in reading, writing and arithmetic, pupils received lessons in colour recognition and telling the time, as well as singing and drawing classes (Figure 3.2).[19] In one class, Henry observed teachers using sensory experience to teach abstract concepts: 'A wooden cube is dabbed on a little one's face. That is "hard—hard". Then a wool ball. "Soft—soft," says the teacher'.[20] Lessons were short. Every twenty minutes brought 'a change of occupation' to allow for the pupils' 'wandering attention' and classes were organised to allow for their differing abilities.[21]

Physical training was 'the same as in English schools—light dumb bells, marching in order, walking on ladder steps, general drill movements for the arms and body'. Henry watched a class of boys practising a 'simple drill—sitting, standing, folding and extending the arms, turning to right and left'—while in the room next-door 'a troop of girls' marched to music (Figures 3.3 and 3.4). Physical training also included vegetable gardening for the boys and sewing and laundry work for the girls.[22] Patients worked in the kitchen and in the wards. Boys judged trustworthy fetched milk from the nearby Kew Asylum farm.[23]

Industrial training, considered by contemporaries as perhaps the most important element, prepared inmates for their intended 'after-life in the world'.[24] By 1892, fourteen boys were making mats so proficiently that the cottages supplied all the asylums with their output. Others manufactured wicker-work furniture.[25] On her visit in 1898, Alice Henry watched male patients cutting willow for basket making, gathering the branches into sheaves and stacking them in a bricked pond until they were ready to be stripped of their bark and dried. Over time, this industrial work expanded to include tailoring, boot mending and mat making for the boys.

However, industrial work in the girls' division was not nearly so far advanced when Henry reported progress for the *Argus*.[26]

Figure 3.3: Girls provide a callisthenic display for the camera, Nicholas Caire, photographer, c. 1900
(Courtesy Wellcome Collection, Public Domain Mark)
In 1900, visitor Alexander Sutherland marvelled at a similar demonstration, taking it as an example of the progress the asylum was making in the treatment of 'mentally deficient' children.

Figure 3.4: Boys walk on ladder steps, assisted by head teacher Theophilus Eastham, Nicholas Caire, photographer, c. 1900
(Courtesy Wellcome Collection, Public Domain Mark)
Walking on ladder steps was one element of the training intended to develop the 'physical powers of the inmates'.

Figure 3.5: Mat making, one of several industrial occupations that formed a key element of training, Nicholas Caire, photographer, c. 1900
(Courtesy Mrs Norma Sutherland)

Figure 3.6: Patients and warders pose with sheaves of willow, used in the manufacture of wickerwork furniture and baskets, Nicholas Caire, photographer, c. 1900, detail
(Courtesy Royal Melbourne Hospital Health Sciences Library incorporating the Victorian Mental Health Library and Photograph Collection)

Figure 3.7: Boys in the tailoring class, Nicholas Caire, photographer, c. 1900
(Courtesy Mrs Norma Sutherland)

In addition to their industrial occupations, residents worked in the wards, kitchen and laundry. Their unpaid labour reduced the cost of maintaining the asylum.

Entertainments and special events broke the routine of the days. Children from the cottages attended the annual asylum picnic.[27] The annual Christmas fete was the highlight of the year. For weeks beforehand preparations absorbed the children's spare time. Each year a Christmas tree, lit with candles and weighed down with donated gifts, formed the centrepiece of the occasion, the room decorated with garlands and wreaths made by the children. After a musical performance for visitors, many of them benefactors, staff distributed presents to the children. In 1903, an *Age* journalist remarked that this was 'a long and tedious task to all but the children, who were willing to go on receiving as long as supplies lasted'.[28] For many years, Mr W.E. Pickells appealed through the columns of the *Argus* for donations of toys and cards for the children's Christmas tree.[29] He was among those 'private friends' who endeavoured to brighten the children's lives. One Kew resident, according to Alice Henry, 'visited frequently, his pockets full of toys and oranges'. Another had 'organised quite a score of entertainments' much to the children's delight.[30]

'Herculean Difficulties'

In her detailed report for the *Argus* in 1898 Alice Henry had remarked on the 'Herculean difficulties' McCreery confronted during the previous decade. The challenges of establishing a new institution were compounded by one of the worst economic depressions in Australia's history, especially in Victoria. The collapse of the Melbourne land boom in 1890, which devastated a wide cross-section of society, was deepened by problems on the London money market, reducing Victoria's capacity to borrow funds. Unemployment had engulfed a third of breadwinners by 1893. The government responded by paring its spending 'to the bone'.[31]

In the asylums, starting wages for newly appointed warders were cut, and annual leave for all staff was reduced from three weeks to two.[32] At the same time the workload in the cottages increased. Despite a dramatic rise in patient numbers, no additional staff had been employed. By January 1895, thirteen staff were caring for 153 patients, three times the number resident at the end of 1887.[33] Even maintaining this number had proved difficult in the straitened economic circumstances. On several occasions, asylum officials felt it necessary to emphasise that a new appointment was 'absolutely necessary'.[34]

Patient care also suffered. In 1892, Inspector Dick reported a reduction in asylum expenditure despite an increase in the number of patients. Although he warned that further reductions must severely compromise patient care, the government cut spending again the following year, partly by allowing less money for the patients' bread and clothing.[35] Overcrowding made matters worse. By 1891 patient numbers had doubled.[36] In a pattern that would recur repeatedly in the history of the cottages, new patients quickly occupied all the available accommodation, necessitating the institution's further expansion. In 1891 two more cottages were built, but the inspector's belief that these additions would provide 'ample' room quickly proved mistaken. Within two years they were full and, by the end of 1894, much overcrowded. McCreery, recently promoted to inspector, declared that the danger to the health of the children made 'the question of extension a very urgent one'.[37]

The situation was exacerbated on 2 August 1895 when a fire broke out in one of the cottages. While the attendants were quick to the scene, low water pressure hampered their efforts to control the blaze. By the time the Kew Fire Brigade arrived, the building was well alight. The *Argus* reported that the inadequate water pressure made the cottage's complete destruction a certainty. The firemen and warders

> centred their efforts on the protection of the other cottages, three or four in number, distant between 30ft. and 50ft. With wet blankets and buckets of water the walls of these were kept constantly wet, and after a hard battle, lasting over three hours, the victory was gained by the firemen.[38]

Thankfully, the inmates of the gutted cottage were at work when the fire started and no lives were lost, but the dormitory, 'workshops, attendants' mess and sleeping rooms' it housed were completely destroyed.[39] Several attendants, called to fight the fire, lost belongings they might otherwise have saved. David Gray claimed £5 13s 6d for his carpenter's tools. John Regan lost virtually all his personal effects, among them a gold double chain and pendant, a gold gilt lead pencil, a silver mounted pipe and his ritual book, in addition to two suits, two shirts, his boxer and soft felt hats, silk and linen handkerchiefs, shaving gear and tailor's kit. David Pittock sought compensation for clothes, toiletries, and his Raleigh Pneumatic Safety bicycle, which, he declared, had 'frequently been of great use in the Govt. service in the pursuit and capture of escapees'. On one Sunday, he claimed, he had 'ridden over 40 miles and captured an absconder when there was no means of using either telegraph or telephone'.[40]

The fire drew public attention to the cottages' inadequate fire safety. The *Argus* urged an immediate inquiry, warning of 'the awful possibilities of a fire at night' if the institution remained unprotected. Its observation

'FOR THE CARE AND TRAINING OF FEEBLE-MINDED CHILDREN' (1887–1907)

was prophetic of events a century later. Again, bureaucratic inertia was to blame. Officials had warned the government about the danger of fire in the asylums for several years.[41] Attempts to remedy the deficiencies at the cottages by installing a new water main and fire hoses at a cost of £200 were repeatedly delayed by the Public Works Department.[42] The fire finally brought action.[43]

McCreery confronted similar inertia in rebuilding the burnt-out cottage and alleviating the detrimental effects of insufficient staff and overcrowding on patient care. A year later, the patients the fire had displaced were still sleeping in tents. Construction of new dormitories proceeded at a 'dilatory' pace. Despite McCreery's repeated complaints to the chief secretary and the minister's urging, the Public Works Department seemed unable to move the contractor to greater efforts.[44] When the official visitors warned that the asylum was 'overcrowded and undermanned', McCreery could only agree. However, there was no prospect of improvement until the new buildings were complete and the asylum rearranged to accommodate more staff.[45]

The overcrowding threatened the health of both patients and staff. In December 1897 the official visitors declared the earth closets 'abominable, the state of things being so bad that no Inspector of Nuisances would hesitate to prosecute'.[46] Within four months, two attendants had contracted typhoid fever.[47] When measles broke out later in 1898, the institution lacked the means to properly isolate the first cases to contain the infection.[48] Mortality rates more than doubled, from 6.5 per cent in 1897 to 14.9 per cent in 1898. By the end of the epidemic, eighteen patients had died, among them little Minnie Lake, only three years old.[49]

In January 1898 Alice Henry reported that the institution was still 'sadly cramped for room'. Forty patients continued to sleep in tents, and part of the newly built dining room had been railed off to provide a temporary workshop in which the workers 'seem to be tumbling over one another for want of space'.[50] Relief was slow in coming. However, in early 1899 the visitors reported that new dormitories for males and females and a new boys bathroom and workroom were imminent.[51] Once they were completed, McCreery optimistically declared 'all present fear of overcrowding

... removed'.[52] More improvements followed, including a new drill room, enhancing the capacity to carry on the asylum's work.[53]

By 1900, staff conditions had also improved. There was new money for extra staff at the Idiot Asylum in 1896, and in 1899 the government granted a wage increase to all attendants and nurses and restored the week's leave lost in 1892.[54] By the turn of the century, with many of the problems of recent years seemingly overcome, the official visitors were expressing 'satisfaction with the condition and working of the Idiot Asylum' and declaring it 'a credit to the Department'.[55]

Figure 3.8: The hospital cook and his resident assistants pose on the steps of the kitchen cottage, Nicholas Caire, photographer, c. 1900
(Courtesy Wellcome Collection, Public Domain Mark)

'A Distinct Advance on Anything Yet Done for the Feeble-minded Children in Australia'?

In a period in which the asylums were the subject of considerable criticism,[56] the treatment of 'idiot' children could be counted one of the achievements of the Victorian asylum system. In 1889 the president of the Psychological

Section of the Medical Congress, Dr Frederick Norton Manning, congratulated Victoria for having made 'a distinct step in advance' of the other Australian colonies by 'commencing a system of special education and training, after English and American models' for 'feeble-minded' children.[57] In 1903, McCreery even boasted that 'the provisions made for these children in Victoria is in advance of that made for similar cases in any part of the world'.[58]

McCreery was keen to publicise the Idiot Asylum's achievements. He and Eastham welcomed visiting journalists, showing them through the institution and explaining the principles of treatment. Organised entertainments demonstrated the children's progress to the press and public benefactors (Figure 3.9).[59] In August 1900, members of the Psychological Society of Melbourne attended an evening's entertainment 'given by 95 children who had shown the greatest improvement under treatment'.[60]

Figure 3.9: An 'entertainment given by the patients before many leading men of Melbourne', Nicholas Caire, photographer, c. 1900
(Courtesy Wellcome Collection, Public Domain Mark)

The fashion for exhibitions provided another opportunity to promote the asylum's successes. In 1896 Eastham entered displays of the inmates' industrial work in the Warrnambool Industrial and Art Exhibition and, in 1901, the Victorian Golden Jubilee Exhibition in Bendigo.[61] The desire to demonstrate the institution's achievements is also evident in a series of photographs taken at this time by prominent Melbourne photographer Nicholas Caire. The quality of the images is outstanding, Caire having carefully framed his subjects to show the institution and its methods to best advantage (Figures 3.2–3.8 above).

Contemporaries were impressed. Judges at the Warrnambool Industrial Exhibition awarded the children a 'gold medal for their display of baskets and mats and general excellence of workmanship'. In a letter to Eastham, the exhibition secretary remarked that the quality of the children's work was 'surprisingly good and would secure ready sale down here properly placed'.[62] Alexander Sutherland, a member of the Psychological Society, expressed astonishment at the abilities of the children he saw, proof of the progress being made: 'On coming away, after two hours filled with surprise at what science in our days attempts and achieves, I felt a strong wish to know how it was all done, and next week went out to see the work in operation'. In a lengthy article in the *Australasian* newspaper, he shared with his readers all he had seen and heard, first at the night's entertainment and then on his tour of the asylum with Eastham. Assured that the 'great majority' of the children were 'capable of great amelioration', he rejoiced 'at all that philanthropy, patience and psychology have been able to effect'.[63]

Alice Henry was more circumspect, explaining to her readers that in comparison to the accomplishments 'in older lands, the work here is in its infancy'. Nonetheless, there was reason to be proud of this institution at Melbourne's door, for it was, she claimed, 'the only establishment of its kind in the whole of the southern and eastern hemispheres'. Moreover, the work of educating and training the children was 'carried on in accordance with the latest teachings of physiology and mental science'.[64]

Were they right? Had the asylum fulfilled the ambition on which it was founded to be an institution for training 'feebleminded' children?

In his first reports, McCreery declared that the program of training had resulted in 'marked mental advance' among many of the patients and an even more noticeable improvement in their 'habits and conduct'.[65] In 1892, he even quantified the institution's success, telling the Intercolonial Medical Congress that an examination of all the children at Kew showed that 'two-thirds have clearly improved'.[66]

Patient histories suggest that some patients did indeed improve. When eight-year-old Edmund Legge arrived at Kew in May 1887, his history noted that he could not speak and was only able to feed himself a little with a spoon. Three years later, he was attempting to form words, doing a little garden work and had 'some idea of simple drill'. The next, undated, entry reported that he could feed himself and was 'generally better at table'. By 1900 he was 'able to do general work, brighter mentally [and] in good bodily health'.[67] The first entry in Henry Stanford's case history described him as 'in good general bodily health, does a little in workshop, understands simple questions and his mind seems open to improvement'. By July 1902, he was working making mats and attending school. Four years later, his history declared him 'one of the best mat makers in the Asylum'.[68]

Other histories noted improvement in more general terms, such as 'some general mental advance' or 'slight general improvement'.[69] However, McCreery's own estimate of the proportion of patients improved suggests that a significant minority received little benefit from admission. In addressing the Medical Congress, he asked his listeners to keep in mind when judging the asylum's results that it was a state institution and, as such, required to admit patients of 'all degrees of mental enfeeblement' regardless of their prospect for improvement, in contrast to the private English idiot asylums, which practised selective admission.[70]

Patient histories do include instances where the institution was seemingly unable to help. Nineteen-year-old Alfred Walters arrived at the asylum on the same day as Edmund Legge, but, where Edmund's history testified to his improvement, Alfred's did not: 'No mental improvement, unable to walk, sits in an easy-chair all day, cannot talk, has severe epileptic fits, bodily health unsatisfactory, gained 2 lbs since admission'. For Alfred, and many other patients, life was very different from that depicted in visitors' accounts and they were rarely mentioned.[71]

Nor were those best placed to judge the institution—its residents—asked their opinion. Visiting journalists had much to say about the patients, particularly about how their difference was written in their appearance. But none reported speaking with them. The silence of the archive makes it difficult to know how its inmates experienced the institution. But the voices of two patients momentarily break the silence, even if only indirectly, their words recorded in their case histories. In May 1904, after four years as an inmate, nineteen-year-old Catherine Hook made her desperate desire for release plain, telling the medical officer that if she were not permitted to leave she would 'commit suicide'. Four years earlier, after several escape attempts, 22-year-old Annie Gately similarly declared that she would kill herself. In both instances, the doctor transferred the complainants to the nearby main asylum, interpreting their distress as a sign of mental disorder rather than an understandable response to their continuing confinement.[72] The women's distress suggests that from the perspective of the people confined the experience was not always the happy one depicted in the public image.

The silence in most case notes makes it impossible to know why particular individuals ran away or were as desperately unhappy as Catherine Hook, but it is possible to speculate more generally. In some cases, the reason seems clear. Thirteen-year-old Rachael Matthews fled the asylum in 1901, only two days after her admission from home. It seems likely that the distress of being separated from her family and confined to an institution filled with strangers prompted her escape. Several weeks later the medical officer reported that Rachael was 'rather more settled', and thereafter she seems to have accepted her confinement.[73]

The separation from family that seemingly caused Rachael to run away was considered fundamental to the success of the training. In McCreery's opinion there was no doubt about the 'advantages of a special training school over home education in cases of idiocy ... home training does not generally turn out a success'.[74] Other elements similarly considered essential to the training of 'idiot' children may have caused inmates distress. Some may have disliked the regimentation contemporaries believed 'essential to the amelioration of disabled and disordered minds'.[75] It is possible that others resented 'the never-sleeping vigilance' officials believed was necessary in the training of 'idiots'. Moral training, intended to teach self-control and to inculcate socially acceptable behaviour such as proper conduct at meals, involved constant observation and correction by staff, both night and day. At night surveillance was potentially intrusive and coercive, extending to the control of what McCreery called 'sexual vices', the practice of which, he asserted, was 'kept within a very limited compass'.[76]

Contemporaries marvelled at how well behaved the children were at meals. Observing the 240 inmates in the dining hall, Alexander Sutherland wondered at the quiet way they took their seats, stood when the hymn was to be sung and then began 'their evening meal of tea and bread and jam, all courteous in passing the viands to each other, the whole meal passing in the comparative silence of subdued conversation'. Sutherland read this as a mark of the institution's achievement. But such remarkable docility might equally be a sign of compliance under a coercive regime.[77]

There were certainly instances of abuse in this period. In January 1906 the senior medical officer, Dr A.A. MacFarlane, caught one of the nurses in the act of striking patient Edith Yorath. Five months later, in a rare recorded example of a resident speaking out, Michael Foley complained to MacFarlane of ill-treatment; one of the attendants, he said, had seized him so roughly that he 'nearly broke my neck'. In November the father of patient William Grant alleged that the warders had 'sworn at, and ill-treated' his son.[78]

MacFarlane noted all these incidents in the patient cases books. Prior to this, the case books record no instances of abuse. However, this apparent uptick is more likely an artefact of record keeping than a true indication of incidence. McCreery retired in August 1905. Medical oversight of the asylum, including the keeping of patient case books, then passed to MacFarlane. There are significant differences in the particulars each man chose to document. McCreery, for example, failed to note family visits or correspondence from relatives. In contrast MacFarlane recorded both, as we saw in the last chapter. It beggars belief that not a single relative chose to enquire after their loved one or visited the cottages in the first eighteen years of their existence. Correspondingly, it is not safe to assume that the silence surrounding abuse before 1906 is in fact indicative of its absence.[79]

Two letters from families do survive for the earlier period. They, too, suggest that the public image did not always match reality. In May 1903, Prahran mother Mrs Fairy wrote to complain that her son was being neglected. On a recent visit she had been shocked to find him 'very dirty' and with bruises on both legs. Two months later, the mother of patient Ernest Colville wrote to the chief secretary, John Murray, alleging that Ernest had 'been grossly neglected and maltreated'. McCreery denied that there was any substance to either complaint. At the very least, however, these letters suggest that the care their sons received did not measure up to these mothers' expectations. 'I did not', Mrs Fairy declared, 'put him there to be neglected but taken care of'.[80]

Visitors made assumptions about how patients felt. In 1898, Alice Henry described the feelings she assumed the inmates' basket making and other trade employments must induce, asking her readers to consider 'the sense of just pride that wakes in a poor, useless child when he first discovers that he can create something; what a link with his fellow-beings to be able to give instead of always receiving'. Inmates may well have felt pride in their achievement. But then again, they may not. Some patients refused to work, Edmund Legge among them, despite the initial 'improvement' observed in his behaviour. But either way, Henry did not ask.

Moreover, Henry's conclusion depends on negative assumptions about children with intellectual disabilities implicit to the discourse of 'improvement'. That such training might create a link between the 'idiot' child and his or her fellow beings assumes the prior absence of that link. In this, Henry's remark reflects the promise on which psychotherapist Joanna Ryan argues nineteenth-century advocates made the case for training 'idiot' children: that it would lift them from the bestial state contemporaries assumed they occupied.[81] As McCreery expressed it in his presentation to the Intercolonial Medical Congress, training in idiot asylums 'humanizes as far as may be, beings who are often more degraded than beasts of the field'.[82]

Other visitors deployed the same rhetorical device to emphasise the Idiot Asylum's achievements. Sutherland began the account of his visit with a recollection of a trip to the Kew Asylum twenty-five years earlier. He recalled the children still living there. 'In those days', he explained, 'it was assumed that the mentally-deficient child was born without human faculty. Its plight was considered to be hopeless, and it was allowed to lounge about as a mere animal that happened to be distressfully like the human race'. He was bewildered then, when he arrived at the Idiot Asylum and saw a gymnastic display already begun: 'Surely these comely, well-grown, smart-looking girls, in their navy-blue dresses, who were going through callisthenic exercises to the music of the piano, could not be the successors of the dingy, slouching creatures whom I had seen five-and-twenty years ago'.[83] Such ideas easily lent themselves to the more pessimistic eugenicist beliefs that would dominate the first half of the twentieth century.

'Results that Justify Its Continuance on the Present Scale'

In 1887, the Idiot Asylum was established as 'an institution for the care and training of feeble-minded children'. By the early twentieth century that mission was under threat. In 1903, the chief secretary, John Murray, expressed doubts about whether the asylum's results justified its cost to the government. Refusing a request for the permanent appointment of a new teacher, he asked: 'Cannot the staff at the Idiot Asylum be reduced without lessening efficiency? The school teaching does not appear to be attended with results that justify its continuance on the present scale'.[84] Murray had already refused to approve other appointments to the teaching staff. McCreery did his utmost to meet the challenge, arguing that, in comparison with similar institutions in England and America, the staff at Kew was small and the asylum worked at a very low cost. To do this, I take full medical and administrative charge, and devote Sundays, Public Holidays and most of the evenings to the work. In this I have neither received nor expected reward, the only recompense I wish for is that the work of sixteen years not be impaired.[85]

Two years later McCreery retired. In February 1907, Theophilus Eastham, the man with whom McCreery had worked so closely, followed. Eastham had sincerely believed that his work might improve at least some of his charges sufficiently 'to fit them to live outside the asylum'.[86] On this measure, the institution failed. Only a minority, about 17 per cent or one in seven of all inmates admitted between 1887 and 1907, ever left the institution.[87]

Admission for most patients consequently marked the beginning of what was effectively institutionalisation for life. More than half of the patients admitted in these years died in the institution.[88] Many quickly succumbed to diseases such as typhoid and tuberculosis. Others grew into adulthood and spent decades in the institution. The status of the asylum as an institution for children condemned others to a similar fate elsewhere. Among the 16 per cent of patients transferred into Victoria's network of public lunatic asylums were those whose temperament and behaviour the medical officers deemed unsuitable for a children's institution.[89] The general asylums could also be the destination of escapees and others considered 'refractory'.

Such was the fate of Edmund Legge, among the first patients admitted in May 1887. Twenty years later, almost to the day, Edmund was transferred to the Sunbury Asylum. By then he was twenty-eight years old. His Sunbury patient file explained that lately Edmund had 'taken to knocking the smaller boys about'. The Kew Asylum superintendent, Walter Barker, believed he 'ought to be in an adult asylum' and 'compelled to work'. Edmund died on 5 January 1965. By then in his late eighties, he had lived for eighty years in Victoria's institutions for the mentally disabled.[90]

Of the 17 per cent of patients admitted between 1887 and 1907 who returned to the community, only a few were able to earn their own living,

'For the Care and Training of Feeble-minded Children' (1887–1907)

most returning to the care of their family.[91] It was this inability of patients to make their way in the world, rather than any dramatic increase in admissions, that caused patient numbers to rise. Of course, there were patients like Edmund who were without family. In other cases, their families may have been unable or unwilling to resume care. The medical officers sometimes vetoed the release of patients if they considered their families insufficiently responsible. But, as Alice Henry observed, the government had made no provision for the children as they grew into adulthood. Hostels were still decades away. In the meantime, most people admitted to the cottages remained there or were transferred into the general asylums.

Edmund's fate, and that of many others, was not the outcome imagined when the Idiot Asylum was established in 1887. By the early twentieth century, however, as fear of the so-called 'feebleminded' took hold owing to the new 'science' of eugenics, lifelong institutionalisation was an outcome many contemporaries would applaud. Ironically, few saw a place for Kew Cottages in protecting society from this newly imagined danger. Instead, indifference and neglect began to take hold.

Chapter 4

'Mental Defectives: A Serious Social Problem' (1907–24)

On 5 July 1907 the Miller family of Geelong received a telegram urging them to come immediately to Kew, where their eleven-year-old daughter Violet was a patient in the cottages. Violet had been desperately ill with typhoid fever for several weeks. Tragically, she died before her family arrived.[1] Her death was one of the first in a severe typhoid epidemic. Beginning in the female wards of the main asylum in February, the infection spread quickly to the cottages. By the time it finally abated late the following year, thirty patients and six nurses had been infected. In all, four patients and a nurse died.[2] In the absence of an isolation ward, the schoolrooms were converted into makeshift quarantine wards, disrupting classes.[3]

In retrospect, the epidemic marked the end of Kew Cottages' life as 'an institution for the care and training of feeble-minded children'. In the first decades of the twentieth century, fear driven by the emergence of a more deterministic eugenics discourse displaced optimism in thinking about intellectual disabilities. Convinced that the so-called 'feebleminded' represented a threat to social and racial health, a new and more diverse generation of social reformers lobbied government to enact measures to 'protect' the community, though with as yet limited success. Meanwhile, in response to local demands for the removal of the asylum from Kew, the Bent state government in 1905 announced a plan for its eventual closure. Dependent on construction of alternative accommodation for several thousand patients, the plan was beset by delays but gave successive governments an excuse to withhold funding for maintenance and improvements. By the early 1920s the cottages were in a dire state. In 1924, forty years after the Zox royal commission had examined the treatment 'idiot' children received in the state's asylums, another royal commission exposed the suffering this neglect had inflicted on the cottages' residents and raised important questions about their treatment, shocking the Victorian community.

'An Up-to-Date Institution Elsewhere'

The 1890s depression had prevented the government from implementing many of the reforms recommended by the Zox royal commission: but the establishment of the Idiot Asylum in 1887 was a notable exception. By the late 1890s, there was increasing concern about the standard of Victoria's asylums.[4] In 1901 prominent physician Dr J.W. Springthorpe sought a position as 'official visitor' to the metropolitan asylums, intending to do what he could 'to improve what almost everyone condemned'. Two years later he addressed the Medical Society of Victoria on the subject. Compared to asylums in America and Britain, Victoria's were very much inferior: inadequately staffed, overcrowded, ill-equipped and insanitary. The use of mechanical restraints was excessive, the cures too few. The cause, he suggested, was government neglect. Springthorpe called on his medical colleagues to help put an end 'to the regime of indifference and neglect'.[5]

On 25 March 1903 thirty members of the Medical Society waited on Chief Secretary John Murray, to 'urge the necessity for immediate and extensive reform in the treatment and cure of the insane'. The campaign drew widespread support. Newspaper editorials weighed in on the side of reform. The Council of Churches and the Presbyterian Assembly passed resolutions supporting the society's actions. Four months after Springthorpe's address, representatives of the medical profession, the churches, women's organisations and parliamentarians attended a meeting at the Melbourne Town Hall organised to 'show that the whole community is interested in the matter, and to give weight to public opinion. Everyone was strongly convinced that the Government should move in this matter'. The meeting resolved that a deputation should again wait on the chief secretary to urge a speedy amendment to the Lunacy Act.[6] The resulting deputation, when it met with Chief Secretary Murray, was nearly one hundred strong.

The campaign had apparently had little influence on Murray thus far. The press criticised his flippant dismissal of those seeking reform. But in responding to this deputation he revealed that in fact a lunacy bill was in preparation.[7] By December, Victoria had a new Lunacy Act. The new Act created a separate Lunacy Department under the control of an inspector-general of the insane. The chief secretary remained ministerial head.[8]

Seeking to recruit the 'very best man' for the new position, the government advertised widely. Given the run-down state of the department, there was little hope of recruiting anyone pre-eminent in the field. An attempt to poach the New South Wales inspector-general of the insane, Eric Sinclair, had failed. Hope lay in attracting a 'young and ambitious man who was finding his reputation'. The position elicited little interest in Australia. There was more in Britain, where salaries were much lower; the successful candidate was one of sixteen British applicants.[9]

Thirty-seven and unmarried, Dr William Ernest Jones was the medical superintendent of Brecon and Radnor County Asylum in Wales. He had dedicated most of his career to the treatment of lunacy, rising through a series of asylum appointments to his present position. The advertisement for the position had emphasised both extensive 'experience in the treatment of insane persons' and 'skill in administration and ability to manage and organise', and it was probably his demonstrated ability at the latter that won him the position. In applying, Jones explained that Brecon and Radnor was 'a new asylum', which he had opened and organised; its 'arrangements', he explained, represented 'the latest ideas of Asylum construction and requirements'. The five testimonials accompanying his application praised his 'excellent professional and administrative skill'.[10]

Jones arrived in Melbourne on the steamer *Oceana* on 14 February 1905.[11] Soon after, he toured the institutions for which he was now responsible. By 1905 there were six 'hospitals for the insane', as the asylums were now officially designated: the two metropolitan asylums at Yarra Bend and Kew, and four country asylums at Ararat, Beechworth, Sunbury and Ballarat (the last reopened in 1893). Between them they accommodated almost five thousand patients, including the 308 inmates in the Idiot Asylum.[12] After the previous decade of neglect, they presented a grim contrast to the modern asylum Jones had recently left. In a report to government, he set out their many deficiencies. Among the principal defects he listed the reliance on gas lighting and the absence of water-borne sewerage systems. The wards were seriously overcrowded and lacking in general comfort. In the kitchens and laundries of the various institutions, workers toiled without the aid of any labour-saving devices. There was no provision for the isolation of patients with infectious diseases.[13]

His impressions of the Idiot Asylum were mixed. While conceding that it did humane and 'useful work', he found the progress of its development difficult to follow. Much of its infrastructure was seriously deficient, its kitchen and laundry dilapidated and dangerous, while 'many of the buildings were too close together, and some of them utterly unsuitable'. All in all, he thought it 'would be very much wiser to remove the idiot children to a suitable asylum in the country or by the sea'.[14]

Jones estimated that modernising the existing asylums would cost £250,000 and asked the government to provide £50,000 each year to do so. In July 1905 the premier, Thomas Bent, allocated £40,000 from surplus revenue for the 'erection, re-arrangement and repair of Lunatic Asylums, and erection of receiving house for inebriates'.[15] News of this spending created consternation in Kew, where the municipal council and a considerable number of residents continued to oppose the presence of the asylum. The recent campaign for lunacy reform had given the objectors a new opportunity to press for the institution's removal. In August 1903, responding to a petition from ratepayers, Kew Council had called a public meeting to consider the question. Attended by several hundred, the meeting considered both lunacy reform, to which it pledged unanimous support, and removal. Frank Madden, MLA Eastern Suburbs, argued the case for the latter on the grounds of the former, arguing the impossibility of modernising the existing asylum, except at very considerable expense. The government should instead sell the land and use the proceeds to build 'an up-to-date institution elsewhere for the proper treatment of the insane'. His proposal met with unanimous approval.[16]

The announcement in mid-1905 of proposed new spending elicited renewed objections from Kew Council and residents. In August the town clerk wrote to the premier on the council's behalf, reminding him of the public meeting and deputation two years earlier and asking him to keep the plan for removal then proposed in mind. No moneys should be spent except to establish elsewhere 'an Institution on modern lines for the curative treatment of the insane'. More spending would only retard removal and 'perpetuate the location of the Asylum' in Kew. The same sentiments were expressed at a well-attended public meeting. In early August another deputation waited on the premier, urging sale.[17]

Jones had in fact proposed the removal of both the metropolitan asylums, but the government had vetoed his suggestion on the grounds of expense.[18] The agitation from Kew apparently changed its thinking. When cabinet met in August 1905 to consider the question of lunacy reform, it adopted a scheme that would see the 'the ultimate removal of the Kew and Yarra Bend lunatic asylums to some locality to be selected'. The land the asylums occupied would be subdivided and sold, the sale proceeds invested in an endowment to provide for future needs.[19]

The decision to surrender the metropolitan asylums could not be effected either quickly or cheaply, however. It depended on providing alternative accommodation for two thousand patients at an estimated cost of £350,000 to £400,000. This was in addition to the cost of modernising and extending the other asylums.[20] In 1907 the government purchased the Mont Park Estate, fourteen kilometres north east of Melbourne, as a site for a new metropolitan asylum. Two years later it acquired the adjoining Strathallen Estate. Together Jones believed the acquisitions provided sufficient land to allow for the closure of both Yarra Bend and Kew asylums.[21]

Jones considered Yarra Bend beyond redemption, and by 1911 the first stages of the new Mont Park Hospital for the Insane were under construction. He hoped the new hospital would be completed in three years. But the project was beset with problems. Construction was so slow that the rising number of patients at Yarra Bend threatened to exceed the capacity of the new hospital and prevent the closure of the old asylum. Mont Park opened in stages but was incomplete for want of funds when war broke out in 1914. The following year the Department of Defence took over part of the hospital, agreeing to build the outstanding central block for use as a military hospital. It would be almost a decade before Mont Park Hospital reverted to civilian use and the Yarra Bend Asylum finally closed.[22] Until then, it was not possible to contemplate the removal of the Kew Asylum. Consequently, it remained, and the Idiot Asylum with it. Nothing had come of suggestions to move the children to a new institution in the country or by the sea. But, with the main hospital again slated for eventual closure, the cottages' future seemed once more uncertain.

'Mental Defectives: A Serious Social Problem'

When the typhoid epidemic finally ended in December 1908, work began to restore the schoolrooms to their original purpose. By late February 1909, disinfected and freshly painted, they stood ready for occupation.[23] With Eastham retired, the recent death of his assistant and the resignation of the remaining teacher, the appointment of a new teaching staff was necessary.[24] Jones proposed recruiting trained teachers from the Department of Education, but Chief Secretary Murray remained unconvinced.[25]

Without teachers, and despite the official visitors' urging, the training of the inmates was allowed to dwindle into 'practical nothingness'.[26] The resulting neglect shocked visitors. In February 1911, Arthur Hauser called at the asylum as a member of a special committee considering 'the question of backward and mentally defective children'. The conditions

Hauser observed appalled him and were in stark contrast to those observed by Alice Henry thirteen years earlier. 'These boys and girls', he reported, 'have been disgracefully neglected. They are untrained in physical habits. Many masturbate openly. Their clothes reek of filth'.[27]

While Hauser made his remarks confidentially, the neglect he observed was in fact already the subject of public criticism. Only weeks before his visit, the *Age* newspaper had condemned the neglect of the inmates' education, contrasting the previously 'very marked and well directed efforts' to educate them under McCreery with the present situation. Now, it declared, 'this humanitarian case of the afflicted has been abandoned by a parsimonious department, and the half-witted child is allowed to drift downward and allowed to become a loathsome and much more expensive burden on the State'.[28] However, the *Age* was not concerned solely with the effect on individual inmates or the cost to government, as its headline—'Mental Defectives: A Serious Social Problem'—suggested. Left untrained, it warned, such children 'must drift downward, a failure and a menace to the community'. This problem, it explained, was engaging attention elsewhere. In England the report of a royal commission appointed to consider the care and control of the 'feebleminded' had found that there were

> numbers of mentally defective persons whose training is neglected, over whom no efficient control is exercised, and whose wayward and irresponsible lives are productive of crime and misery, and of much continued expenditure, wasteful to the State and individual families.[29]

The *Age* was articulating a by-now widely held belief. In the decades around 1900, a convergence of social and racial anxieties convinced many new social reformers in western countries to espouse the eugenic view that the so-called 'feebleminded' were the ultimate cause of a multitude of social problems. 'Feeblemindedness' was, in the words of the English social reformer and eugenicist Mary Dendy, 'an evil which brings all other evils in its train'.[30] Contemporaries like Dendy, convinced of the 'menace of the feebleminded', assumed that mental deficiency was a hereditary defect passed from one generation of the 'feebleminded' to the next, rendering them 'constitutionally inclined' to immorality. This moral debility led in turn to 'profligate breeding' and an ever-increasing number of the 'feebleminded', threatening an eventual decline in the 'overall fitness of the population'.[31] To prevent social, national and racial disaster, contemporaries considered it imperative to impose control where they assumed none existed.[32]

Eight months after the *Age* warned of the dangers of neglecting the 'feebleminded', several papers read at the 1911 Australasian Medical Congress in Sydney expressed similar alarm. In 1885 Dr Fishbourne had testified to the capacity of the 'feebleminded' at the Zox royal commission, declaring that with proper education at least some people would be able to support themselves outside institutions. Now, however, his views reflected the new racial anxieties. Focusing on the question of 'the segregation of the epileptic and feeble-minded', he argued that the latter represented a 'far-reaching source of evil' to which Australia must respond. In failing to act, he asserted, the nation was lagging behind international opinion. To prove his point, he cited evidence from recent British and American investigations, quoting the opinions of Dr Martin Barr, chief physician of the Pennsylvania School for Feeble-minded Children, and Dendy, both of whom advocated permanent segregation of those deemed 'feebleminded'. Opinion was 'gaining ground amongst those who have studied the subject that legislative interference should be invoked to check the appalling increase of that most hereditary of diseases, feeble-mindedness'. Barr advocated a census of school-age children as a means to determine the prevalence of 'feeble-mindedness' and as a first step toward 'permanent sequestration', a remedy that would protect both society and the 'feebleminded'.[33]

In his paper Dr Harvey Sutton, school medical officer with the Victorian Department of Education, emphasised the problems created by the presence of 'feebleminded' children in schools where, he asserted, they were 'so much grit in the hub of the educational machine'. Sutton argued that they should instead be taught in special schools, which would act as clearing grounds to determine who among them should be segregated. The general public, he declared, must be convinced of 'the need for the care and control of mental defectives'.[34] A third paper contributed by Liverpool doctor E.M. Steven, and read to the congress on his behalf, took an even more radical stance. Concerning 'the treatment of mentally defective children from a national standpoint', he suggested that the 'question of emasculation', while 'abhorrent to many', deserved serious consideration. It would 'undoubtedly materially reduce the roll of the inhabitants of your prisons, lunatic asylums and destitute homes'.[35]

After discussion, the delegates decided to tackle the problem by determining the prevalence of 'feeblemindedness' in Australasia and initiating a 'popular campaign throughout the Commonwealth to educate the people on the problem of the Feeble-minded'.[36] In Victoria, the campaign took a number of approaches. Sutton and others of like mind addressed interested organisations on the subject.[37] Articles, reports, and discussion appeared in the pages of the *Australian Medical Journal*.[38] In March 1913, the Victorian branch of the British Medical Association convened a special meeting to 'arouse medical interest' in the subject.[39] The *Age*, already persuaded, lent its support, publishing a steady stream of articles and editorials emphasising the dire consequences of allowing the 'feebleminded' to go uncontrolled.[40]

William Ernest Jones, Victoria's recently appointed inspector-general of the insane, played a prominent part in the campaign. His career in England had coincided with rising alarm there, and he arrived in Victoria already convinced of the danger.[41] In 1911 he was elected to the central committee established by the congress to oversee the campaign and census, in addition speaking publicly of the urgent need to act.[42] In subsequent decades Jones became one of the key advocates for eugenic control of the mentally deficient.[43]

By March 1913 the results of the investigation into the prevalence of mental deficiency initiated by the medical congress were in. The Victorian committee had conducted a census, asking state and private schools to count the number of 'mentally dull, feebleminded, imbecile and idiot children' among their pupils. These were the standard categories used to classify degrees of mental deficiency, organised from least to most severe.[44] Doctors were asked to provide the same information about their patients, to allow for those children who did not attend school. The census included the 324 inmates of the Idiot Asylum, representing 7 per cent of the reported total of 4709: 7 of the patients were classified as 'mentally dull', 30 'feeble-minded', 154 'imbecile' and 133 'idiot'. Organisers suspected their total figures were an underestimate; returns from private schools and doctors had been poor. Even so, they believed, the results revealed 'a problem demanding solution by legislation'.[45]

Accordingly, in April 1913 Jones introduced a deputation representing the medical profession to Murray, then acting premier, and the minister of public instruction, Sir Alexander Peacock. After presenting the results of the recent investigation into the prevalence of 'feeblemindedness' in Victoria, the deputation reiterated the prevailing beliefs about the 'feebleminded': the strongly hereditary character of their 'defect' (so intensely so, according to one speaker, that 'given a feebleminded father and a feebleminded mother, it was absolutely sure that there would be 100 per cent. of feeble-minded children'); their inherent tendency to breed prolifically and without restraint; and their alleged susceptibility to crime and vice. What was needed, the deputation told the ministers, was a 'proper system' of control. The system they proposed encompassed special and residential schools for 'mentally backward and defective' children, a residential colony to segregate 'adult defectives', and legislation to allow for compulsory segregation. Queried by Murray about how far they proposed to go regarding special legislation for segregation, Jones replied that the intent was 'segregation for life in a large number of cases'. Industrial training to make the inmates of such institutions useful would ease the financial burden on the state, but any cost would in reality constitute an economy by reducing expenditure on the hospitals, gaols, and other institutions in which the 'feebleminded' inevitably washed up. The question of sterilisation the deputation thought too radical for the present.[46]

Murray proved receptive. Institutional segregation on the lines the deputation described, he said, 'appealed to him as about the most practical, practicable and common sense way of dealing with the question'. His experience as head of the Neglected Children's Department had crystallised in his mind the necessity for the state to maintain 'life-long control' of the 'feebleminded'. He agreed with the view that educating 'mental defectives' was futile. His remarks, no doubt galling to McCreery, also a member of the deputation, explain his previous refusal to support the educational mission of the Idiot Asylum. He pledged to recommend the deputation's proposals to cabinet but warned that there was the question of cost to consider.[47]

Despite this positive response, attempts to control the 'feebleminded' made little headway over the following decade. After considering the deputation's proposals, the government announced its intention to introduce legislation and directed Jones to prepare a bill authorising compulsory institutional segregation.[48] When Jones visited England shortly afterward, he took the opportunity to study the legislation relating to the care and control of the 'feebleminded' then before the British parliament. He came away unimpressed, believing its provisions too much tied up in 'red tape'. Proper provision could be made, he thought, by an amendment of the Victorian Lunacy Act.[49] Two years later he concluded that additional legislation was

> not entirely necessary, inasmuch as the present method of certification, inspection and segregation could readily be used … owing to the fact that the definition of "lunatic" in our Act is so wide as to embrace high grade imbeciles or other similar mental defective persons.[50]

Whether because of this opinion or otherwise, no new legislation followed.

Institutional segregation of the 'feebleminded' made similarly limited progress. Initially Jones envisaged the Idiot Asylum playing only a minor part in the scheme to control the 'feebleminded', believing it unsuitable 'to receive anything [*sic*] but the very lowest grades of mental defect'.[51] In 1911 he proposed transferring the small number of educable children at the Idiot Asylum—by his estimate physical drill and manual training would improve half of the 320 inmates, forty to fifty of whom would 'more than likely to benefit from elementary educational training'—to a new institution. Together with the 'backward' and 'feebleminded' children from the Neglected Children's Depot, they would constitute 'the nucleus of a proper training institution for the defective and feebleminded and higher grade imbeciles'. But this and subsequent suggestions to establish such an institution fell on deaf ears.[52]

This left only the Idiot Asylum. By mid-1914, Jones seemed to be changing his mind about the role it could play. Improving the cottages and providing teachers for the educable inmates was, he now argued, the best means to fulfil the urgent need for 'a residential institution for the training of mental defectives'.[53] However, here too his efforts met with little success.

Schooling had been suspended since the chief secretary's refusal to authorise the employment of teachers in 1909. When the *Age* criticised the lack of any education for the 'feebleminded' in January 1911, Jones seized the chance to press for the resumption of teaching. In a public statement he revealed that his proposals had been ignored, effectively charging the government with refusing to act on 'his advice or provide the necessary co-operation to carry out urgent reforms in his department'.[54]

Director of Education Frank Tate responded by appointing a committee to investigate the education of 'feebleminded' children, of which both Jones and Arthur Hauser were members. The committee discussed education at the Idiot Asylum at some length, including the qualifications and experience necessary in the teaching staff, and what the training should entail, the latter reminiscent of the regime under Eastham. The committee recommended the establishment of a school for fifty children. However, after visiting the cottages, a shocked Hauser declared that no teacher could be expected to work there until 'decided changes' were made.

The committee consequently made its recommendation contingent on certain structural alterations and extensions, including repairs to the existing schoolroom and the erection of open-air classrooms, then in vogue. It went so far as to identify a site for the latter in the boys exercise yard. It estimated the cost of these alterations at £1000, in addition to the £550 per annum allowed for teacher salaries. But subsequent events suggest that establishing a school at the Idiot Asylum was not a government priority. When the committee's proposals went to cabinet, the recommendation for a special day school in Bell Street, Fitzroy, was approved, but the recommendation for a school at the cottages was passed over in silence. The Bell Street school was expanded in 1915 with the opening of a branch in Montague.[55]

Attempts to recommence teaching on a more modest scale met with no more success. In 1916 Jones proposed employing two female teachers, at a cost of £350 per annum. The scheme foundered on the question of which department should bear the cost of the teachers' salaries. While treasury considered that the Department of Education should do so, the minister of public instruction, H.S.W. Lawson, disagreed. In December 1916, the money allocated for the teachers' salaries was struck off the estimates and 'the matter thus postponed'.[56] Despite Jones's repeated urging, teaching would remain in abeyance for more than a decade, its absence depriving the inmates of the opportunity of an education.

Despite some reconstruction, which included a new nursery for younger children (Figure 4.1), by the early 1920s The Children's Cottages was in need of 'a great deal of attention and expenditure'. Connection to the sewer was incomplete, despite the typhoid known to be endemic in the institution and only held at bay by routine vaccination. Some of the wards were in need of remodelling. Some of the 'bigger boys' continued to sleep in worn-out 'wood and canvas sleeping tents' for want of other accommodation. Proper covered ways or corridors between the buildings remained unbuilt, as did improved amenities for staff.[57]

In 1922 a series of articles in the *Argus* revealed just how dilapidated the cottages had become. In the dormitories, long-broken windows went unreplaced, while defective drainage rotted the timber walls. In the wooden and canvas dormitories the walls were torn, exposing the inmates to the cold, while gaping holes in the wire doors and windows left the more 'helpless' patients to be tormented by flies. The asphalt paths between the buildings were so broken up that they endangered the safety of staff and patients. It was, the newspaper declared, 'a case of housing human beings under the worst conditions'.[58]

'MENTAL DEFECTIVES: A SERIOUS SOCIAL PROBLEM' (1907–24)

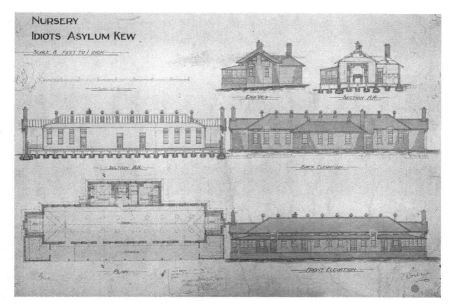

Figure 4.1: Nursery, Idiots Asylum Kew, Plans
(Courtesy Public Record Office Victoria, VPRS 3686/P0017, MHK 1.29)
In 1914 a new nursery for thirty or forty children was added to the cottages. Superintendent Gamble's belief that it heralded other improvements went unfulfilled. By the early 1920s the cottages had fallen into a terrible state of dilapidation, the result of sustained government neglect.

Why had reconstruction made so little headway? One reason was the ongoing opposition to the presence of the institutions in Kew. Any sign of building provoked renewed protest. In early June 1917 the district's parliamentary representatives, William McPherson and James Merrett, waited on the chief secretary, Donald McLeod, to express their constituents' concern that any investment in new buildings at Kew would diminish the likelihood of the institutions' removal. Pressed by McPherson, the chief secretary explained that, while removal remained the government's policy, the delayed closure of Yarra Bend and the difficulty of funding the substantial cost of a new institution to accommodate the Kew patients would slow removal. Neither man seemed especially sympathetic to these difficulties or to the patients living in the run-down institutions. Instead they reiterated their protest that any new building violated previous promises to close the institutions.[59]

FAILED AMBITIONS

Wartime economies did not help, but the parsimony did not end with the coming of peace.[60] Writing in response to the *Argus* revelations, Kew's recently retired superintendent, Morris Gamble, endorsed practically everything it reported. The cause, he declared, was government neglect: 'If he who wins the palm should bear it, then equally he who incurs the blame should shoulder it'. In his view, the 'entire blame for the bad condition of affairs as to the buildings in Kew and other asylums' rested with 'the Chief Secretary and the Treasurer, who ... [had] systematically withheld money needed for the general upkeep from the Lunacy Department on the plea of economising'.[61]

The consequences of this 'economising' for those living and working in the Children's Cottages were made particularly stark when typhoid struck the institution again in March 1922, only weeks after the *Argus* exposé. With the isolation ward in ruins, it proved impossible to quarantine the sufferers, increasing the danger of the infection spreading. Nor could special nurses be employed for want of accommodation. The official visitors feared the flies that 'more or less covered' the 'helpless' patients confined to chairs were a 'probable source of contagion' because of the failure to fly proof verandahs with netting.[62]

For many patients the absence of anything with which to occupy their time exacerbated the deprivation of their material circumstances. In March 1923, Dr Springthorpe reported finding 'some 95 patients lolling about a bare yard some 70 yards square, doing nothing', their 'only amusement one unused football'.[63] Five months earlier another of the visitors, Mr G.T. Howard, suggested that 'something more might be done to brighten the lives' of the patients through the provision of such amusements as 'music: magic lantern: moving pictures: toys, skipping ropes &c' but with apparently little effect.[64] The modest nature of his suggestions provides some insight into the monotony and deprivation of inmates' lives.

'An Indictment Against the Whole Community'

In December 1923 a new medical officer took charge of the Children's Cottages. Dr Reginald Ellery, twenty-seven, had graduated from medical school the previous March. Unable to obtain an appointment elsewhere, he accepted a position as a junior medical officer at Kew Hospital for the Insane. In December 1923 he was transferred to the cottages. Less than a year later, in November 1924, he found his actions the subject of a royal commission, after members of the attendant staff accused him of maladministration and cruelty to the patients.[65]

The allegations were initially investigated by the inspector-general of the insane. After three days of hearings, Jones concluded that the charges were malicious, 'deliberately engineered' by an attendant with a grudge against Ellery and supported by false statements from one of the nurses. Jones considered their actions serious enough to warrant charges of misconduct.[66] The threatened investigation into their actions was slow in coming, however, delayed by procedural problems and a seeming reluctance within the department to pursue the issue further.[67]

Little detail of the charges had yet become public. But that was about to change. In early October 1924, under the headline 'Kew Asylum in a Ferment', the populist left-wing Sydney newspaper *Smith's Weekly* carried a long report on its front page. On the same day, the Melbourne *Truth* reported on the 'Kew Asylum Scandal'. In typically sensational style, they revealed that 'allegations of an astounding nature' had been made against Ellery at a recent departmental inquiry, some 'too revolting to print' but relating to 'wanton' acts of 'cruelty including in one instance the extraction of an idiot boy's teeth to cure him of a habit of biting his clothing to shreds'. Outraged by this and other alleged cruelties, the attendants had reportedly risen in 'revolt', complaining to the inspector-general through their union. They alleged the resulting departmental inquiry had been 'farcical' in its favouritism, with Ellery exonerated and the attendants accused of conspiracy and perjury.

Rather than demand that verdict be withdrawn, however, the union sought to have the charges investigated 'in their proper place'. When no such investigation eventuated, they had turned to the newspapers to bring the scandal to the public's attention. Both newspapers called for an 'open' and independent inquiry, *Truth* arguing that if there was conspiracy, as alleged, the chief secretary should not be satisfied to leave the matter lie. 'Why', it asked, 'should inquiries as that of Kew be hushed up? Why should the public have to rely upon distorted and garbled details which filter through official channels and leave them undecided and worried in mind?'[68] Both papers continued to run hard on the issue, publishing follow-up articles that quoted extracts from the sworn affidavits of staff detailing instances of patient ill-treatment and accusing the government of 'a conspiracy of silence'.[69] However, the prospect of a new inquiry seemed to have reached a 'dead end'.

Kew's medical superintendent, Joseph Hollow, had declined to lay charges against the staff. In such circumstances the chief secretary, Thomas Tunnecliffe, told the press that 'he could not see how another inquiry could legally be ordered … The Lunacy Act made no other provision. In any case, the occurrences which were the subject of the previous inquiry were now five months old'.[70] If this was an attempt to deploy 'hush hush tactics', as *Truth* alleged, it failed. The Mental Hospital Employees Association continued to agitate.[71] Two days later, Tunnecliffe announced the appointment of a board of inquiry. While the allegations 'had been already thoroughly investigated by Dr Jones as a departmental inquiry', the complainants had not accepted the findings, and in those circumstances 'a public inquiry was the only convincing mode of procedure'. The 'public conscience was particularly sensitive to the treatment received by helpless and irresponsible persons such as the inmates of Kew Asylum'.[72]

In late October the government appointed a royal commission headed by Police Magistrate A.A. Kelley to investigate the truth of the complaints, with Frank Menzies of the Crown Law Department assisting. Frank's younger brother, Robert Menzies, then a prominent lawyer and later Australia's longest-serving prime minister, represented Ellery.[73] The only royal commission into Kew Cottages in their 120-year history, it exposed the terrible state to which years of government neglect had reduced the institution. It also raised important ethical questions about the authority of doctors to subject people with intellectual disabilities to non-therapeutic and experimental treatments without their consent.

In 1924 no external authority existed to oversee medical practice in mental hospitals.[74] The appointment of the royal commission provided an opportunity for outside scrutiny. It was Frank Brennan, counsel representing the attendants and nurses, who interrogated the actions of the medical men most closely (Figure 4.2). Brennan, already a member of the Commonwealth parliament, would be appointed attorney-general in the Scullin Labor government. His questioning of the medical staff exposed how the belief that people with intellectual disabilities were somehow less than human rationalised treatment that was otherwise unjustifiable.

Figure 4.2: Frank Brennan in the 1920s, T. Humphrey and Co.
Melbourne (192?), detail
(Courtesy National Library of Australia)
Brennan's interrogation of witnesses at the 1924 royal commission raised important ethical questions about the right of doctors to subject people with intellectual disabilities to treatment without their consent.

Brennan, in contrast, argued that the need to gain consent applied whether the patient was intellectually disabled or not. His pursuit of these questions marks him as an important, if hitherto unrecognised, figure in Australia's disability history. His thinking on the subject of the treatment of patients with intellectual disabilities was not only shaped by his 'deep respect for the law' but perhaps by his personal circumstances as well. Brennan's eldest daughter Mary, born in January 1917, was intellectually disabled. By 1924, she was six years old. Beloved by her father, in later years she would become 'the keystone of his life'.[75]

Hearings commenced at the cottages on 5 November. Prior to their beginning, Commissioner Kelley, accompanied by counsel and the press, toured the institution. The *Age*'s account of the inspection was coloured by its attitude towards people with intellectual disabilities. What the visitors saw, it declared, could produce 'nothing but a revolting and depressing effect upon them. Any large idiot asylum must produce such an effect on visitors who are not acquainted with such institutions'. But leaving the 'pitiful mental state' of the inmates aside, its report confirmed how bad conditions had become:

> The buildings are old, far from hygienic, and in many parts dilapidated. The wards, dining rooms and other divisions of the buildings are permeated by a nauseating musty odour. The furnishings are old and frayed by wear, and the accommodation for patients and for the staff is unsuitable and apparently inadequate.

The dominant characteristic was one of 'deep and settled gloom'.[76]

The commission's subsequent hearings revealed something of the hardships the overcrowding and want of amenities inflicted on patients. For many years, around eighty male patients were taken from the wards to an airing court in which the old drill hall stood. With almost all the glass in the windows broken, the doors and floors defective, and no fireplace or other heating, it provided little comfort or shelter. Until recently the patients had been moved to the disused schoolroom on cold winter days.

'MENTAL DEFECTIVES: A SERIOUS SOCIAL PROBLEM' (1907–24)

While far too small to accommodate them all, its windows were at least intact and its fireplaces provided some warmth.

When the official visitors condemned the schoolroom as unsafe in early 1924, the children were left to shelter in the drill hall, where 'they were many times found crying from the effects of the cold weather, some huddled together into corners to obtain warmth from one another; others standing or sitting on a floor saturated in places with urine'. Other 'crippled' children spent their days in an old, unheated wooden annexe to one of the cottages in which a three-inch gap between the asphalt floor and walls provided 'ventilation'. The transfer of inmates from the hospital to make more space for sick patients created corresponding overcrowding elsewhere. Even much-needed repairs inflicted privation. For eight weeks during the previous winter, fourteen or so 'crippled children' had to be bathed in the open air, there being nowhere else available while the bathroom usually used for the purpose was repaired and sewered. Kelley criticised all this as 'altogether inadequate' but concluded that in the current state of the institution there was no alternative, there being 'insufficient buildings at the institution to accommodate the idiot patients under ideal conditions'.[77]

As earlier press reports reveal, these conditions were not new. And, as Kelley observed, the staff, given their considerable years of service at the cottages, must have known that the recently appointed Ellery could not be held responsible for them. On the contrary, among the exhibits tended to the commission was a lengthy list of improvements he had effected. It was partly on this basis that Kelley concluded that the charges levelled against Ellery were 'actuated by animosity' and with the intention of displacing him as medical officer rather than from concern for the patients' wellbeing. He attributed this animosity to changes Ellery 'made in the management and affairs of the institution and the rearrangement of the male staff'.[78]

The commissioner nevertheless also acknowledged a broader context of antagonism and distrust between the medical and attendant staff. He noted that some two or so years earlier 'the Council of the Victorian Branch of the Hospital Employees Association of which most of the attendants of the Idiot Asylum are members passed a resolution expressing no confidence in Dr Jones'. When they made their charges, the staff had not done so to Hollow, the medical superintendent, as regulations dictated, but through their union to the inspector-general. This, Kelley suggested, was because they believed 'that they were not likely to receive proper consideration of their grievances'. Hollow had previously failed to consider other (unrelated) complaints from the attendants.[79]

Despite concluding that the charges were motivated by animosity toward Ellery, the commissioner did not discount all the evidence he heard. He judged that 'speaking generally', the nurses and attendants had 'given truthful evidence of certain facts which have been for the most part admitted'. He counted among these facts the hardships inflicted on the patients, for which the recently appointed Ellery could not be blamed. Significantly, however, he also accepted as truthful evidence relating to aspects of his treatment of the patients that were new.[80]

In addition to their charges of maladministration, the staff had accused Ellery of cruelty. This included demonstrations by him of catheterisation and the use of nasal and oesophageal tubes in 'forcible feeding' for the benefit of the nursing staff, experimental treatments for epilepsy, injections of the drug apomorphine hydrochloride into 'excited' or 'violent' patients, and his allegedly improper extraction of patients' teeth.[81]

The previous internal inquiry had already established that Ellery did indeed perform the procedures alleged on a number of occasions. The question then became whether he had done so with good or sufficient cause.[82] At issue, as Brennan recognised, was how far the discretion of the medical officers extended in their treatment of patients.[83] His questioning forced the doctors to articulate their understandings of their authority versus the rights of patients, eliciting some disturbing revelations.

For much of the nineteenth century, asylum attendants received no formal instruction in nursing the insane. This changed in the late 1880s and 1890s, when the medical officers initiated a system of training, as part of a push to transform the asylums into hospitals. If asylums were to become mental hospitals, the reasoning went, then attendants must become nurses, akin to their counterparts in general hospitals. The scheme was initially

'Mental Defectives: A Serious Social Problem' (1907–24)

voluntary, and many attendants refused to participate. In 1905 the new Lunacy Act empowered the newly appointed Jones to introduce compulsory training. Permanent appointment, wage increments and promotion all depended on satisfactory completion of the course. The first lectures and examinations were conducted in 1907.[84] In 1911 Mary J. Grant, a nurse at the Idiot Asylum, won the gold medal awarded to the candidate with the highest marks in the senior nursing examination.[85]

It was in this context that several nurses asked Ellery to demonstrate the use of the catheter and feeding tubes, and he obliged. Crucially, he conducted the demonstrations on patients who did not require the procedures. This was apparently a new departure. Matron Molloy testified that she had never in her thirty years' experience seen other doctors demonstrate such procedures 'on patients who did not need the operations'. Her evidence that 'very few patients at the asylum ever required catheter treatment, and if the nurses who were studying for the examinations had waited for actual cases to occur before having the demonstrations they would be waiting still' explains the resort to patients who did not need the procedure.[86] It also raises a question about the relevance of hospitalisation to the work of the cottages.

Nonetheless, to the objection that none of the patients had needed the operations, the medical officers testified that it was Ellery's responsibility to provide instruction, particularly if the nurses requested he do so. The nurses, Hollow declared, 'must be instructed. They have a right to receive instruction'. When Brennan asked whether 'It would be quite wrong to use the catheter on patients who were perfectly healthy and did not require it—merely for demonstration', Hollow disagreed: 'This is a procedure to increase knowledge, and one must consider the principle of the end justifying the means in many of these cases'. Ellery was of the same mind.[87]

Clearly, the medical officers believed that the pursuit of knowledge trumped the patients' rights. They made the same argument to defend the experimental treatments for epilepsy Ellery had administered and his use of apomorphine hydrochloride to sedate patients. Hollow argued that:

'Experiments were necessary if the medical staff was to keep abreast of modern methods of dealing with mental cases'. Ellery believed it a legitimate part of his role as a medical officer to conduct 'reasonable experiments'. While conceding that the patients were admitted for their own and the community's protection, he asserted the right of the medical officers 'to conduct certain experiments' on the patients that would 'enable us in time to deal with defectiveness and find out the cause and treatment'.[88]

In all this, the consent of the patient seemed to be more or less irrelevant. Consent, Ellery testified in relation to catheterisation, was immaterial, excepting that in its absence 'the operation could not be performed because they would resist'.[89] He had regularly taken patients' blood for a study into the relationship between syphilis and mental deficiency conducted by the departmental pathologist, Dr Lind. Statistical rather than therapeutic, the study was analogous to the demonstrations because participating patients received no benefit. It was not, Hollow said, the practice to ask their permission before taking their blood because, he agreed with Menzies, it would not be 'possible to get results of any accuracy if you did that'.[90] In one instance, Ellery had resorted to chloroforming a patient after she resisted.[91]

Brennan pressed the medical witnesses to explain these views, and by so doing argued that such treatment was unlawful. He began by asking if they could cite any examples in which similar procedures were performed on sane patients solely for the purposes of demonstration? In what circumstances, if any, would they do so on such patients? Would it be acceptable if the patient was anesthetised, for example? Under his questioning the medical officers agreed that 'in the interests of science' it was acceptable to treat mentally defective patients differently, to do things to them that could not be done to patients outside without their consent.[92] How then, he asked, did they justify this difference in treatment? On what legal or other authority did they rely? What rights had the patients forfeited other than the 'necessary restraint that is put upon them as mental defectives', which permitted the doctors to treat them as they had?[93]

Consent, Brennan argued, was paramount. The patients' passivity when so treated, or their ignorance of their legal or moral rights, did not justify

'MENTAL DEFECTIVES: A SERIOUS SOCIAL PROBLEM' (1907–24)

treating them without their consent for purposes other than therapy. No matter the procedure, he asserted, without consent the doctor was 'taking from the person of a fellow creature something against his will'. A procedure carried out without consent could not be justified on the basis of its degree of harm or its contribution to knowledge. In acting without their consent, the patients were being treated in ways that were unlawful in respect to free men. 'Why', he asked Ellery, 'should the weak and helpless pay tribute to knowledge that no one else is required to pay?'[94]

The answer seemed to be because they were at hand. Certainly, Ellery answered the question in those terms. It was, he said, 'Because they are only the weak and helpless that are in this institution'.[95] His remark reflects the sense of entitlement he and the other medical officers seemed to feel. They ventured various answers to Brennan's question about the authority that sanctioned their actions. The inspector-general, for example, argued that the medical superintendent was 'the legal guardian' of the patients but conceded that he did not know whether such guardianship bestowed 'any measure of right whatever to interfere with their persons, outside the necessary restraint that is put upon them as mental defectives'.[96] Such testimony suggests they had given the question little actual consideration, believing their qualifications as medical men conferred sufficient authority. Asked if he would expect a 'junior medical officer' such as Ellery to consult him 'before he embarked on any experiment, or would he have a degree of judgment in that', Hollow replied, 'Not necessarily; it would be left to his own judgment. He is a qualified medical man and he is quite qualified to carry out therapeutic measures'.[97]

They conceded there were limits. Ellery excluded anything that would endanger the patient's life or cause 'real pain that would be hard to bear'. Nor did he hold with 'speculative' experimentation, 'just to try anything which comes along, but if there is a reasonable ground of hope that some benefit may accrue, then it is certainly reasonable to try it'. Hollow agreed that no 'dangerous experiments' should be conducted on the patients. However, the 'characteristic' insensibility of 'idiots' provided a degree of latitude not permissible with 'normal' people. Ellery explained that he did not consider the pain of an injection 'as pain, especially with this class of people, whose sensibilities are reduced'. Hollow justified catheterisation on the same grounds. It was not usually 'a painful procedure and particularly in these cases where the sensibility is diminished very much, both psychically and physically'. This presumably negated any embarrassment the patients may have felt.[98] The supposed insensibility of 'idiots' also provided a defence to the allegation that Ellery had improperly extracted the patients' teeth.

Dental hygiene, or the lack of it, was a longstanding problem in the asylums. Until the previous February, the department had not employed a single dentist, despite repeated requests to governments for the money to do so.[99] Faced with 'a considerable leeway to make up', the new dentist, Mr Govett, had only been able to make a 'rough examination' of the patients at the cottages by the time of the commission's hearings. He testified that their 'mouths were in a very septic condition, and in great need of dental attention'. The only patients whose teeth did not require treatment were those that were 'edentulous' or, as Menzies put it, 'those who have not teeth at all'.[100] Ellery had reported on the urgent need to treat the patients' teeth soon after he began working at the cottages, suggesting that if no money was forthcoming dental hospital students might be recruited to assist. The question for the commission was not whether there was a need for dental treatment but whether any of the many extractions Ellery performed were done 'for other than good or sufficient cause' or in improper conditions, as alleged.[101]

The commission focused on two instances. In the first, Ellery had extracted teeth from six or seven patients in the female airing court in the presence of other inmates and had allowed two nurses to try their hand at removing teeth from the patients. There was much dispute among witnesses about the circumstances, including whether Ellery had taken proper steps to prevent infection and if the patients present had been frightened by the proceedings.[102] Here, the alleged insensibility of 'idiots' again provided a defence. Hollow conceded that patients witnessing the extractions 'would probably manifest some symptoms of fear, perhaps, but it would not effect [*sic*] them. They would forget it immediately; it would have no permanent effect upon them'. Their 'sensibilities', he explained, 'are very much diminished in every way, both the psychical and physical sensibilities of mentally sub-normal patients are very much diminished'.[103]

Here, too, Brennan raised the question of whether this would be done to other people. Nonetheless, it could at least be argued that it was therapeutic. The same could not be said for the second occasion the commission examined. This was the 'cruelty' to which *Smith's Weekly* had referred when it first broke the story. Ellery had indeed extracted teeth from a patient to prevent him habitually tearing his clothes. A 'special coat with closed sleeves' had failed to stop him; he had freed his fingers by biting the ends out of the sleeves. In consultation Ellery and Hollow then agreed that, providing the patient's 'teeth were unsound', Ellery should extract them. Unsurprisingly, Ellery found on examination teeth in various degrees of decay. He removed three, but 'was compelled to desist' after the patient 'became refractory'. The extractions failed to prevent him from tearing his clothes and he was subsequently confined in a camisole (a modified straitjacket in which the hands were confined by the patient's side). While the medical officers defended their actions as in the patient's interest, Hollow argued that '[i]f he tore his clothes he would not be properly clothed'. It is hard to see this as anything other than an attempt to manage difficult behaviour in the interests of institutional routine, made possible by disregard of patient rights and assumptions about their diminished sensibility and the entitlement of doctors to act on their own authority.[104]

By the end of its hearings the commission had heard from thirty attendants and nurses, the medical officers and sundry other witnesses. It had heard nothing from the patients. Questioning one of the nurses about why she thought the demonstration of force feeding of patients was acceptable, Brennan observed that the patient also 'had a point of view'. While she had 'never thought of it', Brennan had in fact suggested calling patients to testify. His proposal provoked a discussion between commissioner and counsel about the capacity of the patients to do so.

Brennan argued that he had spoken with two patients and thought they might be examined to ascertain if their evidence was 'of any value … Some of these patients are intelligible and apparently intelligent'. They were certainly aware of the commission being held in their midst. According to Hollow, it was 'a matter of general discussion' among them.[105] Asked by Brennan if some of the patients were 'fairly bright', Nurse Lohman replied: 'Oh yes, I saw one of them reading about the commission in the paper the other day'. Her remark elicited laughter from those present, presumably provoked by the idea that any of the patients could or would have any interest in the commission.[106] Mr Frank Menzies, counsel assisting the commissioner, suggested that an expert assessment would be required. It should not be left to a layman such as Brennan to 'determine whether a witness is sound and rational'. But any chance that the patients' point of view would be heard ended when the commissioner declared 'that the matter of the inquiry can be determined without calling evidence of persons who are probably idiots'.[107] These of course were the very people on whom the procedures were performed.

This was not the first time that people with intellectual disabilities were silenced by the assumption that they were incapable of giving formal testimony. Seven years earlier, patient Frank Dawson told the senior attendant that he had seen another warder 'doing "dirty things" to' a fellow resident the previous evening. The victim subsequently corroborated Dawson's account of the assault in the most explicit terms, and, when questioned by the medical officer, both victim and witness 'adhered to their statement'. Despite the clarity and consistency of their account, the medical superintendent and inspector-general agreed that there was no prospect of successfully prosecuting the perpetrator because 'the witnesses' were 'of such a low average of intelligence that the court' was unlikely 'to accept their evidence as sufficiently reliable to convict on' and there was 'no sane witness to give any sort of corroborative evidence'. They agreed to take no further action against the perpetrator, having already sent him away from the institution shortly after the assault, so avoiding the public exposure of a trial.[108]

Commissioner Kelley provided no reasoning for his conclusions, confining his remarks strictly to the detail of the charges against Ellery and his findings, so it is difficult to know how far the arguments of counsel influenced him. The findings suggest that where he judged there was a therapeutic rationale he found the treatment acceptable. Into this basket fell the use of apomorphine hydrochloride, the experimental treatments for epilepsy and extractions of teeth (although he considered Ellery 'should not have performed the extractions on the airing court in the presence of other patients and he should not have permitted the nurses to extract teeth').

He also considered taking blood to study the relationship between syphilis and mental deficiency 'reasonable' and 'of great assistance to valuable scientific research'. But the caveat to this finding, and those on the demonstrations conducted for the benefit of the nurses, invoked a limit. When taking blood caused 'a patient to become excited and refractory it should be discontinued and the use of chloroform should not be resorted to'. The use of patients to demonstrate procedures they did not need he considered unacceptable. These findings seem to give some consideration to the balance between the rights of patients and the benefit derived. Overall, however, he found no evidence of 'cruelty wilfully and deliberately practised' on the patients in any of these actions, as alleged.[109]

The commissioner also discussed the question of administration, although the terms of reference allowed him to do so only as far as the question touched on 'the complaints dealt with at the inquiry'. His finding was highly critical of the inspector-general: 'Whatever urgent claims other activities may have had upon the money allotted by Dr Jones, the comfort of the children referred to should', he declared, 'have found a place amongst the most urgent much earlier than the present time'.[110] Jones in turn blamed the economies of successive governments, writing in his annual report that the commission had revealed the failure of previous ministries to effect his 'various recommendations for the improvement and reconstruction of the Institution'. He softened his criticism with the observation that government inaction was 'no doubt' due 'to the necessity for an extreme economy attributable to the strain entailed on the State's finance as a result of war'.[111] On the question of where blame should be assigned, the press was in agreement.

The Melbourne newspapers reported extensively on the commission's hearings. Ellery later recalled reporters arriving each morning, 'clambering out of a "Herald" newsvan'.[112] In the wake of the hearings, the press praised 'the obvious penetration and impartiality' of the commissioner's report, believing its findings dealt out censure in proper proportion to the culpability of those immediately involved. Ultimately, however, they argued that blame for the terrible conditions could not be assigned to any one individual. Rather, the report was 'an indictment against the whole community which, through its Governments, has paid so little heed to repeated pleadings'. The report must be a catalyst to reform. 'Anger', the *Herald* declared:

> must turn against those who, in blindness to the real responsibilities of government, have scraped and saved money at the price of such suffering. It has been the boast of Victoria that it has managed to get along for years so cheaply. Can we be glad, when we read Mr Kelley's description of the conditions at the Kew Asylum of the extra shillings we have saved in taxation?

The public, the *Age* declared, had 'consented to three decades of doing nothing' since the Gillies government had promised to remove the Kew Asylum elsewhere more than thirty-five years earlier. All agreed the government must finally act on that promise.[113]

In the wake of the commission, the department transferred Ellery to the Sunbury Hospital for the Insane. Despite being a demotion, the transfer was the making of his career. In Sunbury's superintendent, Dr John Adey, he found a mentor. Ellery would become 'the most prominent psychiatrist in the country during the interwar years', earning 'a reputation for alternative and radical methods of treating the mentally ill'.[114]

Three of the attendants were dismissed and others transferred. It was the question of the fairness of their dismissal that dominated debate in

84

the weeks after the commission concluded.[115] Almost nothing was said about the rights of the patients. Nor did this matter concern those who continued to interest themselves in the question of mental deficiency over the next decade.

Chapter 5

'A New Deal for Mental Defectives' (1924–39)

In 1924 the *Herald* published a series of articles to garner public support for measures to prevent the 'multiplication' of the 'mentally defective'. The series began with a visit to the Children's Cottages. There, the author asserted, on 'the scrapheap of society', could be seen the consequences of inaction. In language that is both highly offensive and hard to read today, he described the more severely disabled residents as 'human vegetables'. However, they did not in his view pose the greatest threat to society. It was the so-called 'feebleminded' who represented the most significant danger: people who, while having 'few outward signs of mental derangement', allegedly lacked the capacity to manage their lives without resort to 'vice, violence and crime'. The author lamented that the state lacked the 'machinery' necessary to control them.[1]

The *Herald* was among a wide array of individuals and organisations lobbying government to control the 'mentally defective' in the interwar decades. Meanwhile, in Kew, a reinvigorated campaign demanded removal of the Mental Hospital from the district. Even as these campaigns swirled around them, life in the cottages went on. The memories of Edward 'Ted' Rowe, who lived in the cottages from 1925 to 1933, provide a rare insight into everyday life for residents. His recollections suggest that the royal commission did little to mitigate the deprivations they endured.

Governments began to act on concerns about mental deficiency in the 1920s, but progress was slow, hindered by Victoria's political instability and a reluctance to spend, especially during the financial turmoil of the Great Depression. By the eve of the Second World War, however, Victoria had established the foundations of a system of institutional care. But there was seemingly no place for the cottages in these plans. In 1936, the government announced the closure of the Kew Mental Hospital, beginning with the Children's Cottages. While the Kew Council was elated, residents and their families confronted an uncertain future.

'Dealing with the Menace of the Feeble-minded'

Following a public meeting in June 1918, a deputation from the Association to Combat the Social Evil met with John Bowser, chief secretary in the Lawson conservative government, to argue 'the necessity of adequate provision for the feebleminded'. The association's primary purpose was the containment of sexually transmitted diseases, which contemporaries frequently linked to a failure to control the activities of 'feebleminded' individuals in the community. The association's membership neatly illustrates the breadth of concern, including doctors, psychologists, social workers, Protestant clergy, and representatives of many women's organisations. The deputation urged the establishment of residential schools for 'feebleminded' children and industrial colonies to provide permanent care for them in their adulthood. It also called for 'the immediate formation of after-care committees' to supervise the 'feebleminded' in the community.

The deputation rehearsed the now familiar arguments about 'the menace of the feeble minded', arguing that the two special schools in Fitzroy and Montague (South Melbourne) were inadequate to protect the state against the 'vice and criminality' to which the mentally deficient were allegedly prone. Nor, Miss Glendenning from the Free Kindergarten Union of Victoria asserted, did they prevent them 'propagating their species'. Day schools left 'feebleminded' children too much to their own devices and free to mix with other children. As Angela Booth, secretary of the Association to Combat the Social Evil, argued:

The morals of the feebleminded are never high, and those of the lower grades distinctly depraved. When you take into consideration the imitative faculties of children, think how wrong and injurious it is that these children should be allowed to contaminate the normal children with whom they associate.

Segregation in residential institutions would protect against these evils. However, the deputation also claimed segregation served a humanitarian purpose by providing the 'feebleminded' with 'a decent chance of a happy life'. Unable to care for themselves, the 'feebleminded' would be protected. Separated from 'normal' children in ordinary schools, with whom they could not compete, and carefully graded according to their degree of 'defect', they could receive training more appropriate to their capacities, making them useful and happy, whether in self-supporting colonies or perhaps in suitable work in the community.[2]

Over the next decade, an array of individuals and organisations pressed government for a policy to deal with the menace of the so-called 'feebleminded'.[3] In 1921, the Australian Natives Association pledged its support to the campaign for institutional segregation in industrial or farming colonies.[4] In 1924 the Women's Section of the Victorian Farmers Union offered to help 'to educate the public mind on the necessity for action'.[5] Women's organisations were also among the 'more than thirty societies and organisations interested in human welfare and humanitarian work', which came together to form the Society for Mental Defectives Colony Association in March 1923. Some months later, a 'monster deputation' from the association waited on the acting premier, Sir William McPherson, to ask that the government 'make some definite promise with regard to the course by which the crying evil of mental defectives in the midst of the community should be dealt with'.[6]

Government ministers expressed their sympathy but were slow to act.[7] Victoria's political instability was partly to blame, as alliances between the various political parties waxed and waned.[8] A reluctance to spend on social services, shockingly exemplified by the revelations at the Ellery royal commission, also played a part. In 1923, a suggestion to transfer the children at Fitzroy and Montague 'to a farm school in the country' where they could be 'properly segregated and systematically educated' was rejected on financial grounds.[9]

Successive governments considered the question anew, appointing a series of expert committees to advise on how to deal with 'mental deficiency'. With key members in common—notably Director of Education Frank Tate, Dr Richard Berry, professor of anatomy at the University of Melbourne, and W. Ernest Jones, inspector-general of the insane, all three men committed eugenicists—the various committees' recommendations were consistent. These were: the establishment of a child-study clinic to identify and classify children with 'mental deficiency'; training in special and residential schools; 'after-care' colonies for the adult 'feebleminded'; and, finally, legislation to establish the necessary legal authority to compulsorily segregate those who posed the greatest 'danger' to the community.[10]

In 1924, the short-lived Prendergast Labor government planned to establish a large colony for 'mental defectives' at Janefield at an initial cost of £35,000, but the proposal lapsed when the government lost office.[11] Two years later, the conservative Allan–Peacock government purchased 'Travancore', a mansion on ten acres in Flemington, as a residential school for 'backward' children.[12] Admitted between the ages of six and twelve, children would remain in the school until, approaching adulthood, they were boarded out or transferred to a residential colony. To provide for this 'ultimate institution', the government had purchased a 600-acre property, 'Bundoora Park', part of which was being used as a convalescent home for mentally ill returned servicemen. About fifteen kilometres north-east of Melbourne, it was in Jones's view an ideal site for a farming and industrial colony.[13]

Each new proposal provoked protest, revealing the fear and repugnance many in the community felt toward 'mental defectives'. Ironically, their objections echoed the arguments made for such institutions. In September 1924, 500 Janefield and Bundoora residents signed a petition arguing that a colony at Janefield 'would create a menace to women and children' and cause families to leave the district. Few wanted such institutions in their neighbourhood. The local member, William Everard, argued that Mont Park Mental Hospital was a far preferable location, but 'if more space was needed perhaps some of the buildings in the decadent [*sic*] mining towns might be utilised'.[14] In a deputation to the chief secretary the following year, local councillors and residents of Travancore expressed fears about the effect of the new institution on their property values and its 'psychological effect upon the minds' of the children at the nearby state school.[15]

Both conservative and Labor chief secretaries, Dr Stanley Argyle and Thomas Tunnecliffe, attempted to allay residents' fears, arguing that the 'mentally defective' were neither criminals nor lunatics but people whose mental 'development had been arrested'. Both ministers stressed that the proposed institutions were educational rather than curative, intended to train rather than treat. While many inmates would have to be permanently segregated, others through training would become 'useful citizens'. Inmates would be kept strictly within the bounds of the institutions, and, in any case, no dangerous or serious cases would be admitted. Argyle assured protesters that Travancore would 'be no idiot asylum'.[16]

While the Allan–Peacock ministry had taken the first steps toward establishing a system to deal with the 'mentally deficient' with its purchases of Travancore and Bundoora, the state had no legal power to segregate or control people considered 'mentally defective'.[17] In October 1926 Chief Secretary Argyle tabled a mental deficiency bill to create the necessary authority, but it lapsed owing to more pressing parliamentary business.[18] Three years and two changes of government later, Argyle introduced a similar bill. He firmly believed that the hereditary nature of 'feeblemindedness' posed a serious danger.[19] Without a system to deal with 'mental deficiency', the state must inevitably suffer 'inestimable loss and harm, both monetarily and in physical and mental deterioration, resulting from the uncontrolled reproduction of a lower type'.

Argyle supported his argument with 'concrete examples' from Victoria's public institutions, including the Children's Cottages. A study by the cottages' medical officer, Dr Ryan, concluded

> that of 234 cases [over five years], heredity was a contributing factor in
> at least 72 instances, including 42 cases in which there was insanity or

nervous instability on one side or the other, and sometimes on both. These 42 cases cost the State at least £3000 a year.

While such evidence was hardly convincing proof of the overwhelming influence of heredity as a cause of 'mental deficiency', Argyle declared that it demonstrated 'the result of allowing such people to wander at large to reproduce their species'.[20] Accordingly, the bill established formal processes to identify, certify and commit to institutions, voluntarily and otherwise, those individuals judged to be 'mentally defective'.

However, as Argyle explained, the government did not propose to commit all those deemed 'mentally defective' to institutions. Citing recent statistical surveys that purported to show alarmingly high numbers of 'mental defectives' in the community, he declared that establishing institutions to accommodate even a 'small proportion' of them was impossible and 'would cost the State a mint of money'.[21] The bill thus provided for guardianship in the community as an alternative to institutionalisation, and for the boarding out of 'harmless' inmates from state institutions to private persons, or their placement in employment, subject to certain conditions.[22]

The bill was, as Argyle conceded, exceedingly complex. To assist his parliamentary colleagues he circulated an explanatory pamphlet, which included a diagram illustrating 'how mentally defective persons were to be classified under the Act' (Figure 5.1). Following English precedent, the bill's third clause defined four categories of mental deficiency. 'Idiots' and 'low grade imbeciles'—defined by the bill as people who were 'unable to guard themselves against common physical dangers' or, in the case of 'imbeciles', were 'incapable of managing themselves or their affairs'— would continue to be certified under the Lunacy Acts and admitted to the Children's Cottages. 'Higher grade imbeciles' and the 'feebleminded'—those whose 'mental deficiency', while not so severe, nonetheless required care, supervision and control for their own or others' protection—together with 'moral defectives' (individuals in whom 'mentally deficiency' was 'coupled with strongly vicious or criminal tendencies') would be certified under the new legislation and treated according to its provisions. The bill thus proposed to extend the state's power significantly, to encompass individuals who could not be certified under the Lunacy Act.[23] In this schema, the cottages constituted one among a constellation of institutions set aside as the inspector-general had long argued they should be for the lowest grades of 'mental defect'.[24]

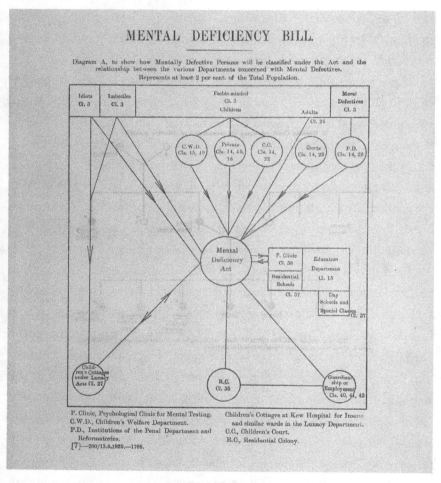

Figure 5.1: Mental Deficiency Bill, Diagram A
(Courtesy Public Record Office Victoria, VPRS 4723/P, Unit 513, File Mental Deficiency Bill 1929)
Part of the explanatory pamphlet circulated to members of parliament, this diagram illustrates how the 1929 Mental Deficiency Bill proposed to classify people deemed 'mentally defective'. The Children's Cottages are shown at bottom left, set aside 'for lowest grades of mental defect'.

While accepting the need to deal with the problem, subsequent speakers expressed reservations about the bill. Thomas Tunnecliffe, the minister responsible for the appointment of the Ellery royal commission in 1924 and now deputy leader of the Labor opposition, argued that in proposing the legislation without establishing the necessary institutions Argyle had 'put the cart before the horse'. With the scandal of the cottages in mind, he argued, the public would only accept the far-reaching powers embodied in the bill after the government demonstrated its capacity to care properly for 'mentally deficient' children. Families, too, required that assurance before they would willingly surrender their children to institutions.[25]

Maurice Blackburn, lawyer, civil libertarian and the Labor member for Clifton Hill, expressed the strongest objections. He argued forcefully against the provision for involuntary committal against the wishes of parents: 'I am not willing to agree to any provision that will enable children who are able to lead happy and, within limits, useful lives, to be torn from the arms of parents and committed to institutions'. Society, he declared, had no right to demand they should 'suffer for the welfare of the race'. Better, too, that 'feeble-minded' delinquent or neglected children be boarded out to other families than 'cooped up in a Government institution'.[26] On 8 October 1929 the Legislative Assembly passed an amended version of the bill, but the McPherson government collapsed before the Legislative Council voted on it.[27]

Fear of the so-called 'feebleminded' persisted. For some, the problem of 'mental deficiency' seemed so grave that it warranted radical action. In October 1933 James Disney, the Labor member for Melbourne West in the Legislative Council, called on the conservative Argyle–Allan government to confront the problem head on: 'Other nations', he declared, 'were dealing with it. If the subject is not faced fearlessly, the British race will degenerate into a third-class race'. Arguing that sterilisation was the means to 'get at the root of the evil and stamp it out', he proposed 'that every boy and girl should be medically examined at, say, the age of fourteen or fifteen years, and if found mentally afflicted, he or she should be sterilized'.[28]

As Disney suggested, elsewhere laws to sanction sterilisation of the 'unfit' were already in place or under serious consideration. In 1927, in the landmark case *Buck v. Bell,* the United States Supreme Court declared involuntary sterilisation constitutional, the presiding judge Oliver Wendell Holmes famously proclaiming: 'Three generations of imbeciles are enough'. In the wake of the decision many states rushed to legalise sterilisation. In Britain, a government committee was investigating the efficacy of voluntary sterilisation as a means to control 'mental deficiency'. In Germany, Hitler's National Socialist government had recently implemented a program to sterilise the 'hereditarily afflicted', a category that included people with intellectual disabilities. Speaking in support of Disney in parliament, the member for North-Eastern Province, Albert Zwar, suggested this might prove a model to emulate.[29]

In Melbourne, where the press reported on these developments, the question of sterilisation was also the subject of debate among women's organisations throughout the interwar period. The National Council of Women raised the issue at national and international conferences,[30] and affiliated organisations also discussed the issue independently. In April 1934, for example, the Victorian Federation of Mothers Clubs and the Women Citizens' Movement organised a meeting to allow their members to hear opposing views on the question.[31] Three months later Disney attempted to introduce a private members bill to implement his proposal. The idea proved too contentious for the government. Disney was forced to abandon the bill after the attorney-general, Albert Macfarlan, refused to allow the parliamentary draftsman to assist in its framing.[32]

Others, while sharing Disney's conviction that something must be done, rejected sterilisation as an effective means to eliminate 'mental deficiency'. Critics argued that the sheer number of sterilisations needed to make any significant difference to its prevalence would create public outcry. Nor would sterilisation have any effect on the non-hereditary causes of 'mental deficiency', such as birth injuries, alcohol, or venereal and other infectious disease.[33]

By the early 1930s the campaign to deal with 'mental deficiency' had made limited progress. Eleven state governments had held power since the end of the Great War. Two 'mental deficiency' bills had failed despite bipartisan support. Parlous finances delayed the opening of Travancore for several years.[34] Until then, the Kew Children's Cottages remained Victoria's only specialised institution for people with intellectual disabilities.

What was life like for the people living in the cottages? Few, whether reporters, parliamentarians or royal commissioners, bothered to ask them. However, some residents' voices from this period do survive. Edward 'Ted' Rowe spent eight years in the cottages after being admitted in March 1925. In 2006 he shared his memories with historian Corinne Manning, providing a rare first-hand account of everyday life in the Kew institution.

'I Just Did What I Was Told'

Abandoned as an infant in January 1921, Ted Rowe spent his early childhood in the care of the Children's Welfare Department. In early 1925, however, the matron at the Royal Park Children's Depot requested his removal to the Kew Children's Cottages. In the certificates authorising his admission she declared him: 'idiotic in his behaviour, irritable and inclined to hurt other children and cannot be taught habits of cleanliness and intelligence'. In her opinion, he showed 'no capacity for being taught anything'. Two doctors, who examined him as the law required, agreed, certifying that his physical appearance and behaviour indicated 'idiocy'. His behaviour was deemed inappropriate for his age, particularly his apparent inability to speak more than 'a few words' and his tendency to laugh 'merrily at everything and nothing'. On 5 March 1925, aged four and a half, Ted was admitted to the cottages.[35]

His early progress there revealed how subjective judgments of 'mental deficiency' could be. Within weeks, he mastered the habits of cleanliness the former matron claimed were beyond him, and could understand 'simple directions'. After ten months his case notes reported he was: 'Considerably improved. Clean in habits' (Figure 5.2).

Figure 5.2: This image of Edward 'Ted' Rowe smiling at the photographer is one of two that survive in his patient case file
(Courtesy Kew Residential Services, Department of Human Services)

Ted arrived three months after the royal commission exposed the appalling conditions at the cottages. In the wake of its revelations the government authorised a plan of 'improvements and additions' (Figure 5.3).[36] However, it took three years at a cost of £42,000 before the cottages were finally sewered and the old gas lights replaced with electricity. A new nursery and dormitories added extra accommodation, and a new dining room reduced overcrowding at meals. New covered ways connected the various buildings, providing shelter from the elements.[37] In October 1927, after more than a year's absence, Dr Springthorpe expressed his pleasure in the Official Visitors' Book at 'the very real improvement': 'The place looks a new one, the approach, the new buildings, fresh painting etc. have quite transformed it. Relatives can now take a pleasure in visiting, and the improved surroundings cannot but react favourably upon the conduct of [patients (?) illegible]'.[38]

'A New Deal for Mental Defectives' (1924–39)

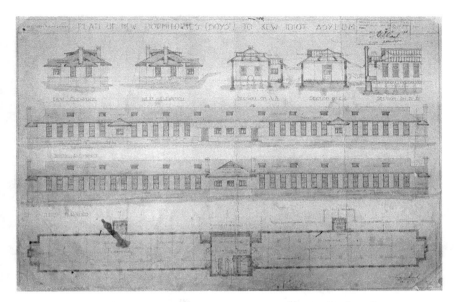

Figure 5.3: Kew Idiot Asylum Plan of New Dormitories (Boys)
(Courtesy Public Record Office Victoria, VPRS 3686/P0017, MHK 1.41)
This plan shows the extent of the new boys' dormitories built in the wake of the revelations at the 1924 royal commission. The scale of the building reflects the ever-increasing number of residents.

While Springthorpe was impressed, Ted's recollections suggest that everyday life in the cottages remained bleak. Inmates slept in crowded dormitories on uncomfortable, straw-filled mattresses with a single blanket and quilt.[39] In contrast to the official visitor's observation that the food was 'well cooked and good',[40] Ted remembered it as neither appetising—inmates referred to the porridge as 'the glue'—nor sufficient. In Ted's words, 'You had to eat them otherwise you starve'. The patients' clothes similarly reflected the poverty of institutional life; 'like prison clothes', he recalled, the material was rough against the skin (Figure 5.4). Their unmistakably 'institutional' character is evident in the photographs that survive in his case history.

Ted's memories reflect the regimentation and monotony of institutional life, with each day beginning with the ringing of a bell, signalling time for breakfast, and ending with trooping back to the dormitories 'all in one like brown cows' to be locked in together for the night.

Figure 5.4: Ted Rowe shares his recollections with Dr Corinne Manning in 2006
(Courtesy Edward Rowe, private collection)

In February 1925 Springthorpe observed that both the 'male and female playgrounds' were 'quite bare. Cannot they be made more attractive—even somewhat therapeutic or for exercise or amusement?' he asked. Six years later nothing had changed: 'Rather pitiful', Springthorpe wrote, 'to see a number of the boys simply sitting in the airing Court'.[41] It was this 'sitting around here like monkeys', as Ted described it, that saw him agree to work.

Work was considered a key element of training when the Idiot Asylum was established in 1887. While formal training had gradually dwindled into nothingness, the employment of patients continued. Ellery recalled inmates working 'in the kitchen where the soup cauldrons were boiling, in the monotonous whir of the sewing room, knee-deep in the shavings of the carpenter's shop or dirty-handed in the garden'.[42] Ted worked in the laundry folding sheets and on the asylum farm, where he milked cows and helped grow vegetables, as well as doing chores in his ward. In 1929 the inspector-general reported that 'the main [mental hospital] laundry and the Children's Cottages are carried on with patients' labour—materially diminishing the employment of paid staff'.[43]

By the 1930s, however, the use of patient labour was attracting criticism. In February 1937 *Truth* newspaper reported that 28-year-old May K., a patient at the cottages, had sustained serious injuries while working in the kitchen. In its typically sensationalist style, it declared that the patients who worked in Victoria's 'mental homes' were 'little better than chattel slaves working without pay'.[44] Four months later *Truth* raised the issue again. Reporting the case of a 27-year-old cottages patient it dubbed the 'Forgotten Girl', who worked caring for younger children and making clothes for the institution: 'She is practically unpaid. Her labor is exploited by a department which, soullessly, does nothing for her in return'.[45]

While conceding that few patients received any payment, officials argued that work contributed to patients' 'contentment' and wellbeing.[46] Staff certainly valued residents who were willing and able to work. In his autobiography, Ellery referred to the working patients as 'usefuls', probably reflecting common cottages' parlance, and the 'usefulness' or otherwise of patients was a consistent theme in their histories.[47] For patients, finding ways to 'get along better with the staff' was very important given the power staff wielded over their everyday lives. Work may also have provided some sense of purpose and fulfilment in the otherwise monotonous institutional routine.[48] Caring for other residents, as did the 'Forgotten Girl', may have fulfilled the need 'for affection and attention' otherwise absent in institutional life.[49]

Ted Rowe remembered the loneliness and bewilderment of institutional life without family and his distress when other families came to visit: 'when I'd see the others I'd start to cry and "Wish I had my mummy and daddy coming to see me"'. Some of the nurses responded to his unhappiness with a kind of casual cruelty, telling him that he was to blame: '"Oh you must've done something wrong because they don't want to see you". Or, they tried to get them to come and see me and "they wouldn't come"'. Others were kinder, one nurse consoling him, saying, 'I'll be your parents'.

By his own admission, Ted was a favourite with the staff, the 'nurses' pet'. In his view, this was because he 'behaved' himself, but the mild degree of his disability and his responsiveness perhaps influenced their affection for him.[50] His case notes describe him as 'a happy little chap', and the photographs in his file, which in their informality resemble family snapshots, show a 'bright and cheerful' child, smiling back at the photographer. Evidence suggests that some staff shared the repugnance felt toward people with more severe disabilities. In his autobiography, psychologist Stanley Porteus recalled visiting the cottages in early February 1913 accompanied by the medical superintendent Dr Morris Gamble, who remarked bitterly of a patient described by Porteus as 'a hydrocephalic imbecile': '[W]ouldn't you think that God Almighty would be ashamed of creating something like that?'[51]

Ted's recollections suggest he negotiated institutional life by 'behaving himself'. His remarks about other patients' complaints of mistreatment reflect this strategy: 'Someone said they treated us like dogs. Well I said it was your fault, I haven't been treated like a dog. I just did what I was told, see, that was it'. His remarks illuminate case notes that describe other 'well behaved' patients or those who sought to make themselves 'useful'.[52] Ted's recollections also suggest that the experience of patients who 'misbehaved' could be quite different from his own. While Ted found a way to negotiate life at the cottages, other inmates continued to find it unbearable, one telling him of his wish to 'get away from here'.

Ted's recollections reveal, where the archive does not, that recaptured escapees were severely punished, so much so that he was not 'game to escape': 'You could hear them yelling out, "No, no, no!" They knew they were going [to] get the strap on the backside though. Gee they hit them'. Other patients also witnessed beatings. In October 1935, *Truth* investigated the accidental death of six-year-old Allan Barnes, reporting that his mother was told by another resident that Allan 'had been beaten'.[53]

The Ellery royal commission exposed other usually hidden methods used by staff to punish 'unruly' patients. Giving evidence, nurse Annie Corry testified that coming on duty one evening she found a patient confined to a single room without clothing or blankets and was informed by the nurse on duty that her confinement was 'for punishment' and she was to have no food because she had been 'tiresome and using violent language'.

Corry testified that when Dr Ellery discovered the patient he ordered her dressed and released to sit by the fire to get warm.[54]

Legally, seclusion was permissible for medical or surgical treatment, to prevent violence or for 'persistently destroying property', but it required authorisation by the superintendent or medical officer. Its use as punishment was explicitly prohibited.[55] The confinement Corry described was clearly illegal. However, the commission chose not to investigate further.[56]

Relationships with other patients were also a significant aspect of institutional life. For Ted, friendships with other inmates made institutional life more bearable. Among the handful of 'good things' he recalled about Kew were the many friends he made and the time he spent playing cricket and football with them. The importance of such camaraderie is clear from instances in which it was absent. In 1911, fourteen-year-old John Heaney told the medical officer that he had attempted to cut his throat with a piece of tin because 'he wished to die—that boys were unkind & his mother does not want him'.[57] Case histories reveal that other residents endured physical or sexual assault at the hands of fellow patients.[58]

One of Ted's fondest memories was the day he and several other boys rushed through the open gate that separated the boys and girls exercise yards. Kisses were briefly exchanged before staff discovered the boys and sent them hastily back to their 'own side of the fence'. His recollection emphasises how strictly staff attempted to control relationships between the sexes. Nineteenth-century asylums were constructed to segregate the sexes as a matter of propriety. The eugenic concern and resulting moral panic about the menace of the 'feebleminded' only intensified the determination to keep the sexes apart. Attempts by residents to circumvent the restrictions met with repression and punishment. When 21-year-old Louisa Thomson began showing what the doctor characterised as 'amatory tendencies, wandering up to' the fence dividing the male and female divisions and 'refusing to come away', the staff dragged her away by force.[59] Nonetheless, some residents were able to establish sexual relationships. In September 1922 staff caught Ruby Jones and another patient 'making towards the strawshed'. Questioned, Ruby admitted that she had been 'out before' with this resident and 'other boys'.[60]

When Ted arrived at Kew Children's Cottages in 1925, the school had been closed for almost twenty years, despite the repeated lobbying of Inspector-General Jones for a resumption of teaching.[61] In 1928, in the context of the recent developments in mental deficiency policy, Jones tried again, arguing the Education Department was abdicating its responsibility to provide education 'for all classes of children', including 'mental defectives'. With the expected passage of a Mental Defectives Act and the establishment of new institutions, the training of the children at Kew was an immediate imperative. Jones believed a tenth of the 400 children in the cottages would 'benefit from educational training of a simple character'. Another half, he thought, would be 'materially improved by simple manual and industrial training'.[62]

The Education Department, which had expanded its interest in special education over the previous decade, agreed to establish a special school at the cottages. On 20 February 1929, a new school staffed by two department teachers opened.[63] Official reports commended their enthusiasm and the 'good results' achieved. In November 1930, in a performance reminiscent of those at the Idiot Asylum, the pupils entertained one of the official visitors, singing 'in very good style' the patriotic World War I song 'Australia Will be There'. He also praised the 'remarkably good' standard of their manual work.[64] Later that year a display of their handicrafts in an exhibition of work done by 'backward' children in the state's special schools drew favourable comment.[65]

By 1932 Ted was attending classes and 'getting on well'.[66] However, only thirty-four of the cottages' four hundred inmates were judged suitable to attend when the school opened, consistent with the view that only a small minority of residents were 'educable'.[67] Others felt their exclusion. In 1937, one of the visitors reported that 'Noel Muller was persistently begging' to 'be taught to read and write' saying 'his mother has not taught him these things'.[68]

Such judgments made a significant difference to residents' lives. In marked contrast to the empty monotony most inmates endured, pupils at the school spent their weekdays learning to read and do elementary arithmetic; drawing with pencils, chalk and pastel; doing physical drills and playing games. They also worked at various manual crafts. The boys made mats—producing '150 in the year, said to be worth some 15/- each'—the girls sewed with raffia and did cane work.[69]

In March 1933, after several years delay, the new residential school at Travancore opened. Soon after, Ted was transferred there. His memories of Travancore reveal the differences between it and the now nearly fifty-year-old and seriously neglected cottages: 'I liked Travancore it was a lovely place. All the people were nice there. They're the ones who put me out on the job'. In his case the transfer was the first step toward life outside institutions.[70] For the residents he left behind, to whom no such opportunities were offered, a seemingly empty life in a rundown institution loomed. However, by now the future of the Children's Cottages was once more in doubt. Finally it seemed that the decades of uncertainty about the fate of the Kew Mental Hospital, and with it Kew Cottages, would be resolved in favour of removal.

'Almost Like the Rock of Ages'

In May 1929 Dr Springthorpe addressed a public meeting at the Kew Town Hall, convened by the Kew Council to discuss the removal of the asylum from the district. Calling for the construction of a new hospital 'for the curative treatment of the insane' elsewhere, Springthorpe observed that the old asylum 'was almost like the Rock of Ages, because nothing had been able to shift it' since 1871.[71] Previous agitation had elicited a commitment to close both Yarra Bend and Kew asylums. The closure of Yarra Bend, deemed beyond restoration, had taken precedence, but the war had drawn out its surrender. The last patients were finally transferred to Mont Park in September 1925.[72] However, in 1929, the Kew Asylum, now officially renamed the Kew Hospital for the Insane, remained.

The 1929 protest meeting was part of a reinvigorated campaign for removal. In May 1928 the North Kew Progress Association urged council to lobby the Hogan government.[73] Days later Kew Council argued that making any improvements at the cottages breached the 'clearly defined' policy of previous governments to remove the asylum. It was also wasteful to spend 'further public money on an out-of-date Institution, which Medical Experts have for many years condemned as a Hospital for the treatment of the unfortunate Insane'.[74] The new MLA for Kew, Wilfred Kent Hughes, also urged removal, declaring a suburb less than four miles from the GPO was not the 'right situation for a mental hospital'.[75]

However, as with the earlier surrender of the Yarra Bend Asylum, any closure confronted significant obstacles, notably finding alternative accommodation for the thirteen hundred patients in the main hospital and cottages. By the late 1920s, years of government neglect had resulted in serious overcrowding in all the hospitals for the insane: by the inspector-general's estimate 'to the extent of at least four hundred patients'. Each night, staff made up beds on the floors of corridors and day rooms for patients with nowhere else to sleep. However, replacing the old hospital was expensive, the inspector-general calculating that a 'modern institution' would cost 'at least £450,000' (the modern equivalent $35,000,000). A country site, as Kent Hughes suggested, would make visiting expensive and difficult for patients' relatives.[76]

The Hogan government proved unwilling to replace the Kew hospital with a new institution elsewhere, citing the need to provide adequate accommodation for existing patients and the state's current 'financial position'.[77] However, with the election of the new McPherson conservative government in late 1928, opposition to the retention of the asylum gained traction. Chief Secretary Argyle had long been staunchly opposed to the presence of a hospital in Kew. As mayor of Kew between 1903 and 1905 he had campaigned hard for its removal.[78] In early 1929 the press reported his intention to move the hospital to a site further from Melbourne, funded by the sale and development of part of the hospital's 400-acre site as a 'garden suburb'. The remaining land would be reserved for a park and scenic boulevard.[79] However, when Kew Council convened the public meeting at which Springthorpe spoke, support for the proposition was far from universal.[80] Kent Hughes's attempt to outline the case for removal met with much interruption and argument from the back of the crowded hall, where a 'strong force' of hospital warders gathered. Mr W.G. Higgs expressed a more well-mannered opposition, proposing an amendment to the motion stipulating that the government renovate and extend the hospital if it was not in a position to remove it.[81]

A former federal treasurer and a resident of Kew, Higgs had recently established the Society for the Welfare of the Mentally Afflicted. Founded to promote the wellbeing of patients in the mental hospitals, the society quickly became a thorn in the flesh of the administration. At public meetings and in the press, it alleged ill-treatment and neglect of patients, the wrongful detention of men and women who were actually sane, and called repeatedly for a royal commission to investigate the administration of the department. It also consistently opposed the removal of the hospital from Kew.[82]

Moving his amendment, Higgs argued that 'the welfare of the 1,300 patients in the asylum and the convenience of their relatives' must be the main consideration. The secretary of the Mental Hospital Employees Association, Mr C.A. Loughnan, seconded Higgs's amendment, reflecting his members' opposition to moving away from Kew. The meeting ended in disarray when the chairman refused, amidst 'shouting and jeering', to declare whether the original motion in favour of removal was won or lost.[83]

Kew councillors argued that the opposition expressed at the meeting was motivated by self-interest and did not represent the opinion of the City of Kew. Removal 'was for the welfare of the people, and a national matter'.[84] Several weeks later the council and Kew Progress Association, which also favoured removal, met with the premier, Sir William McPherson, to seek his support.[85] Cabinet did in fact consider the proposal over the following months, ministers inspecting both Kew and Mont Park in an effort to decide how to proceed.[86] However, the McPherson government collapsed in December 1929 without a decision. The next two governments left the future of the hospital unresolved, pleading insufficient funds either to extend the hospital or to move it elsewhere.[87]

In 1933 criticisms from Higgs revived the question of Kew's future. In a letter to the *Argus* he condemned the overcrowding in the mental hospitals, citing figures from Kew, where patient numbers exceeded the number of beds in both the main hospital and the cottages.[88] The *Herald* dispatched a reporter to investigate. The truth of Higgs's allegations was obvious in the splintered floors, 'the paucity of fittings, the crowding of bed alongside bed in many wards, the cupboard size rooms where inmates slept on mattresses on the floor and the pervading atmosphere of makeshift'. Only in the new nursery and schoolroom at the cottages did he find anything to commend. The dreadful state of the hospital demanded immediate action. Why, if the government intended to remove it, did it not do so immediately, or otherwise make the necessary improvements?[89] The answer, according to the new premier, the recently knighted Sir Stanley Seymour Argyle, was the perennial one: want of money. Argyle conceded the hospital was 'an old and out-of-date building, and that there was overcrowding. "But", he asked, "where was the money to be found with which to build another asylum"'.[90]

As a former federal treasurer Higgs was notably sceptical. Citing the significant sums spent on unemployment relief—by his calculation almost £5 million in the previous three financial years—Higgs argued that the government could easily have spared the money needed to renovate Kew. 'If the Flinders street railway station and the Old Treasury building can be renovated out of the unemployment relief fund', he asked, 'why not the mental hospitals, which need the renovation more and for a more urgent purpose, relieving pain and suffering?'[91] In fact, news that the state government offices would be remodelled, at a cost of £40,000, had appeared on the same page of the *Argus* as his letter criticising the overcrowding in the hospitals.[92] The cost was comparable; the inspector-general estimated the cost of the alterations to improve the hospital to be between £60,000 and £80,000.[93] Argyle, however, was committed to removal and was inclined to believe, as Kew Council did, that any spending on improvements was a waste of money.[94]

The mentally disabled were rarely a priority, even in the best of times, and these were financially the worst of times. Both the Argyle government and its Labor predecessor under Edmond (Ned) Hogan chose to combat the Depression by severely cutting public expenditure.[95] Tellingly, Argyle argued that because 'the care of the insane was a social service that was not reproductive it was impossible under present stringent financial conditions to undertake the heavy expenditure of building a new asylum'. This decision, to wait on better times to remove the hospital rather than make improvements, condemned the patients, including the inmates of the Children's Cottages, to endure the deplorable conditions in the meantime.[96]

In April 1935, Argyle's government lost office without making any final decision as to the fate of the hospital. In marked contrast to previous administrations the new conservative government, led by Albert Dunstan, immediately tackled the problems in the mental hospitals. Flagging his intention to modernise accommodation for the mentally afflicted the new chief secretary, Brigadier Murray Bourchier, observed that, since the government had taken responsibility for the care of those who, like the mentally disabled, were 'unable to maintain themselves', it was incumbent on them to provide 'suitable and adequate accommodation', an argument notably ignored by previous administrations.[97]

Before it lost office, the Argyle government despatched the director of mental hygiene on a six-month fact-finding mission to study mental hospitals and 'deficiency colonies' in England. His report to the Dunstan government included a recommendation to remove the mental hospital from Kew.[98] A cabinet subcommittee appointed to consider his report subsequently condemned the old hospital as 'completely obsolete, quite unsatisfactory for its purpose and likely to have a detrimental effect on patients, retarding their chances of recovery'. A 'new hospital was imperative' (Figure 5.5).[99]

In late April 1936 the Dunstan government announced its decision to build a new mental institution at Bundoora, some miles north of Mont Park, at a cost of approximately £300,000. Borrowings would finance construction of the new hospital, pending the subdivision and sale of the old Kew Asylum reserve.[100] The press praised the Dunstan government for acting where so many previous administrations had failed to do so, the

Herald declaring that it 'could take credit for making a decision which has been required of Governments for more than a generation'.[101]

Finally, it seemed the immovable would yield. The Kew Council was 'jubilant'.[102] At the same time as the council was campaigning for closure, social reformers continued to call on government for a policy to deal with the problem of 'mental deficiency'. The outcome of that campaign would shape the closure of Kew Cottages and the future of their residents.

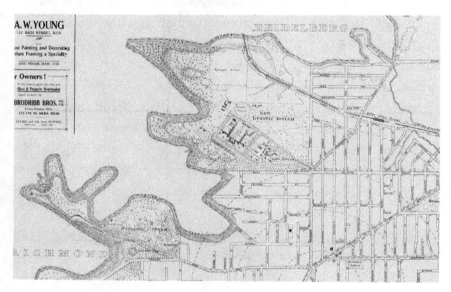

Figure 5.5: A 1921 map of the municipality of Kew showing the Mental Hospital and Cottages, detail, *Municipality of Kew*, Melbourne Publishing Co.
(Courtesy State Library Victoria)
On this map, the Kew Mental Hospital and Cottages are referred to by their older names, the Kew Lunatic and Idiot Asylums and are bordered by residential streets. Beginning in the late 1920s, a reinvigorated campaign for removal resulted in a decision to move the institutions elsewhere.

'A New Deal for Mental Defectives'

By the end of 1935, five hundred inmates were crowded into the Children's Cottages' dismal surrounds. Travancore, opened two years earlier, was already at capacity, home to sixty children with a waiting list nearly as long.

The mental hospitals accommodated nearly seven hundred more 'mentally deficient' patients, some of whom had 'graduated' from the cottages to make space for new admissions. The want of accommodation prevented the department from accepting cases from the Children's Welfare Department, Berry Street Foundling Home and other religious and charitable institutions.[103]

For some, these figures suggested 'an alarming increase in the number of mental defectives'.[104] What they certainly reflected was the lack of provision governments had thus far made for people with intellectual disabilities. Excluding the mental hospitals, the Children's Cottages and Travancore provided accommodation for fewer than seven hundred people and that only at the cost of significant overcrowding.[105]

Concerned, social reformers called on the government to establish new institutions specifically for the 'mentally defective'. Their arguments combined the enduring conviction that the 'feebleminded' constituted a menace to social and racial health with a paternalist concern for their 'protection'. The president of the Travancore auxiliary, Mrs F.R. Quinton, was among the most indefatigable campaigners for the cause. Established in June 1931 under the auspices of the Victorian Federation of Mothers' Clubs, the auxiliary worked to raise funds for Travancore and campaigned to extend provision for the care of 'mentally deficient' children.[106] Appealing to other women's organisations for support, she asserted that Victoria was 'reaping a harvest of criminals, imbeciles and progenitors of imbeciles because of upward of half a century of neglect by those in authority to grapple with the problem'.

At the same time, that failure inflicted a 'serious injustice' on the 'mentally deficient'. Rather than a form of mental disease, 'mental deficiency' was a permanent arrest in mental development resulting from hereditary or other causes. Consequently, those afflicted were unable to take responsibility for themselves. It was wrong, in the absence of 'mental deficiency' legislation, that they had to be subjected to the stigma of certification under the Lunacy Act in order to receive the supervision and control necessary to ensure their 'protection'.[107] Consequently, the passing of 'mental deficiency' legislation was one of the campaigners' main aims. They were also anxious to see a colony established to which the children of school-leaving age at Travancore could be transferred and, with further training, become to some degree self-supporting.[108]

In November 1935, the inspector-general, recently returned from his overseas tour, turned his attention to the want of accommodation. He recommended the expansion of Travancore and the establishment of a 1000-bed colony at Janefield, modelled on the new Middlesex Colony in England.[109] In fact the Dunstan government had recently approved expenditure of £32,000 toward the establishment of such a colony.[110] In 1936 it approved further spending to extend Travancore. To provide for the nearly one hundred 'mentally deficient' children in the Children's Welfare Department, it authorised the conversion of the old Pleasant Creek Hospital in Stawell, 235 kilometres northwest of Melbourne, for use as a residential institution and school for one hundred children.[111]

Jones retired the following year, after thirty-two years as head of the Department of Mental Hygiene. In that time, he had campaigned tirelessly on the need to control the 'mentally defective'. With the establishment of the residential schools at Travancore and Pleasant Creek and planning for the new Janefield colony underway, the foundations of the system of institutional control he and others had long advocated was finally in place.[112] However, with the failure of the 1926 and 1929 bills, Victoria still lacked a 'mental deficiency' Act.

The establishment of the new institutions made the need for legislation more pressing. In its absence the state lacked any 'legal authority to detain or control many of the children at the institutions'.[113] Accordingly, in October 1939 the chief secretary, Henry Bailey, introduced a new 'mental deficiency' bill to parliament. Narrower in scope that its predecessors, it focused on establishing the legal power to commit and detain people beyond the reach of the Lunacy Act, providing for both voluntary reception and compulsory committal. Explaining the necessity for the legislation, Bailey resurrected the old arguments about the propensity of the so-called 'feebleminded' to fall into immorality, delinquency and crime. To counter that danger and provide care to those presently denied it, the government intended to establish 'proper colonies' where individuals deemed 'mentally defective' could be accommodated and trained to become 'socially useful' and thus, the belief went, 'happy'. However, before this was possible, the government 'must have the legal power to commit them to these institutions'.[114]

By early December 1939, parliament had passed the bill, although its proclamation was delayed pending the establishment of the necessary institutions. As with its predecessors, it received support from across the political spectrum.[115] The press praised the legislation as socially progressive. Borrowing the language of US President Franklin D. Roosevelt's administration, the *Age* declared it 'a new deal for mental defectives'.[116] It was not, however, a new deal for all.

Many people concerned with 'mental deficiency' objected strenuously to the indiscriminate mixing of people with different degrees of disability, as at the Children's Cottages. During the debate Sir Stanley Argyle, now leader of the opposition, recalled his horror at seeing on a visit to the cottages 'ordinary, partly educable, defective children herded together with congenital idiots'. Other speakers shared his abhorrence of people with more severe disabilities. The so-called 'feebleminded', they believed, could only be degraded by continuing contact with such 'lower grades'. Thus classification was considered key.[117]

The process of classification began with the legislation, which excluded 'idiots' from its definition of 'defective'. Their treatment, and that of patients for whom 'nothing can be done in any way of curative treatment or training', was, Bailey explained, to remain for the time being under the provisions of the Lunacy Act. The administrative structure of the department had already been reorganised to reflect this division, with the creation in 1936 of a Mental Defectives Branch to oversee Travancore, Pleasant Creek and Janefield but notably not the Children's Cottages. While Bailey expected that eventually 'all the mental defectives' could be brought under the Act's provisions, in the meantime the focus was very much on the 'higher grades'.[118] Travancore, where a psychological clinic to study the problem of 'mental deficiency' had been established in 1938, would act as a 'clearing house'. There, psychologists and psychiatrists would assess and classify 'mentally deficient' children, to determine to which institution they should be sent. As at the Middlesex Colony in England, visited by Jones on his overseas tour, a new 'chain of villas' at Janefield would allow classification and segregation according to the degree of the individual's mental 'defect'.[119]

When the Legislative Assembly passed the bill in 1939, the deputy speaker, Ernest Coyle, described the legislation as 'of a most humanitarian type'.[120] Many residents of the Children's Cottages and their families, already confronting the uncertainties of closure, would have cause to doubt this claim as the new policy played out.

Chapter 6

'A Hillside of Sadness' (1939–50)

The decision to close the Kew Children's Cottages together with the 'new deal' in 'mental deficiency' policy finally seemed to promise some relief for the residents of the rundown institution. But it was not to be. The decision to prioritise the needs of the so-called 'feebleminded' over people who were more severely disabled, along with the effects of World War II, which brought the department's building program to a halt, left the residents of the cottages stranded in an institution still slated for removal and falling further into ruin.

As ever, it was those who lived in the cottages and those who cared for them who bore the cost. Parents, however, were becoming increasingly unwilling to do so in silence. By 1945 they were beginning to speak out publicly about conditions. Their appeals for improvement were met with public sympathy as ideas about intellectual disabilities began to shift and the community grew increasingly uneasy about the treatment of the mentally disabled. By the late 1940s that concern had grown sufficiently powerful to force reform.

'Sorrowing Parents'

Once, and often twice, a week Mr and Mrs Jarvie travelled from Carnegie in Melbourne's inner south east to Kew to visit their daughter Laurel, who was admitted to the Children's Cottages in 1935. However, in early 1938 the Jarvies discovered that the closure of the cottages would make seeing their daughter all but impossible.[1]

Cabinet formally approved the closure in April 1936. While construction of the new colony at Janefield had yet to begin, existing buildings on the site provided sufficient accommodation for one hundred patients. In November 1937 thirty female patients were transferred there from the cottages. In 1938 'all the girls of higher mental grade' followed.[2] For 'the helpless type' of patient the government had approved construction of new wards at the country mental hospitals in Ararat and Beechworth at a cost of £40,000.[3]

In February 1938 the Jarvies learned that Laurel, assessed by the cottages' superintendent, Dr Rogerson, as an 'idiot', the lowest grade of mental deficiency, was among the patients selected for transfer to Beechworth. For Laurel and the other patients also chosen to go, a future in the wards of the old mental hospitals loomed. For the Jarvies, the decision threatened to further separate them from their daughter, as a distraught Mrs Jarvie explained in a letter to the chief secretary, H.S. Bailey, asking him to intervene: 'If our unfortunate girl is sent away from Kew', she wrote, 'it will be all but impossible for us to visit her excepting at rare intervals'. Such a decision 'would be cruel'.[4]

Asked to comment on Mrs Jarvie's letter, the director of mental hygiene argued that policy, with its emphasis on classification and segregation, must take precedence over any objections. The 'lower grade' patients 'must necessarily be sent to the country institutions'. Their transfer to a farm colony like Janefield was impossible:

> its inhabitants must be capable of a certain amount of training, either mental or physical, in the endeavour to fit them for an independent existence, or, failing that, to enable them to live happily in the institution as useful and industrious components of the colony.

There was, he concluded, 'nothing to prevent relatives making other arrangements for the care of these patients if they so desire'.[5] In the absence of any state support for community care, this remark seems particularly callous.

More objections followed, as parents learnt that their children were among the patients to go to the country asylums. It would be impossible, Mrs M. Thomas wrote from Bentleigh, to visit her four-year-old son Donald if he were transferred to Ararat: 'it is so far away and so expensive and we could not afford the fare'.[6] Families also worried about the hurt the separation would inflict on their children. One St Kilda mother wrote of the 'bitter disappointment' her daughter would feel if she could not see her. Mr Forster of Glen Iris was certain his son Ebenezer would miss his family's 'weekly visits very much' if sent to Ararat.[7] Their fears were certainly warranted: Ted Rowe's memories attest to the loneliness and grief of an institutional life without family.

While families made their appeals individually, their letters echo each other's distress. Perhaps this simply reflects the similarity of their circumstances, but we cannot discount that such dedicated visitors may have come together in the cottages' visiting rooms to share their pain. Their letters, among the few from family to survive in the archive, foreshadow the increasingly vocal advocacy of parents yet to come. Whether through their initiative or not, others rallied to their cause. The president of the Society for the Welfare of the Mentally Afflicted, W.G. Higgs, consistently argued that relocating the hospital to Melbourne's outskirts would inflict hardship on the hundreds of families who visited regularly. Now he spoke out in support of the cottage children's families. 'Sorrowing parents', he declared in a letter to the press, were 'almost heartbroken because of the threatened removal of their loved ones from the Children's Cottages'.[8] Replying to the appeals, Chief Secretary Henry Bailey promised that 'every effort' would be made to keep those children whose parents lived in Melbourne and wanted to continue visiting in the metropolitan area.[9] By late 1938, 176 patients had been transferred to the country mental hospitals.

By early 1939 alternative accommodation for the remaining patients was exhausted and transfers ceased.[10] Resident numbers at the cottages had now fallen from 500 to 276.[11] Paradoxically, the transfers intensified the existing overcrowding. Staff transferred with their patients (the reason many opposed the closure), and, with fewer staff, patients were concentrated into fewer wards.[12] At the same time, admissions continued. In 1938, thirty-six new residents were received and in 1939 another seventy-seven.[13]

Construction of accommodation for 'at least 300 hundred children of low intellect' was required before the cottages could finally close.[14] The department's attention was elsewhere, however, focused on expanding accommodation for 'the better types of children' able to be 'taught manually or intellectually'.[15] Construction of the new colony at Janefield, modernisation of Travancore, and improvements at Pleasant Creek to better fit it as a residential school received priority, the director promising the department would turn its attention to 'housing of the lower grade imbeciles' when these projects were complete.[16]

At the cottages, patient numbers continued to rise. Closed wards were reopened, effectively reversing the decision to abolish the cottages. Fearing accusations of broken promises, by early 1941 the government was considering how to accommodate the 'residue' of residents.[17] Meanwhile, the cottages were the subject of renewed criticism. Addressing the Mental Hospital Auxiliaries on 10 February 1941, its president, Mrs Edith Pardy, condemned the conditions. Pardy had been inspired to establish the auxiliary in 1933 after hearing a lecture on 'A Day in the Life of a Patient in a Mental Hospital'. Adopting the motto 'I shall light a candle of understanding in thine heart', the auxiliary sought to foster a better public appreciation of mental illness. It strove also to bring 'comfort and entertainment' to the patients' lives and quickly embraced the cottages, donating toys, clothes and sweets and organising picnics, parties and outings for those of the residents able to participate.[18]

As auxiliaries president and, from 1939, an official visitor to the mental hospitals, Pardy could speak with authority about conditions. Her remarks reflected the increasing gap between the cottages and the newer institutions. 'Compared with the girls' home at Janefield', conditions were 'appalling': 'The wooden floors are splintered, the cots are battered, and the bed linen old and grey. The whole effect of the place is drab'. Even if the intention to close made building repairs impractical, still 'furnishings could be improved' and the cottages kept 'cleaner and made more comfortable'.

The *Age* and *Argus* reported Pardy's remarks and, given her profile, they carried significant weight.[19]

A week later, Chief Secretary Bailey instructed the director of mental hygiene to plan and cost alternative accommodation for those at the cottages, although he seemed more intent on deflecting criticism than making real change. A memo explained:

> The Minister feels that this Department should place itself in a position to be free of criticism by pressing for this work to be done. If funds cannot be made available or the Public Works Department cannot then encompass the work, the responsibility will not rest upon the Department of Mental Hygiene.

In April the director costed removal of the cottages' residents to a self-contained institution on the Janefield site at £125,000.[20]

There was little hope it would proceed. By the end of 1941 the diversion of both 'manpower' and materials to the war effort had all but halted the department's building projects. The attack on Pearl Harbour in December, and the rapid advance of the Japanese army south, only intensified the demand on resources.[21] A new institution to accommodate the patients in the cottages receded into an indeterminate future. In the meantime, the buildings fell further into dereliction.

'A Hillside of Sadness'

For parents the longstanding neglect of Kew Children's Cottages made the decision to surrender their children to the institution even more difficult. Speaking to the meeting of the Mental Hospital Auxiliaries in 1941, Mrs Pardy confessed that conditions at the cottages were so appalling that she 'could not honestly recommend any mother of a defective child to place her child there'.[22] For many families, however, there probably seemed little choice. Parents caring for children with intellectual disabilities at home continued to confront many of the same difficulties as their predecessors.

The testimony they related to certifying doctors between the wars is strikingly similar to that of parents in previous decades, recounting the constant care their children needed and the difficulties their behaviour sometimes caused, whether through wandering from home or acting destructively.[23]

Nor did prevailing ideas about 'mental deficiency' offer much encouragement to parents to care for their children at home. Both expert and popular opinion advised parents to institutionalise their children, both for their children's sake and to protect the family. 'Jacqueline Gore', the women's columnist for the *Weekly Times*, consistently counselled parents who sought her advice to admit their children to the cottages, despite the neglected conditions. The care they would receive would far exceed any parents could provide, and their children would be happier among others 'similarly backward'.[24] Much of the advice assumed that mothers were somehow inadequate to the task. Experts argued that in comparison with themselves mothers lacked the necessary knowledge to train their children. Moreover, keeping a child at home was believed to threaten the wellbeing of the entire family. Occupied with caring for their 'backward' children, mothers would tend to neglect their 'normal' children and the creation of 'a happy home life'. More and better institutions were considered the solution to all these problems.[25]

Families caring for children at home were not necessarily persuaded by such ideas.[26] Nonetheless, whatever constellation of reasons finally impelled parents to relinquish their children, there seems little chance that admission to the cottages brought any peace of mind. In 1927 Dr Springthorpe observed that with recent improvements families would 'be able to take pleasure in visiting'.[27] His remark recognised the toll of worry and pain the neglect of the cottages exacted from families.

In 1945, one mother decided to speak publicly about her feelings. Writing to the *Herald* under the pseudonym 'Distracted Mother', a choice that spoke eloquently to her state of mind, she described the pain of having a child confined in such dreadful conditions. Perhaps the bare boards, the ragged clothing or the 'coarse and unappealing' meals did not matter so much to the inmates:

But when one walks into a ward where there are children sitting in bed with flies swarming over the sores on their faces, and then realises that one's own child has to sleep in that same ward I wonder who could guess a mother's feelings.

She ended her letter with an appeal to the community: 'Too many people are willing to forget the people who exist in mental homes. They are human beings and deserve better treatment' (Figure 6.1).[28] Other parents had advocated for their children with doctors and politicians, but 'Distracted Mother' was one of the first to do so publicly. Her letter encouraged other parents to speak out. A week later 'Another Mother' wrote to express disgust at the conditions: 'You have to see it to believe that conditions such as these could exist for Australian children'.[29]

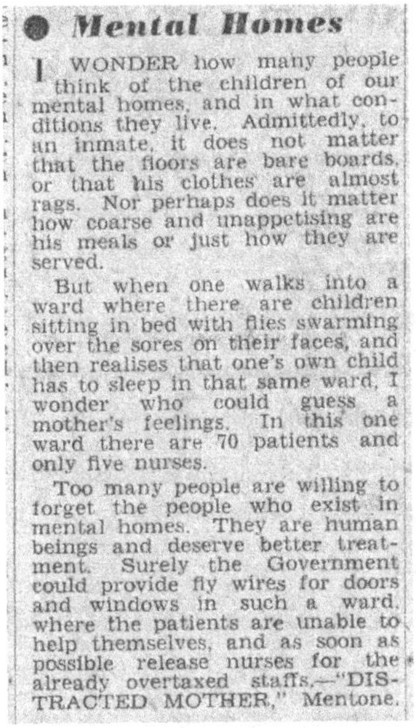

Mental Homes

I WONDER how many people think of the children of our mental homes, and in what conditions they live. Admittedly, to an inmate, it does not matter that the floors are bare boards, or that his clothes are almost rags. Nor perhaps does it matter how coarse and unappetising are his meals or just how they are served.

But when one walks into a ward where there are children sitting in bed with flies swarming over the sores on their faces, and then realises that one's own child has to sleep in that same ward, I wonder who could guess a mother's feelings. In this one ward there are 70 patients and only five nurses.

Too many people are willing to forget the people who exist in mental homes. They are human beings and deserve better treatment. Surely the Government could provide fly wires for doors and windows in such a ward, where the patients are unable to help themselves, and as soon as possible release nurses for the already overtaxed staffs.—"DISTRACTED MOTHER," Mentone.

Figure 6.1: 'Mental Homes'
(Courtesy *Herald*, 29 December 1945, 7)
'Distracted Mother' was among the first parents to advocate publicly for better treatment for Kew Cottages' residents. Her letter to the editor elicited sympathy and calls for action from readers of the *Herald*, arguably reflecting the emergence of more positive attitudes toward people with intellectual disabilities.

Other readers also wrote to express their sympathy and condemn the conditions. The buildings were 'not fit for cattle' in the view of one correspondent who had recently visited.[30] The department's excuses—that wartime restrictions and rationing had disrupted its plans to rehouse Kew residents at Janefield—received short shrift.[31] 'These Our Brethren' declared that its explanation did 'nothing to allay the disquiet felt by all decent people'. Immediate renovations should not be set aside because Janefield might 'some day' be extended to accommodate Kew residents. Nothing should delay helping 'afflicted people who are so dependent on the kindness of others'.[32] Then parents would at least have 'peace of mind'.[33]

There was one notable exception to these sentiments, however. In a letter published two weeks after that of 'Distracted Mother', cottages staff voiced their resentment at the criticisms. While unnamed, 'Distracted Mother' and her advocacy seem to have been the target of much of their bitterness. Why, they asked, did 'people who find the conditions so deplorable leave their children' in the institution? Why were so many 'infants and very small children' admitted, adding to 'the strain on the staff', when they could be cared for at home as easily as 'normal' children the same age? Would 'it not be better if persons interested gave some practical aid to the patients and staff, instead of letter-writing?'[34]

'Distracted Mother' had not in fact criticised the staff, but her letter clearly created discord within the cottages. A week after her first letter, she wrote a second in order to clarify that she did not blame the staff. On the contrary she felt 'only admiration for their work which is ill-paid and done in trying conditions'.[35] Why then had they responded so bitterly? One explanation may be the 'trying conditions' to which she referred.

During the war, nurses had resigned from the department in significant numbers to take up the better paid and more congenial work the war created. All attempts to arrest the exodus and recruit replacements failed. The remaining staff worked long hours of overtime without respite. Without their dedication and 'self-sacrifice', the director conceded that the hospitals would be unable to function. The end of the war brought no relief. With the relaxation of wartime controls on employment, resignations increased.

By early 1946 the staff of the mental hospitals was three hundred nurses short. There were simply too few nurses to care properly for patients.[36]

At Kew Children's Cottages, staff–patient ratios were shockingly high. 'Another Mother' described a nursery ward in which four nurses cared for seventy-two patients, many of whom were 'helpless little children who have to be hand-fed'. Even in the midst of the crisis, however, the policy prejudice against the more severely disabled persisted. 'At Janefield', she told *Herald* readers, 'the equivalent ward has only 30 patients and four nurses'.[37] For staff who persevered in these circumstances at Kew, public criticism may well have felt like an attack.

One correspondent wondered if the government even knew what conditions were like. Two weeks after the *Herald* published 'Distracted Mother's' letter, William Barry, the minister for health and housing in the recently elected John Cain (Snr) Labor government, decided to find out. Horrified by what he had seen, he told the press he had 'declared war' on the cottages, promising to transfer the patients as soon as possible. The next day cabinet approved his plans for new buildings at Janefield.[38] As so often before, this promise to improve the lives of the cottages' residents went unfulfilled. When the Cain government lost office in November 1947, the new buildings were still in the planning stage. The two successive conservative governments repeated the same pattern. After inspecting the cottages, responsible ministers in each new administration expressed their shock at the terrible conditions. In 1947 Albert Dunstan declared them 'a grave reflection on modern civilisation'—but redressive measures did not follow.[39]

Postwar governments certainly confronted severe shortages of materials and labour. Even within these constraints, however, governments accorded other social issues precedence over the mentally disabled. More than a decade of depression and conflict had created a severe housing crisis. In 1945 newly constructed buildings at Larundel Mental Hospital were converted into temporary housing for homeless families. In these circumstances the Department of Mental Hygiene's building program made virtually no progress.[40]

When *Herald* journalist Rohan Rivett visited Kew Children's Cottages in September 1948, he found 'a hillside of sadness'. Rivett was a well-known and trusted journalist. Formerly a war correspondent, he had announced the invasion of Singapore by Japanese forces on BBC radio before himself being captured and spending three years as a POW on the Thai–Burma Railway. His account of that experience, *Behind the Bamboo Curtain*, sold over 100,000 copies. After the war Sir Keith Murdoch recruited him to the *Herald*.[41]

Even on a lovely spring morning, Rivett told his readers, the cottages were not a pleasant place to visit. He was especially struck by the deprivation their residents endured. The cottages lacked virtually every comfort or amenity to distract the inmates from their endless days. No splash of colour relieved the drab monotony in the crowded dormitories. Outside, the more disabled patients sat along the verandahs or in rows across the open hillside. Rivett was pained to find over forty others, girls and women of varying ages, confined within a wire enclosure (Figure 6.2). He saw nothing that reflected any credit on the current or previous governments or on the department.

Figure 6.2: Women and girls at Kew Cottages confined behind wire, 1948
(Courtesy Kew Cottages Historical Society)
Visiting the cottages in 1948, journalist Rohan Rivett was shocked to discover some forty or fifty women and girls confined within a wire enclosure. Visitors had long remarked on the bare yards in which residents spent their days, with little to distract them from the monotony of institutional life.

'A HILLSIDE OF SADNESS' (1939–50)

Only among the staff—'short-handed and over-worked' but enduring despite the appalling conditions—did he find anything to commend. For their stout-hearted endeavours he expressed an overwhelming gratitude. The 'only ultimate solution' was to abandon the cottages and transfer the patients to a modern institution. There must be, too, proper funding for amenities to enliven the patients' lives.[42]

Rivett's article touched many readers. For one mother in particular, the article helped ease the isolation she felt, moving her to share her experience. On the advice of a Collins Street specialist, she and her husband had admitted their baby daughter to Kew. Her experience reflected the extra toll of grief parents felt relinquishing their children to an institution so neglected. At first, she wrote, 'I broke my heart over the place' but after visiting regularly she found some comfort in the 'wonderful work' of the staff. They also helped her understand that it was 'no fault of ours' that their daughter had come 'as she did'. Born with a congenital heart condition, their baby died after six weeks at the cottages. Friends seemed not to understand their particular sadness, and so they did not speak of it. Now, she wrote, she felt 'a little rested' that others could understand and write about 'something' she had felt but could not express.[43]

So many other readers wrote or telephoned with expressions of sympathy and offers of help that the *Herald* was inspired to open a week-long toy appeal. Donations flooded in. Drivers doubled-parked their cars outside Newspaper House in Collins Street to deliver armloads of toys. One determined man travelled by tram and train to deliver a 'heavy wooden rocking horse'. A city business donated fifty teddy bears. So many were the donations that the baskets set out to receive them had to be cleared half a dozen times a day, the gifts taken in newspaper vans to storage. After only four days, the *Herald* declared the appeal closed.[44]

The next day a procession of *Herald* vans made its way to the Children's Cottages, where the patients received the donations 'with cries of joy' (Figure 6.3). In the weeks after the appeal, visitors to the wards saw 'children nursing dolls and wheeling prams' and, in the nursery, cots 'well supplied with soft toys'. The public donated so many toys that there were enough for the children at Janefield and Beechworth.[45] Why did the public respond so generously to the *Herald*'s appeal?

Figure 6.3: 'Joy Comes to "Hillside of Sadness"'
(Courtesy *Herald*, 15 October 1948, 1)
In 1948, children crowd round Matron Harris as she distributes toys donated to the *Herald*'s toy appeal. The appeal reflected the belief that people with intellectual disabilities were 'grown-up children'. While fear of the 'feebleminded' was beginning to subside, the idea that people with intellectual disabilities were 'forever children' would continue to justify institutionalisation.

Rivett had certainly made the need clear, writing movingly about the patients' deprivation. Perhaps readers also responded to the way in which both he and the *Herald* appeal represented the residents. While Rivett used the language of deficiency to refer to the patients—they were 'incurably defective'—the overtone of menace with which the 'mentally defective' had so often been associated was missing. The residents of the cottages were rather tragic 'children'. Of several small children in one of the cottages' bare rooms, Rivett observed that while 'some of them might live to be adults in years' none among them 'would ever have the mentality of a normal child of 12'.

The appeal for toys reflected this understanding of intellectual disabilities. The newspaper assured its readers that, while some of the patients were 'adult in age and appearance', mentally they remained 'young children. For them the toys will be as welcome as for the toddlers'.[46] This idea, that people with intellectual disabilities were 'grown up children', derived from theories of child development first conceived in the late nineteenth century. According to this thinking, 'mental deficiency' resulted from diseased inheritance or other causes that rendered normal development impossible. The 'feebleminded', their development permanently arrested, were left, in the words of American psychologist Henry H. Goddard, 'perpetual children'. For those convinced of the menace of the 'feebleminded', the idea explained their alleged propensity to vice and provided a paternalist rationale for control. Lacking adult self-control, the 'feebleminded' must, without protection, inevitably succumb to immorality and crime.[47] However, even as fear of the 'feebleminded' subsided, the idea that people with intellectual disabilities were 'forever children' would continue to justify the need for permanent care. Eternal childhood implied eternal dependence.[48]

Despite its success, in the absence of government action the appeal could do little to improve the material conditions of the cottages. But the emotions that inspired it, and the generosity of the response, were part of a groundswell of concern about the treatment of the mentally disabled that would soon force reform.

'Our Out-dated Asylums'

In December 1946 the *Herald* published a series of articles under the banner, 'Our Out-dated Asylums'. Written by journalist Denis Warner with the intent to drive reform, they described in shocking detail the 'dismal, sometimes horrifying' conditions in Victoria's mental hospitals.[49]

Forced to defend the government in parliament, the minister for health, William Barry, rejected Warner's claims as 'substantially untrue', arguing that he lacked the necessary medical knowledge to appreciate the inherent difficulties of treating 'mental disease'.[50] There were, however, medical men with the requisite knowledge willing to lend their support to the *Herald*'s campaign. Writing to the newspaper in early January, two prominent psychiatrists, Drs H.F. Maudsley and John F. Williams, declared much of Warner's criticism entirely justified and called for a royal commission 'to inquire into the present deficiencies of an outmoded and starved department'.[51]

Critics of the Mental Hygiene Department had called for a royal commission for over a decade, to no avail. For several months the Cain Labor government followed the example of its predecessors, refusing to appoint any inquiry. Both minister and director argued that the department was neither underfunded nor outdated. Rather, its difficulties resulted from the present abnormal economic and social conditions. In the meantime, concerned citizens took the task of inquiry into their own hands. After inspecting the Kew Mental Hospital, delegates of the East Kew Women's Community Club resolved to make 'a survey of world standards in mental hospitals' to present to the minister. Church representatives proposed their own investigation. The Association of Friends and Relatives of the Mentally Ill, founded by Mrs Rosa Gilbert in November 1945 to campaign for better conditions, publicly criticised the department's 'out-dated methods'.[52]

Finally, the demand for an inquiry grew too insistent to resist. In July 1947 Barry announced the appointment of a committee to inquire into conditions in the state's mental hospitals. Chaired by the former director of mental hygiene, Dr W. Ernest Jones, it included representatives of the Catholic and Protestant churches, the Returned Services League and the Hospital Employees Federation. Given these appointments, the press doubted whether the committee could shed any light 'on the problem of how to bring our treatment of the mentally ill more into conformity with modern practice'. Editorials were particularly critical of the government's decision to entrust the 'expert direction' of the committee to the 75-year-old Jones, given his previous oversight of the department the committee was now tasked to examine, rather than pick a younger medical man more conversant with modern treatment. The National Council of Women of Victoria also deprecated the appointment of 'former administrators' and protested that no woman representative had been included in an inquiry 'concerned with matters so vital to women patients'. Nor, as the *Sun* observed, was a representative of any patients included, even by proxy.[53]

Released seven months later, the report vindicated the *Herald*. The committee admitted that

> far too much of these allegations is true, that most of the older institutions are out of date, that insufficient money for maintenance, equipment, and advancement has been provided, and this parsimony is of many years standing. Overcrowding does exist and considerable improvement in the clothing, feeding, and amenities is imperative. Perhaps the greatest need is a substantial increase in staff, particularly in the female side of the hospitals.[54]

In the time between the committee's appointment and its report, Victorians elected a new Liberal government under Thomas Hollway. Perhaps concerned by the limitations of the previous inquiry, the new minister for health, Charles Gartside, proposed inviting 'a leading psychiatrist' from England to advise the government on mental hygiene. Professor Alexander Kennedy, chosen by the government with the assistance of the British Council, was reportedly 'one of Britain's leading young psychiatrists'. He arrived in September 1949 and spent the next six weeks assessing the state's existing system of mental hygiene and its future needs.[55]

Widely reported by the press, Kennedy did not mince words, and his impressions made difficult reading for Victorians. The standard of patient care was 'most unsatisfactory' and 'quite out of keeping with the otherwise highly civilised conditions of living in the State'. Conditions at Kew Mental Hospital were especially bad; any first time visitor, he wrote, must be horrified. The hospital should be pulled down as soon as possible. He commended the press for reminding the department of its responsibilities.[56]

Kennedy's recommendations encompassed all aspects of mental hygiene. In many respects he considered that Victoria had fallen far behind modern practice. In the case of 'mental deficiency', however, he proposed no change of direction. The department had made 'a fine but belated effort to improve conditions in recent years by the establishment of a well-organised nucleus of institutions', but the small scale of that effort was, he declared, 'quite inadequate'. The 1939 Mental Deficiency Act had not been proclaimed because the state's existing institutions could not accommodate all those seeking admission. The Mental Hospital Inquiries Committee recommended the expansion of Janefield to accommodate one thousand residents as well as the extension of Pleasant Creek. Kennedy's recommendations far exceeded this number. Immediate plans should be made to accommodate a minimum of three thousand 'defectives' in institutions, with the 'full realisation' that within ten years institutions to confine three thousand more would be necessary. He based his estimate of future requirements on 'the expectation rate in the UK, which in most respects appear to be very similar to those in Victoria'. Separate institutional provision for the different grades of 'mental defectives' should also continue.[57]

While Kennedy did not refer explicitly to Kew Children's Cottages, his remarks about the damaging effects of 'the older accommodation' reflected his assessment. 'Many mothers', he observed, 'having seen some of the accommodation to which their children might be sent, have preferred to keep them at home to the detriment of the whole family and especially of normal brothers and sisters'. This, the alleged harm done to families caring for children with intellectual disabilities, was the dominant principle underpinning Kennedy's recommendations on 'mental deficiency' policy. It was 'difficult to imagine the cost in unhappiness and inefficiency to the State which must be caused by the fact that mental defectives, through lack of provision, are having to live with their families'. Policy should also ensure that the 'mentally defective' were afforded the necessary protection to live 'satisfactory' lives.[58]

Kennedy's recommendations also encompassed provision of services outside institutions. Some, such as guardianship schemes for high-grade 'defectives', and hostels, would ensure both protection and control. The belief in the menace of the 'feebleminded' lingered also in his remarks on their propensity to 'become involved in crime'. Overall, the extent of his recommendations for institutional expansion suggests he envisaged a great number of people with intellectual disabilities living 'satisfactory' lives in institutions.[59]

Neither the Mental Hospitals Inquiry Committee nor Kennedy's report envisaged a place for Kew Children's Cottages. Appalled by the conditions, the 1948 Mental Hospitals Inquiry Committee recommended their 'urgent and entire immediate evacuation'.[60] It also proposed a new board of three commissioners to oversee the administration of mental hygiene, including 'mental deficiency'. Kennedy was in broad agreement with the need for a new mental hygiene authority. A bill to establish it was already drafted by the time he presented his report in 1950. With Dr Catarinich, the present director of mental hygiene, on the verge of retirement, Kennedy recommended advertising widely for his replacement to ensure the appointment of a man willing to act boldly to reform the department. Responding to the report, the minister for health, Charles Gartside, promised legislation to give effect to Kennedy's recommendations. An international search for a successor to Dr Catarinich began.[61]

PART TWO

A PASSION FOR REFORM

Chapter 7

Eric Cunningham Dax and the Reform of the Kew Children's Cottages (1951–60)

In the immediate postwar years, the portfolio of the Ministry for Health became something of a poisoned chalice for Victorian members of parliament. Over three years between 1946 and 1948, five men held the position of minister, and each at some point during his term of office expressed horror at the prevailing state of affairs at the Kew Children's Cottages. Yet none of them could find the initiative, nor the resources, to do much to improve the terrible conditions at what many people now considered one of Victoria's most notorious institutions. The Mental Hygiene Authority Bill, which went before parliament in October 1950, was a belated acknowledgment by the Victorian government that something needed to be done.

The new legislation included many of Professor Kennedy's recommendations, and the bill received bipartisan support. A spirit of optimism and new ways of talking about people with intellectual disabilities infused the debate about the future of mental health services in Victoria. Many parliamentarians expressed the hope that an outdated custodial system might eventually be replaced by community services, preventative social reform, and more modern forms of treatment. The MLA for Barwon, Thomas Maltby, noted that an 'enlightened community' should be doing more for people with mental illness and people with intellectual disability than confining them and treating them in 'penal institutions'.[1] George Fewster, MLA for Essendon, also argued for a clean break with the past. Fewster called past practices 'woefully inadequate' because they deprived mental patients 'through no fault of their own' of ordinary citizens' rights. He urged that 'no time should be lost' in bringing the 'wonderful provisions' of the *Mental Hygiene Authority Act* into operation.[2]

In his report, Professor Kennedy had recommended that the Board of the Mental Hygiene Authority should comprise six to eight members drawn from a wide range of professions representing law, health, mental disability, and academia.[3] Yet, when it passed, the *Mental Hygiene Authority Act* only made provision for a board of three, two of whom would have to be psychiatrists.

Seventeen people—all men—applied for the three positions on the board. It appears that in the early 1950s most considered overseeing the reorganisation of the Victorian mental health services a job suited to men only, despite the claims of the National Council of Women to the contrary. Views about overseeing an institution were the same; every superintendent in the state was a man. So, when the minister for health described the search for candidates as an exhaustive process, he would not have thought the candidates would be anything other than male. There were eight applicants from Great Britain and nine from Australia. The successful appointments were announced on 26 June 1951. Ultimately, the Victorian cabinet settled on an 'Englishman, a Victorian and Tasmanian', as the *Argus* put it, to oversee a complete renovation of 'Victoria's mental health treatment system'.[4]

Englishman Eric Cunningham Dax, physician, consultant psychiatrist and superintendent at Netherne Hospital, Coulson in Surrey, was appointed inaugural chairman at a salary of £3000 a year. At 43, Dax was the youngest of the three appointees. The deputy chairmanship (£2500 a year) went to Dr Charles R.D. Brothers. Mr Eric Ebbs (£2000 a year) took the final position on the board. Charles Brothers was 46 years old and had extensive experience in the field. For more than eight years, he had worked as a senior consultant psychiatrist in the Tasmanian public hospital system.

He was also the director of the State Psychological Clinic and chairman of the Tasmanian Mental Deficiency Board. Given the third position on the board was primarily administrative, Ebbs, a 54-year-old secretary in the Department of Health's tuberculosis section, seemed suited for the job.

In the *Advocate*'s reckoning, the Mental Hygiene Authority had been designed to give the mentally ill in Victoria a 'new deal', and, for many observers, this was long overdue.[5] Now, at last, 'those who have mentally sick friends or relatives' could be 'assured of a new and thoroughly modern deal for mental patients with the appointment of Dr Cunningham Dax'.[6] Another correspondent looked forward to seeing immediate improvements—new buildings, better clothing and proper segregation—that would alleviate the situation for those poor 'unfortunate waifs' at Kew.[7]

If the make-up of the new Mental Hygiene Authority provoked significant interest in the local press, it was the chairman who excited the most curiosity. Dax's reputation, it seemed, preceded him. The *Argus* noted that he was not 'easily deterred by red tape'. Nor was he 'afraid to use unorthodox methods of treatment'. Once, the *Argus* reported, Dax had brought a group of patients together and played Mozart's Concerto in F for the Oboe. When the music stopped, Dax and his colleagues had provided the patients with painting materials and instructed them to paint whatever they wished.[8] The key message was that Dax was an innovator, a rebel and exactly the sort of person the decrepit Victoria mental health system needed. The *Argus* special representative in London wrote in July 1951 that 'we have done a great thing, I believe, to get such a man'.[9]

Eric Cunningham Dax

Eric Cunningham Dax was born on 18 May 1908 in Eastwood, a small town ten miles north of Nottingham. Dax's father, Henry Dax was a 'pleasant, graceful man' and a third generation apothecarist whose business was on the verge of collapse by the time Dax was born. Henry Dax was softly spoken, not particularly 'clever' or 'promising' and therefore nothing like his wife, Alice Mills, who was a 'highly intelligent' and 'very practical woman'.[10] Alice Mills was a socialist and a suffragette 'with very firm views' who had taken her first job, aged thirteen, at a post office in Liverpool. In 1895, because of her exuberant commitment to various socialist and suffragist causes, she was transferred to a new post office on the Isle of Man, though the transfer did little to curb her radical ways. By 1905, having married Henry Dax and moved to Eastwood, Mills had established a reputation as a controversial figure in town. She rode a bicycle, attended suffragette meetings and refused to 'drape her windows with Nottingham lace', all of which caused some consternation in a small, largely conservative town like Eastwood.[11] Alice Mills had a sharp wit, and she was not afraid to speak her mind. The author, D.H. Lawrence, for one, trusted her critical eye, and in 1908, while she was confined to bed and awaiting the birth of her son, Mills informed Lawrence that an early draft of his first novel, *The White Peacock*, required further work. Of the four chapters Mills read, only two were any good. 'The other pair', Mills told Lawrence, could only be described as 'very bad'.[12]

Dax and his sister Phyllis, who was born two years after him in 1910, grew up in a bustling household surrounded by their mother's liberal friends and books. Dax did not much like school, but he was an excellent student and excelled at almost anything he attempted. At high school he was a house captain, senior prefect and played soccer and cricket in school teams. When he graduated in 1929, he was offered a place at Cambridge but chose instead to study medicine at St Mary's Medical School at London University. Dax studied psychiatry and gained clinical experience at Barnwood House, a private mental hospital in Gloucester, and in the psychiatric unit of the London County Council General Hospital in Lewisham.[13] He graduated with honours in 1934 and by the late 1930s was exhibiting an aptitude for administration and looking for a job to match his capabilities. In 1939, he applied unsuccessfully for the position of deputy medical superintendent at the Bracebridge Health Hospital. Later that year, however, he was appointed deputy superintendent at Netherne Hospital, a 2000-bed psychiatric institution in Surrey.[14]

When Dax arrived at Netherne in 1939 he considered the hospital 'a wretchedly bare place' that was led, if that was the right word for it, by Dr L.M. Webber, an 'indecisive' superintendent who was 'largely afraid to make new moves'.[15] In Dax's candid assessment, Dr Webber had surrounded himself with mediocre, indifferent medical staff who fulfilled some routine requirements but nothing more. When Dr Webber died in 1941, the 33-year-old Dax was elevated to the position of superintendent

Almost immediately he began to make changes. He recruited new staff to overhaul the way that the hospital operated. Nineteenth-century custodial principles, which had defined the way the hospital had operated since it first opened in 1909, were eschewed in favour of more democratic principles such as an 'open-door' policy, which allowed patients free access to the grounds at any time. Dax also introduced new, modern treatments such as electro-convulsive therapy and prolonged sleep insulin coma, which, he believed, enabled most 'chronically depressed patients [to be] discharged'.[16]

Another of Dax's initiatives, and one that he would repeat in Victoria, involved opening the hospital up to inspection. Dax invited the public and journalists to visit whenever they wished to scrutinise the changes that were taking place. Those who took up the offer were usually impressed. One *New Statesman* journalist wrote in 1949 that, under Dax's stewardship, Netherne had become 'one of the best half-dozen hospitals in this country'. The journalist exclaimed, rather grandly, that, as they unlocked their doors, hospitals like Netherne were 'unbolting the dungeons of the human mind and setting free the imprisoned selves'.[17]

The contributions Dax made to the modernisation of the Netherne Hospital are documented in a comparative history of the hospital that credits Dax with a number of achievements including: the maintenance of standards of care during the Second World War; the appointment of the first social worker in 1942; the development of occupational therapy programs; and a rapid expansion of out-patient facilities.[18] By the time he left England to take up his new post in Victoria, Eric Cunningham Dax had transformed a mediocre hospital into one that could be considered, as he put it, 'among the best in England'.[19] Others viewed the Dax era at Netherne in a similar light. He left with the best wishes of the hospital's management committee, which expressed 'deep appreciation' for his work over the past decade and wished him 'every happiness and success in his new sphere of work'.[20]

While Dax and family voyaged for six weeks on the cargo ship *La Cordillera*, tradesmen in Melbourne worked around the clock to ensure that his new home in Kew and his new offices in the CBD would be ready when he arrived. The new Mental Hygiene Authority was housed in an old Georgian building at 300 Queen Street. The stuccoed brick building, once the home of a former mayor of Melbourne, required some urgent repairs. The *Argus* described it as a 'square, squat, treble-floored building', akin to a 'woman running late for a party' who had applied her make up 'rather hurriedly'. New carpets were laid on the ground floor, but at the end of December the staircases were still wet with paint and scaffolding obscured three sides of the building. A magnificent new switchboard stood idle with no telephonist to use it, and the new telephones had not been 'taken out of their cardboard boxes, much less connected'.[21]

By the time Dax and family disembarked in Sydney—the last leg of the journey would be by aeroplane—tradesmen were still 'trying valiantly' to get everything right. Great anticipation greeted Dax's arrival in Melbourne. Psychiatrist and chair of the 1924 royal commission Reginald Spencer Ellery captured the mood of optimism, seeing Dax as a focal point for the modernisation of a decrepit mental health system:

> The eyes of Victoria are now focussed upon this mild-mannered man who left his art classes in an orderly asylum in Surrey to rectify the discrepancies and supply the deficiencies of half a century's inadequate administration of the State's lunacy department. Pious hopes are vested in him by those who watch him roll up his shirt sleeves and face his tasks.[22]

'A Terrible Reproach to the Public Conscience'

In some respects, the situation Dax encountered in Victoria was not dissimilar to that he faced a decade earlier at Netherne. Like the Netherne Hospital, the Victorian mental health system was already at a crossroads between two eras when Dax took up his position in 1952. Moreover, as an Englishman abroad, Dax timed his transition into a new job to perfection. Soon postwar Australians would look to the United States rather than Great Britain for new ideas and leadership. However, Melbourne in the 1950s was still Anglophile and welcoming to an Englishman with Dax's credentials. Being both English and a man, and also a person with a reputation for reform, Dax seemed to promise much.

Dax was helped by having more resources at his disposal than all those who came before him. His predecessor, Dr Catarinich, had been forced to run his understaffed 'strange department' from 'one little office' tucked away somewhere inside the Treasury. The establishment of the Mental Hygiene Authority and the refurbishment of its new headquarters in Queen Street was proof that the Victorian government now had an appetite for change. Also, a shift in thinking about the hospitalisation of the mentally ill was already taking place at a policy level. All of this offered Dax an unprecedented opportunity to draw a line through the past and implement his program of reform (Figure 7.1). Dax, as the journalist Osmar White put it, 'was coming to work in a field where, to our shame, there is almost limitless opportunity for reform'.[23]

Osmar White knew the situation well. During two months in mid-1951, he investigated the history and administration of the Mental Hygiene Department and inspected some of the worst mental hospitals in the state. He interviewed doctors, nurses, attendants and, when the opportunity presented itself, some patients as well. The announcement of Dax's appointment provided White with an impetus to report his findings, or 'the facts and an authoritative interpretation of them' as the *Herald* stated. The exposé was framed as a series of open letters to Dr Cunningham Dax. The first appeared in the *Herald* on 28 August 1951.

Figure 7.1: Eric Cunningham Dax in Sydney 1955 with hospital matrons: left to right, Miss Homes RP, Miss Pruer (Larundel) and a matron from a Sydney hospital
(Courtesy the Royal Australian and New Zealand College of Psychiatrists)

It was titled 'Their Misery is Our Shame' and revealed to Dax (and the public) the 'facts about our mental hospitals'. The terrible conditions in such hospitals, wrote White, 'would have aroused a fury of indignation in Britain 50 years ago'.[24]

White called the conditions of the mental hospitals 'a terrible reproach to the public conscience and a damning indictment of State administrations, past and present'. He wrote of the tragedy of Royal Park, where 'men and woman whose only illness is age' were forced to spend the last months of their lives in 'the tense horror of the acute ward'. He described the building delays at Larundel that had rendered the hospital virtually vacant since 1945. But he saved his most evocative prose for the 'poor mentally defective children' who were living in the decrepit old cottages at Kew. The aged, filthy buildings, wrote White, had more in common with 'medieval Bedlam than a modern institution for the care of the sick'. At Kew Cottages, a handful of doctors, nurses and attendants were 'heroically' fighting an ever-encroaching squalor to 'give a little happiness and warmth to those who are doomed to live and die as idiots'. Repeated promises by successive governments for new buildings and better funding had never materialised. The cottages were a sad summation, wrote White, of the only home available to 'hundreds of miserable children, whose mental defect is far less than the moral defect of a community which permits them to be so housed and clothed'.[25]

Apart from an aptitude for incisive and evocative prose, Osmar White had a flair for being in the right place at the right time. As the *Herald*'s top war correspondent during the Second World War, White was among a handful of Australian journalists present during the Allied liberation of Paris and the only Australian journalist present at the German surrender at Remis in 1945.[26] After the war, White returned to the *Herald*. His investigation of the Victorian mental health system fortuitously just preceded Dax's arrival.

Special investigations of this kind become a recurrent feature in newspapers at home and abroad in the postwar years. For some journalists, it could be a way of burnishing a reputation. Not long beforehand, White's colleague at the *Herald*, Dennis Warner, had enhanced his career with the first serious investigation into the conditions of some Victorian psychiatric hospitals. With the help of staff at the Kew Mental Hospital, Warner donned a white coat and stethoscope. His four-part series, which called for a royal commission, was supported by several leading psychiatrists.

The *Herald*'s unsuccessful insistence on a royal commission suggests its exposés were not simply about sensationalism and selling newspapers. Its staff believed the Fourth Estate (the press) could report and campaign at the same time to effect social change. Cecil Edwards, the editor of the *Herald*, emphasised this principle in reflecting that 'if [a headline] was all we wanted, we had it: shriek in the night, and then onto the next sensation'.[27] He insisted on approaching sensational material 'from a different direction' and believed that it could be used to marshal 'public support' and to force a 'reform in a system'. A good newspaper, Edwards believed, should 'flash the light of publicity on problems and needs that have been neglected or abandoned'. A good newspaper had to 'identify itself with the community's life' and should be 'prepared to tap the strings of charity for those who cannot help themselves'. Under Edwards' leadership, the *Herald* embraced this tradition and forged a reputation for campaigning on what it considered issues of civic virtue, such as vandalism, sly grog, or communism. Osmar White's investigation into the Victorian mental health system occurred within this context of campaigning for social causes. His series was not unique but it was timely because mental health had become a potential issue in the next state election.

White's series of open letters outlined certain qualities—patience, political nous and strength—that Dax would need to properly tackle the problem at hand. But the articles also identified some structural issues that had plagued the system for more than thirty years. White bemoaned the Department of Mental Hygiene's inability to attract and retain sufficiently trained staff. And he castigated the inefficient, 'indifferent and ignorant' Department of Public Works, which rarely prioritised the urgent and repeated requests for more buildings to cope with the overcrowding that plagued so many Victorian institutions.[28] Much to the chagrin of some members of parliament, White laid most of the blame for the deplorable conditions at the feet of indifferent politicians and public servants. Bill Fulton, the minister for health, sought to downplay the severity of the *Herald*'s assessment and called Osmar White a 'scurrilous writer' who had 'a very limited knowledge' of the truth of the situation. The minister for public works, Percy Byrnes, went even further, accusing White of wilfully misrepresenting the facts.[29]

Like Osmar White, Catarinich, by now acting director of the Mental Hygiene Authority, believed that the problems were mostly systemic. Unlike White, he did not believe that the problems could be resolved by one man. When Catarinich sat down in August 1951 to write his final annual report he emphasised this point. For thirteen years Catarinich had worked in a difficult job in trying circumstances. Now, he was keeping the seat warm for Dax, and this would be his last report. In a reflective mood, he thanked the 'various Ministers to whom I have been responsible for

ERIC CUNNINGHAM DAX AND THE KEW CHILDREN'S COTTAGES (1951–60)

their sympathetic attitude towards myself'. If Professor Kennedy's report had singled him out for some of the severest criticism, Catarinich viewed the situation through a slightly different lens. 'The difficulties at present confronting the Department are not the result of indifference or a lack of appreciation of the many issues involved', wrote Catarinich, but rather a matter of priorities and the inevitable result 'of many urgent and essential activities which had preference over the claims of the mentally ill'. He also suggested that those who looked to Dax and the newly formed Mental Hygiene Authority to bring about a revolution should be more cautious. 'The Authority will have an uphill task to fulfil', he wrote, and it would be 'wrong to expect the new Authority to perform miracles'.[30]

Yet miracles, of a sort, were exactly what Dax had in mind. A month after the announcement of the new Mental Hygiene Authority, Geoffrey Hutton, the *Argus* special representative in London, had visited Dax at his home in the United Kingdom. Dax, who was confined to his sick bed due to 'an attack of pneumonia', was nevertheless able to convey to Hutton 'something of his plans, his methods, and his beliefs', and it was clear that Dax's experience at Netherne would provide a blueprint for his Victorian program of reform.[31] He promised to open the hospitals up to public scrutiny and introduce new treatments. He would encourage people to take on voluntary roles within the network of Victorian institutions so that they might begin to 'break down the wall of fear and prejudice which separates the inside of the mental hospital' from the outside world. Dax was quick to point out that he had no intention of transforming Victoria's mental health system within a couple of weeks. 'What I want to do first', he said, 'is sit back and collect information'.

He reiterated the same sentiment at Essendon Airport on his arrival on 28 December 1951, where some journalists and a distinguished group, including Minister for Health Fulton, had gathered to welcome him. They were bemused as Dax immediately broke with protocol by talking to the press. When asked if he had heard anything of the conditions in Victoria's mental hospitals, Dax admitted that he had read some critical reports but refused to comment further until he had seen things for himself. 'I am a new boy at present', he said, 'and eager to learn all I can'. His doorstep press interview caused some consternation, and later Dax explained that 'I had no idea that public servants did not talk to the press … so I talked quite openly'.[32] Fulton was as surprised as anyone by the turn of events and sought, as quickly as possible, to bring the impromptu press conference to a close.

Getting to Work

As well as his wife and four children, Dax brought his ageing parents, Henry and Alice Dax, to Australia. Before taking the job, Dax had been quite clear that his salary package should include a car and suitable accommodation to house his extended family. The Victorian government had acquiesced to all his demands and provided him with a new FX Holden and a two-storey Edwardian mansion—known as *The Gables*—in Kew. The government had purchased the twelve-room mansion from the American Embassy in January 1949. At the time, Fulton had announced that the building would be transformed into much-needed accommodation for thirty-five nurses who were living in the most 'appalling conditions' at the Kew Mental Hospital next door. The nurses would have to wait. If Dax and his family were living cheek by jowl with his workplace, his children had plenty of freedom to roam; Susannah Dax, the youngest daughter, recalled she had 'the whole of the Kew Mental Hospital as a playground'.[33]

While his family settled into their new home, Dax turned his attention to the job at hand. On New Year's Day in 1952, his fourth day in Melbourne, Dax strode into the new offices of the Mental Hygiene Authority, leapt lithely up the stairs and got to work. From that moment, wrote one former colleague, 'the Department felt the impact of Eric Dax's personality'. Another colleague, Herbert Bower, was less impressed. He thought the new chairman presented 'as a rather upper-class Englishman who looked down on the colonials'. But Bower also intimated that the new Mental Hygiene Authority 'needed a foreigner' because someone 'from the outside' could get things done that one could never 'do locally'.[34] It is worth noting, however, that the structure of the new Mental Hygiene Authority gave Dax more resources, more freedom, and more autonomy than his predecessor had ever had at his disposal.

The Mental Hygiene Authority never quite became the fully autonomous, self-contained unit that Kennedy envisaged in his report. For instance, the authority remained subject to the provisions of the Public Works Act when carrying out any maintenance or repair work on the institutions under its control. It was also subject to the provisions of the *Public Service Act* for all non-clinical staff appointments. But, as a quasi-division, or branch, of the Department of Health, the Mental Hygiene Authority nevertheless had 'a considerable amount of autonomy'. Dax as chairman reported directly to the minister for health, who, at the beginning at least, gave him plenty of freedom to do as he pleased. Dax appreciated the freedom and recalled later that 'no one has been so utterly lucky as to come to a job like that and to have had a very free hand'.[35]

The primary function of the authority was to formulate, control and direct the general policy and administration of the Mental Hygiene Act. Its remit was: to improve treatment and develop measures 'for the prevention of mental defect, disorder and disease'; to conduct research; and to arrange for the provision and control of all institutions licensed as mental homes.[36] The authority met roughly once a fortnight and the roles of each board member were clearly defined. Eric Ebbs was responsible for essential services, overseeing the budget and the appointment of non-professional staff. The deputy chairman, Charles Brothers, was chiefly responsible for professional staffing matters at the various clinics and institutions and supervising the pharmaceutical, medical, and other ancillary departments. This left the chairman to focus on the bigger picture. He was responsible for the coordination of overall policy, the building program, and public relations.

One of the first things Dax did was get Catarinich—the man he was replacing—to take him on a tour of his new domain. Catarinich and Dax got along well together, and, in his first annual report, Dax commended Catarinich for helping 'us over the transition period with the utmost kindness and unstinting assistance'. As well as providing the three members of the Mental Hygiene Authority with 'the benefit of his remarkable and detailed knowledge', Catarinich took them on a guided tour of every institution in the state.[37] On 7 January 1952, they visited their first Mental Hospital in Ballarat. A few days later they visited the Mental Hospital at Kew, and soon a rumour was going around that, during the visit, Dax had immediately begun 'ripping bars off the windows' with his bare hands. On an oppressively hot day the following week, the group went out to Sunbury. On that tour, Dax, by his own report, was surprised to find his colleagues struggling to keep up with his pace. At one point he recalled glancing back only to find his three companions drenched in sweat and wilting in the heat. It might have been around then, Dax recalled, that some started 'wondering what sort of a fool' they had brought all the way out from England to take control.[38]

In his first two months, that is by March 1952, Dax had visited Kew, Ballarat, Sunbury, Mont Park, Bundoora and Beechworth. He developed an understanding of the network of receiving houses, clinics, mental hospitals and 'mental deficiency' colonies that were now part of his domain. In total, the authority was responsible for twelve institutions of various sizes that looked after 6386 patients with mental illness and a further 746 'mental defectives'.[39] The largest mental hospital was Mont Park, which held 1658 patients, while the smallest, Bundoora, held just over 200. The Kew Cottages, with 492 patients on the books, was the largest institution for people with intellectual disabilities. Dax thought that, overall, the mental hospitals were in a worse state than the institutions for people with intellectual disabilities. In fact, while doing his rounds, he was surprised to find most of the services for 'intellectually subnormal children' in relatively good condition. He thought Travancore—the clinic for diagnosing cases of 'mental deficiency'—and its accompanying residential centre in 'good working order'. He was also impressed by the two 'mental deficiency' colonies at Janefield and Stawell. Within this small network of Victorian institutions, Dax was able to glimpse what he called the 'nucleus of a valuable programme' of services for people with intellectual disabilities.[40]

When he visited the Kew Cottages, however, Dax was shocked by what he saw. He had read Osmar White's articles about Kew but even so, was shaken by what he encountered. Dax later admitted that he had 'never seen anything like the Kew Cottages' before.[41] He first noticed the whole place smelt 'of stale food, excreta and unsatisfactory drainage'. In one building, he came across a table laid with a black tablecloth only to discover that it was, in fact, a table covered by a thick, heaving layer of flies. He was appalled by the open drains and the way that 'some of the sewage emptied onto the adjacent fields'. And he was distressed by the sight of small children wandering about the place in oversized, filthy clothing: second-hand adult football jerseys, old army jackets and 'whatever hats they could collect'. During the day, the children played in a dilapidated old shed. At mealtimes, they 'ate from tin bowls with their fingers', and at night they slept on 'straw mattresses', thirty to forty children to a room. In most rooms the paint was peeling from the walls, and there was dirt and grime everywhere (Figures 7.2 and 7.3).

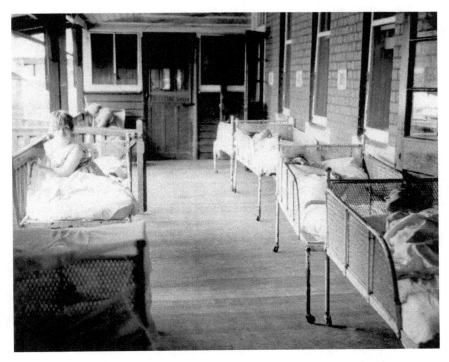

Figure 7.2 Cots spilling out onto the verandah of one of the units at Kew
(Courtesy Kew Residential Services)

Figure 7.3: A toilet block at Kew Cottages
(Courtesy Kew Residential Services)

Little wonder then that, at their inaugural meeting on 18 January 1952, the Mental Hygiene Authority acknowledged that renovations at the Kew Cottages were a 'matter of extreme urgency'. Dax, Brothers and Ebbs all agreed that most of the buildings at Kew would have to be 'completely renovated and modernised in so far as it is possible'.[42]

Dax regarded those first few months of 1952 as 'the emergency': a time 'when conditions demanded immediate improvement', both at some of the mental hospitals and at institutions for people with intellectual disabilities. As such, one of his earliest acts as chairman of the Mental Hygiene Authority was to instigate a program of spring cleaning in nearly every institution in the state. He 'issued soap and scrubbing brushes' to the wards in all institutions and ordered all staff to start 'scrubbing from top to toe'.[43]

At the Kew Cottages everyone got involved. Patients and staff worked beside each other scrubbing away decades of grime. Dax noted wryly in one interview that although this 'wasn't exactly psychiatry ... it was good clean fun'. Other superficial improvements soon followed. The ill-fitting, second-hand clothing was discarded, and patients were encouraged to wear their own clothes. At some point, tradesmen regularly appeared on site. They repainted the buildings and repaired whatever they could. The library was renovated, and new furniture was installed in the nurses' accommodation. By the end of May, a new, modern school building was erected to provide 'a balanced programme of training ... music, games and handicrafts' (Figures 7.4 and 7.5). New play equipment was installed in the grounds. When the minister for health visited the cottages on 11 June 1952, the institution was looking better than it had in years. Fulton applauded the Mental Hygiene Authority's commitment to implementing 'significant change'. He declared it the 'beginning of a policy of improvement' that would one day realise his dream of mental hospitals and general hospitals being run along 'similar lines'.[44]

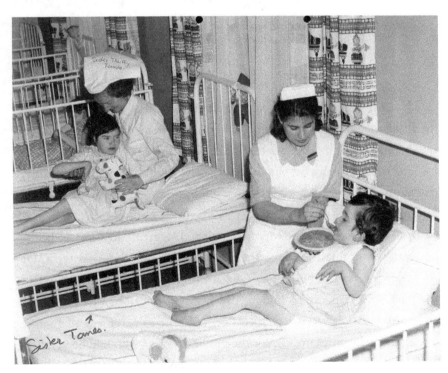

Figure 7.4: Two nurses attending to two young residents
at Kew Cottages
(Courtesy Kew Residential Services)

Figure 7.5: A group of young male residents and three nurses in one of the education/therapy rooms at Kew Cottages
(Courtesy Kew Residential Services)

Over fifty years later Dax said he had no idea how the initial improvements at the cottages were funded, adding, 'I don't think I thought very much about the finances' at all.[45] That job fell to Eric Ebbs. Fortunately, by 1952 some money had begun to flow. The Mental Hygiene Authority's first annual operating budget, at just under £3 million, was almost twice as large as the £1.6 million budget Catarinich had administered in his final year as director of the Mental Hygiene Department.[46] The authority's budget grew annually and, by the middle of his first five-year term, Dax was working with a budget of £4.2 million. The significant growth of the authority's operating budget did not go unnoticed by other public servants, and Dax recalled 'a certain amount of resentment' in some circles. He felt some concern for the public servants who had been asking, without success, 'for money for their departments for some time', but he was also convinced that the Mental Hygiene Authority 'needed it more than anyone else'.

Untangling Mental Illness and Intellectual Disability

As Dax and the Mental Hygiene Authority navigated a path through the first months of 'the emergency' in 1952, they were also considering the best way to reorganise the entire Victorian mental health system. The minutes of their earliest meetings reveal the issues they faced. On 18 January 1952, the authority acknowledged that a guiding principle for the reorganisation of the mental health services should be decentralisation, to allow 'all people, in all places, at all times' to receive the treatment they required within a 'reasonable distance from their homes'. Two weeks later, Dax, Brothers and Ebbs considered the best ways to publicise their work. They decided that 'at the appropriate time, the press should be informed of what has been done already, what is in course at present, and of plans for the future'. On 25 February 1952 they discussed the proclamation of the *Mental Deficiency Act*, which although passed in 1939 had not officially become law. Their attention to this piece of legislation indicated that they sought to untangle services for intellectual disability and mental illness.[47]

From the outset, Dax had made it clear that people with mental illness and people with intellectual disabilities required different treatment, care and control. Services for people with intellectual disabilities and those with mental illness had ostensibly been segregated in 1937 with the creation of two branches within the Department of Mental Hygiene. The Mental Hygiene Branch was responsible for care and treatment of the mentally ill, while the so-called Mental Defectives Branch was responsible for the care and treatment of people with intellectual disabilities. Each branch operated their own network of institutions and associated clinical services. However, when Dax had toured Victoria's network of institutions, he was surprised to find that mental illness and intellectual disability 'remained fused together' in several institutions. At Beechworth he discovered 'a hell of a lot of intellectually handicapped people' in a hospital that was supposedly a hospital for the mentally ill.[48] In Sunbury, the story was similar. Even at Kew, which contained two separate institutions on the one site, Dax reported that people with intellectual disabilities and mental illness 'were all mixed up together'.

Dax pinpointed the crux of problem to the *Age* in late 1952, remarking that all of Victoria's institutions for people with intellectual disabilities were designed for children. As a result, '1000 adults of subnormal intelligence' had ended up living 'tangled up with the mentally ill' in mental hospitals, because there was nowhere else for them to be housed. Dax was convinced that this was not helping either group of patients. By 'living in close proximity', he said, the 'mentally ill and the intellectually sub-normal adults are having a detrimental effect each on the other'.[49]

Publicly and privately, Dax lamented the lack of legislative distinction in Victorian mental health service policies between 'the mentally-ill, who were of normal intelligence, and the mentally-retarded, who might never become mentally ill'. At a meeting of the Kew Hospital Welfare Group on 7 March 1952, Dax highlighted one fundamental difference between these two groups when he declared that 'about 80 percent of the mentally ill can be cured'. This meant that the pattern of services for the mentally ill essentially revolved around treatment, rehabilitation and follow-up care in the community. By contrast, for intellectual disability there was no cure, which meant the pattern of services for people with intellectual disabilities revolved around custodial care and training. Dax spoke to this theme on 29 June 1952 when he urged parents of children with intellectual disabilities to accept their fate: 'Parents should not hope against hope that their child will grow out of its backwardness and become normal when it grows up'.[50] It was impossible, as Dax put it, to 'give a person more intelligence than he already has'. But you could teach such people to use whatever intelligence they had and 'to make the most of it'. If taught a trade, Dax said, 'a mentally retarded child … can advance in life as much as a normal child'.

The desire of the Mental Hygiene Authority to place 'into operation' the 1939 *Mental Deficiency Act* was essentially a desire to legislate for the complete administrative separation of services for people with intellectual disabilities from the services for people with mental illness. On the one hand, such a desire was progressive in the sense that it acknowledged the fundamental principle that people with intellectual disabilities and people with mental illness required different (and specialised) forms of treatment, care and control. On the other hand, it was regressive (or outdated) in the sense that it meant implementing an Act that was heavily infused with the now discredited 'science' of eugenics to justify such measures. Perhaps Dax was less concerned with the subtleties of the legislation than he was with what it could achieve. Perhaps he viewed the Act as nothing more than a useful tool that could be used, once and for all, to untangle services for two divergent groups of people.

The 1953 annual report reveals the scope of reforms that Dax believed the proclamation of the *Mental Deficiency Act* could achieve. He argued that the proclamation of the Act would 'necessitate a significant expansion of the Mental Hygiene Authority'. In hindsight, there is something almost guilelessly optimistic about the vision for the future that Dax presented on the page, one that pictured the establishment of new residential buildings for adults and children with intellectual disabilities across the state. At least two thousand extra beds were needed, he explained, to 'place residential care and training of retarded children and defectives of all ages on a sound basis'.[51] Dax envisaged new clinical and social services designed specifically for the care and training of children with intellectual disabilities. He also imagined a thriving network of day centres run by volunteers that would cater for 'children in the medium range of backwardness' and the formation of an entirely separate administrative and medical branch of the Mental Hygiene Authority that would concern itself only with intellectual disabilities. 'Extra buildings would be required to house the staff, statutory and medical records' of this new branch, wrote Dax, because existing facilities were inadequate to accommodate even the present 'small mental deficiency section in the department'.

The authority's 1953 report outlined a bold vision for the reorganisation of services for people with intellectual disabilities. The request for 2000 additional beds—an increase of more than 200 per cent—suggests that the institutional model of care remained the central pillar of the

Mental Hygiene Authority's reforms. But Dax also pointed out that, 'when considering the requirements for the care and training of children and adolescents, it must not be thought that residential provision is always necessary'. He had been impressed with the rapid development of day centres at several metropolitan and regional sites across Victoria, and he saw 'many advantages for this method' of care. Dax also saw much that was good in facilitating an ongoing connection between a parent and their child with an intellectual disability. He suggested that daily association within this family unit might lift some of the stigma around intellectual disabilities because parents who spent more time with their children were 'more apt to be proud of their achievements, no matter how limited'. As such, Dax was inclined to support the establishment of day centres whenever possible. By 1953, the Mental Hygiene Authority was subsidising each child at approved day centres with an annual ex-gratia grant of £12 per child. 'Too much credit cannot be given to the various organisations ... which have inaugurated Day Centres during recent months', wrote Dax, who made it clear that this network of centres remained an essential part of his overall plans.[52]

To achieve this overarching plan—for the current 'situation to be remedied' as he put it—the chairman explained that finance would need to be 'assured' because no building plan could 'be completed overnight'. Rather, the building program would require various branches of the Department of Public Works to operate seamlessly together. Dax imagined the timely and orderly 'allocation of the services of experienced architects, engineers, draftsmen, and applied specialists in sufficient numbers to expedite finalisation' of his plans. At the time, he probably thought he could implement his program of reform. Certainly, some things, like the segregation of services, would eventually happen, though beyond Dax's timeline. But fiscal constraints, a ponderous bureaucracy and, ultimately, changing ideas around intellectual disability ensured that much of what Eric Cunningham Dax articulated in his vision for the future would never be realised.

Chapter 8

The Tipping Campaign and Public Support (1961–65)

In April 1952, Dr J.V. Ashburner was appointed to the position of psychiatrist-superintendent of the Kew Mental Hospital, which still had oversight of the Kew Cottages. Ashburner was largely impressed with the changes being implemented by Eric Cunningham Dax and the government's commitment to implementing reform. In his first annual report, the superintendent noted the arrival of a new social worker and two assistant therapists, who were providing 'a great benefit to patients'. Ashburner also referred to the appointment of an extra thirty-two 'male and female' nurses at the cottages as a 'welcome addition'. Like many mental hygiene professionals, he was optimistic about the future. 'At the Children's Cottages a new era has begun', he wrote, and 'step by step as opportunity offers, the replanning is being put into effect'.[1] However, he added, this 'brief record' of achievements should not obscure everything that still 'remains to be done'. For many decades Kew had been neglected on 'the assumption that it would be closed', which meant that 'decay and gloom and stench' were everywhere. One problem, as far as Ashburner was concerned, was that 'methods designed to save every last penny' tended to waste precious time. Of even greater concern were the 'present methods of maintenance, administration, and requestioning', which slowed everything down and ultimately hampered any attempts at reform.

Fighting Red Tape

On this latter issue, as well as many others, Ashburner and Dax saw eye to eye. Because the Mental Hygiene Authority remained subject to the provisions of the *Public Works Act*, Dax could not determine capital funding for maintenance or repair work on the institutions under the authority's control. He could only make requests for finance and wait for these to be approved or denied. Dax chafed against such constraints for many years. The minutes of the Mental Hygiene Authority meetings during the 1950s and 1960s offer a glimpse of the limitations under which the authority often operated. They also reveal how Dax's eagerness to spend money allocated to the authority—the government promised £6 million over four years—was tempered by the parsimony of the Department of Public Works, which refused many of his requisitions.[2]

As early as August 1952, the authority expressed its concern to the minister for public works about the frequent delays in responding to urgent requisitions for capital and maintenance works at its institutions. On 4 September, a special meeting of the Mental Hygiene Authority voiced growing concerns about these delays. Dax invited Mr Symes from the Public Works Department to the meeting to discuss why so many requisitions had been deferred or delayed.[3] There was little change, however, and the department continued to show scant regard for the authority's program of reform. Being ignored in these encounters infuriated Dax, who now considered himself to be in an ongoing and unwinnable battle against the department's decision makers for every last penny. 'I blasted them up hill and downhill', Dax later recalled, 'we never called each other by our Christian names as there was too much fighting'.[4]

These frequent battles nevertheless saw much-needed funds flow to the Mental Hygiene Authority's bottom line. Indeed, gross expenditure rose by almost 30 per cent—from £2,142,690 to £2,996,344—during Dax's first full year as chairman of the authority. Of that, nearly 9 per cent (£248,491) represented expenditure by the Department of Public Works on maintenance and capital works, so perhaps the fights were worth the trouble. Of course, most funds went towards the maintenance of mental hospitals through the Mental Hygiene Branch, whose budget was almost twenty times larger than the budget of the Mental Defectives Branch. But the Mental Defectives Branch budget also increased significantly in Dax's first year—from £127,667 in 1952 to £160,454 in 1953—a more modest but still significant 25 per cent rise. These were tangible improvements, and the average weekly expenditure per patient rose by almost 20 per cent (from £5 15s 7d to £6 16s 11d) in one year.[5]

Even so, Dax thought the budget completely insufficient for what he was trying to achieve. While Ashburner could laud the progress of the reforms taking place at Kew, Dax found it difficult to ignore all that still required his attention and continued to issue vehement protests to the Department of Public Works. In September 1953, he called his budget 'woefully inadequate' and bemoaned the fact that 'little progress has been achieved in regard to maintenance and capital works'.[6] What little money he could scrounge together was spent on a 'certain amount of overdue work … amongst which was a school and nurses' hostel at the Kew Cottages'. Though feeling generally discouraged, Dax was not afraid to express his dissatisfaction with what he considered an inefficient, defective system. The 'present system is extremely cumbersome', he wrote, 'and there seems to be little reason why, if firms are available to supply goods at contract prices, the hospital secretaries should not be able to contact them directly for requirements, providing the expenditure was within the approved limits'. Dax could not fathom how a 'system which requires months of waiting for items, which could be bought in a few minutes' was going to help him implement urgent reforms. Such an inefficient system, he predicted, would eventually produce 'frustration and irritation throughout the department'.

Half a century later Dax reiterated his attack on the Department of Public Works. They 'were just sitting on their rear quarters doing absolutely nothing', Dax recalled in one interview, 'I was ringing up day after day to demand this and that, then going to the newspapers about it'.[7] Ever since he had spoken to journalists on his first day in Australia, going to the press had become a part of Dax's *modus operandi*. One of his friends,

Keith Benn, later recalled that 'his style was so entirely different to the old public service method'. He 'would get on the radio and he'd say anything', and he was always ready to offer a comment 'on any relevant event'.[8] Dax himself had been quite upfront about his commitment to transparency when he first took the job and frequently noted that any event, no matter how confronting, 'should be faced as openly as possible'. But his willingness to talk to the press was also rooted in his belief that the newspapers and the broader public were on his side. Dax was convinced that the press 'felt that somehow or other they were involved ... I mean they were on our side you see, so straight away it wasn't a matter of complaining against us, it was a matter of complaining against the government'.[9]

Dax's relations with the press highlight the role the media has played in shaping the history of the Kew Children's Cottages and public perceptions about intellectual disability. Ever since the *Argus* reported in May 1887 that a new institution for people with intellectual disabilities would soon be 'ready for occupation', the goings on at the cottages were covered in the local press.[10] And Kew Cottages captured public attention like no other institution in the state, perhaps because it was a place essentially created for children. A century after it was built, one observer remarked that Kew Cottages had 'an almost iconic status in the minds of many families and the local community'.[11] The frequent press exposés about the atrocious conditions at Kew, together with repeated calls for enquiries and royal commissions, had for decades kept the plight of the 'poor waifs' at Kew at the forefront of many people's minds. And again after 1950 the media played an important role in forcing reluctant governments to institute reform at Kew and other institutions across the state.

Honesty and openness with the press was one thing, but public relations was quite another, and Dax proved just as adept at managing the message as he was at making an honest appraisal of any situation. If there was any doubt about Dax's talent as an astute spin doctor, it could be resolved by the minutes of the third meeting of the Mental Hygiene Authority, where Dax, Brothers and Ebbs openly discussed the best ways to publicise their work.[12] Dax knew that, if he was going to get the funding the Victorian government had promised, he would need to fight for every pound. Speaking (or leaking) to the press was just one of the ways that he could remind the government of the commitments it had already made. It was a risky game and one that Dax played, for the most part, with a deft touch. Occasionally, however, his leaking did more harm than good.

On 13 May 1952 Dr Barry Mulvaney, honorary psychiatrist at St Vincent's Hospital, delivered a public lecture at the University of Melbourne during which he claimed that 'slippery politicians' were already reneging on their promises to support Dax as he went about the 'gigantic task of improving the conditions in mental hospitals throughout Victoria'. Premier William McDonald was not impressed with Mulvaney's mudslinging, and two days later he dismissed Mulvaney's remarks as 'unnecessarily offensive'. Then he proceeded to sling a bit of mud of his own. McDonald would not vouch for the existence or otherwise of 'slippery politicians' he said, but he was quite certain about the existence of 'some very foolish critics' in the press. The following day, Dax released a conciliatory statement declaring that everything was proceeding as planned. According to the *Argus*, the gist of Dax's statement was that 'works to improve Victoria's mental hospitals' were 'in progress' and that no contracts had been cancelled 'because of financial difficulties'. Although this was not quite true, it was exactly what the government wanted to hear. The premier thanked Dax for his 'fair, clean and concise statement of the actual position', which, he said, had put 'the question of mental hygiene in its proper perspective'.[13]

If Dax was occasionally guilty of overreach, more often than not his skills in public relations on behalf of the Mental Hygiene Authority fuelled public confidence in what he and his colleagues were trying to achieve. It probably helped that Dax cultivated friendships with the media in order to get his message across. He took journalists from various news outlets to lunch at the Windsor Hotel, a grand, nineteenth-century luxury hotel and restaurant on Spring Street and situated conveniently across the road from Parliament House. He also invited journalists to his home in Kew. Dax's son Richard recalled that 'journalists were always at the house', and that, in a way, they almost became 'a part of normal life'.

Edmond William (Bill) Tipping, a journalist at the *Herald*, spent more time at the Dax residence than most. Dax met Tipping and his wife, Marjorie, shortly after arriving in Australia. He immediately connected with them, declaring them 'wonderful people' who became 'great family friends'. Tipping was just as fond of Dax, and in 1963 he managed to convey some of this affection when he wrote a personal profile about Dax for the *Herald* that sought to explain something of the man's character and charm. 'I think it is his eyes that impress you most when you meet this 55-year-old', wrote Tipping. He described Dax as a 'slim, fit and vital Englishman who regards himself very much an Australian now'. Dax, Tipping wrote, 'likes normal people because they are normal and entertainingly unpredictable' and he 'likes abnormal people because ... they're just people who are rather more unpredictable than normal people'.[14]

Edmond William Tipping

Edmond William (Bill) Tipping was an impressive assemblage of eloquence, wit and talent who had an enviable capacity for getting on with the job at hand. He was a University of Melbourne man, a part-time punter and a raconteur with an acerbic wit. Tipping was born on 27 August 1915 in Moonee Ponds and educated in Toorak, at St. Kevin's College, where he became school captain in 1933.[15] By the time he had made his way to the University of Melbourne, Bill Tipping had his finger in a number of different pies. He studied law, edited *Farrago*, the university newspaper, and he ran the debating club in his spare time. He also worked part time as a correspondent for the *Herald*. In early 1939, Tipping published an interview with Percy Grainger in the *Herald* that caught the attention of Sir Keith Murdoch, who thought it unconventional but enlightening. By November 1939, the world was at war and Tipping had parlayed his Grainger article into a full-time job.

Bill Tipping was a large, jowly man who wore his hair short and smoked a packet of cigarettes a day; both habits he had picked up—along with a serious bout of tuberculosis—during his spell as a private in the Australian

Imperial Force in the Second World War. When he was discharged from the army in March 1944, Tipping took a job as a public relations officer in the Royal Australian Air Force. When the war ended, he returned to his job at the *Herald*, and within five years had risen to become chief of staff.[16] As a newspaperman, Tipping set great store in placing himself at the forefront of those events about which he wrote. He was blessed with considerable vitality, and he used his drive and enthusiasm to great advantage when chasing a story. His ability to get to the heart of the matter gave his readers a sense that they were on assignment with him, capturing the moment. His colleagues commended 'his eye for detail' and his propensity to 'absorb information at extraordinary speed'. Tipping, as one former colleague put it, was also a forceful campaigner who 'was never happier than when exposing an injustice or helping to make somebody's life a little better' (Figure 8.1).[17]

Figure 8.1: Edmond William Tipping, journalist and social commentator
(Courtesy Kew Residential Services)

When Tipping died in 1970, 3DB radio presenter Gerald Lyons declared that 'I doubt that any one man living has done so much in human terms to make the problem of mentally retarded children known and accepted'. Lyons was referring to two articles that Tipping had written almost twenty years earlier about a young boy with intellectual disabilities, whose parents had kept him on a leash tied to a stake in their suburban back yard. Bill Tipping's story of 'Michael', the boy who was tied to a stake, struck a chord with many Victorian readers at the time and ultimately became the catalyst for a fundraising campaign, the Tipping Appeal, which lasted two weeks and raised almost £50,000—about eight times the minimum wage of the day—for the children at Kew.[18]

Later, when he was asked about the Tipping Appeal, Eric Cunningham Dax was coy about the whole affair. 'Someone must have told Tipping about the boy', Dax said in more than one interview, before moving on to other subjects. The Kew Cottages' first social worker, Irene Higgins, also believed that it was Dax who alerted Tipping to the boy tied to the stake. But she had a slightly different view of the whole affair and suggested that the campaign was more staged managed than it looked. Higgins recalled that sometime in April 1953, Dax had told her a 'story about a child that was sort of on a leash'.[19] When she went to investigate, Higgins found that 'the poor parents were wonderful parents' but also that their son could climb a 'bare wall'. Given that they lived next door to a butcher who 'had a cauldron of fat in his back yard', the parents had been terrified that their son would climb over and 'hurt himself'. As Higgins recalled, the parents, desperate to get on with their work—they ran a small business from their home—had tied their son to the stake for his own protection. But Higgins was convinced that this was not the story that Dax wanted people to hear. Dax 'didn't like it', she recalled, he wanted the story to have a hint of malevolence; he wanted it to be 'sort of horrible'.

Cecil Edwards, Tipping's boss and the editor of the newspaper that actually ran the two-part series, was convinced that a neighbour had first alerted the press about the boy tied to a stake. But his account throws further light on what Higgins intimated was the stage-managed nature of the affair. Edwards had first been informed about the boy in March 1952, but he was not sure how to deal with it at the time. Under Edwards' editorship in the late 1940s and early 1950s, the *Herald* had played a significant role in exposing the terrible conditions in a number of institutions across the state. Edwards was proud of his paper's achievements. He believed that in exposing these conditions his paper could 'make the government and the community meet their responsibilities'.[20] But he also believed that such exposures had inadvertently discouraged parents from sending their children to institutions such as the Kew Cottages. He was convinced that such campaigns had scared parents 'into refusing to send their pitiable child to the cottages, and into retaining a burden that was certain to grow intolerable'. Edwards wondered how many more parents like Michael's 'were forced by the unbearable present into ignoring their inexorable future'. All of this crystallised in his mind that the story of the boy who was tied to the stake 'should be presented, not as a one-day wonder of reputed cruelty, but as a cautionary tale that might awaken government and people to do their duty'.[21]

Edwards contacted Dax, who sent his own experts to examine Michael. Next, Dax and Higgins convinced the parents to admit their child to Kew, where, they were promised, he would be placed in a newly refurbished ward. While Dax set about arranging for Michael's admission, Edwards deliberately assigned the story to Tipping, who had 'a spastic child' and therefore faced 'a similar though not identical problem'.[22] Tipping spent a few days on the investigation, and his first visit to the parents of Michael was carefully orchestrated to coincide with the arrival of the police because, as Edwards put it, to 'investigate and publish without telling the police would make it seem that we cared less about ending the abuse than getting our headline'.[23] A few weeks later, Tipping visited Michael in the newly refurbished ward at Kew.

By early April, the story was ready for publication, and, although it had hints of cruelty, it was not the 'horrible' story Higgins believed that Dax had so desired for its shock value as publicity. As Edwards later admitted, the cruelty at the heart of the story was 'the peg for a greater theme'.

And that theme— the necessity for reform—was close to the hearts of Edwards, Tipping and Dax. The intention of the articles, as Edwards later explained, was to ensure that the Kew Cottages would be transformed into a place 'to which distracted parents would not be afraid to send their unfortunate children':

> There must be adequate funds and staff to provide kindly, firm, constant supervision which was impossible for parents to maintain while they were earning a living, running a home and bringing up a normal family. There must be comfort, cleanliness, good food and every care to make as pleasant as possible the lives of the children whose brains would never grow up.[24]

All of this, of course, fed nicely into the program of reform Dax was trying to implement. And, as Dax no doubt knew, the public exposure would also apply timely pressure upon a Department of Public Works that was failing to respond to his own 'polite' demands (Figure 8.2).

Figure 8.2: Run-down buildings at Kew Cottages
(Courtesy Kew Residential Services)

The Tipping Appeal

As a writer, Tipping preferred substance over style. One colleague at the *Herald*, Keith Dunstan, explained that 'Bill Tipping was never a pretty writer' because 'he hated that sort of thing'. Tipping, said Dunstan, 'wanted to give the impression he was talking direct, as if across a dinner table'. But there is very little of this direct style in the two articles that explore the story of Michael, the boy tied to a stake.[25]

The first article appeared in the *Herald* on 6 April 1953, and with a few deft strokes Tipping set a tragic scene. 'Michael is 6, blue-eyed, fair, freckled', wrote Tipping, and he 'looks very much like your 6-year-old or mine—but he isn't. He's so different that until a few weeks ago he spent most fine days tied to a stake in a backyard'.[26] The *Herald* had found Michael sitting in the dirt. He was chewing a piece of rubber and humming quietly to himself. Strewn around him in the dirt were several pieces of torn-up paper, and a handful of toys also lay just within reach. Michael, Tipping explained, 'is mentally retarded, but he's as active as any normal child', and he 'can get into all the dangers that a normal child can get into'. Tipping reported that Michael's father had just come out to give his son a drink when the police (and the *Herald*) arrived on the scene. What followed next might have been a scene ripped straight from any midday matinee. As the two detectives untethered Michael from his rope, his mother 'cried bitterly' and took him in her arms. 'The world will say we've been cruel', she sobbed, 'but we haven't'. She explained how she would send her son to an institution if only there was one she trusted, adding: 'I will never send him to those terrible Kew Cottages as long as I live'.

The irony was that the press, which had shone a light on the terrible conditions at Kew, now took a leading a role in rehabilitating the cottages' reputation. It is difficult to say what, or who, prompted this shift in thinking about how the press might be utilised, but the effects were soon apparent.

Tipping explained how Michael's mother shunned Kew 'because of what she had read' about the conditions at 'the infamous Kew Cottages'. And at the heart of the story was the message that parents of children with intellectual disabilities 'faced a tragic problem' that was not easily resolved. Michael's parents had tied him to a stake 'because they couldn't face the only alternative—to send him to Kew'. Michael's mother told Tipping a familiar story of a family coming to terms with the reality that their child had an intellectual disability. The initial belief that he was a 'normal healthy child' had given way to concern that her son would be unable to talk despite trips to 'doctor after doctor'; finally the realisation set in that his situation was 'hopeless'. Now, she did not know what to do. 'I don't want to part with him', she said, though she agreed she would put him in an institution she 'trusted'. However, she would never consent to placement in Kew 'unless they took him there forcibly'.

Tipping did not write this story as one of abject cruelty and did not blame the parents. The boy was 'well looked after' and 'his parents love him', wrote Tipping, 'there is no doubt about that'. Instead, Tipping bemoaned a civilised society that treated some of its most vulnerable families with such scant regard. He also conveyed the problems facing parents who chose to look after their children at home. Tipping himself was well versed in these problems as his own son, Peter, had recently turned five, and he had personal experience of the lack of support networks for families raising their children themselves. He explained to his readers that those caring for a child with an intellectual disability at home did so knowing they would have to manage on their own.

Tipping's second article in the *Herald* the next day followed Michael in his new environment at the Kew Cottages. It was a clear attempt to rehabilitate the reputation of institutional care. Two accompanying images set the scene, the first a smiling, neatly dressed nurse attending to a handful of children in Michael's new ward (Ward F4). Two well-appointed cots are visible, and on the other side of the room a small shelf displays a neat row of toys suggesting the children in F4 do not want for entertainment. Tipping added that the walls of F4 were freshly painted in an array of bright colours to stimulate the children. A second image provides a stark contrast to this cheery scene, revealing an unrenovated ward (Ward F2) with two lines of tightly packed beds squeezed into a dreary room with paint peeling from the walls. A headline above the two images states the obvious: 'things are better for some children at Kew' than they are for others.[27]

Tipping's second article argued things were certainly better for Michael now he was at Kew. Michael was pictured sitting in the sun completely transformed in just a few weeks. He was dressed in bright red overalls, his hair was brushed, his shoes polished, and his cheeks had a ruddy glow. Tipping explained that Michael was lucky being placed in a refurbished ward at Kew with 'modern comforts' providing a sense of security. Michael, Tipping reported, 'is obviously happy at Kew'. Michael's mother acknowledged her son was better off in this new environment than he was tied up to a stake in his own backyard. 'Hope is written all over this corner of Kew', wrote Tipping, adding 'if there were more wards like F4 there would be hope too for many of the 400-odd other children' at the cottages. It was a call to action. 'F4 proves what can be done', Tipping concluded, 'if only adequate funds were made available'.

Figure 8.3: Positive photographic images of residents could change perceptions of Kew Cottages. 'Working Girls': circa late 1960s. Dolly Stainer [back row, far left], Katie Collins [back row, far right], Ellen Wilson [in front row, second from left]
(Courtesy Kew Cottages Historical Society Collection).

Bill Tipping's articles touched a nerve in the wider community, just as Osmar White's articles had done a few years earlier. Cecil Edwards, the editor of the *Herald*, acknowledged as much when he noted that 'as soon as the articles were printed, letters began to flow in and they showed that the problem was more common than I had imagined'.[28] One mother in Albert Park wrote to the *Herald* about her own little boy who was just like Michael. 'I would not hesitate to send him to the Kew Cottages', she said, 'if I thought he would be in "Michael's" ward'. Another mother explained that she was 'the mother of one of the little patients at the Kew Cottages', though 'unfortunately not in Michael's ward'. Tipping's articles had 'heartened' her, not because it exposed the many problems with institutional care but rather because it placed a timely spotlight on the problem of intellectual disability and how such people were perceived in the community. 'These babies should not be regarded as outcasts', she wrote, 'the tragedy of having a loved child retarded mentally is made a very bitter burden by public apathy'.[29]

Incredibly, and if only for the briefest of moments, the Tipping articles also woke some other people from their apathy to the plight of more than 400 people (children and adults) with intellectual disabilities living in squalor at Kew. A day after the second article, the *Herald* announced that two readers had sent in money to 'help improve conditions'. One man from St Kilda enclosed a cheque for £5 5s 'for the provision of a few comforts for the poor little aimless souls of F4'. He expressed the hope that 'many of your other readers, shocked and humbled as I am, might similarly help'.[30] Another donor, a mother of three 'normal children', sent in £5 with a similar purpose, urging the *Herald* to run a campaign along the lines of the Good Friday Children's Hospital Appeal. 'We had no intention of running an appeal' at the time, Edwards later recalled, but as money started to flow in—£265 in just two days—Edwards was forced to change his mind.

On 10 April 1953, the *Herald* announced that it had opened 'an appeal for a fund to help the mentally retarded children at Kew Cottages'. When he was informed about plans for the appeal, Dax expressed his delight and

THE TIPPING CAMPAIGN AND PUBLIC SUPPORT (1961–65)

promised that every penny raised 'would be set aside to modernise and renovate' the institution's most dilapidated wards. He estimated that it had cost £3500 to refurbish ward F4 and predicted around £30,000 would be needed to raise all wards to a similar standard.

Money flowed into the offices of the *Herald* from all over the state. There were large donations from prominent Melbourne philanthropists and from businesses such as Holden and the Savoy Hotel, perhaps seeking to add some lustre to their brand. Thousands of donations came from ordinary Victorians who wished to play their part. The *Herald* relished reporting stories of individual contributions because it gave some sense of the scope of the community's response to the campaign. On 14 April, Frank Richardson, a member of North Balwyn Bowling Club, donated £100 and challenged other bowlers to match his generosity. The following day, a woman walked into the *Herald*'s offices and handed over five £10 notes for the appeal. She left no name. Others donated what they could afford. Hundreds of people sent in £1 and many more sent in less. Even children got in on the act. In Caulfield, three schoolgirls set up a bazaar on Bokhara Road to sell an assortment of knick-knacks and second-hand clothes. And, over in Altona, a thirteen-year-old schoolboy named Neville Johnstone took up a collection at his school to give thanks for his own health and strength. 'I think you are doing a marvellous thing in helping these unfortunate little children', he wrote, and 'I want to do my bit'.

The appeal ran for two weeks, and the *Herald* kept up a running commentary on its progress as it rolled through the latter half of April 1953. Even before it had entered a second week, politicians acknowledged what had evidently become a groundswell of community support. The member for Ivanhoe, Michael Lucy, told parliament that 'the *Herald* must be congratulated for the fine effort it is making to help Victoria's mentally ill'. Meanwhile, Bill Barry, the minister for health, whose department oversaw operations at Kew, could hardly keep quiet. He struck a note somewhere between helplessness and concern. 'The government would like to carry out the renovations', but it 'could not find the money', he said on one occasion.

A few days later he tried again. He admitted that mental hospitals had been 'neglected over the years', but he defended his government's record, claiming that adequate funding had 'been provided for maintenance' despite an 'unexpected deterioration in State finances'. Each explanation sounded a little too defensive. Then, to make matters worse, Barry was trumped by Premier John Cain, who announced on 14 April that the Victorian government would match every pound the appeal raised. In his daily column for the *Herald*, Bill Tipping thanked the premier for his pledge and predicted that 'this appeal will snowball now', which proved correct.[31] Over the first six days of the appeal, the *Herald* had raised £3761 10s 5d. By the second week of the appeal, the *Herald* was receiving more than £2000 each day.

The Tipping Appeal closed on 24 April 1953, having raised £23,891 5s. The Victorian government's contribution brought the total to £47,783: a significant amount of money. Today, £47,783 is roughly equivalent to $500,000. At the time it represented just under one-sixth of the entire expenditure of the Mental Defectives' Branch for the 1953–54 financial year. Ashburner called the appeal a magnificent voluntary effort and claimed that it was evidence of a community 'solidly behind all efforts to improve the lot of the mentally ill, and particularly the retarded child'.[32] In a letter to the editor published in the *Herald* on 29 April, Dax was equally effusive in his praise. He offered his 'grateful thanks' to the 'many understanding and kind-hearted' people who had contributed to the campaign, reiterating his promise to spend all the money on refurbishments at Kew. Dax also drew a link between the appeal and his ongoing campaign to erase the stigmatisation of intellectual disability and institutional care. For too long parents had been ashamed of having a child at Kew Cottages and 'suffered in silence', wrote Dax. If the appeal had shown anything, it was that those feelings of shame were unwarranted, and that parents could now 'be sure that they have the goodwill of a large, generous and understanding public'.

Personal Stories of Residents of Kew Cottages

One striking feature of Bill Tipping's articles about Michael is that they told a personal—though heavily stage-managed—story of intellectual disability. Michael's story reminds us that individuals are at the heart of the history of the Kew Cottages. But how can we tell this more personal history of intellectual disability? How can we write about the patients who were not necessarily privy to the changes taking place around them but whose lives were affected by such reforms? Katie Holmes has written that institutional histories tend to explore the experiences of those who cared for the patients in institutions and that 'a persistent challenge for historians has been to hear the voices of the patients themselves'.[33] The problem, of course, is that there is often very little in the archives about the individuals who lived in such institutions. What little evidence that does exist—case histories for instance—tends to privilege the medical information over all else, and more often than not an individual is presented as little more than the sum of their symptoms or diagnoses. Case histories are also rightly hedged by restrictions on use.

How then should we write about Donald John Herbert Salt, a ten-year-old boy whose case history is longer than most and who was admitted to Kew two months after the Tipping articles appeared? Donald Salt was born in Ormond on 23 November 1942, and we know from his case history that he was diagnosed as a 'Congenital Mongoloid' at birth, though today, of course, we would refer to such a diagnosis as Down syndrome. We know that for ten years his mother and father (who died in 1948) had tried to raise him at home. And we know that Donald Salt was a voluntary admission. Perhaps his mother, Elizabeth Salt, had misgivings—like Michael's mother—about placing her child at Kew. Perhaps, though we have no way of knowing, she had relented after reading the Tipping articles in April 1953. Admissions certainly rose sharply in the years following the Tipping Appeal. For example, between 1950 and 1953, the population at Kew Cottages had remained fairly static; there were 505 patients on the books in 1950 and only 509 patients in 1953. But between

1954 and 1957 admissions to Kew rose by more than 40 per cent. And by 1960 there were 856 patients—508 males and 348 females—'under care' at Kew (Figure 8.4).[34]

Figure 8.4: A consultation between a mother of a child with intellectual disability and a nurse at Kew Cottages
(Courtesy Kew Residential Services)

What else do we know about Donald Salt? The most diligent reading of his case history only gives us the briefest insight into what sort of a person he might have been. Salt was a 'cheerful' and 'bright' boy whose personal habits 'were unobjectionable', as one admitting doctor put it at the time. He could not read or write, nor could he count. He could not even answer the simplest questions. But he was an 'affectionate' and 'social' boy, words that hint at how distressing it must have been for his mother to leave him at Kew. Donald Salt was placed at the Kew Cottages on 3 June 1953, and when Ashburner assessed him for the first time he wrote one line: 'Mongoloid. Slow feeder. Attending School. Clean & well behaved'.

So, in a more modern reading of such a diagnosis, Donald had Down Syndrome, which means from his conception a genetic mistake gave him an extra chromosome and a different trajectory in life.

Did Donald Salt settle in well at Kew? Did he make any friends? Was he comfortable in his new environment? None of these questions are easy to answer, but in 1954 Ashburner noted that Salt's general health was good and that he had 'progressed somewhat over the past twelve months'. He also noted that Salt was a 'friendly and sociable' boy who gave 'no trouble'. Dr Wilfred Brady, who replaced Ashburner as superintendent of the Kew Cottages in 1955, made a similar point the following year when he wrote that Salt was 'well behaved', 'friendly and cooperative'. Indeed, Salt's good nature is something of a recurring theme and a reminder that being friendly and cooperative was a choice he made. He might have chosen to play up or cause trouble, like many other residents at the institution, but Salt chose to be an exemplary resident. He worked hard to help out around the wards, and his good deeds did not go unnoticed: 'a good ward worker', wrote Brady in 1965. The gratitude of the staff must have been a boon for Salt because he was a boy who thrived on praise. Salt, explained one staff member, was 'easily pleased with a kind word'.

In the middle of the 1950s it was not uncommon for doctors to instruct parents of young children with an intellectual disability to place their child in an institution and forget about them. If Elizabeth Salt received such advice, it was advice she chose to ignore. After she placed her son at Kew, she visited him once or twice a year for two decades, though a note in Salt's case history in 1974 stating that he is 'rarely visited' offers the first hint that Elizabeth's visits became more sporadic from the mid-1970s. By 1979—when Elizabeth Salt would have been 81—the evidence suggests that the visits had stopped altogether. By now Donald Salt was a full-grown man, though staff had only begun referring to him as such after he turned 23 in 1964. He was 38 years old, 'rather obese', and his health had begun to deteriorate. He was also on a new regime of medication that meant that his epilepsy was now under control, but he was unsteady on his feet, his speech was slurred, and his eyesight was poor. When he could, he continued to help around the place, and he remained a cheerful and friendly patient. 'Salty', as one occupational therapist wrote in 1979, 'relates well to all staff and at time with peers'.

Donald Salt's health continued to deteriorate over the next decade, and by 1985 he was completely blind and partially deaf. He was still 'quite capable' of looking after himself and he could 'still find his way around', but he had been forced to give up helping out in the wards in 1974. Now, he spent most of his time in his own ward 'due to blindness'. No one visited him anymore, yet he remained a 'pleasant and cooperative man'. In May 1992 it was becoming clear that Donald Salt did not have long to live. Most days, he could hardly breathe, and on 14 May 1992 he woke with an 'elevated temperature and bilateral basal creps'. He was treated with Panadol, Augmentin, Bisolvon and Flagyl. By 18 May, his condition was 'considered to be terminal'. He died at Kew Cottages on 1 June 1992. He was just fifty years old. A coroner's inquest into his death four months later found that Donald Salt had died of 'natural causes'.

It is a difficult and sometimes distressing task to write about the experiences of residents living in Kew Cottages because often there is so little that can be told. Can something of Donald Salt's experiences really be salvaged from a medical case history that conveys so little of his point of view? What of Bill Tipping's own son, Peter, whose case history no longer exists? We know very little about his experiences except what can be gleaned from other sources. We know, for instance, that Bill and Marjorie Tipping 'reluctantly' sought a place for their son at the Kew Cottages in 1960.[35] He had just turned twelve. We also know that he died there three years later, but we know little beyond that. And what of Michael, the boy who was tied to a stake? In 1955, two years after he was admitted to Kew, Michael was transferred from the relative comfort of Ward F4 to 'Little Pell', a ward that had a reputation as one of the most squalid at Kew. For Michael, the benefits of being at the heart of the Tipping Appeal were obviously short lived.[36] But can we say that the story of Michael, or Donald Salt, or Peter Tipping is indicative of what life was actually like for some of those who lived in the Kew Cottages? Some questions are impossible to answer, some viewpoints impossible to retrieve. We build our fragile narratives from the sources available to us, working between the gaps left by the silent.

What we do know is that, as Donald Salt and Michael settled into their new accommodation in 1953, some significant renovations were finally getting underway. In the Mental Hygiene Authority report for 1954, Ashburner remarked on the extraordinary fact of 'building or other activity in at least nine places' at Kew Cottages.[37] Indeed, even the briefest perusal of the annual reports of Kew Cottages in the middle of the 1950s reveals themes of activity, improvement and reform (Figures 8.4 and 8.5). It is worth noting, of course, that the renovation of Kew Cottages was just one part of the renovation of an entire system that was taking place at the time. Between 1952 and 1962, the Victorian government, under Labor's John Cain senior, and then from 1955 under Henry Bolte's conservative coalition government, built, refurbished and added more public health facilities than in any other period of the state's history. The dramatic increase in funding for capital and maintenance works in the early 1950s emphasises this point. In 1951, public works expenditure on Mental Hygiene services was £526,254. Two years later that amount had more than doubled to £1,297,361. But even 'this apparently heavy expenditure', warned Dax, 'is no more than a fraction [of that] which is urgently required'.

A comprehensive list of major capital works underway by September 1954 also conveys something of the scale of developments across the state.[38] At Travancore, new classrooms and a new recreation room were under construction. Janefield would soon have a new occupational therapy centre, a new school building and a newly refurbished concert hall. At Pleasant Creek, the story was more or less the same. New classrooms and a new ward for boys were constructed. Meanwhile, at Kew, a dilapidated old cottage, formerly the office of the head matron, was transformed into a new ward for babies, and the 'reorganisation and modernisation' of two other wards (£23,300) was almost complete. A new boiler house (£13,000) was built so that hot water would be more readily available across the entire institution, and an occupational therapy centre (£16,390) was under construction.

Figure 8.5: Kew Cottages residents out in one of the play areas
(Courtesy Kew Residential Services)

Figure 8.6: Toddlers at Kew Cottages enjoying some time outside
(Courtesy Kew Residential Services)

Soon, electricians would begin the delicate task of rewiring every cottage in the institution (£15,900). But the minutes of the Mental Hygiene Authority's meeting on 5 April 1954 reveal a baffling fact—hardly any of this work was being funded by the Tipping Appeal. A year after Tipping's articles had galvanised a community to act, only £943 of the £47,783 raised during the subsequent appeal had been spent on renovations at Kew.[39] The Tipping Campaign had solved one ostensibly intractable problem—a lack of finance—only to expose another: bureaucratic red tape.

All of the work at Kew was also causing another significant problem, though it is one that Ashburner must surely have foreseen. As each cottage was remodelled, accommodation had to be found for those residents displaced by the renovations. By mid-1954, the other cottages were struggling to cope with the increased demand. In June that year, Ashburner warned Dax that 'unless we can have more cottages soon … the conversion of the old cottages will have to stop'. On the issue of new capital works however, the Department of Public Works continued to drag its feet. Ashburner, Dax and the Mental Hygiene Authority must have had some idea about how slowly the wheels of government turned when contracts had to be let and tenders called, but by the second half of 1954 they were getting impatient. In late September 1954, Dax resorted to a familiar ploy; he invited Bill Tipping to visit the cottages and report on the progress of renovations at Kew.

Tipping's article for the *Herald*, titled 'There's a lot to be done yet out at Kew', did not bury the lead. Tipping wished to make an objective appraisal of the situation—'let's be fair about this', he wrote—and acknowledged that significant progress had been made since his last visit.[40] He noted how a handful of cottages had been refurbished and that staff in these new wards appeared happier than before. He noted that children now sat 'down to meals on chrome chairs at brightly coloured Laminex tables', and he called the construction of the new occupational therapy centre one of the 'most significant changes at Kew' in years. But Tipping was 'shocked to see all that had not been done because of Government delay'. The '*Herald* money was designed to fix things speedily', he wrote, but things were 'hastening slowly out at Kew'. What infuriated Tipping most was that the delays were mostly caused by needless 'red tape'. The Department of Public Works was simply too 'slow getting the buildings up', wrote Tipping, who bemoaned a government and bureaucracy that failed to act with any urgency on the matter of Kew. He challenged Premier Cain to visit the institution to see things for himself. The community had done its bit, explained Tipping, it was now 'up to the bureaucracy to pull its weight'.

When pressed on the issue, the premier expressed displeasure at the delays, but he deflected blame onto the Department of Public Works. Even a meeting in early 1955 between Tipping, the premier, and the minister for public works, Samuel Merrifield, failed to resolve the impasse. During that meeting, Merrifield explained that 'schools could be slapped up in next to no time', but the requirements for 'building a hospital' were completely different. As a result, the refurbishment of the Kew Cottages continued to hasten slowly through the latter half of the 1950s.

In 1955, Dax reported that 'renovations, alterations, and additions at Kew Cottages during the year have reached the stage that conditions are such that about half the children are now housed satisfactorily'. It was a step in the right direction, although Dax's optimism would have been tempered by the new superintendent's annual report, which focused on issues caused by overcrowding. Dr Wilfred Brady, who was just settling into a job he would hold for the next ten years, reported that 1955 had been 'a difficult year'. Most wards were still 'grossly overcrowded', storage facilities were basically non-existent, and the toilets in a number of wards required urgent attention.[41]

By 1958 however, even Brady—not one for unbridled enthusiasm in his reports—was beginning to express a cautious optimism when referring to the renovations at Kew. He reported that four new wards had been built in the northern corner of the institution, and all were now occupied. Brady was also beginning to notice a better mood among staff working at the institution because they now had 'a very good idea of the type of accommodation which is being aimed at'.[42] A year later Brady wrote that 'more than in any other year the ward situation has improved',[43] and, by 1960, Dax and Brady were taking stock of all that had been achieved: 272 new beds had 'been put up at Kew Cottages' in four years, and an additional 146 new beds were on the way.[44] Even so, the institution was still not keeping up with the demand. At Kew, there were 770 residents and a waiting listing of 211.[45] The story was more or less the same at other institutions across the state. Every institution was at capacity, and many parents were clamouring for their child to be admitted as soon as an opportunity presented itself.

How things had changed. Ten years earlier the Kennedy Report had identified a problem of convincing parents to place their children in institutional care. Back then, Professor Kennedy had noted that 'many mothers of idiot children, having seen some of the accommodation to which their children might be sent, had preferred to keep them at home to the detriment of the whole family'.[46] Even in 1953, 'Michael's' mother had expressed a similar sentiment when she outlined her reasons for keeping her son tied to a stake. But repeated exposés in the *Herald* and other newspapers, as well as a program of significant and well-publicised reform, meant that by the 1960s the notion of institutional care had been rehabilitated. Now all classes of Australians saw the institution as a place for the care of their children. Conditions at the Kew Cottages and other institutions were still far from ideal, but, for many parents of children with intellectual disabilities, institutionalisation had become a viable— and even a respectable—alternative to raising their child at home. Eric Cunningham Dax could not have been more pleased. As far as he was concerned, the growing demand for institutional care was a good thing that could be easily explained:

> The better conditions within the intellectually handicapped training colonies has removed many of the fears and prejudices that parents had in the past towards their children entering. In consequence there is a great deal more demand on the available accommodation.[47]

Chapter 9

The Kew Cottages Parents' Association (1958–70)

On a hot November morning in 1975, Bev Coutts and Joan Westgarth, two parents with children in the Kew Cottages, wandered through the grounds of the institution to double check preparations for the annual fete. For the second year running, the task of organising the Kew Cottages fete had fallen to them. Soon, Coutts, Westgarth, and an army of visitors would be able to relax and enjoy the fun. But first they had to ensure that everything was in place.

The inaugural Kew Cottages fete had been held in 1961. Back then it was a humble affair consisting of a handful of stalls, a fairy floss seller and a hamburger stand. And, for the first few years, the fete had perched uneasily on the edge of the institution, just inside the Princess Street gate. However, as time passed and the fete grew, it had crept further and further into the grounds of the cottages until by the 1970s it essentially took over the entire institution for one day each year. The food offerings of fairy floss and hamburgers were now augmented by sandwiches, ice cream, tea, coffee and cake. There was a book stall, a Christmas card stall and a stall selling precious stones. At one end of the institution, a miniature train was installed for the residents and other children to enjoy. At the other end, pony rides were on offer for anyone willing to put their money to a good cause.

By the 1970s a tradition had also developed whereby a TV or radio personality officially opened proceedings. In 1975 that 'honour' fell to

Bruce Mansfield. On that warm November morning, Mansfield opened the fete 'in a very friendly way', which 'seemed to set the atmosphere' for the rest of the day.[1] The fete was well attended and the Victorian premier, Rupert Hamer and his wife, April, put in their usual appearance, though how long they stayed is unknown. The day was a great success with a record $15,555 raised for the residents at Kew.

'The fete was a grand event back then', recalled Astrid Judge in her 2007 memoir of growing up at Kew.[2] Judge, the daughter of a psychiatrist who lived and worked at Kew, spent a good part of her childhood at the cottages, and she attended the fete almost every year. Judge recalled that people with no direct connection to the institution came annually to 'offer their support'. But, for her, the day really belonged to the residents (Figure 9.1). Someone dressed as Elvis Presley often appeared and was mobbed by enthusiastic fans. Astrid Judge recalled the music, dancing and laughter that seemed to be such a feature of every fete.

Figure 9.1: Some of the older residents having a cup of tea
(Courtesy Kew Residential Services)

Such scenes would have been inconceivable twenty years earlier. How had this come about? Astrid Judge provided the explanation. The 'young and energetic' Kew Cottages Parents' Association had made these festivities possible. The association was formed in 1957, but the story of its origins stretches back to the early 1950s and the appointment of the first social worker at Kew.

Origins of the Kew Cottages Parents' Association

As early as 1950, there had been discussions within the Department of Mental Hygiene about employing a social worker at Kew to act 'as a contact between relatives and the cottages'. P.O. Spicer, the official visitor, Metropolitan Mental Hospitals, recommended such an appointment to the minister for health 'on humanitarian grounds alone'. Spicer firmly believed that a social worker would mitigate the 'fear and mistrust' many parents felt about placing their children in the cottages. The following year, the Mental Hygiene Authority searched for a suitably qualified person who could divide their time equally between the Kew Mental Hospital and the Kew Cottages. The authority eventually hired Irene Higgins, a young Polish woman resident in Australia for just over ten years (Figure 9.2). It was Higgins' ideal job, although most people would have shunned working in two of Victoria's most stigmatised institutions.

Irene Higgins was a petite, softly spoken woman who, by her own account, had always wanted to leave a mark on the world. At the age of nineteen, she enrolled in social work at the University of Lwow in Polish Ukraine. When she was twenty-three, by which time Europe was lurching towards war, Higgins had graduated and was considering a move abroad. She left home and family for Australia in late 1938 and settled, initially at least, in Perth. There she found a husband but little recognition for the profession of social work. 'Nobody knew what my profession was', Higgins later recalled, which meant that everyone tended to think of her as some sort of teacher or instructor. To broaden her expertise, she embarked on further study in Perth, this time in psychology at the University of Western

Australia. After short stints living in Brisbane and Sydney, Higgins and her husband settled in Melbourne in 1945. By then, Irene Higgins was 28 years old, the mother of a young boy and still trying to find her way in the world.

Figure 9.2: Irene Higgins
(Courtesy Kew Residential Services)

In 1946, Higgins took a job at the Society for Crippled Children and Adults, a small organisation that provided counselling and social services for people with disabilities. Higgins first visited the Kew Cottages in 1950, when she accompanied a young mother who was contemplating placing her child there. Like everyone who encountered the institution in those days, she was shocked by what she saw. 'It stunk to high heaven', Higgins later recalled.[3] Yet, where many recoiled from the squalor at Kew, Higgins saw an opportunity to make a difference. When she left the cottages that day, she promised herself that at some point in the future she would return to work with the children at Kew.

Neither Kew Cottages nor the Kew Mental Hospital had ever employed a social worker, and when Higgins joined the staff at the Mental Hygiene Authority there were only two other social workers employed in the entire department. There was no job description and certainly no predecessor upon whose labours she might build. Irene Higgins started from scratch in a place dominated by the medical profession—mostly men—for more than sixty years. Higgins was able to develop her strategies and her caseload as she saw fit. The superintendent made that clear when he instructed Higgins to assess any observable problems and devise her own plans as to how they might be tackled.[4] And so, for the first few months, Higgins simply walked around the site to get her bearings and a sense of how the two institutions worked.

In those early months, Irene Higgins got to know every building, every unit and every ward in each of the institutions at Kew. The first social worker at Kew, roaming the grounds in her long winter coats and expensive shoes, must have been a curious sight. She took copious notes, and she introduced herself to the residents and staff. Higgins soon conceptualised her role as a link or 'liaison' between the community and the institution. In particular, she bemoaned the extent to which families were ignored by the staff running the institution. There was 'no one there to talk' to the parents of prospective residents, Higgins later recalled, and no one to 'explain to them what was going to happen to their child'. Higgins believed that the parents of residents at Kew 'were isolated, often ashamed and lonely in their problem'.[5] Whenever it was possible, she talked to those who visited their children. For parents more accustomed to staff making themselves scarce on such occasions, conversations with Higgins could be a welcome or a jarring experience. A community activist herself, Higgins was surprised that parents had made no effort to 'meet or organise'. The nurses, for their part, rarely understood why a mother or father would place their child in such an institution in the first place. The result, in Higgins' judgment, was a frosty and antagonistic relationship between parents and staff.

To tackle this problem head on, Higgins raised the idea of a parents' association at a senior staff meeting in 1953. At the time, she envisaged an organisation that could contribute to the welfare of the children at Kew but also educate itself to gain a better understanding of the problem of 'mental retardation'. While most staff could see the logic in such a proposal, they were wary about having a parents' organisation operating inside the cottages. The problem, as ever, was a deep mistrust between parents and staff. The sentiments expressed at the meeting, Higgins wrote, 'pointed out the difficulties that staff often encountered in dealing with parents'.[6] Most staff felt that their job was hard enough already. Further scrutiny would only make matters worse. No one, wrote Higgins, wanted a 'a group of aggressive busybodies who would criticise the staff for certain conditions that they had no power to change'. The proposal was rejected. Discouraged, Higgins let the matter rest.

In 1955, Irene Higgins took six months unpaid leave to accompany her husband, a CSIRO scientist, on a research trip to Europe. By the time she returned, the Mental Hygiene Authority had begun the delicate task of separating Victoria's 'mental deficiency' and psychiatric services. Although the *Mental Deficiency Act* had still not been proclaimed (it never would be), Eric Cunningham Dax was now exploring other ways to get around the problem. Section 34 of the *Mental Hygiene Act*, which allowed the director of the Mental Hygiene Authority to 'proclaim any house or building in Victoria … a mental hospital', ostensibly provided a solution. By proclaiming the Kew Mental Hospital as one institution and the Kew Cottages as another, Dax could create two administratively separate institutions: one devoted to people with intellectual disabilities, the other to the mentally ill. Each institution would have its own superintendent, its own psychiatrists and its own specially trained nursing staff. And each would operate independently of the other.

In April 1956, H.J. Martin, secretary of the Mental Hygiene Authority, wrote to the secretary of the Department of Health that 'the Authority regards the legal separation of these institutions as a matter of urgency'.[7] And, although it was not until 1958 that the administrative separation of the Kew Cottages from the Kew Mental Hospital was finally complete, preliminary arrangements for the separation of staff were already underway when Irene Higgins returned from Europe in 1956. By this time, too, her role had changed. When she returned to work, Higgins was surprised (and relieved) to discover that she was no longer required to spread her attentions between two institutions. She could now devote all her time to the residents at the cottages. Five years after she made it, Higgins was able to deliver on her promise that one day she would work for the children at Kew.

As she settled into her new position, Higgins revisited her idea of a parents' organisation, though this time she tried a different tack. She 'decided to proceed slowly' and to approach parents directly. First, Higgins wrote to five 'carefully selected' couples and told them of her plan. Later, in explaining the reasons for her new approach, she recalled that she wanted to form a nucleus of parents who 'would themselves profit' from membership of such an organisation, but 'who would also be capable' of driving any fledgling organisation forward.[8] When the members of this provisional organising committee first met in the middle of 1956, they discussed what the aims and objectives of their organisation might be. Next, they sent letters to parents of Kew Cottages residents across the state, inviting them to attend the inaugural meeting of what the committee was now calling the Kew Cottages Parents' Association. The meeting was slated for late December 1957, and Higgins asked Dr Ashburner, who had recently been transferred to Bendigo, to open proceedings with a lecture on 'mental retardation'. She asked Dr Wilfred Brady, the new superintendent at Kew, to chair the meeting (Figure 9.3). Irene Higgins was convinced that, because so many parents lived in regional Victoria, the meeting would be relatively small. If she expected a sedate and polite affair, she was in for a surprise.

On a warm evening in December 1957, more than 130 people gathered at the local hall in Bouverie Street, Carlton North. Higgins, wary of creating any further tension between families and staff at Kew, had decided the meeting would be better held at a venue offsite. Every parent who attended had at least one thing in common: hardly anyone knew each other. On an entrance table, the provisional organising committee laid out name tags for all the invited parents, but less than half of the attendees were willing to disclose their identity. The stigma of having a child with an intellectual disability meant many of the name tags were untouched, and many parents remained unbadged.

Figure 9.3: Dr Wilfred Brady, new superintendent at Kew
(Courtesy Kew Residential Services)

The first meeting of the Kew Cottages Parents' Association was a fractious and fiery affair. Dr Ashburner gave a measured talk about how the association might operate and then opened the meeting up to a debate about what the purpose of the organisation might be. Within minutes the meeting had degenerated into a direct attack on the shortcomings at Kew. One mother recalled that 'we yacked and blew our tops about the conditions at the Cottages'.[9] Higgins, for her part, recalled that 'many parents were aggressive, bitter, insulting and almost threatening'.[10] Later, what stuck in Higgins' mind was the image of the two exhausted men—Ashburner and Brady—who had borne the brunt of the parents' anger. It is curious that, for someone so attuned to the experiences of parents of children with intellectual disabilities, Higgins did not have more sympathy for them. But, in this instance at least, she came down firmly on the side of her professional colleagues at Kew.

If anger and aggression were the defining features of the association's inaugural meeting, there was also an undercurrent of relief that parents now had a platform from which to voice their concerns. In the mid-1950s it was not common for people to talk openly about their children's intellectual disabilities. Some parents buried their problems and grief entirely or turned their attention to other things. Others, like June Epstein, were simply tired of the 'pity or commiseration, shocked silence or false reassurance' they received from friends and neighbours who knew almost nothing of what their lives were really like.[11] The meeting allowed many people to talk openly and realistically about their children to people who understood. Many probably shared what one parent remembered as feeling 'an immense outburst of relief, of pent-up emotion'. At that first meeting, she wrote, 'we all realised how important it was that we had met ... of finding out that others felt as we did'.[12] Epstein made a similar point, declaring 'although we were nearly all strangers to each other, the relief of being able to talk with people who understood was indescribable'.[13]

On 18 December 1957, a newsletter announced the establishment of the Kew Cottages Parents' Association. The first parents' association attached to a state-run institution for people with intellectual disability had begun. When Brady noted in the 1957 annual report that the parents' association had been created 'largely through the efforts' of the Kew Cottages' first social worker, he was succinctly describing a process that had taken Higgins four and a half years.[14] The inaugural president of the association echoed Brady's sentiments when she later wrote that, 'looking back, it is easy to realise that no one could have stopped us had we spontaneously formed the association ourselves. But everything must have a starting point, and in this case, it was Mrs Higgins'.[15]

Early Days

In terms of establishing an immediate membership base, the inaugural meeting of the Kew Cottages Parents' Association was a success. The association was open to all parents of residents or those whose child was on a waiting list to enter Kew Cottages. More than half of those who attended the first meeting—seventy in all—joined the new association. June Epstein, author, musician and sometime schoolteacher, was elected as foundational president. Epstein and her husband, Julius, were both well versed in the challenges parents faced in raising a child with intellectual disabilities at home. In September 1952, June Epstein had given birth to her second child, a son whom she and her husband named Carey. Shortly after his birth, Carey Epstein contracted encephalitis, which left him with severe intellectual disabilities. For four years, the Epsteins raised Carey—and his older brother—at home. By 1957 they were convinced they could no longer provide the care that Carey required. In March that year, the Epsteins drove their son to Kew Cottages, admitted him, and left in tears. Much later, June Epstein wrote that leaving her young son with the charge nurse at Kew was one of the most challenging and confronting decisions she ever made.

Most members of the Kew Cottages Parents' Association were proud that their association was the first parents' organisation attached to a state-run institution, but it was not the first parents' organisation to advocate for children with intellectual disabilities. In the late 1940s, groups of parents unwilling or unable to place their children in institutions had begun organising across Australia, mirroring more broadly a phenomenon that was taking place across much of the western world. The first parents' association had been established in New South Wales in early 1947, when the Sub-Normal Children's Association of New South Wales was formed by a group of parents who had been meeting regularly while their children were examined at the Royal Prince Alfred Hospital in Sydney. Later that year, parents of children with intellectual disabilities in Victoria formed the Helping Hand Association, which aimed to advocate for the 'thousands of mentally handicapped children' living 'unhappy, frustrated' and unfulfilled lives across the state.

In other states across Australia, parents of children with intellectual disabilities quickly followed suit. In South Australia, the Mentally Retarded Children's Education and Welfare Society was formed in August 1950 at a meeting of parents concerned about the lack of facilities for their children. And a year later, the Slow Learning Children's Group was established in Western Australia for much the same reason. Each group had its own aims and philosophies, though most sought to establish special schools, occupational centres, sheltered workshops and residential institutions in the hope of supplementing the already overcrowded and underfunded government facilities and services. By 1956, most of these voluntary parents' groups were federated under an umbrella organisation known as the Australian Council for Mental Retardation, which presented a united front to improve the quality of life of people with intellectual disabilities.

Such groupings were part of the massive expansion of civic and community organisations after 1945. Postwar Australians were a generation of joiners; they joined country women's clubs, lions and rotary clubs, swimming clubs, and other organisations in unprecedented numbers. Melanie Oppenheimer has explored this huge expansion of voluntary and civic organisations and linked their emergence to the voluntary spirit that grew during the Second World War and flowed into postwar voluntary associations, including those for people with disabilities.[16] When the NSW premier, Sir William McKell, declared in 1946 that 'citizens should share with the State the responsibility for assistance to disabled people', he was explicitly invoking this principle of civic duty.[17] McKell's comment conveniently ignored the fact that a lot of parents—usually mothers—had been caring for their disabled children for many years without any assistance from the state. A few years later, Eric Cunningham Dax echoed McKell's sentiments—more eloquently perhaps—when he said that voluntary groups would have a crucial role to play in the reorganisation of the Victorian mental health services.

Given that it was only established in 1957, the Kew Cottages Parents' Association was somewhat late to the parent advocacy scene. In fact, by the time that it was formally established, some parents' organisations had been operating for almost ten years. This was as true for Victoria and other Australian states as it was for similar parents' organisations around the world. Indeed, if there was a heyday for parent advocacy and parents' associations, it was immediately after 1945. In the United Kingdom, for instance, the organisation that later became Mencap and advocated for the right to education for those labelled 'ineducable', and to provide services for people with intellectual disabilities in the community, was founded in the mid-1940s.[18] And in the USA, the first meeting of the New Jersey Parents' Group for Retarded Children occurred in 1947. It ultimately led to the formation of the National Association of Parents and Friends of Mentally Retarded Children in 1950.[19]

Such parents' organisations emerged across the Anglophone world to provide forums for advocacy and support for families with a 'handicapped' relative. The Kew Cottages Parents' Association mirrored this world-wide development. And, like many of its Australian counterparts, the association soon joined the umbrella body, the Australian Council for Mental Retardation.

In other respects, however, the association had to navigate its own path because it was defined by its attachment to the Kew Cottages and, by implication, its attachment to institutional models of care. This meant that in the early days the organisation struggled to form a coherent identity. Ethel Temby captured this confusion when she noted that, after the first handful of meetings, we still 'didn't know what we were volunteering to do'.[20] Many members recalled strenuous disagreements at those early meetings. One woman was probably being diplomatic when she described the parents' association as a 'warm, friendly group' where there was 'plenty of difference of opinion'. That difference of opinion sometimes turned into heated arguments, which usually revolved around whether the association should be a benevolent or an advocacy organisation. 'Some were already concerned with educating the public—and ourselves—on the fact of mental retardation', Epstein recalled, while 'others thought that we should immediately be raising money for the benefit of the children'.[21] Most agreed that improving conditions at Kew, either by direct action or by pressure at government levels, should be a key priority. Eventually the association settled on a mission that combined all of these concerns.

The objectives of the association, as outlined in its constitution, were broad enough to ensure that it could be many things to many people. The association would 'work for and promote the care, education and welfare of the retarded'; it would provide 'comfort' to 'parents and families of the retarded'; it would 'encourage and help' staff at the Kew Cottages; and it would 'disseminate information on mental retardation for the education of the public and the benefit of the retarded'. Here, then, was the blueprint for an association that was committed, as the final objective of the constitution put it, to doing the things 'necessary to give retarded persons an effective way of life'.[22] The language of the association paralleled that of the time, although it had moved on from terms such as 'idiocy' or 'feeble minded' commonly used a generation earlier. It focused on what people lacked rather than what abilities they might have. They were 'retarded' from the normal, not with a dis-ability and certainly not 'differently abled' as advocates might say today.

If the lofty ideals outlined in the constitution represented a goal towards which the association might strive, the members remained pragmatic about what they could achieve. Frank Dale, who replaced June Epstein as president of the association in 1958, acknowledged as much in one letter when he noted that 'the results of our activities will always be intangible', but that did not mean their efforts would be in vain. In those early years, this group of young and enthusiastic parents, motivated by a spirit of civic responsibility and the idea that everyone should do their bit, set to work to improve the lives of the residents at Kew, spurred on by the fact that these were their children.

In order to meet the twin demands of fundraising and advocacy outlined in its constitution, the association established two further subcommittees: a Finance Committee to oversee fundraising, and a Publicity Committee (later Information Committee) to gather and disseminate information with 'the aim of correcting the many misapprehensions that are held regarding mental retardation'.[23] But one of the association's most important funct-ions, at least in the early days, was as a self-help group for the parents themselves. Temby recalled the relief she felt in being able to talk 'to someone with a shared experience' because it offered her 'a way to counter the terrible isolation' and 'terrible loneliness' of her situation. One of the fathers noted how important it was for him to talk 'to people who were having the same sort of problems'. Talking was never 'going to stop the problems' or 'make them go away', he admitted, but it could do 'a lot of good'.[24] One mother, who outlined in some detail how the association had irrevocably changed her relationship with other parents at Kew, raised an important distinction between thinking about the individual and collective experiences of intellectual disability. In her letter to Irene Higgins, this young mother recalled that before the association was established she had been 'reluctant to talk to other mothers ... because my own feelings were so raw' and because each mother 'was so sadly absorbed in her own baby, so plainly sorrowing over what the baby should have been'. The letter bears extensive quotation, because it captures something of the way that an organisation like the Kew Cottages Parents' Association could transform a private matter, or private grief, into public or shared concern. 'We went to that first meeting full of emotion', she wrote, 'afraid we would not be able to control our tears':

> To my surprise my own experience in getting inside the hall was a feeling of tremendous sympathy for all those other parents whose children were mentally retarded. My private sorrow seemed just a little part of a mountain of sadness. Well after the first meeting the emotion was largely gone. We were letting off steam and making plans and getting to know each other. On Cottages visits we kept our eyes open for friends. We lost our shyness of talking to strangers because we had found that to talk to other parents gave us a fellow feeling that was warming.[25]

What this mother cherished most was being part of a collective with shared problems and concerns, because it was the collective that provided her with the comfort, understanding and support that she so desperately desired. 'Only those who have attended' a meeting of the association, she wrote, 'can know what the fellowship there can do for the parents'.

By simply coming together parents were doing something different from what they had done before the war. Until then, parent advocacy, if it existed at all, was individualised because families were isolated and had no means of knowing or connecting with others in a similar situation. In this sense, parent advocacy was muted, personal and largely disjointed. Collective advocacy could be more energetic and more persistent, and it could create a sense of togetherness among the parents of children at Kew.

One mother, Beryl Power, who joined the association shortly after placing her son Geoffrey at Kew in 1965, noted that there was a 'natural progression' to becoming an advocate. 'When told by a charge nurse you could not do anything unique for your own child', Power explained, you 'moved on first to trying to help them by doing whatever it took to help everyone in the ward in the hope they would get some spin-off, then to everyone in the Cottages, then to representing all mentally retarded people in the State'.[26] Power inadvertently invoked sociologist C. Wright Mills' distinction between personal troubles and public issues that have 'to do with matters that transcend these local environments of the individual and the range of his inner life'.[27] By turning their 'personal troubles' into 'public issues', the members of the Kew Cottages Parents' Association were attempting to legitimise and valorise their own concerns.

Benevolence, Fundraising and Welfare

What, exactly, were the primary concerns of this fledgling association of parents? The short answer is the terrible conditions at Kew. It is tempting to view the establishment of the Mental Hygiene Authority in 1952 and the subsequent decade of reform as a time when the most pressing problems at the Kew Cottages were finally resolved. And some of the promotional material for the cottages at the time did nothing to suggest that this was not the case. For example, a photograph of the new nursery ward from the early 1960s depicts an almost idyllic scene. In the image, a young nurse in bright white scrubs attends to a baby in a charming wicker bassinet with the devotion any mother would show for her firstborn child. Two other babies—in equally well-kept bassinets nearby—are discernible in the image, and it appears as if they are patiently awaiting their turn. There is evidence that the staff-to-resident ratio in the nursery ward was generally lower than in other wards and also that staff did, in fact, try to create a homely atmosphere for the babies in their care.[28] But the image of the devoted nurse—which was used in a number of promotional campaigns for the Kew Cottages in the 1960s—painted a misleading picture of institutional care.

The Kew Cottages' first paediatrician's description of the way in which the institution operated during this period was probably closer to the mark. Dr David Pitt arrived at Kew in January 1959, just as the institution was, as he put it, 'slowly emerging from its long, dark night'.[29] Pitt thought the cottages overcrowded and inadequately staffed, which was true enough, even in 1959. It was not unusual for one staff member to be responsible for forty residents during the day and up to eighty residents during the night. This meant that rudimentary duties such as bathing, feeding and cleaning trumped what might be considered more meaningful interpersonal interactions between residents and staff. Sociologist Erving Goffman's classic account of 'total institutions' throws light on the way the Kew Cottages operated. In *Asylums* (1961), Goffman described the parallel existence of two worlds in most institutions, one of the staff and the other of the inmates, 'jogging alongside of each other with points of contact but little mutual penetration'.[30] At Kew Cottages there were tensions between providing an appropriate standard of humane care on the one hand and ensuring that the institution operated efficiently on the other. Goffman emphasised that the staff and inmates each 'conceive of the other in terms of narrow hostile stereotypes'.[31] While we may know little of what cottage residents thought of staff, there is no doubt that the staff objectified many residents as 'hard work'. This meant that the care offered by the nursing staff at the cottages could be mechanical, brusque and devoid of any meaningful interpersonal connection.

Many parents who placed their children at Kew in the late 1950s and early 1960s were distressed by the dehumanising nature of the care their children received, yet, as Goffman observed, staff often felt superior and righteous about the work they did in institutions. Beryl Power recalled being 'appalled' after she visited her six-year-old son, Geoffrey, in 1965. She recalled finding him with a group of other children playing, if you could call it that, in a large bare playroom with no furniture or toys. At one end of the room, a nurse was sitting on a stool. She was knitting and holding onto a can of air freshener at the same time. Another nurse was on duty at the other end of the room, but her only job, as far as Power could make out, 'was to clean anyone up who had been incontinent'.[32] Power was distraught to observe that 'nobody rated any attention other than just being watched'.

One of the principles of the Kew Cottages Parents' Association was to improve the physical environment and lift the standards of daily care at Kew. From its earliest days, the association engaged in vigorous fundraising efforts to achieve this goal. All fundraising was organised by the Finance Committee, whose members, Epstein recalled, 'worked like beavers' in those early days. Even so, the initial efforts of the association were quite modest. One campaign sought to raise enough money to equip each ward with TVs, radios and a suitable array of toys. Another involved a working bee of diligent mothers arranging fifty-four vases of plastic flowers 'to brighten up the wards, and help the children appreciate colour'. Later, the association turned its attention to the outdoor areas and to procuring new play equipment (Figures 9.4 and 9.5). An old, decommissioned tram was installed outside the main playroom at the northern end of the institution. Further south, an old car was set up in the courtyard just outside Ward 14A. The association's newsletter reported in 1961 that these new pieces of 'play equipment' were proving 'very popular with the children' and that soon, tyre swings would be put up so that children could 'enjoy themselves actively' without becoming a 'danger to their playmates'.[33] A brief albeit uncritical history of the Kew Cottages Parents' Association paints these early endeavours as significant contributions that improved the lives of the residents at Kew.[34] Later, more formalised fundraising efforts would improve conditions at the institution more substantially.

Figure 9.4: Residents on the play equipment
(Courtesy Kew Residential Services)

Figure 9.5: Residents keeping cool in the summer heat
(Courtesy Kew Residential Services)

The initial importance of the association was that it fostered a sense among parents and staff that they were all part of one community. In that sense it straddled those two worlds of staff and clients that Erving Goffman detected in all total institutions. For more than half a century, the institutional system had largely disempowered parents by restricting their involvement in their children's lives once they were placed at Kew. The institutional model of care was founded on the notion that mothers and fathers relinquished their children to the state. From the moment a child was admitted to Kew, the responsibility for that child's care shifted from the parents to the nursing staff. The prevailing medical view was that, from that point on, parents should play no further role in their child's care. By maintaining relationships with their institutionalised children, the members of the Kew Cottages Parents' Association began to challenge some of the key tenets underpinning institutional care.[35] A new spirit of maternalism was injected into Kew's life, as mothers in particular—who played the most active roles in the association—began to negotiate a new place for themselves and a new place for maternal care within the context of the institution.

Irene Higgins, who witnessed these developments, was immensely pleased. Later, she explained that the association's first successful representations allowed many mothers and fathers to play the role of 'caring, vigilant parents', while also relieving them of their feelings of 'redundancy and guilt'.[36] Higgins was also pleased to note how the association's work was leading to improved relations between parents and staff. As early as December 1959, when the association organised its first coffee party to celebrate the staff, Higgins noticed a remarkable 'change in the attitude of the staff towards parents'. Expressions of gratitude and appreciation were more common than criticism, she observed, and parents could 'discuss their difficulties' with most staff members in a constructive, non-confrontational manner. Some of the association's mothers would have said the same thing. One mother recalled that, as she and others 'came into close contact', an alliance was formed 'between parents and staff' because each realised the other was doing their best in incredibly difficult circumstances. Beryl Power made a similar point when she recalled that, once she became a liaison representative to her son's ward, it 'helped so much to improve what had been a strained relationship with the charge nurse'.[37]

A heartfelt note in the newsletter from December 1964—by which time the coffee party had become an annual event—offers an insight into just how much the once frosty relationship between staff and parents had changed:

> I sometimes wonder if the staff at the Cottages really know that we are grateful for the devoted care they all give to our children day by day and the whole year through. It is a wonderful job that they have undertaken for us and our children ... Perhaps that is the most important reason we have our Coffee Party about this time every year. Even if we don't put our feelings into words, just by being present we are saying "Thank You"![38]

It probably helped that the lines of communication had been formalised with the appointment of a liaison officer in 1961 and the establishment of a Liaison Committee in early 1964. The Liaison Committee was conceived as a body that could act as 'a link between the staff and the Parents' Association' and consult on the most effective and equitable way to spend any money raised.[39] To this end, the committee appointed a parent representative to each ward to ascertain what was most needed at any given time. Slowly, inextricably, the Liaison Committee wove itself into the daily life of the institution. It provided wards with much needed amenities such as air conditioners, new clothes and toys. It organised various therapeutic and educational programs, and it ran birthday parties for individual residents. And every Christmas, the committee bought presents for each resident in the institution.

By the mid-1970s, the Kew Cottages Parents' Association could confidently assert and celebrate its contribution to improving conditions at Kew. In October 1974, Robin Coutts, the president of the association, acknowledged as much when he wrote in the *Newsletter* that their organisation had begun at 'a time when conditions at Kew were deplorable'. Coutts argued that the situation had improved immensely over the years and that 'the Parents' Association has played a direct role in this improvement'.[40] The association had also grown over the years, and it now had a membership of more than 560 families and two regional branches: the Latrobe Valley branch, established by Fred Badenhope in 1961, and another branch in Geelong, established by Harry Kirby in 1966. More than ever before, parents felt more at home and connected to Kew Cottages. Through their fundraising, activism and lobbying, some parents had reclaimed their status and identity as mothers and fathers within the institutional regime. It probably helped that reforms introduced by the Mental Hygiene Authority now generally encouraged family and community involvement with mental health institutions across the state. One mother, who managed a stall at the 1983 fete, invoked this sense of community when she set down her feelings about the annual Kew Cottages fete:

> Apart from the obvious and necessary function of raising money to buy additional comforts for our retarded children and adults, there is, I believe, a secondary and possibly more important aspect to our big day. Standing in my stall looking out, I see a happy village interacting with community, and the community interacting with the village.[41]

Advocacy

If the fundraising of the Kew Cottages Parents' Association was inward looking and focused primarily on helping improve the conditions within the institution, the advocacy of the association was outward looking and represented an engagement with the wider community and the outside world. When the Kew Cottages Parents' Association's publicity material explained the problems of coping with children with intellectual disability in psychological terms, they were unconsciously mimicking the approach of other parents' organisations across the western world.[42] Like their counterparts abroad, what these parents were demanding was inclusion in an imagined community of ordinary Australian families. These parents sought to deflect some of the responsibility for their problems from themselves (and their children) onto society. They argued that greater community acceptance and better public understanding could become factors in resolving some of the difficulties associated with intellectual disability. In doing so, they suggested that the problem of intellectual disability was not necessarily located in the child with the intellectual disability, but rather in the community's failure to accept and accommodate that child.

As advocates, members of the parents' association sought to educate the public about their children and, more broadly, to counter the stigma of intellectual disability. This educational/advocacy role fell to the Information Committee, which was initially convened by the husband-and-wife team of Ethel and Allan Temby shortly after the association was established. A 1962 charter outlining the Information Committee's key roles evoked the United Nations Declaration of the Rights of the Child and reveals the committee's core beliefs. The charter declared that 'all people in all countries' needed to take responsibility for 'all children' and 'promote the realisation that our level of intelligence should never be the factor deciding whether the educational, welfare or training facilities we need are made available to us'.[43]

One of the committee's main roles was to collect, collate and sift through relevant information, so that members of the association could educate themselves (and the public) about intellectual disability. A second role was to consider how this information could best be used. Some could 'educate the public through information leaflets and through talks to any groups that will listen', while other information could help arouse public concern over the deficiencies in the mental health services. To this end, the committee was conceived chiefly as an aggregator and disseminator of information about intellectual disability, a topic that was not generally well understood at the time. June Epstein, who made numerous speeches to church groups, schools and various clubs, recalled that she 'was surprised to find how little people seemed to know about retardation, and how genuinely they wanted to find out'.[44] The committee attempted to fill in these gaps in public knowledge. By doing so it could, as Ethel Temby put it, 'refute folklore and old-wives' tales—and seek out the truth for its own and the public benefit. It could seek the causes of community attitudes, and by explaining them bring about change'.[45]

Making a commitment to 'correcting the many misapprehensions that are held regarding mental retardation' was one thing, fostering change was another. But the members of the Information Committee were confident in their ability to change perceptions. Temby captured this sentiment when she wrote that 'we hope to influence thinking that the time will soon come when no one fears to acknowledge a retarded child'.[46] One way of achieving such a goal, as far as the parents' association was concerned, was through honest dialogue and 'by talking freely, and being quite unselfconscious about their children'. This was quite a revolutionary idea. For respectable mothers and fathers to openly discuss a child's intellectual disabilities in front of others was no easy task. Yet one parents' association leaflet urged parents and the public to do just that.[47] The association acknowledged that finding the right way to talk about intellectual disabilities might be difficult and urged the public to show their acceptance 'by being neither overly conscious nor under-interested in the handicapped person and his family'.

When the parents who were members of the association explained the problem of intellectual disability to the public, they drew on their own experiences of stigma and social isolation. To some extent, they had been radicalised by a strong awareness of their position in society as parents of an intellectually disabled child. Every parent in the association had first-hand experience of such stigmatisation, and every parent had a story to tell about the hurt and suffering they had experienced over the years. In her memoir, June Epstein recalled the many times that neighbours crossed the street after her son was diagnosed, so that they would not have to talk to her about her situation. Another parent, Bill Westgarth, recalled the difficulties his children faced in the schoolyard when peers teased them about their 'mad brother'. Even some of his adult friends 'were a bit frightened' of his son, Westgarth recalled: 'We didn't lose any friends or anything like that', he said, but people still 'didn't like him wobbling over' to them. Westgarth acknowledged the hurt he felt when he witnessed such reactions. It also baffled him, he said, because 'I don't know why they'd be frightened of a little fella like that'.[48]

In this context, it is probably not surprising that the publicity material highlighted the mental anguish and social isolation many families experienced. 'No blame and no stigma should touch the families of these children', one leaflet declared. Others stressed that mental retardation could appear in any family and that 'no race, no religion, no standard of education, no economic circumstance ensures freedom from intellectual handicap'.[49] Still others directed their efforts to overturning old eugenic ideas, emphasising that intellectual disabilities were not hereditary, the result of poor hygiene or of an illness contracted by the mother during pregnancy. Under the influence of the eugenic movement, intellectual disabilities had been presented as a threat to society from lower class, sexually aggressive juvenile delinquents.

After World War II, a preoccupation with visions of an idealised middle-class family, with a mother at home raising psychologically healthy children, led to a rising concern for intellectual disabilities to be seen as a problem facing entire families.[50] The family became the centre of public concern, and solutions to the problem of intellectual disabilities were increasingly aimed at helping the rest of the family as much as the child with an intellectual disability.

In stressing the need for social acceptance and the human rights of their children, these parents were developing a deeper understanding of intellectual disability, what it meant, and how it might be dealt with. This broadened understanding would have radical implications and consequences that few members of the parents' association could ever have foreseen.

Chapter 10

Normalisation Emerges
(from 1970)

In late February 1974, Rob Coutts, president of the Kew Cottages Parents' Association, remarked in his report on what he referred to as 'an upsurge in interest' in 'mental retardation' in Victoria and a growing interest in Kew Cottages in particular. It had reached the point, wrote Coutts, that it was now not unusual to witness groups of visitors coming 'to observe parts of the operation' at Kew.[1] For some people, Kew Cottages was no longer the notorious institution it had once been. For others, like Irene Higgins, who believed that it was 'now one of the best institutions of its kind in Australia', the institution had been returned to its former glory, though whether such a halcyon period had ever really existed is doubtful.[2]

What, exactly, would a visitor to Kew have witnessed in 1974? A decade earlier, the institution was transformed by an extraordinary period of renovation and growth. The original cottages were renovated and refurbished, and a further seven cottages built from scratch to cater to what seemed like a never-ending demand for residential places. The Dax period had come to an end in 1969 when the chairman of the Mental Health Authority resigned to take up a new position co-ordinating community health services in Tasmania. When news got out that Dax was finishing up in Victoria, some pundits immediately put it down to his 'differences with the State Government'. When questioned on the matter, Dax admitted he had had the occasional run-in with the government, but he also claimed that differences of opinion had nothing to do with his decision to start afresh. 'I've been with the Mental Health Authority since 1952', he explained, and 'with the aid of the Government we have been able to achieve quite a lot'.[3] All of this was true enough, and, by 1974, the refurbishment of the Kew Cottages had been replicated—to a certain extent—in every other institution for people with an intellectual disability (and for people with mental illness) across Victoria.

Figure 10.1: A young resident practising skills of good hygiene fulfilling the programs at training centres of this post 1970 period
(Courtesy Kew Residential Services)

Expansion of Services

Indeed, by 1974 there was a web of services for people with intellectual disabilities that stretched out across the state. How effectively such services were operating remained open for debate, but all commentators agreed that things were better now than in 1952. At the heart of the web was Travancore, a small school and residential centre located in Flemington that had been established in 1933. Part institution and part diagnostic clinic, Travancore housed and offered some sort of formal training to a handful of children with intellectual disabilities up to the age of fourteen. Essentially, Travancore was a reception centre for children who might have an intellectual disability but who were also 'capable of receiving benefit from special instruction'. As one observer noted, the institution had been established to 'provide education and domestic care' but also to 'promote all-round development, physical, intellectual, emotional and social, to the fullest extent possible'. But residential spots at Travancore were always limited, and, according to the Mental Health Authority, there were only thirty-six children 'on the books' in 1974.[4]

The Travancore Clinic, which operated out of the same address, justified Travancore's preeminent position at the heart of Victorian services for people with intellectual disabilities. It was at the Travancore Clinic that most 'mentally retarded children' in Victoria were 'thoroughly examined' and the extent of their disability revealed to parents. It was here too that expert advice was offered to parents about the 'care and management' of their children. Thus, at Travancore, parents learnt whether their child needed to be placed in an institution and which one might best suit their needs. Earlier, Kew Cottages was the only choice, but by 1974 the options for prospective parents were quite varied and a lot depended on the diagnosis at Travancore.

Including Travancore, there were now twelve state-run institutions that offered residential placements for children with intellectual disabilities in Victoria, though, since the proclamation of the *Mental Health Act 1959*, all such institutions were now called 'training centres'. The Victorian government had proclaimed the Act on 11 November 1962. The new act overhauled the *Mental Deficiency Act*, which, though never proclaimed, had provided Dax with some of the tools required to update the decrepit Victorian mental health system. Few, however, would have mourned the earlier Act's demise.

The new Act separated the mentally ill from the mentally disabled and provided for easier admission and discharge. It was underpinned by the principle of education rather than that of control. If there was a consensus among interested observers, it was that this legislation was long overdue. When it passed through both houses of parliament in 1959, Dax noted that it was perhaps the 'most important step forward' for that year.[5] When it was finally proclaimed in 1962, Brady was equally pleased. He noted that 'it would appear that the new Act has many advantages in the intellectually handicapped field'.[6]

What would have gratified both men equally is the fact that the nomenclature of the *Mental Health Act* reflected contemporary understandings of intellectual disabilities. If the language is jarring today, at the time it represented a significant break with the more derogatory language of the past. Mental 'retardation' was defined as 'suffering from an arrested or incomplete development of the mind', and, while the legislation still made provision for different grades of 'mental retardation', the language had changed here too.[7] Severely, moderately and mildly 'retarded' replaced the more antiquated terms 'idiot', 'imbecile' and 'feeble minded'. The new Act also 'necessitated a rearrangement and reclassification of both patients and hospitals', which meant, among other things, that 'mental defective institutions' would now be referred to as 'training centres'. The new nomenclature was a nod to the fact that intellectual disability was no longer viewed in eugenic terms as a problem that might be mitigated by incarceration and sterilisation. Rather, the problem of intellectual disability had become a problem of appropriate education and social welfare.

Of the twelve training centres across Victoria, Kew and Sunbury were by far the largest. If a child was not placed at Kew, then he or she was likely to end up at Sunbury because, between them, the Sunbury Training Centre and the Kew Cottages accounted for more than half of the beds in Victoria. Like Kew, Sunbury was overcrowded, understaffed, and generally catered for the most severely intellectually disabled. By 1974 it held 895 residents, making it the second largest institution in the state.[8] Despite these difficulties, training or educational programs were a part of the fabric of the institution. According to Dr T.J. Leonard, the super-intendent, Sunbury aimed to foster some 'degree of independence on the part of residents'. This meant that some staff tried to 'improve the level of self care competencies' of the most 'severely and profoundly retarded' residents, while others worked with more 'moderately or mildly retarded' residents to build their 'capacity for occupational and social adjustment'.

A child with more moderate intellectual disability might end up at Sandhurst or Janefield. In 1955 the Mental Hygiene Authority had established a training centre in Bendigo for adolescent boys. This new institution, which Dax hailed as 'a major development' at the time, became known as the Sandhurst Boy's Centre and would provide accommodation for up to a hundred residents. It was reserved for boys over the age of sixteen. On 3 March 1955, a group of twelve boys was sent from Kew Cottages to Bendigo. Over the next few months, further groups were transferred from the Pleasant Creek Training Centre (Stawell) and Janefield (Bundoora) and, by the end of June 1955, there were forty-three boys living at Sandhurst. The new residents 'settled down very quickly', and by all reports they seemed to 'be appreciative of their new surroundings and way of life'. The secretary at Sandhurst, Mr Nugent, closely monitored developments detecting 'many hearting signs' and was convinced Sandhurst had made 'a very satisfactory start'. Eric Cunningham Dax was equally pleased, declaring the new institution 'an unqualified success', and commenting that 'improvement in the mental and social outlook of the boys' was 'most noticeable'.[9]

By 1974 68 boys were in residence at the Sandhurst Boys' Home, which had become a visible part of the broader Bendigo community. The superintendent at Sandhurst, Dr John Bomford, thought the 'trainees'—as residents were known—were 'very well accepted in the local community'. Bomford attributed this to their 'high standard of dress and their good manners and behaviour in public'. Such positive behaviour stemmed from the 'comprehensive training programme' at Sandhurst. For some years, Sandhurst had been preparing young men to lead conscientious and useful lives in the world outside, Bomford noting in 1974 that most ex-trainees who returned to visit the centre appeared to be living 'prosperous and responsible lives in the community'. He also remarked that the Sandhurst training program now included a more formal educational curriculum, which offered 'a wide range of subjects and activities ... designed to improve the trainees' overall education'. The program was conducted with 'a different group of lads every afternoon' so that every boy attended the classes 'one afternoon per week'.[10]

Catering as it did for students with a moderate intellectual disability, Sandhurst was essentially a sister institution to the Janefield Training Centre, which ostensibly catered for female residents of a similar age and disability. The Janefield Training Centre was an old Red Cross Tuberculosis Sanatorium that had been converted into an institution for girls with intellectual disability in 1937. However, a general shortage of residential positions at most institutions across the state meant that by 1945 Janefield accepted a mixture of males and females, although girls generally outnumbered boys by more than two to one.

The Janefield Training Centre lay on about 900 acres of farmland in Bundoora, 18 kilometres from the centre of Melbourne. The large swathes of arable land meant that Janefield was usually viewed by administrators as an important part of any expansion plan. In 1953, Eric Cunningham Dax had outlined his own vision for Janefield, which involved transforming the existing 157-bed institution into a self-sustaining mega-colony for a thousand children and adolescents. That vision never eventuated, but by 1974 there were 480 children—302 females and 176 males—'in residence' at Janefield, and, like their counterparts at Sandhurst, most were responding well to the 'new activities' that were now a part of their everyday routines. Music therapy and occupational therapy programs were running at Janefield on most days, and teachers from the Special School Centre had also recently commenced 'educative programmes' for some of the more 'severely retarded children'. Dr Denys Berrange Brink, superintendent at Janefield, reported that these activities were yielding good results and 'being met by a gratifying response from the children involved'.[11]

In 1974, other options for prospective parents seeking to place their child in an institution included the training centres at Ararat (385 residents), Beechworth (244 residents) and Warrnambool (123 residents), all annexes to larger institutions for people with mental illness. This was an imperfect arrangement that mixed the two streams of residents. There were also smaller residential options at Kingsbury (31 residents) and St Nicholas (156 residents) and, for the most mildly intellectually disabled children, there was the Pleasant Creek Training Centre in Stawell (192 residents).[12]

The rapidly expanding network of day centres was another option that parents might have explored in 1974. The Victorian government was now funding the establishment of such centres on a four-to-one basis. In 1974 alone, seven new ones had been established. Another eight centres were expected to be completed the following year. Alan Stoller, the chairman of the Mental Health Authority, thought the day training program 'a most successful venture and one of which Victoria can be very proud'. Parents were probably still the main driving force behind most of these centres, but Stoller also noted that the Department of Education had recently assumed 'greater responsibilities for the education of the mentally handicapped' attending day centres across the state.[13]

The strong emphasis on education and training, so evident in the reports on most institutions and day centres at the time, is also discernible in contemporary reports about Kew. By 1974 Kew Cottages held 919 residents, which represented more than a quarter of all people on the Mental Health Authority's books. At Kew, the problem of overcrowding had diminished (but not disappeared), and few believed that a solution would be forthcoming any time soon. Each year, Dr Alan Stoller would raise the issue of overcrowding in his annual report. However, each time he also added that the government was aware of the 'need to expedite the provision of additional accommodation to alleviate' desperate shortages of beds in most institutions across the state. In spite of the apparent intractability of this problem, four new training and education centres now provided a variety of educational programs for residents. The programs in these centres were designed to improve independent living skills or offer residents stimulating activities outside of their living accommodation. Of course, the usual problems of understaffing meant that some residents could not access these new opportunities, and other residents received truncated or less than adequate sessions. Yet Irene Higgins, for one, was impressed with what she referred to as the 'tremendous changes' that had occurred at Kew. She recalled that, when she started working at the institution, the children had very few opportunities for extra activities apart from being 'washed, clothed and fed'.[14]

Now there was a structure to the overall operation of the Kew Cottages, and a lot more attention was devoted to ensuring residents could have access to some form of meaningful activity throughout the day. Also, some Kew staff now came from other—nonmedical—professions. There were still doctors and nurses, as there always had been, but there were also dentists, occupational therapists, speech pathologists, biologists, and schoolteachers. Higgins had remarked upon this welcome development as early as 1963 when she noted that the staff at Kew Cottages had grown over the years to become 'representative of many disciplines'.[15]

Of course, the changes taking place at the Kew Cottages were also occurring in many institutions around the world. If anything, the Kew Cottages were late to the party, for the implementation of new forms of education and training in overseas institutions for people with intellectual disability had largely begun towards the end of the 1950s, a few years after the publication of Maxwell Jones's influential book, *The Therapeutic Community* in 1953. Jones, a Scottish psychiatrist, bemoaned how traditional institutions isolated and estranged the very patients they sought to treat, increasing their disengagement and dependence with each passing day. In essence he argued that a more multidisciplinary and inclusive approach to institutional care might offset the worst effects of institutions upon patients.[16]

In the early 1970s, Higgins described in some detail how the principle of education and training now underpinned many daily routines at the cottages. Training, Higgins noted, usually began with a child's arrival at the institution. It involved a nurse teaching the children in the infant's ward 'to hold the spoon and eat, to hold the cup and drink, to sit up, to sit on the potty chairs' or to take his or her first steps. As the children grew and were moved to the toddlers' ward, they received further training to 'become used to certain routines' such as 'bedtime' or going to the toilet or 'basic table manners'. Higgins claimed that nurses operated like mothers, watching children go 'off to kindergarten', welcoming them back home and always taking pride in their 'good behaviour, appearance and advancement'. Like all good mothers, she wrote, nurses 'make each little one feel at home … and happy, as well as training and teaching each child to achieve the highest level of development of which he or she is capable'. Higgins did not offer an opinion about the gendered nature of the role the Kew Cottages nurses played in this scenario, but clearly few questioned the assumption that it was women, predominantly, who would be called upon to provide care, comfort and domestic training to the children at Kew.

Higgins revealed that the residents at the Kew Cottages were now more active and occupied than ever before. Some attended kindergarten or the special school. They also had regular sessions at the Occupational Therapy Centre or the Physiotherapy Department. 'Further training and teaching' opportunities occurred in each residential ward where, Higgins wrote, little tasks were allocated 'such as setting the table, drying the crockery, or sweeping the floors'. All of this had proved of 'very great advantage to the children', who now had far less 'time for quarrels or misdeeds'.[17] Another staff member agreed, noting that 'when people started to get dressed and go out of the ward every day … all those macabre behaviours disappeared'.[18] Such observations revealed Kew Cottages had changed due to improved attitudes towards its residents. Intellectual disabilities could no longer be considered only as a medical problem. The new approach demanded the involvement of other professions in order to ensure the residents' lives reached their fullest potential.

These changes in societal attitudes were hinted at as early as 1962, when Dr Brady noted changes in volunteerism at Kew: 'over the recent years the growth of knowledge and understanding on the part of the general public has resulted in a change in the emphasis in their "giving" to this institution'. For as long as Brady could remember, toys, or money or in-kind work had been the main focus of 'giving' to Kew. But now, he wrote, an 'increasing number of inquiries' were being received from 'individuals and groups as to the value of visiting the children, making contact, getting to know them, playing with them, and taking them for outings' (Figures 10.2 and 10.3).[19]

Normalisation Emerges (from 1970)

Figure 10.2: Residents enjoying the view from a bayside pier
(Courtesy Kew Residential Services)

Figure 10.3: Residents enjoying an outing to the beach
(Courtesy Kew Residential Services)

Changing Attitudes

What had prompted this 'growth of knowledge and understanding on the part of the general public'? Why were public attitudes to people with intellectual disability shifting? The answer is complex. Politicians and legislators played an important role by proclaiming the *Mental Health Act*—the first piece of intellectual disability specific legislation—in 1962. The different tenor of postwar debates on the *Mental Health Act*, when compared to prewar debates on the *Mental Deficiency Act*, reveals how much contemporary attitudes to people with intellectual disabilities had been transformed. In the 1930s, debates on 'mental deficiency' legislation revolved around the segregation and exclusion of people with intellectual disabilities from civil society, predominantly for the good of the broader community. Back then, Sir Stanley Argyle, a prominent eugenicist, spoke of how a 'community' should be 'divided into two main groups'. One group consisted of 'those who can independently adjust themselves to social surroundings in a satisfactory manner'. The other group consisted of 'those who cannot so adjust themselves without assistance from others and who require special surroundings and control, or supervision'. Argyle believed that the community needed to be protected from the 'imbeciles' and 'mental retardants' who made up the latter group and who, he said, have 'no mind, and who are incapable of having any'.[20]

Two decades later, the debates were more concerned with education and training, and building appropriate supports and services, to assist people with intellectual disabilities to participate more fully in society. A key reason for this shift in thinking around intellectual disability was that the Nazi regime in Germany had followed eugenicist ideas to their horrific logical conclusions. After this, no government—in Australia or elsewhere—could flirt with policies based on the 'science of eugenics'.

By 1959, the debates around intellectual disability had assumed a softer, more inclusive tone. Buckley Machin, a Labor MLC, confirmed in the parliament his party's support for the *Mental Health Act*, saying he was happy to see 'people of all types and of all political persuasion who have interested themselves in the care of the mentally ill'. But it was Bill Fulton, the former minister for health, who revealed in supporting the new Act how much contemporary understandings of intellectual disability had shifted. Fulton declared in a moving speech: 'I have seen children who could not speak or walk', who 'through care, attention and the skill of physicians and surgeons' had become 'useful citizens'. He also referred to the stigma associated with so much of the language around intellectual disability and mental illness. Fulton was talking for many when he told parliament that 'it is time we discarded certain terms that were in use 200 years ago but which are now outmoded'.[21]

The debilitating effects of stigma and shame were something almost every parent of a child with intellectual disabilities could understand. The Kew Cottages Parents' Association—as well as other parents' organisations—had played a part in changing public attitudes towards intellectual disabilities. June Epstein perhaps exaggerated a little when she recalled that parents precipitated 'a revolution' that 'brought about several remarkable changes' over the years. And they changed themselves. Parents, as Epstein pointed out, were now less inclined to be 'ashamed' of their children than formerly. They talked openly of their children and in doing so 'helped in the development of a new, healthier attitude towards mental handicap'.[22] Parents were also more inclined to acknowledge that many people with intellectual disabilities 'can and do grow', as Epstein put it, 'in direct proportion to the teaching given to them'. As such, they demanded better access to education. If that was not always forthcoming, they established day centres of their own, 'where new ways of teaching were discovered, new gains reported' and 'new research undertaken'.

Parents seeking to shift public attitudes to intellectual disability were also supported by an ever-increasing number of medical professionals who argued that intellectual disability was not just a medical problem. In November 1969, Dr Athel Hockey, an expert in mental disability from Western Australia, explained this relatively new idea at a Melbourne meeting of the Australian group for the scientific study of 'mental deficiency'. 'The treatment of mental deficiency in children is basically a social problem' she told her audience.[23] Public acceptance of intellectual disability was still quite 'limited' in Australia, due to 'old wives tales and childhood impressions' that 'die hard'. Hockey hoped that the public might come to realise that people with intellectual disabilities were better served 'in an environment suited' to their needs, which paralleled those of other individuals, rather than in heavily medicalised environments.

Parents, activists, medical professionals and politicians seeking to change public attitudes and to assert that intellectual disability was a social, not a medical, problem tapped into the activism for social justice that characterised the 1960s and 1970s. They shared with other civil rights movements a similar optimism about solving social problems. In the same way as Black American or Indigenous Australians pushed for civil rights, disability advocates and their allies emphasised that people with intellectual disability were also on the margins of society. They made the same demands for social justice, equality and community responsibility. They also used similar methods to raise consciousness and bring about change by drawing on the language of civil rights, racial inequality, and citizenship to make their point. They declared that people with intellectual disabilities were citizens who should have the same rights as everyone else. People with intellectual disabilities should 'no longer' be the object of shame and derision', argued Epstein, nor 'even of pity and handouts'. She argued they should have access to education, a place in the community, to care and protection where necessary, and to employment. That way, Epstein suggested, a person with an intellectual disability might 'experience the dignity and self-respect of the citizen who knows he is making a contribution to the community'.[24]

Epstein's arguments about citizenship hints at another philosophical concept—human rights—that came to dominate thinking about the problem of intellectual disability in Australia and elsewhere in the world. Indeed, during this period, a nascent disability rights movement began to argue that people with intellectual disabilities were of equal worth to others in the community and had the same human rights as any other individual, including the right to personal safety and the right to a meaningful life.

The extent to which such ideas gained traction in the broader community is difficult to ascertain. If contemporary newspaper reports are any guide, public attention between 1970 and 1972 was more focused on what the *Age* referred to as the 'money pinch' hitting the Mental Health Authority than on the rights of people with intellectual disabilities.[25] But, at this time, certain sectors of the community looked beyond budgetary issues to engage in a broader conversation around the rights of people with intellectual disabilities. In May 1971, for example, the *Age* framed an article about the 'glaring neglect and deficiencies' in services for people with intellectual disabilities as 'discrimination against the basic rights of a fairly large section of the community'.[26] On 20 December 1971, the United Nations General Assembly highlighted the issue by proclaiming the Declaration on the Rights of Mentally Retarded Persons, which enshrined the right of people with intellectual disabilities to 'proper medical care', 'economic security', and 'protection from exploitation'.[27] The Declaration, which also stressed that 'the mentally retarded person has, to the maximum degree of feasibility, the same rights as other human beings', was the first international statement asserting the equal rights of people with intellectual disabilities.

The Idea of Normalisation

Within this developing picture of intellectual disability evolved a new paradigm—normalisation—which further shifted thinking about intellectual disability in Australia and around the world. The concept of 'normalisation' was initially developed in the early 1960s by Bengt Nirje, executive director of the Swedish Association for Retarded Children, and Niels Erik Bank-Mikkelsen, a member of the Danish National Board of Social Welfare. Normalisation represented a cluster of ideas and assumptions relating to intellectual disability that eventually captured a large following among workers in the field around the world.[28] Nirje and Bank-Mikkelsen, for instance, described 'normalisation' as allowing for 'an existence for the mentally retarded as close to normal living conditions as possible' and 'making normal, mentally retarded people's housing, education, working and leisure conditions'.[29]

One of Nirje's chief concerns was that institutional confinement created a stifling and unnatural environment that thwarted the innate desire of individuals to control their day. Normalisation extended to the most mundane tasks, such as getting out of bed at a time of the individual's choosing, washing, getting dressed and eating (Figures 10.1 and 10.4).[30] Nirje argued that normalisation also related to how an individual moved in, used and explored their community. They should, whenever possible, utilise community agencies and facilities rather than remaining dependent on specialised settings. They should replicate and enjoy the normal rhythms of everyday life including work, leisure time with family and friends, and holidays or vacations. Nirje's articulation of normalisation was a practical statement of rights for people with intellectual disabilities to be regarded as human beings—or as citizens—by asserting their equality on an everyday level with others.

Figure 10.4: Young men learning to knot a tie
(Courtesy Kew Residential Services)

The concept of normalisation was elevated to a principle in 1972 in Wolf Wolfensberger's influential book, the *Principle of Normalization in Human Services*, in which he developed the ideas around the concept of normalisation and introduced it to the English-speaking world.[31] Wolfensberger, a well-known psychologist with a reputation for innovative thinking about intellectual disability, was influenced, like many others, by the underpinning ideas of the sociologist Erving Goffman's theory of deviance. According to Wolfensberger, mentally disabled people were viewed as deviant not as a result of their own choosing but because of their 'observed quality', which was viewed as 'negatively value-charged'.[32] He was convinced that structural problems within services for people with intellectual disabilities inadvertently called attention to their uniquely devalued qualities. In spite of their best intentions, service providers or well-meaning policy makers exacerbated the problem by reinforcing problematic, or counterproductive, ideas about people with intellectual disabilities as eternally 'childlike' or 'subhuman'. In his book, Wolfensberger painted a picture of a vicious cycle that undermined people with intellectual disabilities at every turn. He argued that service systems that relied heavily on large-scale residential institutions, sheltered workshops, special schools and other segregated programs, highlighted the mostly devalued—or 'deviant'—qualities of people with intellectual disabilities. Once labelled as 'deviant', they absorbed these devalued qualities and assumed roles that violated social norms, which in turn served only to reinforce further those devalued qualities.

In order to end the labelling process—and the dehumanisation that accompanied such labels—two things needed to change. First, Wolfensberger insisted that significant effort needed to be put into assisting people with intellectual disabilities to assume socially valued behaviours. Second, people with intellectual disabilities needed to be integrated into the socially and culturally normative settings that made up such a significant part of everyday life. Eventually, integration became for Wolfensberger and many of his disciples a moral means to an even greater end. In order to integrate mentally disabled citizens into daily life, human services providers would have to commit themselves not only to the principle of normalisation, but also to fine tuning normal institutions to 'provide the framework for a cathedral of human dignity'.[33] This sort of dignity, of course, could never be satisfactorily achieved in an institutional environment, because institutions largely reinforced the *status quo*. Only in normal community settings could mentally disabled people learn behaviours that would lead to social acceptance, fuller participation in mainstream life, and the erasure of negative labels and hence stigma.

Victorian Committee on Mental Retardation

The concept of normalisation represented a comprehensive challenge to the segregated nature of the intellectual disability service system. Although we know that the concept resonated with parent advocates, health care professionals and people with intellectual disabilities alike, it is not clear how such thinking spread across the Victorian community as a whole. We know, for instance, that the key ideas underpinning the principle of normalisation were widely disseminated by its proponents through prolific writing and publication and through the development of exhaustive training programs. And we also know that, at some point, many interested observers in Victoria were grappling with these ideas and trying to work out how they might be applied in an Australian setting.

Ethel Temby, the president of STAR Victoria, an independent community organisation advocating for people with intellectual disability, was one such interested observer. In the early 1970s, Temby travelled to the USA to see first-hand how normalisation-based approaches were being implemented. Temby was a former member of the Kew Cottages Parents' Association and a founding member of STAR, which emerged from the parents' concerns that it was essential to change broader community attitudes toward intellectual disabilities. Temby returned from her excursion convinced that such approaches could work in an Australian context. 'I got desperate about the fact that I was getting stuff from overseas from everywhere', Temby recalled, from 'Canada, the USA, Britain, Sweden,

New Zealand and occasionally Denmark'. She 'was getting wonderful ideas about things that were happening in this area of life overseas', she said, and so she 'kept putting bits and snatches in the newsletter about them'.[34]

In Victoria, some young professionals working in intellectual disability services were also receptive to these new ideas. Brendan Lillywhite, for instance, who worked at Kew Cottages in the 1970s, recalled starting to question the degrading policies and procedures that underpinned his work:

> You'd walk through Kew and you'd see people, you know, in a ward. Or you'd see people being toileted, where there'd be no toilet doors on and they'd be all around ... I guess it was an impression of an 18 or 19 year old and it was just a bit like: Well, you know, shit, what is going on here?[35]

Irene Higgins, still at the Kew Cottages, speculated on what normalisation might mean for the residents living there. Normalisation 'does not mean that one is attempting to "produce" a normal person', she wrote in the early 1970s, but rather that 'one is attempting to provide a normal type of life for that person' (Figure 10.5). Higgins noted that residents should as far as possible be treated with 'dignity', should 'achieve maximum independence', and should be allowed 'normal opportunities for privacy'. And she mused that it would 'be interesting to see how many normal patients' at Kew would 'agree that they are given all these'.[36]

A fundamental turning point in terms of the embrace of the concept of normalisation in Victoria—though few may have recognised it as such at the time—was the October 1974 announcement by the Liberal premier, Rupert Hamer, of the formation of a committee 'to inform him on all matters concerning retarded persons'.[37] This emerged after the *Age* newspaper led a sustained public campaign and fundraising appeal—the Minus Children Appeal—to raise money for improvements at Kew. Like the Tipping Appeal twenty years earlier, the Minus Children Appeal tapped into a well-established tradition that combined emotive reporting with a plea to the public and the government to do something to assist the poor children at Kew.

Figure 10.5: A young resident enjoying normal playtime
(Courtesy Kew Residential Services)

Judged by this standard alone, the campaign was a resounding success; the appeal raised two and a half million dollars. Even so, Don Trescowthick, chairman of the Minus Children Appeal, ignored or was unaware of past fundraising efforts when he boasted that 'never before in the State of Victoria have we seen all sections of the community joined together so forcibly to achieve an appeal target'.[38] He also missed a more significant point: that the Victorian Committee on Mental Retardation—rather than the fundraising efforts—would bring about greater change.

The committee met for the first time on 19 December 1974. It was chaired by the psychiatrist, Jack Evans, and included Ethel Temby and Gil Pierce. Pierce and Temby were both well informed about the rapid transformations in the field of intellectual disability taking place in countries like the USA and Canada, which, Pierce recalled, were already 'well down the deinstitutionalisation and community support path'.[39] The committee's terms of reference were broad. It was tasked with researching current local conditions and developing recommendations for reform. If the task of overseeing the project fell to Jack Evans, he was less involved in the practical details than some of the other committee members. That work, according to Gill Pierce, was carried out by members who were more versed in the art of policy formation:

> At that stage the key players were the psychiatrists, and they weren't good planners and they weren't good policy people and they weren't good managers, so a lot of the work of that report fell to me, and Ethel Temby, and to somebody from the Education Department ... we did the real work.[40]

By June 1977, the committee had completed an interim report, and by then it was already becoming clear that it would recommend significant reforms.

The Mental Health Authority was relatively quick to see which way the Victorian Committee on Mental Retardation would lean. Therefore, well before the committee handed down its findings, the authority was already making significant changes to the way it would operate into the future. The annual report for 1974—by which time the committee had just convened—did not hint at the significant changes about to take place. If anything, it is largely similar to any number of other annual reports that had preceded it over the years. It weighs improvements such as new buildings and new day centres against more intractable problems such as overcrowding, run-down facilities and staff shortages. The preceding year had presented the usual 'considerable difficulties in regard to the provision of facilities', wrote Dr Stoller, and 'as mentioned in last year's report' the numbers on the 'urgent waiting list' remained largely unchanged. That large-scale institutions remained a firm part of the Mental Health Authority's plans in 1974 is also clear from Stoller's note on the progress of work on a new institution under construction in Colac. Stage one of the project was already well underway, and Stoller believed that the new training centre would accept its first residents in the middle of 1976.[41]

Two years later—and half a year before the Committee on Mental Retardation tabled its interim report—the Mental Health Authority was already announcing major reforms across its entire system of services. And the principle of normalisation was at the centre of these new reforms. The 1976 annual report noted that the 'modern concepts of normalisation' had precipitated a 'complete re-orientation in thinking regarding the needs of the mentally retarded and ways of coping with these needs'.[42] One of the shifts taking place was in the way professionals were now treating or caring for people with intellectual disabilities. The report noted that the 'medical and nursing approach' to intellectual disability was inexorably being replaced by a 'psychological, social and educational approach'. This was probably the first official acknowledgment by the Mental Health Authority that intellectual disability should be viewed as a social rather than a medical issue.

The report also noted another equally important development in acknowledging that a movement 'away from hospital-type buildings and institutions towards hostels and group homes ... in the community' was occurring 'throughout the world'. What this actually meant for Victoria's web of existing institutions was not entirely clear, but the Mental Health Authority did point out that the 'emphasis must be on providing service facilities and service personnel rather than fixed purpose hospital-type bricks and mortar structures which, by their very nature, must mould the patient and associated helper to the limited form of use'. In future, the authority noted, government funding would also 'need to be diverted from the building of major structures such as at Colac, to the provision of support services' in the community.[43]

It is an astonishing experience, after reading through two decades of Mental Hygiene/Health Authority annual reports highlighting the significant growth of institutions and considerable increases in funding for segregated intellectual disability services, to then come across a report that signals a complete shift in thinking about how services for people with intellectual disability should be organised. But that is exactly what the 1976 annual report did. The report accepted, as self-evident, 'the right of the retarded person to live as normal a life as possible as defined by normal community standards'. It accepted too, that normalisation 'is now universally regarded as the underlying principle in the provision of services for the handicapped'. It also noted that, in future, the Mental Health Authority would be committed to 'the fostering of a life lived in normal community surroundings, making use of normal community facilities'.[44] What this meant for the new institution still under construction at Colac was now becoming clear. Victoria's newest institution had accepted its first residents in 1976, but the second stage of works was halted in 1977 after the interim report of the Victorian Committee on Mental Retardation criticised institutional models of care as out of date.

The final Report of the Victorian Committee on Mental Retardation, tabled in 1978, would serve only to further reinforce this dramatic shift in thinking about intellectual disabilities. It made 137 recommendations, and most of those were underpinned by the principle of normalisation. In many respects, the report was a blueprint for the reform of the entire intellectual disability service system, which, the committee noted, had been inadequate for 'a number of years'.[45]

Intellectually Disabled Persons' Services Act 1986

Though it never used the word 'deinstitutionalisation', the Evans Report made it clear that the Victorian government should commit 'to the provision of residential services other than in large scale institutions'. That the Victorian government was at least willing to countenance such an idea was clear enough in its decision to cease work at Colac. It was later confirmed in its popular decision in 1981 to close St. Nicholas Hospital, a small institution for severely disabled 'children' in Carlton, although it lingered until 1985. Another major recommendation, though one the Victorian government was less inclined to implement, was 'that an independent Office of Mental Retardation be created' to oversee the 'provision and administration of services for retarded persons'.[46] There had been a long-held view among many observers that the interests of people with intellectual disability were not best served while the Mental Health Authority remained subsumed within the Department of Health. Subsequent reports over the next decade would continue to push the Victorian government toward creating such an office and also toward taking a stronger stance on the issue of deinstitutionalisation.

If legislative action on these two issues was slower than some might have hoped, a further report in 1984 by Victoria's health commissioner, John Rimmer—'Report of the Committee on a Legislative Framework for Services to Intellectually Disabled Persons'—provided enough impetus to push the Victorian government into action. The Rimmer Report recommended that the government craft new legislation—to replace the *Mental Health Act*—that would enable it to begin implementing many of the recommendations of the earlier reports; to embark on an overhaul of all its services for people with intellectual disabilities; and ultimately to commit to a policy of deinstitutionalisation.

As a result, the Labor government under John Cain Jr introduced the Victorian *Intellectually Disabled Persons' Services Act*, which passed through both houses of parliament in 1986. Twenty-four years earlier, the *Mental Health Act* had provided the basis and rationale for a distinct web of services, designed specifically for people with intellectual disabilities and founded on the assumption that the welfare of such people was best served in large-scale, congregate care facilities. The new *Intellectually Disabled Persons' Services Act* would provide the basis and the rationale for pulling this web of services apart.

The foundational principle underpinning the *Intellectually Disabled Persons' Services Act* was undoubtedly normalisation. But the new legislation was also quite explicit about protecting the rights of people with intellectual disabilities and outlining the mechanisms by which this might be achieved. Indeed, the statement of principles underpinning the Act illustrates the extent to which these two philosophical ideas—normalisation and human rights—were embedded in the new legislation. For instance, the first principle noted that 'intellectually disabled persons have the same right as other members of the community to services which support a reasonable quality of life'. Furthermore, the fourth principle could have come straight out of the writing of Bank-Mikkelesen or Nirje. It stated that 'the needs of intellectually disabled persons are best met when the conditions of their everyday life are the same as, or as close as possible to, norms and patterns which are valued in the general community'.[47] Essentially, what the new Act provided was official recognition that people with intellectual disabilities had the same needs and rights as all other citizens. However, because of a disability they required special, well-planned and ongoing support. Just as importantly, the new Act also laid the foundations upon which a movement for the closure of residential institutions could be built.

Suddenly, in 1986, things began to move fast. Before the *Intellectually Disabled Persons' Services Act* was even proclaimed, the minister for community services, Caroline Hogg, engaged the consulting firm Neilson Associates to work with the newly established Office of Intellectual Disability Services on a plan for the redevelopment of these services across Victoria. The 'overall objectives' of such a plan would be 'to provide intellectually disabled people with an array of services and opportunities' that would not only 'meet their personal needs' but also 'provide them with a basis for leading a normal and dignified life'.[48]

By August 1988, the *Ten Year Plan for the Redevelopment of Intellectual Disability Services* was complete. Essentially, the plan provided a basis for effectively 'implementing the Intellectually Disabled Persons' Services Act 1986'. It made 267 recommendations that covered, among other things, appropriate management structures, residential services, education, and the justice system. In order to provide the overarching framework for the implementation of its recommendations, the report advised the government to declare two things: first, 'its commitment to opening up all government provided and funded general services to people with intellectual disabilities'; and, second, to 'ensure that its protective provisions relating to the treatment of individuals with an intellectual disability are applicable to all government agencies'.[49]

The Ten-Year Plan did not recommend the closure of all institutions across the state. But the recommendations dealing with issues around accommodation for people with intellectual disabilities were clearly weighted against large-scale congregate care. For example, one recommendation suggested that the government should 'adopt the policy of supporting the provision of normal community housing for people with intellectual disabilities, where flexibility in the types of homes available can be ensured'. As for large-scale institutional models of care, it was clear that the Ten-Year Plan favoured a policy of deinstitutionalisation wherever it was practicable. The plan pointed out that 'the development of effective community-based accommodation and services' would ultimately render residential training centres superfluous, except in the most extenuating circumstances.

As far as the Ten-Year Plan was concerned, there were only four needs that might 'be met in institutional settings in the future': (1) services for psychiatric treatment of people with intellectual disabilities, which would be provided for at Kingsbury; (2) a secure facility for offenders with intellectual disabilities, which would be provided for at Sandhurst; (3) specialist support services for people in behaviour management programs, which would be provided at Colac; and (4) accommodation services for people with intellectual disabilities realised under Section 20 of the *Intellectually Disabled Persons' Services Act*, that is to say, people charged with criminal offences, who could be housed at St Gabriel's Training Centre, in Balwyn.[50]

If interested observers needed convincing as to where the Ten-Year Plan stood on the issue of deinstitutionalisation, they did not need to look any further than the key outcomes outlined in the plan. Looking ten years into the future, the plan envisaged a time when there would be no child 'resident in Training Centres or large-scale congregate facilities' and where there would also be a significant reduction 'in the numbers of adult clients resident in all forms of large scale congregate facilities'. What that meant for the web of institutions across Victoria was spelled out more clearly in a section of the plan devoted to 'the future of training centre facilities'. Janefield, Pleasant Creek, Sandhurst and Sunbury—which accounted for more than two thirds of all residents with intellectual disabilities—would be closed.[51] And what of the oldest institution for people with intellectual disabilities in Australia? The Kew Cottages, according to the Ten-Year Plan, should 'be closed progressively', and the site on which the cottages stood should 'be redeveloped'.

Chapter 11

A Disastrous Fire (1996)

The hope of the 1988 *Ten Year Plan for the Redevelopment of Intellectual Disability Services: Final Report*, that Kew Cottages should be 'closed progressively' had not eventuated by early 1996, but efforts at normalisation at the cottages, now called Kew Residential Services, were being made. Then disaster struck, changing the trajectory of the cottages' future for ever. The blackest of Kew Cottages' often dark days was 8 April 1996, when some residents with intellectual disabilities died late at night in an inferno in Building 37. In many ways this disaster was a long time coming because the cottages, through much of their 111-year history to that time, had been substandard and a risk to health and wellbeing.[1]

In 2005, several members of the Kew Cottages history research team were shown through a burnt-out building. Viewing the chaos of charred debris, then almost a decade old, was a sombre experience. It seemed largely untouched and just as it might have been once the smoke cleared and the fire cooled all those years earlier. The remains of charred personal effects were still strewn about, and blackened and twisted metals beds stood starkly against burnt-out and collapsed walls and ceilings. With all the features of a rabbit warren, including the remains of rooms and doorways leading off everywhere, the dormitory seemed like a death trap, and indeed it was.

Inferno

Building 37 was erected in 1960 to house forty residents. It was later divided into units 30 and 31 in an effort at normalisation. However, in 1993, far from disappearing, Building 37 was modified to respond to the pressure of numbers at Kew and to boost the building's capacity to sixty-four beds. By 1996 further efforts at normalisation had produced more modifications. Building 37 was 70 x 20 metres in size and in the process of being converted into five flats, with bedrooms adjoining a kitchen, bathroom and living room. According to the floor plan of the same-sized and similar adjoining building, units 28 and 29 had six flats and forty-eight beds. It revealed a similar labyrinth of flats with kitchens, day rooms, bathrooms and shared bedrooms, with a plethora of connecting corridors and doors (Figure 11.1). However, in early April 1996, Building 37's modifications were unfinished, and the fire sprinkler system was not operational.

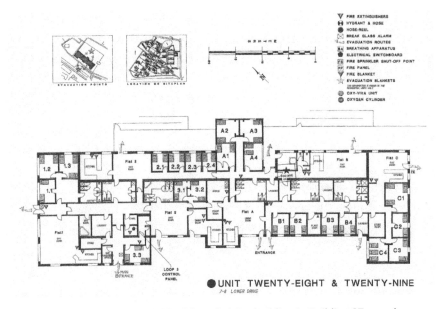

Figure 11.1: Units 28 & 29 of the adjoining building to Building 37 reveal the same labyrinth of rooms and doorways
(Courtesy Kew Residential Services)

It rained on the night of Easter Monday 8 April 1996. The forty-six residents of Building 37 were bedded down as usual behind locked doors to prevent wandering. Two carers, one for each unit, were on duty. At 10.49 pm a fire erupted in Flat E of Unit 31, Building 37. Initially, the carer of Unit 31 was oblivious to the outbreak because the alarm system was centralised elsewhere on site.[2] The Melbourne Fire Brigade (MFB) was alerted at 10.56 pm. However, owing to a deficiency in the internal Kew fire alarm system, the MFB operations officer who rang Kew Residential Services to confirm was told there was no fire. Soon after, the cottages' central staff alerted the carers in Units 30 and 31. Upon checking, they discovered thick smoke in the roof space of Flat E in Unit 31 and alerted the central office at Kew, which then contacted the MFB.

The MFB, based at the Richmond Fire Station, arrived with great rapidity at 11.01 pm. Fire officers went to Kew often, mostly in response to false alarms, and knew the layout well. But they took every call-out with equal seriousness and always took three instead of the usual two fire-fighting appliances because of the potential problems of rescuing people with intellectual disabilities. Upon arrival, the MFB officers witnessed flames shooting from the roof of Unit 31. Other fire units arrived shortly after. Fire officers quickly checked the spread of the fire into Unit 30 and focused on the centre of the fire. However, it had engulfed Flat E and spread into Flats B, C and D. A later coronial inquiry found the residents in Flat E had by this stage probably died from smoke inhalation before there was any chance of rescue. Officers engaged the fire in Flat E, which was now filled with black smoke and flames rolling across the ceiling. Flames also burst through the windows and began to melt the aluminium shutters. After fifteen minutes of fighting the fire through locked doors, and with temperatures reaching 600° Celsius, officers were ordered to withdraw as the roof timbers and walls began to collapse (Figures 11.2 and 11.3). The fire was under control by 11.29 pm.

The evacuation of the residents of Building 37 on the night was horrendous. The building, with its labyrinthine corridors and multiple locked doors, was filled with black smoke down to a half metre from the floor in some areas. The fire's heat quickly became intense. Kew Residential Services staff had to evacuate residents with mobility problems, diminished hearing and vision, psychiatric and intellectual disabilities, and possibly impairment due to medication as well. Some residents had no appreciation of the dangers, and, once rescued, several tried to re-enter the building.

A Disastrous Fire (1996)

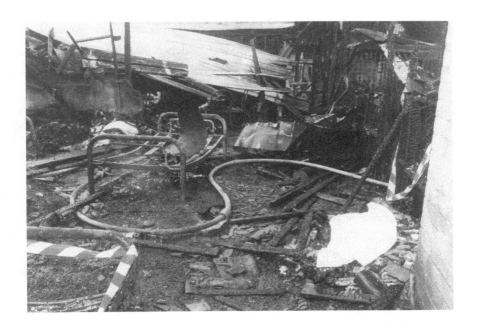

Figures 11.2 and 11.3: Interior of Unit 31, Building 37, after the fire
(Courtesy Victoria Police)

One MFB fire fighter, Ian Morris, recalled the confusion inside: 'The residents were all over the place. There was evidence that they were moving around within the building. Some were still in bed, others were in the corridors and we also located one in the toilet'. Morris found two men still inside Flat C, either asleep or smoke affected. He tried to rouse them and lift them out, but, being 'worn out' by fighting the fire in intense heat, he sought help to carry them out.[3]

Later forensic investigations concluded the fire began in bedding in Bedroom 1 of Flat E. The subsequent Coronial Inquest found that the occupant of one of the three beds in that room was the likely cause of the fire. He was given the pseudonym of 'Paul' to protect his identity during the investigation, as he 'did not understand the consequences of his actions'.[4] The evidence was not rock solid, but he was the only resident from Flat E to escape the fire. 'Paul' had a habit of collecting things. In the past, and significantly on that day, he had a cigarette lighter he had found during an excursion. It was confiscated. Later at the cottages, he acquired another, probably left by a staff member, which was again confiscated. The Coronial Inquest found 'Paul' had the motor skills to operate a lighter and, after being evacuated from the fire, was again discovered with an operational lighter. The state coroner, Graeme Johnstone, whose investigation uncovered 'Paul's' previous fascination with lighters over several years, declared: 'it would seem that the failure to record incidents of this nature or to read files thoroughly was not an unusual practice among the staff'.[5] However, Johnstone praised staff overall for their bravery during the fire. He also commended the firefighters.

Of the ten people in Flat E, all grown men, nine died from burns and smoke inhalation. The press called them 'the innocents'. They had lived in institutional care for a total of 286 years, most of those spent at Kew: an average of about thirty years each. Their disabilities were such that today they would not be in an institution. Their details in brief are as follows. Alan Negri 61, in institutional care at Sunbury since his twenties, but not at Kew Cottages until Caloola's closure in 1992. Joseph Raymond 35, who suffered from Down Syndrome and was at Kew from 1969. Adrian Edmunds 39, who also had Down Syndrome and was at Kew most of his life. Thomas Patrick Grant 36, resident at Kew since he was ten and admitted for 'mental retardation'. Shayne Newman 38, who suffered from cerebral palsy and had been at Kew since 1972. Bruce Mark Haw 39, who suffered from Fragile X syndrome and was resident at Kew from 1961. Stanley Matthews 42, who suffered from cerebral palsy and was admitted to Kew in 1959. Peter Arthur Bernard 37, who had autism and was admitted in 1964. Ronald Aldridge 31, who was in Kew most of his life and remained unknown to his four siblings until his death.[6]

The Reaction

Melbourne awoke to the tragic news on 9 April. Of course, an institutional fire was not unique in Melbourne, or elsewhere for that matter. Those with long memories might recall that six elderly women had died in a fire at the Kew Mental Hospital in July 1968, and the staggering number of thirty men died in August 1966 in a conflagration at the William Booth Men's Home in Little Lonsdale Street.[7] However, the fire on Easter Monday 1996 led to an extraordinary outpouring of grief and concern not only for the dead but also for those still living at Kew Cottages. The people of Melbourne were now clearly attuned to the suffering of those with intellectual disabilities. And the expression of concern once again revealed the role the press played in prompting this response.

Both Melbourne dailies, the *Age* and the *Herald Sun*, expressed shock and alarm, as did the television news. The front-page headlines of the *Herald Sun* over the next two days in massive-size font boomed 'NINE DIE IN DORM FIRE' and 'DEATH OF 9 INNOCENTS'. On 10 April the *Herald Sun* devoted seven full pages to the fire, in addition to an editorial, letters to the editor, the initial tributes in the *in memoriam* columns, and an emotive cartoon by Mark Knight of a hefty fireman carrying a slim resident in striped pyjamas with the caption: 'They Ain't Heavy … They're Our Brothers'. Aerial and ground images of the burnt building were splashed across the pages (Figure 11.4). The tragedy was magnified by an MFB statement that sprinklers recently installed in the units were six weeks away from being operational, having been delayed because asbestos was found in the roof of the building.[8]

Figure 11.4: Aerial view showing the burnt-out section of Building 37 the morning after the fire
(Courtesy Victoria Police)

The *Herald Sun*'s editorial on 19 April opened with the challenge that 'the test of a civilised society is how to help those who cannot help themselves'. It reflected on the deaths of these men in horrendous circumstances, the locked doors and sprinkler inadequacy, and the failure of government to staff the units properly (a ratio of one staff member to twenty-three residents being judged totally inadequate). It concluded that a cut in funds of 17 per cent over four years, with recreational programs being 'slashed from 39 hours to six, does not seem to meet community expectations'. Paul Gray, a journalist, wrote that the Kennett Liberal government, in power since 1992 and recently re-elected, needed to end constant cuts to community services. He pointed to the two, often-conflicting, motivations then characteristic of government service provision—first, economic rationalist ideas arguing that community services should be curtailed and individuals made to be more self-reliant, and second, the view that normalisation should be further encouraged to end nineteenth-century attitudes to institutionalisation. He concluded: 'even before yesterday's fire all the evidence pointed to the need for a vigorous re-think of the entire government approach to institutions and care for those in most need'.[9] The *Australian* newspaper's headline on page one, atop fire images and diagrams of the facility and locked doors, also took an anti-government line: 'Killer Fire Inquiry Demanded'.[10]

The *Age*'s page one headline 'Disaster was "Avoidable"', was accompanied by four pages of articles, diagrams, maps and dismal images of a burnt-out building and people in grief. Its coverage focused on three things: the tragedy of the inoperable sprinklers due to delays over asbestos; the denial by Premier Kennett that government cutbacks had anything to do with the fire; and the belief by parents of Kew residents that cutbacks were to blame. Geoff Welchman, president of the Kew Cottages and St. Nicholas Parents' Association, stated that funding for Kew was never a priority, and for fifteen years his group had 'pushed and pushed for an upgrade of the services'. One report said some of the men in Flat E died in their beds, others as they tried to crawl to the door. MFB Inspector Ron Haines said it was the worst fire he had witnessed in twenty years: 'They had little chance'.[11]

Opinion pieces flowed, discussing economic rationalism, government funding cuts and staffing reductions. The Victorian Advocacy League for Individuals with Disability (VALID), Victoria's peak body for people with intellectual disabilities and their families, joined the conversation. Kevin Stone, its director, issued a press release outlining questions to be addressed at the coronial inquiry about staff-to-resident ratios, locked doors and budget cuts. The media release said $47 million or 17 per cent had been cut from a budget of $300 million over three years, $32 million from accommodation services alone. The previous Labor government, led by Joan Kirner, pledged $30 million over three years to bring services into the twentieth century, but budget restraints by the Kennett government had caused that to be shelved. Kevin Stone called for the reintroduction of the pledged amount and urged that it be made recurrent.[12]

The context of these recent government cuts was that Australia, and the world, had experienced a recession, soaring interest rates, and rising unemployment in 1990. In Victoria, the Pyramid Building Society collapsed with debts of $2 billion and the State Bank of Victoria failed as well, leading to the resignation of the Labor Premier John Cain Jr, who had told the public the circumstances of these institutions were not dire. The Kennett government came to power in 1992 and began instituting deep budget cuts and the controversial economic rationalist policy of privatisation and sale of government assets and infrastructure. Over several years the government privatised and sold off water, gas and electricity utilities, prisons (including the 140-year-old Pentridge Prison), and other government properties. It was the biggest shake-up of government ownership in the nation's history. A neo-liberal agenda was the main driving force, but cost savings in tough times were also a motivation. Both motives affected Kew Cottages.

Elizabeth Hastings, the disability discrimination commissioner at the Human Rights and Equal Opportunity Commission, argued for taking a different tack. This reflected her own disability. She first experienced discrimination as a child in 1957 when banned from immigrating to Australia with her English family because of her physical disability.[13] The ban was overturned, although her family had to pay her passage from the United Kingdom. Hastings rose above that dismal start to become a psychologist, board member and, later, a leading disability rights activist, all before disability discrimination legislation was in place. Hastings' response to the Kew fire was to place it in the framework of equality before the law. 'I have not heard', she wrote, 'the more obvious question raised as to whether it is legal to lock people in rooms without working fire protection systems'. Hastings, who was confined to a wheelchair, discussed the many legal failures to assist those with disabilities, despite disability having been added to anti-discrimination laws in 1986. She added: 'In general, police, courts and other personnel in our justice system have limited awareness of dealing fairly with people who have a disability'. The courts in particular, she continued, have failed to provide legal frameworks to protect those with a disability 'from the violation of their fundamental rights'.[14]

The *Age* referred to a confidential report of 1995 by the Department of Health and Community Services, which detailed overcrowding, staff shortages and safety issues at Kew Residential Services. The report stated that 'the physical condition of Kew is generally poor and would require a major investment to bring it up to an accommodation standard of the quality that would be expected today'. It added the comment that it would be a 'questionable investment' given the trend to deinstitutionalisation. But Jude Wallace, who had earlier recommended the closure of Caloola, and Ben Bodna, the former Victorian public advocate, both declared the state government had failed in its duty of care. Wallace called for a far-ranging inquiry into the treatment of the intellectually disabled. This call was backed by the peak body for people with intellectual disabilities, VALID.[15]

The *Age*'s Insight team embarked on its own four-week investigation, termed 'Victoria's Forgotten People'. In mid-May its investigative team revealed a system in crisis, as well as in breach of its own state *Intellectually Disabled Persons' Services Act* (1986) and probably of United Nations' conventions as well. The Insight team found that hundreds of people with an intellectual disability in institutions were exposed to fire risks; that too many were being subjected to unnecessary treatment with mood-altering medications; and that a thousand cases a month of chemical restraint, seclusion or aversion therapy were never investigated. Outside the institutions it was no better. It was estimated that there were 40,000 people with intellectual disabilities in Victoria, but 26,500 were not on state registers and thus were receiving few or no services. About 3,600 were waiting for urgent or crisis accommodation, and 1,400 people were living with parents aged over sixty. Indeed, a survey of seventy carers of children with an intellectual disability in the Echuca region found that five carers were in their nineties, eight in their eighties and fifteen in their seventies. Throughout the system there was a large unmet need, yet, despite this, the state government over three years had cut $42.3 million from the intellectual disability sector.[16]

The Insight team also referred to a 1995 community visitors' report to the Office of the Public Advocate, which slammed Kew Cottages for the eighth time for poor provision of community activities for residents. The report, which suggested conditions at Kew had slid back to those of over a generation earlier, was also critical of the access given to visitors by Health and Community Services. According to the visitors' 1995 report, people were moved from their beds at 7 am, showered, then sat in a day room with thirty other residents 'doing nothing day after day. The major highlight for these people is the arrival of breakfast, lunch, dinner and supper'. Only 217 of 640 residents at Kew Residential Services had access to community programs. Some experienced stress, being couped up with thirty others all day, and chemical restraint was used to keep others under control. The visitors found some units were without hot water. Several had no toilet paper or a locked kitchen because a few residents stuffed the rolls down the toilet or drank excess coffee. All were made to suffer the consequences of actions by these individuals. Many were denied access to their bedrooms during daytime hours, forcing them to sleep on couches or watch television all day.[17]

One of the saddest of ironies was that, on the morning after the fire, a letter to the editor appeared in the *Age*, written and published just hours before the tragic inferno. The letter was from Robert F. Riddiford of Thornbury, who asked why a society that cheerfully spent $80 million on renovating Parliament House, $30 million to demolish the still usable Gas and Fuel buildings (where Federation Square now stands) for the view, and $25,000 on the premier's Parliament House dining table, could not afford to fund Kew, 'so that its residents, completely innocent of any wrongdoing can eat as well as prisoners?'.[18]

Within a week, the Melbourne dailies had published several dozen letters from concerned and outraged members of the public. Many authors attacked the government's cost cutting and lack of staff at Kew. Alan Jones of Macedon, a former nurse in government hospitals, left such work because of the effects on the weak and vulnerable of reduced funding and under-staffing in public institutions: 'If you speak out you are pro-union, pro-Labor, and anti-management and anti the current Government'. The fire was 'blood on the hands of this Government'.[19] Vivien Millane of Kew, who worked for a school, pointed to the different fire safety expectations at her workplace and those at Kew, yet the vulnerability of Kew residents demanded 'the highest standard of care'.[20]

Some correspondents wanted Kew closed as quickly as possible. Anne McDonald of Brunswick wrote 'we lock them up, we bear the blame for their deaths and for their lives', and Rosemary Crossley, who had agitated for the closure of St. Nicholas Hospital over fifteen years earlier, declared 'the residents of Kew deserve no less'.[21] Vic Symons, of Hyde Park in South Australia, added: 'it is clear the retention of these Dickensian facilities is nothing less than a human rights issue'.[22] More measured was David Green, a community visitor at Kew and the state's public advocate. To Green, each resident was an individual, who 'has a history and a future and that future is profoundly affected by the future of Kew Residential Services itself'.[23] John Hanrahan of Balwyn simply penned a poem that began: 'They died as they had not lived, on their hands and knees'.[24]

If the public was shocked by the fire, parents and family of those with intellectual disabilities, wherever they were living in Victoria, were traumatised. An 'Angry and sad mother of Elwood', who had a 'severely disabled son' but not residing at Kew, wrote to the *Herald Sun* to say she was 'devastated by the Kew disaster'. It was 'heartbreaking' to place a child in care, but, with staff and funding cuts, it was now 'terrifying' as well. Children in care, who were the victims of chance, must be given all the care of the home. She pleaded with Premier Kennett: 'get your priorities right and really look at the situation'.[25]

Those with children in Kew itself were highly traumatised, given the immediacy of the event to their own family member's situation. Rosalie Trower said parents had pleaded for more funding and services for years, as Kew Cottages 'slid into crumbling decrepitude'. But none, she added, 'envisaged such a cataclysmic disaster as the inferno that engulfed the nine trusting men as they slept'.[26] Zoe and Don Anderson, parents of Bruce, aged 34, who escaped with serious smoke inhalation, were relieved but terrified by thoughts of his vulnerability. He could not speak and communicated by a basic sign language, so his reaction at the time and later can only be guessed at. He was still recovering in hospital, with his Kew carer, a young man named Yohan, by his side. The Andersons were scathing about the government's policy: 'a case of economic rationalism gone mad'.[27] Elizabeth Silke, sister of Peter Otis, hoped for a positive outcome from his death, while his brother Paul noted ironically that, ignored in life, 'they only wanted to know about him in death'.[28]

All parents nevertheless expressed their unreserved praise for the staff and firefighters who saved so many. James Ballinger of Quambatook, stepfather to Joseph Richmond, one of the victims of the fire, said visiting Kew monthly with Mary, Joseph's mother, was like visiting family: 'we can't speak highly enough of the staff'. However, he was tortured by the question of why Joseph, who had Down Syndrome, was in Kew at all.[29]

Many of the Kew Residential Services on-site staff were as devastated as Kew families. During the fire, staff had run into the burning building repeatedly to help fire fighters rescue the residents. The two night staff in Building 37, Chea Earpeng (Peng) and Bartful Frlan, were especially commended by the coronial inquiry. Nurse Julie Carpenter, interviewed in 2006, said that Peng, a Cambodian refugee, had entered the building time and time again. He collapsed from smoke inhalation and had to be rescued and sent to hospital. Peng suffered a 'total breakdown', and Carpenter concluded: 'I don't think he'll ever work again in his life'.[30] Helen Wilson, who arrived for work the next morning after the fire, recalled the fire trucks, police and ambulance vehicles everywhere, and remembered of the staff, 'everyone was just like walking ghosts that day, honestly, yes it was just awful'.[31]

In the aftermath of the fire, the public was presented with intimate stories of residents and their families through the efforts of newspaper feature writers. Geoff Welchman, president of the Kew Cottages Parents' Association, and his wife, Elsie, had a healthy eleven-month-old son, David, who in 1957 contracted encephalitis and suffered severe brain damage. They cared for him until he was six, despite his destructive behaviour, which took its toll on Elsie as well as David's three siblings. In the sixties they helped found the Oakleigh Centre for those with intellectual disabilities. Similarly, the Andersons, Don and Zoe, helped establish a special school for those with autism. Indeed, as we have seen, many facilities and most advocacy groups were formed by the efforts of parents. Others sought improvements as individuals. John and Anne Dusink's son John, who was in Unit 30, escaped the blaze. He had been admitted twenty-five years earlier, and, since that time, they had raised $350,000 for the residents by selling cheap jeans from their house. The Dusinks declared that services had plummeted in recent times and the residents had been 'forgotten because there is no vote in disabled people and they are powerless to speak out about how they are forced to live'.[32]

Rosalie Trower had a similar story. Her son Steven contracted chicken pox when twelve months old, suffering encephalitis and brain damage as a result. Her husband Eric was a seaman, whose absences resulted in Rosalie Trower caring for Steven mostly alone. She found a day care placement for him in Oakleigh, one of the few available. She met the Welchmans at the Oakleigh Centre. When Rosalie became ill, a residency was found for Steven at Greensborough. As Steven grew, Mrs Trower, along with other parents, founded the Kindloin Group for disabled adults at Balnarring, funded by an opportunity shop in Armadale. Unfortunately, Steven had a fall while collecting garbage bins for the Kindloin Centre, the much-loved job that gave him such pride. He suffered further brain damage and had to leave the centre at Balnarring. Rejecting a place at Caloola because of potentially violent inmates, and now alone as her husband Eric Trower had died, Rosalie sought a place for Steven at Kew Cottages in 1983. When told there was no room at Kew, Trower threatened to take Steven home and administer a drug overdose, so 'he can die with dignity in his bed with his little dog'. She finally gained a place later that year. Kew Cottages was good for Steven, then aged 28, and remained so for a decade before services were cut after 1992.[33]

Premier Jeff Kennett quickly deflected calls for a judicial inquiry from the state opposition and elsewhere by declaring such a tragedy should not be politicised. Kennett rejected the idea that cuts to staff and funding were a factor, and said his government was trying to address 150 [*sic*] years of neglect. A police and coronial inquiry would direct his government's response to the fire, and a judicial inquiry was unnecessary.[34] Rosalie Trower and Hilda Logan, whose autistic son Andrew aged 40 had been in residence at the cottages for 28 years, were both outraged at Kennett's comments. They pointed out that government cuts, especially the 10 per cent in 1992, were responsible for 'the miserable life our children have been leading'. Residents' programs had been cut from thirty to six hours a week, and thrice-weekly swimming sessions had all but ended as staff were cut from 161 to 51. The residents' daily food budget was just 65 per cent of what Langi Kal Kal prisoners received. The two women added: if 'those men had not lived in rabbit warrens, they would not have perished'.[35] Myra Hilgendorf, mother of Johanna 49, who had been in Kew since 1983, simply said of Kennett: 'He's trying to dodge the issue'.[36]

An *Age* editorial called for a wide-ranging judicial inquiry, believing government assurances of a review of safety were inadequate. It pointed to a long string of fires in institutions, including 381 in supported accommodation in 1992 alone.[37] Others echoed these calls, including legal and welfare groups such as the Brotherhood of St Laurence and the Kew Cottages Parents' Association. The Australian Democrats senator-elect, Lyn Allison, presented a petition with 1,080 signatures in support. However, over five weeks later, the Kennett government again declared its faith in a forthcoming coronial inquiry, which many believed would narrowly focus on fire safety and ignore budget and other wider issues.[38]

The government's opposition to a wider inquiry revealed a deep disinclination to improve services at Kew in this climate of deinstitutionalisation. Expenditure would have seemed unnecessary to those planning the facility's eventual closure. In April 1995 the Kew Cottages Parents' Association, which represented a thousand parents of 641 residents, had issued a writ against the Victorian government. It claimed the *Intellectually Disabled Persons' Services Act 1986* imposed a duty of care on government not to reduce services for those in Kew Cottages. The government lodged an appeal before the case went to court, claiming the allegations were scandalous, vexatious or frivolous, and were an abuse of the process of the court. Justice Geoff Eames ruled against the government in August 1995, so the government took the Eames' decision to the Court of Appeal. At the time of the fire no date had been set for this appeal. However, the fire reignited the resolve of the parents' association, led by Geoff Welchman. Its solicitors, Blake Dawson Waldron, filed for a priority listing.[39] The association was told that Premier Kennett was playing hard ball, threatening to charge legal costs to individual parents if the parents' litigation failed.[40] In August 1996 the Court of Appeal unanimously dismissed the government's efforts to stop the case.[41]

Deeply emotional memorial services for the nine residents were held, including one in the Kew Cottages Rose Garden on the day after the fire. The editor of the *Age* later wrote that 'a mood close to despair gripped many Victorians. Despair, tinged with a touch of guilt; they were the forgotten people and, because we had forgotten them, nine of their number had perished cruelly and needlessly'.[42] Individual family tributes and funeral services followed. Father Jim Scannell, a former chaplain at the cottages, organised an ecumenical memorial service at Sacred Heart Kew on the corner of Glenferrie and Cotham roads on 12 April. The service was attended by hundreds of people connected to Kew. One year later the Kew Cottages Parents' Association erected a small granite stele with each man's names engraved into it.[43]

Condolences rolled into the parents' association.[44] Many were from other disability groups in Victoria, interstate and beyond, including a telegram from Rescare New Zealand. Others were from those who had worked at Kew, including the social worker Irene Higgins, now a committee member of the Older Women's Network Victoria, based in Ross House, Flinders Lane. Higgins wrote: 'most of our members are grandmothers, great-grandmothers or great aunts. Many of us have had contact with intellectually handicapped people—in our own families, friends or through work'.[45] Other cards and letters were from businesses linked to Kew, and a few came from unions, veterans' groups and private citizens. Some like the Victorian Council of Social Services extended sorrow and also promised action. Patsy Morrison, its executive director, wrote that her coalition group had initiated lobbying. The group had also partnered with five researchers at the *Age* to produce an investigative report because 'the issues at Kew Cottages are symptomatic of an appallingly dysfunctional service system'.[46] The Daimaru Emporium sent four boxes of clothing.

The Kew Cottages Parents' Association organised an ecumenical service at St Paul's Cathedral on 17 April. Premier Jeff Kennett apologised owing to a 'prior engagement', an excuse many of the Kew parents found offensive. Over 1,500 people attended, including nine residents of Kew bearing red roses and candles. Dignitaries who attended included the governor, Richard McGarvie, John Brumby (leader of the opposition), and the local member and state attorney-general Jan Wade. The music was by Val Pyers' notable Victoria Chorale. The dean of Melbourne, Bishop James Grant, gave the address. Bishop Grant recalled that, despite the efforts of Dr Cunningham Dax and the Minus Children's Appeal to improve the lives of those at Kew over the years, the residents were never a jewel in Victoria's crown, remaining 'the poor relation in terms of priority and resource'. However, 'their deaths can yet be fruitful beyond their imagining' by making Kew Residential Services a centre of excellence for research, training and the care of people with intellectual disabilities: 'this is the missing jewel in our State's crown'.[47]

Perhaps surprisingly, many Kew parents wanted Kew Cottages to remain. Bruce, son of Heather de-Pyper Bottomley-Tipping of Wonthaggi, entered Kew aged seven after contracting meningitis and suffering a stroke and constant seizures. His mother said he was admitted to Kew in 1963 after violent and destructive behaviour towards property and family members. She became a volunteer at Kew and regularly took Bruce on outings. He loved the staff, who returned his feelings, she said, despite him being 'a fair cow at times. He's very big and very intimidating'. Kew was needed, she added, as 'there is no way people like my son can be integrated into society. It sounds good in theory but it's just not practical'.[48]

Those who headed the Kew Cottages Parents' Association held similar views and desired a bright future for the cottages and their children there. June Guest, a former president of the association, rejected calls for Kew Cottages to close by those who did not know it intimately. She declared that Kew parents, and those who worked closely with the residents, knew their children's needs best. Not every institution was bad, and not every person with an intellectual disability could live outside them. She called for Kew Cottages to return to the admired model it once was, and to become a village 'where independent group living is combined with overall supervision and there is, also, congregate care for those who need it'.[49] Rosalie Trower also wanted the cottages to stay and become a centre for excellence in care, as Bishop Grant had suggested.[50] Geoff Welchman agreed, saying even the government believed that 450 of the 641 at Kew 'will need to stay in congregate care, with their friends and family on tap'.[51]

Kew parents faced massive opposition to their desire for their family members to remain at Kew Cottages, given the shift in the discourse around intellectual disability to normalisation and deinstitutionalisation. However, their resolve hardened despite the fire, and many supported a cluster-housing alternative. Don and Zoe Anderson, whose son Bruce survived the fire, wrote to Premier Kennett in late April with a series of questions about funding, one being why the association's cluster-housing scheme proposal was constantly shelved?[52] A copy of their letter in the association's files was marked 'NO reply'. Mary Walsh, of the Australian Parent Advocacy group based in Bundaberg Queensland, wrote to the association to express sorrow about the fire. Walsh added that, when interviewing a top bureaucrat in Community Services Victoria in 1991, she had advised him to listen to parents and 'slow down the process of de-institutionalisation'. He replied: 'we have made a commitment to close these places and put these people into the community. We will do that'.[53]

After the fire, however, the government began renovations at Kew Cottages in response to public criticism over conditions and in recognition that any closure of Kew Cottages would take time. In early July, the *Age* obtained a confidential report by consulting engineers, Umow Lai, completed in August 1994. It had stated that sleeping areas at the cottages in 1994 put residents at great risk. Some areas had no fire detection; exit signs and emergency lighting were not provided for some buildings; bedroom walls and bedding were highly flammable; and staff numbers were insufficient in the event of an emergency.[54] However, government action, even after the fire, was less than adequate. The Kew Cottages Parents' Association president, Geoff Welchman, stated that the $1.8 million sprinkler system installed since the fire only covered dormitories and bedrooms and not kitchens and living areas.[55] The government seemed to be doing the bare minimum because moving people out was still high on the agenda. Once again Kew Cottages suffered materially because it was seen as temporary. And Geoff Welchman was again outspoken when forty Kew residents, most of whom had been affected by the fire, were moved into community-based housing: 'They've been burnt out of their homes and now they're being shot into the community'. He vowed to press on with the association's Supreme Court action.[56]

The Coronial Inquest officially opened on 14 October 1996, intensifying the pain for families six months after the fire. Peter Aldridge was still struggling to come to terms with the loss of his brother Ronald 31, who tragically was unknown to Peter until he died in the fire. He applied for the case file on his brother, but his request was denied as the coroner needed the files of the deceased. Peter Aldridge met staff at the funeral, who told him of Ronald's sunny nature, his love of toy cars, and how, being a resident for forty years, Ronald 'ran the place'. Aldridge, whose family lived in Ararat, wistfully remarked that his late brother Ronald could have been placed in Aradale, which had been open when Ronald was placed in care: 'we could have had him out at weekends and visited him'.[57]

As the inquiry opened, Rosalie Trower, mother of Steven and a parents' association committee member, wrote: 'old wounds open, our hearts again bleed for the innocent, gentle boys and we parents continue our struggle'. She added, no doubt aware of the narrowness of the inquiry: 'we parents

A Disastrous Fire (1996)

pin our hopes on our Supreme Court action'.[58] Nevertheless, the association was determined to keep a vigil at the inquiry. It drew up a roster of thirteen parents, beside members of the committee, to ensure it would follow 'the entire proceedings of the Inquiry'. The president, Geoff Welchman, attended every sitting, which heard evidence for a mammoth eighty-one days at the Coroner's Court, and two days on site at Kew Residential Services. It is perhaps not surprising he had by-pass heart surgery not long afterwards.[59]

The Coronial Inquest led by the state's coroner, Graeme Johnstone, produced a meticulous 496-page report that vindicated the claims of parents. Johnstone found the 'State of Victoria' owed a 'duty of care' to the residents of Kew Cottages and the nine who died. Consultants had warned successive governments for ten years, far too long in his view, that fire safety systems were inadequate (Figure 11.5). The present government was commended for making efforts to upgrade fire systems since the fire. However,

> the State of Victoria has contributed to the fire and deaths of the nine residents because, despite all warnings it had received over the decade from 1986, no proper fire safety system was in place at the time of the fire.

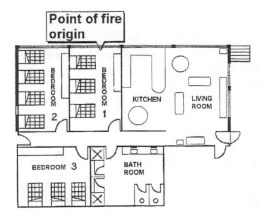

Plan of Building 37, 6 Lower Drive, KRS

Figure 11.5: Drawing of Flat E and the fire's origin for the Coronial Inquest
(Courtesy State Coroner's Office, Victoria)

The state contributed in other ways, which he outlined in detail in the report. No consultants were implicated. Graeme Johnstone was encouraged by the fact that the government began upgrading fire safety after the fire and had committed $75.5 million to fire safety work across all facilities managed by the Department of Human Services.[60] Satisfied, but not comforted, the Kew Cottages Parents' Association withdrew its class action before the Supreme Court, initiated in 1995 and still pending at the time of the handing down of the coroner's report on 17 October 1997.

When the fire destroyed Units 30 and 31, killing nine men, there were about 640 residents in Kew Cottages. The fire sped up the process of normalisation and deinstitutionalisation that had languished in the early nineties due to budget restraints, since both processes promised to be a costly business. A decade later, numbers of residents at the cottages dropped to about a hundred. In 2005, the Kew Cottages historical research team met with many of the parents' association stalwarts to talk about the fire and the cottages' history. There was a sense of exhilaration from parents that Kew Cottages was in the spotlight of research and that someone was taking them seriously after years of lobbying governments. But the pain of remembering the fire was still raw, especially as Kew Cottages were facing imminent and irrevocable closure.

Louise Godwin, executive officer of the association, recalled that the fire was just one of many traumas. She remarked that one Kew mother she had spoken to recently was in the process of seeing her son being relocated from Kew. Godwin commented:

> this 'redevelopment' is forcing every mother to go right back to their decision (all those decades ago) to place their child in Kew. Right back to the sorrow of realising their child had an ID. Back to the moment in which they decided they couldn't cope. Back to the underlying guilt of having placed them in Kew.[61]

Chapter 12

Deinstitutionalisation (1985–2008)

On 7 September 1999, three years and five months after the fire ripped through Building 37 at the Kew Cottages, the Victorian premier, Jeff Kennett, vowed to close the cottages by the end of 2010. Kennett was then two weeks out from an election that he would ultimately lose, though, given his commanding lead in the polls, he was no doubt confident of his ability to fulfil that promise. Kennett's vow was part of a broader Liberal Party community services policy, which included ending large-scale institutions for people with intellectual disabilities. Kew Cottages was a nineteenth-century relic that 'belongs in the past'.[1] Certainly Victorian governments had been committed to deinstitutionalisation, in one form or another, since the Evans Report of 1978. Since then, six institutions for people with intellectual disabilities had been closed, and the number of residents in large-scale congregate care facilities had fallen from 4,439 in 1978 to 873 in 1999.[2]

The Closure of St. Nicholas

The first institution to be closed in Victoria was the St. Nicholas Hospital, which shut down in 1985. St. Nicholas, a small institution in Carlton that housed just over a hundred children with severe and profound intellectual disabilities, did not necessarily fit into the framework for deinstitutionalisation as envisioned in the Evans Report. This report recommended that adult training centres in country areas should be closed first. But, in other ways, St. Nicholas was a prime candidate for closure. First, it was a gloomy, old institution, whose main buildings were in need

FAILED AMBITIONS

of urgent repair. Second, the institution 'occupied 1.25 hectares of prime real estate' close to Melbourne's CBD. It was anticipated that the sale of the property would easily cover 'the costs involved with relocating the residents to less restrictive accommodation within the community'.[3] Finally, the institution had been the subject of intense public scrutiny and debate in the late 1970s. This was sparked by a ward assistant, Rosemary Crossley, who claimed that some of the residents at St. Nicholas were of average intelligence and should never have been placed in an institution. No one wanted that sort of attention, and it was perhaps no surprise then that, when the Health Commission recommended the closure of St. Nicholas in 1981, the Victorian government offered its full support.

Four guiding principles underpinned the closure of St. Nicholas. First, people with intellectual disabilities had the right to live in the community. Second, irrespective of the level of their disability that right should stand. Third, such people should have access to a day program located somewhere beyond their place of residence and access to generic services (as distinct from specialist services) wherever practicable. A fourth principle was that the care provided by staff in any newly established community residential unit should be family-like, rather than custodial, although what that meant in practical terms was never clear.

It is worth briefly considering the language used in relation to group homes. Researchers have probably not paid enough attention to understanding the most salient characteristics of living environments, and we tend to fall back on simple descriptors such as 'institution' and 'group home' without offering clear conceptual or operational definitions of these terms. Essentially, a community residential unit is a shared group home for people with intellectual disabilities, where between two and five people live together, though each resident has their own bedroom. Yet, like so much of the language surrounding intellectual disability, the term 'group home' carries the added burden of stigmatisation. Group homes were first known as 'Community Residential Units', although new terms later emerged such as 'Specialist Disability Accommodations' (SDA) and 'Service Level Agreements' (SLA).

In the two years after it was announced that St. Nicholas was to close, various working parties carried out the detailed planning needed to relocate a hundred people into community residential units. In practical terms, this meant the purchase of twenty-three houses situated in ordinary residential settings, and near to transport, local shopping strips, and parks. Each house would accommodate two to five residents and would be funded to provide essential equipment such as portable hoists, specialist furniture and medical equipment. Selection of houses began in April 1983. Each was furnished as comfortably and attractively as possible, and each bedroom was decorated to reflect the incoming resident's individuality or personality. In July 1984, the first St. Nicholas residents were relocated into their newly acquired homes, and on 20 March 1985 the final group of five residents moved out and the institution was closed.[4]

The successful closure of St. Nicholas and the relocation of its residents into the community was without precedent in Victoria. Even so, it is important to remember that, by the early 1980s, the deinstitutionalisation of people with intellectual disability was occurring—at different speeds and to varying degrees—in many countries throughout the world. In fact, by 1985, when St. Nicholas finally closed, the UK, the USA and several Scandinavian countries were further down the deinstitutionalisation path than Australia. And the stated aims underpinning the closure of St. Nicholas—to increase residents' participation in normal life routines, to increase community contact, and to increase the likelihood that residents would realise their potential—would have resonated in any of those countries working to replace their institutions with community services.

Whether the closure of St. Nicholas achieved those aims is harder to say. An evaluation, published in 1988, suggested that deinstitutionalisation in this case had achieved 'some, but not all' of its stated objectives.[5] For example, the report found that deinstitutionalisation had resulted in 'significant improvements in adaptive behaviour', greater contact between residents and their parents, and had also led to 'more flexible daily routines' and an overall 'increase in leisure activities and holidays'.

However, the evaluation also cautiously noted that, according to the consulting paediatrician at St. Nicholas, the health or physical status of almost one-third of the residents had deteriorated in the two years since relocation, while the physical status of the remaining two-thirds could at best be described as unchanged.

The evaluation also raised another important point, noting that many parents 'felt the project had not been well planned or implemented'. The underlying implication was that the successful closure of institutions in the future might hinge on effective community consultation and an open dialogue with the parents of those residents being relocated into their new homes. Yet, for all their disappointment about the 'lack of adequate consultation', most parents remained 'reasonably confident about the success of the project' as a whole. They were mostly happy with the look and feel of the new homes, and most were also confident that their child would be happy in their new environment. One mother, who 'cried and cried' on the day her daughter moved, recalled the emotion that welled up inside her when she considered the implications of the closure of St. Nicholas. 'I never dreamed' my daughter 'could live in such a beautiful place', she said. 'She's nearly 18', the mother went on, 'when many, many girls move to their own place. And she looks so happy'.[6] As an advertisement for the policy of deinstitutionalisation, you could not get much better than that, and in some respects the closure of St. Nicholas served as a template for the closure of other institutions as deinstitutionalisation in Victoria moved into a more urgent phase.

The Process of Closure Gathers Pace

Some scholars have argued that in the latter half of the 1980s the Victorian government was more interested in the closure of mental hospitals than in shutting down institutions for people with intellectual disabilities.[7] Yet as it closed Willsmere—the mental hospital adjoining Kew Cottages—the Victorian government also prepared to relocate people with intellectual disabilities into the community. However, much of this involved downsizing rather than closing institutions for people with intellectual disabilities. There needed to be a delicate balance: between providing community housing for those leaving institutions on the one hand, and leaving enough community housing places on the other for those moving from living with elderly parents who were increasingly unable to manage. In the early 1980s there was simply not enough housing stock available in community settings to accommodate the needs of both these cohorts.

Two key developments highlighted the government's ongoing and resolute commitment to closing institutions for people with intellectual disabilities. First, in 1986 the Victorian government shifted disability services from the Department of Health to the Department of Community Services, finally signalling its acknowledgment that intellectual disability was a social rather than a medical issue. Second, in 1988 the *Ten Year Plan for the Redevelopment of Intellectual Disability Services* reiterated the government's preference for a policy of deinstitutionalisation wherever it was practicable.

Yet is also true that it was not until the election of Jeff Kennett and his reformist conservative government in 1992 that the actual process of closing institutions in Victoria really gathered steam. In 1992, when Kennett came to power, the Victorian economy was reeling under billions of dollars of debt. Almost immediately, the new premier embarked on a budget-cutting and privatisation program to improve Victoria's fiscal position. By 1995 the Kennett government had slashed funding to public schools and public transport and sacked 7,000 teachers and 16,000 public transport workers. The premier had also initiated a major scheme for the privatisation of state-owned services and utilities.

When he turned his attention to institutions for people with intellectual disabilities, the premier acted in a similarly relentless manner, closing six institutions in the space of six years. Caloola, a large institution in Sunbury, and Mayday Hills, a smaller institution in Beechworth, were the first two institutions the Kennett government closed, both in 1992. The following year, Aradale in Ararat joined the list. When he spoke publicly about de-institutionalisation, Kennett usually linked his desire to close institutions to his wish to see people with intellectual disabilities better included in the wider community. Closure also saved the government money, at least initially. However, Kennett soon realised that not every institution was the same and closing some of the institutions could ultimately become a costly exercise. Despite increasing costs, the government nevertheless persisted with its program of deinstitutionalisation. In 1996, the Janefield and Kingsbury training centres were closed with the assistance of funding from the federal government, and this was followed by the closure of the Pleasant Creek Training Centre in 1998.

In one analysis of deinstitutionalisation in Victoria, Ilan Wiesel and Christine Bigby noted that some institutions were closed despite opposition from residents' parents and staff.[8] Other scholars noted a similar resistance in other places around the world. Indeed, deinstitutionalisation has globally been a highly controversial policy. However, the opposition of parents globally had little impact on the policies of governments already committed to closure. Governments were probably steeled to press on driven by mounting evidence worldwide that demonstrated the superiority of community residential units over institutions, and that residents' quality of life usually improved once they left an institution.

In the Victorian context, evaluations—like the study after the closure of St. Nicholas—stressed the positive outcomes of deinstitutionalisation. These evaluations also provided legitimacy for future redevelopments. The evaluation of Caloola's closure found that, overall, 'the quality of life' of people with disabilities 'improved significantly' after moving into the community, adding that such evidence 'would continue to support the Victorian Government policy of relocation of clients from Training Centres to smaller community-based residential options'.[9] It appeared that deinstitutionalisation, as an overarching policy shaping the lives of people with intellectual disabilities, was here to stay. Even so, in its attempt to close the Kew Children's Cottages, the Victorian government was about to face its biggest challenge from parents yet.

The Closure of Kew Cottages

When Jeff Kennett embarked on a program of deinstitutionalisation in Victoria in 1992, there were more than 2,500 people with intellectual disabilities in institutions across the state. By the time Pleasant Creek closed in 1998, that number had dropped to just under 900 and more than half of those were housed in Kew Cottages. Premier Kennett regarded his vow in 1999 to close the cottages within a decade as simply the finale of the job he had started in 1992. Indeed, the terrible fire in 1996 strengthened his resolve. Yet the task of closing Kew would ultimately fall to a new Victorian premier, Steve Bracks, who, to almost everyone's surprise, formed a Labor government in September 1999 and remained in power for the next eight years.

Premier Steve Bracks announced his government's commitment to closing Kew Cottages and redeveloping the 27-hectare site on 4 May 2001. Bracks described the living conditions at Kew as 'appalling' and 'not of the nature we should have in a civilised society'. At the time of Bracks's announcement, 462 residents lived onsite at Kew, but, under the government's $100 million redevelopment plan, most would be relocated to community residential units across Melbourne and Victoria, making way for a new mini-suburb of 270 homes to be built on the site. Bracks pointed out that 'every cent of the money from the disposal of this property' would be channelled back into disability services. He also sought to assure residents and their families that no resident would be relocated without proper consultation. In fact, the plan included provision for twenty new community residential units to be built on the site. These would provide accommodation for up to a hundred former residents who had lived at Kew for most of their lives. Christine Campbell, the community services minister, who also spoke that day, called the redevelopment of Kew Cottages a 'visionary and innovative' project. For the first time, a community would be built around intellectually disabled residents rather than the other way around. Closing Kew Cottages, the premier added, would be 'a fantastic step on the road to deinstitutionalisation'.[10]

Figure 12.1: Alma Adams, Manager Kew Residential Services Redevelopment
(Courtesy Kew Residential Services)

The Bracks government drew on the experience of other closures by appointing Alma Adams to oversee the closure of the cottages and redevelopment of the site at Kew (Figure 12.1). Alma Adams was a strong-willed, vibrant woman who had already worked at Kew Cottages on two separate occasions in the 1980s. She was also the perfect choice for a difficult job. For one thing, Adams was well versed in the nuances of the theory of normalisation and how it applied to people with intellectual disabilities living in large institutions. Moreover, by the time she returned to Kew 'to get the redevelopment up', as she later put it, she had overseen the closure of the Caloola, Janefield and Kingsbury training centres. When researcher Corinne Manning interviewed her in 2006, Adams recalled that, although the government had committed to closing Kew, the fine details had not been settled at the time. She also acknowledged that, while 'everyone agreed' that people with intellectual disabilities deserved 'a better quality of life than was possible in an old institution', there was 'significant disagreement' about how the redevelopment should proceed. 'I came on board', said Adams, 'to sort of put some flesh' to the government's 'policy commitment'.[11]

Alma Adams would have been pleased that, initially at least, the Kew Cottages Parents' Association appeared to support the government's plans. The association had been quite vocal in the past about its scepticism concerning ideas like normalisation and deinstitutionalisation. Its members challenged the notion that their children would eventually be comfortable or welcome in the wider Victorian community. Many of its *Newsletters* of the late 1990s represented the outside community as dangerous and unwelcoming to children with intellectual disabilities. For instance, a 1997 *Newsletter* claimed those relocated from Kew Cottages faced an 'isolated existence in an anonymous and sometimes threatening suburbia'.[12] The association argued that the cottages constituted a ready-made community that provided 'a safe environment for residents who are essentially very vulnerable people'. Therefore, Alma Adams might well have been shocked when the Kew Cottages Parents' Association welcomed Bracks's announcement in May 2001 as a 'major advance'.[13] That month, the association's *Newsletter* noted that, although it still lacked a number of important details, 'there is much to be very pleased with in this plan'.[14]

Within two years, this goodwill between the parents' association and the Victorian government had dissipated. The *Australian* reported in August 2003 that Kew Cottages had 'become an epic battle ground for one of the great social conflicts of our time'.[15] On one side were the Victorian government and numerous social policy experts who were in favour of 'institution busting', as the *Australian* put it, and who were seeking to dismantle 'the last vestiges of an era when disabled people were hidden away'. On the other side was a group of parents concerned about their children and about whether they could ever live a good life outside the cloistered walls of Kew. Rosalie Trower, a Kew Cottages Parents' Association committee member, articulated these concerns when she told the *Age* that parents were 'fearful and frightened' about where their children would live. 'It's a lonely world out there', said Trower, 'and today's society is not an embracing kind society'.[16]

The parents' association wanted their children to remain on the Kew Cottages site in clustered housing. Their idea of 'clustered housing' paralleled what the Kennett government had done when it redeveloped the Janefield and Kingsbury training centres in October 1997. Alma Adams had overseen those redevelopments too. The Janefield and Kingsbury redevelopment placed 250 former residents into new homes across the state, but also placed another hundred residents requiring a higher level of support into a new housing estate built on the old Janefield site. This facility, named Plenty Residential Services, comprised twenty-three dwellings grouped around prettily landscaped courts—like a normal housing estate—but it was also equipped to protect the privacy and ensure the safety of all residents.

As early as 1988, the Kew Cottages Parents' Association had proposed that any redevelopment of the Kew site should follow a similar format. 'Villa housing at Kew' could have the 'appearance of an attractive housing estate', the association argued, and could consist of homes that would 'be grouped around tree lined streets'.[17] They suggested how each house might be configured and also how such a redevelopment might proceed. That many parents thought the proposal held some merit is highlighted by the fact that the parents' association revived the idea during the Kew fire controversy.

To the consternation of some association members, the cluster housing proposal never gained traction. It was rejected by the Kennett government in 1998 and again by the Bracks government in 2001. A year later, the community services minister, Bronwyn Pike, explained why the Labor government rejected this idea—cluster housing replicated the problems associated with institutions, denying people with intellectual disabilities 'a chance to participate in society'. Pike argued that any form of segregation was 'not in the spirit of inclusion' and that 'a broader base of accommodation and support options' situated within the community was 'the key to inclusion'.[18]

Much later, Alma Adams estimated about 60 of 460 parents strongly supported the cluster housing proposal. If true, it was a very vocal minority. Its adherents were also adept at co-opting other disaffected people to their cause, like Kew locals concerned about how a new housing estate might affect the amenity of their suburb. Soon a heated debate was raging in many Melbourne newspapers about what should be done at Kew. Letters to the editors of all the major Melbourne newspapers captured something of the tenor of the debate. 'I keep hearing people say' that people with intellectual disabilities have a 'right to live in the community', wrote one mother of a resident a Kew: 'Bloody hell, it's also their right not to live in the community'. Another woman with 'cerebral palsy and high support needs' took quite a different position in her letter to the *Herald Sun* in September 2003. The closure of Kew Cottages could not 'come quickly enough', she wrote, and she urged 'parents to let go a bit' and give their 'daughters and sons an opportunity to strive and enjoy their lives in more pleasant surroundings'.[19]

What motivated some parents to oppose deinstitutionalisation so vehemently? Was it fear for their children, fear simply of change, or a paternalist conviction that they still knew what was best for their children and needed to exert that control? The historian Charles Fox has pondered these questions and warns against simple conclusions, reminding us that parents did not hold a 'completely consistent line on the process of deinstitutionalisation'. He suggests some parents struggled with the concept of deinstitutionalisation simply because it reignited conflicted feelings about their original decision to institutionalise their child.

According to Fox, one significant driver of parental opposition to deinstitutionalisation was the belief that their children would fail to thrive outside the walls of an institution. He argues that many parents had 'a bleak dystopian view of the community, of what it was "really like out there"', and provides considerable evidence to make his point.[20] He quotes one parent who described the community as 'at best, uncaring' and at worst 'antagonistic' to people with intellectual disabilities, and another who thought life in the community would be 'troubled' and overly 'frantic'. If Fox seems somewhat impatient with the parents' concerns about the community 'out there', it is probably because in this instance parents were on the wrong side of the debate about human rights. But it is worth remembering that, when parents expressed their opposition to deinstitutionalisation, they were drawing on their knowledge and personal experience of many years of stigmatisation, rejection, and humiliation within the very community they were now being asked to embrace.

In any event, the closure and redevelopment of Australia's oldest institution for people with intellectual disabilities caused fierce and volatile public debate. Several newspaper reporters and columnists were not afraid to let their readers know exactly where they stood on one of the most pertinent issues of the day. When Kenneth Davidson, a columnist at the *Age* and a Kew local, described the plan for redevelopment of Kew as a grubby 'excuse for a public land grab', he was echoing others in the community who had expressed similar sentiments in letters to the press. A *Herald Sun* opinion poll in early August 2003 found that only eighty-one of more than two thousand respondents backed the government's proposal to 'turn the historic site into multi-storey units'. The paper added that a growing number of 'people appear to be in favour of renovating the complex and keeping its long-term residents together'.[21]

A protest was organised and, just before midday on 10 August 2003, hundreds of people gathered at the Kew Cottages to express their opposition to the government's plans. The former chair of the Australian Competition and Consumer Commission, Alan Fels, attended the protest and in doing so leant some prestige to the event. When Fels addressed the protest, he warned the government against the wholesale deinstitutionalisation of people with intellectual disabilities. He raised the spectre of the closure of some mental hospitals in the 1980s, when inadequately resourced community services had struggled to meet consumer demand. This resulted in some former residents being forced to live on the streets. For some people 'a communal arrangement is better', said Fels, and 'there should be a choice rather than a single policy of deinstitutionalisation'.[22]

Alma Adams later reflected on the way that public debate about Kew's redevelopment was hijacked by emotive claims. When Janefield closed, Adams recalled, 'we didn't have any of this stuff to deal with' and 'there wasn't the kind of whole community view that people were being dumped out into the street'.[23] Adams was convinced that there was something almost emblematic about the Kew Cottages that stirred up emotion and clouded judgment. And it is hard to disagree with her point of view. Perhaps the response stemmed from the incessant media attention Kew Children's Cottages had attracted since their inception. Or perhaps it had something to do with the prominent position of the institution itself, nestled on a bend in the river and perched high up on the hill in a prestigious suburb not too far from Melbourne's CBD. Whatever the reason, the plans for the cottages and their residents provoked community responses like no other institution in the state. There was, and always had been, a strong sense that the interests of the broader community were particularly invested in what happened to the Kew Cottages site.

In another interview, Adams elaborated on the iconic nature of the cottages. She claimed that many parents 'had views around the institution which seemed at odds with what the institution actually delivered'. She elaborated:

> they had an idyllic sense of the institution being this beautiful environment, with all the trees. And it is a beautiful environment with trees, but for many people who lived inside those institutions, who hardly saw those trees, their perspective, I suspect, would have been different.[24]

Adams nevertheless sympathised with parents who held such views. 'If I were a parent of someone with a disability', she said, 'I would have a degree of nervousness' about deinstitutionalisation. But she pointed to research that showed deinstitutionalisation worked.

As the Victorian government pushed ahead with its redevelopment plans for Kew, it adopted a similar argument, based on the growing and significant body of local and international research that deinstitutionalisation was successful. Some evidence suggested that 'positive outcomes' were not an 'inevitable result' of moving into the community for all those with intellectual disability.[25] However, most research revealed that 'people in small-scale community-based residences or in semi-independent or supported living arrangements have a better objective quality of life than do people in large, congregate settings'.[26] The Victorian government also drew on local research based on the closure of other institutions such as Aradale, Mayday Hills and Caloola to avoid some of the mistakes of the past.[27]

The End of an Era

In many respects, the process involved in closing Kew Cottages and relocating their residents into the community paralleled the closure of any other institution. Houses had to be sourced and renovated or built from scratch. Decisions had to be made about specific resident groupings and about individual support needs. None of this was new to Alma Adams. But this time Adams was closing an institution in the face of strong parental opposition and a largely negative campaign in the Melbourne press. In 2003, for instance, the Office of the Public Advocate conducted an analysis of the print coverage of the closure of Kew Cottages and found that reportage of the debate had been mostly negative. Between May and August 2003, it claimed, the *Age* had generally run a 'balanced array of articles', but the overall result had been 'heavily influenced by the overwhelmingly negative coverage in the *Herald Sun*'.[28] Perhaps there were no surprises there, but it highlighted the fact that Adams would be closing the cottages under intense scrutiny. Careful consultation and detailed planning would be essential. If something positive emerged from such a negative and divisive campaign and the intense scrutiny over Kew's closure, it was that the residents of the cottages probably benefitted.

Throughout the process, the Department of Human Services assured interested observers that the needs of each individual were being considered. A Resident Assessment Consultation and Planning Team was established to assess each of the individuals to be relocated and to ensure the 'needs and personality of each resident' would be a 'priority in determining where and with whom' each lived.[29] The planning team comprised case managers, therapists from external agencies, and sundry other Kew Cottages staff, who assessed each individual to determine their specific support needs. Next, each resident was allocated a case manager, who consulted with residents, family members, guardians and/or other advocates about preferences and support needs, producing a 'General Service Plan' for each resident. An Intellectual Disability Review Panel provided an independent review of the whole process and signed off on each individual's plan prior to relocation.

One former review panel member recalled it 'added to the quality of the process' and 'ensured that important aspects around the planning process had not been missed'.[30] It also gave parents and advocates 'peace of mind ... that there was someone watching over the process to ensure the best outcomes' for residents.

The choice of the location of the new community residential units was guided by the location of a resident's family, the nature of nearby facilities, the features of the local community and the proximity of day programs. Much thought and planning went into deciding who would live with whom. 'We looked at all the information we had about' each individual, Adams recalled, 'and we then proposed groups of people who could live together' based on that information. Adams also explained that one overt decision that they made early in the process was that people with a certain kind of disability did not necessarily need to live in the same home. The decision 'was around friendships and compatibilities', Adams said, 'it wasn't around support needs'.[31]

On 6 October 2002, the first group of Kew residents—three men and two women—moved out of the cottages and into their new home

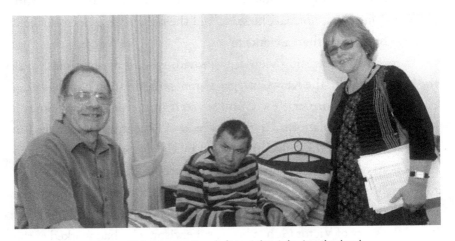

Figure 12.2: Moving Day: left to right, John Leatherland,
Regional Director Eastern Region, Department of Human Services;
Angelo Papadopoulos, resident;
and Alma Adams
(Courtesy Kew Residential Services)

FAILED AMBITIONS

in Doncaster East (Figure 12.2). One reporter from the *Age*, who witnessed the move, referred to the five residents, Robert Cody, Gregory McNamara, Betty-Joy Hickford, Kirsten Campbell and Henry Baker, as pioneers who were making their way out of 'the sprawling 130-year-old residential institution' and moving into a 'spick-and-span new home of their own in East Doncaster'.[32] Cody and McNamara, both 40, were lifelong friends who had lived at Kew for more than thirty years. Campbell and Baker were younger and more recent friends, and, at 51, Betty-Joy Hickford was the oldest of the group. All had been 'picked for their compatibility', the *Age* reported. It added that all were embarking on an 'extraordinary personal adventure' that would involve 'a new life in the community, with up to eight staff to help' around the house.

Their new Doncaster East home, in Banool Quadrant, was well located. It was close enough to the local shops, there was a large reserve a few blocks away and, perhaps most importantly, it was just a short drive to the day centre on Andersons Creek Road. Richard Lindemann, who knew each resident and had worked at Kew for eighteen years, was appointed to the role of house supervisor, and, as far as he was concerned, the main challenge was making the Doncaster East house a home. 'It is hard work making things look normal', he said, 'and the big challenge is to make it a home first, rather than a worksite'.[33]

There was a prevailing view that providing staffing continuity was the best approach. The Kew Cottages Parents' Association had made the redeployment of former Kew Cottages staff into community homes a key plank of their platform after Kew's redevelopment was announced in 2001. *Kew News*—the newsletter issued by the Department of Human Services to inform all about the redevelopment—argued a similar case. *Kew News* tracked the movement of former Kew Cottages staff into the newly developed group homes, even airing their concerns. In June 2004 it told the story of Victor Goh, a house supervisor, who had worked at the cottages for fifteen years. Goh expressed some anxiety about his move and new role. 'I just wasn't sure how we would fit everything in', he said, 'it seemed like there were so many things that had to be organised' and so many 'new systems to get used to'.[34] Neither the department nor the parent's association considered whether former institutional staff might bring with them entrenched institutional views and practices and that this could become a problem over time.

Three more new homes, in Ringwood East, Mitcham and Croydon, were opened in 2002 and a further twelve were opened the following year. As new houses were opened, the older, more decrepit units on the Kew Cottages site were progressively closed. By May 2004, eighty-five former Kew residents were relocated into seventeen new houses across Melbourne and Units 13, 15 and 28 at the Kew Cottages had been closed. In a slightly breathless tone, *Kew News* tracked the progress of each new house and told the personal relocation stories of individual residents and staff. It also kept interested observers up to date with the plans for the redevelopment of the Kew site. The July 2004 issue of *Kew News* informed its readers that while about 80 per cent of the houses in the community had been purchased, only around 20 per cent of residents had been relocated into these new homes. In March the following year, *Kew News* reported that 'all but four of the 73 houses' had been acquired and that all Kew residents would be rehoused by June 2006.

It is not surprising that the department's *Kew News* told a largely positive story of the redevelopment of Kew progressing smoothly. Yet the positive story appears to reflect the reality. Alma Adams recalled that only four of the 360 residents relocated from the Kew Cottages had serious issues during the transition period. The methods by which she arrived at this number were not entirely clear, but other evaluations made a similar point at the time. A 2003 report focusing on the experience of the first thirty residents to exit the cottages found that, in terms of health, safety and happiness, they were better off, and that residents, family members and staff believed this was the case. One staff member remarked that the house in which she worked 'feels like a home', adding that the residents were 'happy' as they had 'their own rooms and the outside garden'. An aunt of another resident explained that the transition was reaping rewards: 'if I ask him if he wants to go back to Kew Cottages he says no'.[35]

The whole process of relocating 360 residents to new homes in the community took just over four years. The final group of residents—five men in their 40s and 50s—moved into their new home in Ivanhoe in August 2006. 'For the five "old boys" from Kew Cottages, it spelled a new beginning', the *Age* reported, and 'for the Bracks government it marked the successful conclusion in moving people into the community'. Of course, the final piece of this puzzle was yet to be completed. There were still a hundred residents in what was left of the Kew Cottages waiting for the redevelopment of the site to begin (Figure 12.3). But offsite, the relocation had been a success to the extent that it had closely followed the plan Bracks had outlined in 2001.

Later, Alma Adams explained that 'there were no delays' in the offsite relocation of Kew Cottages residents. 'That', she said, 'all rolled out as we had planned it would'.[36] However, Adams also acknowledged that there were some significant delays to the redevelopment of the Kew Cottages site, 'where the last 20 houses were going to be'. According to Adams, those delays 'could be summarised as planning and heritage delays', which was a euphemism of sorts for a hard-fought and bitter campaign by some people who simply did not want to see the development at Kew proceed.

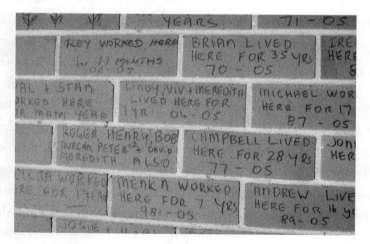

Figure 12.3: Remaining residents and staff in 2005 recorded their time at Kew Cottages poignantly on institutional brick work at the cottages
(Courtesy Kew Residential Services)

Development Battle

In his 2001 announcement, Premier Steve Bracks had indicated that extensive 'permits and approvals' would be required for the redevelopment of the Kew Cottages site. This made it 'difficult to estimate' when onsite construction would begin. Even so, the premier was optimistic that things would be underway by late 2002 or early 2003 at the latest. It proved an underestimation. The first tentative steps in the process began in April 2002, when the Boroondara Council set up a working party of council, community and state government representatives to create an urban design framework for the redevelopment of the site. That framework was not released by the Boroondara Council until February 2003, by which time a coalition between local residents' groups and some members of the Kew Cottages Parents' Association had already formed to express its opposition to the development of Kew. The Kew Coalition, as this loose organisation of groups called itself, had its first significant victory in August 2004, when Heritage Victoria's executive director announced that a significant portion of the 27-hectare Kew site—including six 1880s buildings and an avenue of trees—would be added to Victoria's Heritage Register (Figure 12.4).

Figure 12.4: The cottages *c.* 1900, with the asylum in the background.
Nicholas Caire, photographer
(Courtesy Wellcome Collection, Public Domain Mark)

FAILED AMBITIONS

The heritage listing came as a surprise to the Victorian government and ultimately slashed the number of dwellings any developer could build on the site. Many interested observers acknowledged that it represented a major obstacle to the redevelopment of the whole site. Even so, the government pushed ahead. In November 2004, the Bracks government declared it would 'work with Heritage Victoria' to 'find a solution' and promised to announce a preferred developer for the site by the end of the year. Yet, by 27 January 2005, no such announcement had been made, although the *Age* was reporting that the Walker Corporation was expected to win the tender. In March, the public advocate, Julian Gardner, bemoaned the delay in naming a preferred developer if only because it 'cast doubt over whether Kew ... would close by 2006' as the government had 'promised'. Finally, at the beginning of June, the plans for the redevelopment were released.[37] To no one's surprise, the Walker Corporation won the bid.

The plans for the development provided for a 'new modern housing estate', as *Kew News* put it in July 2005, that would feature 'a community leisure centre and parkland' and twenty houses for a hundred former Kew Cottages residents. A further 480 houses and apartments 'spread across as many as five levels' would be built on the site, and almost one-third of the 27 hectares earmarked for development would be retained as parkland or open space. Under the plans, only three of the six heritage-listed buildings would be retained, and applications to demolish the other three buildings would be lodged with Heritage Victoria as soon as practicable. This meant that the chapel, the old pharmacy and Building 10 would be incorporated into what the developers were now calling a 'heritage precinct'. By contrast, Units 9 and 11 and House Hostel would be demolished. The heritage precinct would include, among other things, a hydrotherapy pool and spa, a gymnasium, and consulting rooms for visiting health practitioners. *Kew News* reported that everyone involved had made it a 'priority' to 'ensure that the facilities will be able to include all former KRS residents in their activities'. The project, which would be built over three stages, would cost $350 million and take close to seven years to complete.[38]

270

When work commenced in late 2006, the plans had been further refined. Now, only 380 dwellings—including the twenty new homes for former Kew Cottages residents—would be built, and most of the dwellings would be detached houses. Given the urgency of closing the Kew Cottages, most of the twenty former residents' houses would be built first, and they were commenced in December 2006. The group homes were initially meant to be spread across the entire suburb, but planning delays and the staged nature of the project meant that most of them were confined to the north-eastern corner of the site. The hundred remaining Kew Cottages residents were living in old Kew Cottages in 'small groupings alongside their future housemates', supported by staff who would eventually be 'working with them in their new homes'. This arrangement aimed to make the transition to their new homes 'as easy as possible'. Alma Adams acknowledged that the integration of a hundred residents into a new community would 'be a different kind of challenge', adding it was important 'to build early connections as the new suburb takes shape and develops it character'.[39]

Finally, on a beautiful autumn day on 20 April 2008, a hundred former residents moved into twenty newly built homes on the old Kew Cottages site. If the move had 'its share of chaos, confusion and last-minute hitches', that was probably because such a logistical challenge had never before been attempted. Despite early teething problems, the move was a great success. While residents unpacked their belongings and explored their new homes, a mobile jazz band roamed from house to house to welcome residents and support staff with a burst of song. At one point, the mother of one of the residents broke into an impromptu dance with her son in the middle of the street. The dance, she said, was an expression of 'her joy and relief that this day had, finally, come'.[40] Kew Cottages was finally closed after 121 years!

For Alma Adams, moving day was an emotional experience. In her final message in *Kew News*, she acknowledged that the period between the opening of the last community house 'off-site' in August 2006 and opening day on site had been 'drawn out'. Yet she was exhilarated to have seen the project through to completion. Of course, that did not mean that the broader project of deinstitutionalisation in Victoria was finished. As Adams pointed out, the move into new, smaller homes in a normal community setting was just 'one step along the way'. Building 'new lives in the community', she said, would take much more than just 'new bricks and mortar'.[41] It was a well-made and prescient point. By the end of the year the *Age* was already reporting that there was 'Trouble in Kew' and that many of the 'site's original residents' had become 'outcasts in their own neighbourhood'.[42] According to Royce Millar, the author of the article, the problems at Kew raised some thorny questions about deinstitutionalisation that had yet to be properly explored.

Trouble at Kew

It is worth considering in more detail what Royce Millar was referring to in his 13 December 2008 article, because, at first glance, he seemed to be exploring the quality of the housing stock built on the former Kew Cottages site. 'The old Kew Cottages site was supposed to be converted into state-of-the-art sustainable housing', wrote Millar, but 'those who bought in' say the government and the developer 'have failed to deliver' on their promises. Millar went on to outline a whole gamut of issues—leaking roofs, problematic heating systems, unfinished gardens and an absence of footpaths across the estate—that had residents up in arms and threatening to take legal action if their demands for compensation were not met. But the article then turned to what Millar called the 'most troubling issue' of all. He explained that some new homebuyers were complaining about the behaviour of former Kew Cottages residents 'relieving themselves in public' and wandering the streets 'with little or no supervision'.

Millar had some sympathy for the former Kew residents who were 'becoming outcasts in the own neighbourhood', he said, but he also noted that the complaints by new homeowners 'have raised the thorniest of questions about deinstitutionalisation'. For one thing, no one had been 'briefed about the reality of living next to intellectually disabled residents', he said, and some new residents were complaining that they had not been informed about their 'disabled neighbours at all'. The article acknowledged that homebuyers should not necessarily expect to be notified of the presence of 'intellectually disabled' people in their neighbourhood, but it had reached a point, Millar said, where there were now tensions across the entire estate. Millar reported that many were concerned that 'an experiment that tore down institutional barriers may yet lead to the saddest paradoxes of all'—that former Kew Cottages residents, who had lived on the site 'forever', were losing what 'limited freedom' they had obtained during the process of closing the cottages.

Royce Millar's article raised some thorny questions about the nature of the redevelopment of the Kew Cottages, about the necessity for stronger and more inclusive communities, and about the subtle differences between the meaning of institutional closure on the one hand and deinstitutionalisation on the other. It also raised questions about the efficacy, or value, of the policy of deinstitutionalisation, by implying that an argument might be made that the interests of some people with intellectual disabilities were better served in large-scale congregate care facilities.

Yet, as indicated above, a substantial body of research analysing the closure of institutions in Australia and around the world had revealed that large-scale congregate care facilities stifled residents' chances to live a meaningful or enjoyable life. Indeed, the research showed those with intellectual disabilities living in small-scale community-based residences had a better quality of life than those in large institutions.[43]

As Australia's oldest institution for people with intellectual disabilities was progressively demolished, and its rundown, impractical buildings replaced by identical, boxy houses, the evaluations of the closure of Kew Cottages revealed a similar story. For all its problems—including those raised by Royce Millar—the transition out of the cottages was a success. The signs that closing Kew led to improved lives were apparent in Gary Radler's 2003 report. Another more detailed report, released in 2012, found that people with intellectual disabilities who left Kew Cottages 'to live in small group homes experienced an increased quality of life'. The authors noted that such findings paralleled earlier Australian and international studies, adding:

> Significant positive changes occurred in the homeliness of their place of residence; the degree of choice they exercised; the community utilisation and personal/social responsibility; their use of community facilities for leisure purposes and other activities; and the size of their social networks.

The report was emphatic that an 'increased quality of life for people with intellectual disabilities results from living in small group homes in the community compared with large institutions'.[44]

Even Royce Millar, who revisited the story of the redevelopment of Kew for the *Age* in 2017, conceded that 'those with disabilities living on the site' appeared 'to be happy enough with the outcome'.[45] Instead of focusing on deinstitutionalisation of the former residents, Millar delved into the murky business of property development. More specifically, he examined Lang Walker, 'the multi-billionaire property developer from Sydney's North Shore' and the hundreds of millions of dollars that remained unaccounted for almost ten years after the redevelopment at Kew had begun. The gist of Millar's 2017 article was that a lack of transparency and poor planning had rendered the redevelopment of the Kew Cottages a 'dodgy deal' that benefited no one other than the developer. It is certainly true that development was plagued with problems from the start and that those problems mounted over time. It is also true that the expected windfall for the Victorian government and for disability services did not materialise from the sale of the land. In fact, at least one subsequent investigation into the redevelopment of Kew found problems with the project and suggested that, overall, it 'had not been in the public interest'.[46]

It is not the purpose of this book to explore the troubled history of the redevelopment of the Kew Cottages site. Nor is there space to delve into the protracted battles between the Walker Corporation, local Kew residents and successive state governments over who was responsible for all that went wrong with Kew's redevelopment. Even so, it is worth noting that the narrative of conflict and chaos that underpins the story of the troubled Kew development can, at times, overshadow the narrative around the closure of the Kew Cottages and the broader story of deinstitutionalisation across Victoria.

Deinstitutionalisation was not a perfectly designed policy, and it did not necessarily deliver on all its promises, but the policy's outcomes were significant and long-lasting for those most centrally involved. Perhaps Alma Adams, who oversaw the whole process at Kew, summed it up best when she said that 'if we had waited to get everything right it might never have happened at all'. And, when viewed from the perspective of the residents of the cottages, deinstitutionalisation must be understood as a successful policy. Indeed, the reaction of many former residents of Kew Cottages to their relocation into the community hints at a largely positive story. One resident, Ralph Dawson, spoke about how much he liked his new home. 'I'm very happy here', he said, 'I've got my keys and my own bedroom', which was obviously more than could be said for conditions at the former Kew Cottages. And, when asked to compare his new home to life in the cottages, another former resident simply replied, 'I like it better here'.[47]

Two years ago, on a cold day in May 2019, David Henderson, one of the authors, visited the old Kew Cottages site for the first time in many years. A few days earlier, it had come to our attention that three heritage-listed buildings had recently come onto the market and would be sold in early June. According to the agent responsible for the sale, each building advertised would offer buyers a 'first-class executive Kew lifestyle' amid 'leafy avenues, luxury homes and tranquil common parklands'. Fourteen years earlier, Lang Walker and the Victorian government had made promises about these buildings too. Back then, the government had promised that the buildings would form the nucleus of a community precinct offering residents a variety of health services and leisure activities. One artist's impression of the precinct, for instance, showed a hydrotherapy pool and spa, a gymnasium and another building fitted out with consulting rooms for a variety of health and wellbeing practitioners. These buildings had also been earmarked to include a small, permanent exhibition on the history of Kew Cottages. But Royce Millar tells us that by 2014 Lang Walker had struck a deal with the government 'to scrap' those plans entirely. Now, seven years later, the buildings were for sale, the agents anticipating they would bring more than a million dollars each, and no historical exhibition about the cottage was in sight on site.

David felt queasy as soon as he got out of the car, and had to resist an urgent desire to leave. The feeling did not dissipate as he walked from one dilapidated building to the next, trying to imagine what it would be like to transform any one of them into a new home. Each building was more than a hundred years old, and each was set on unkempt and scraggy lawns. They looked out of place. They seemed to be perched amongst the newer, almost identical houses that made up the rest of the housing estate (Figure 12.5).

Figure 12.5: Kew Cottages November 2021
(Courtesy Ian McNaughton)
One of the few original buildings remaining after the redevelopment, surrounded by modern housing. The old asylum tower is still visible, though now part of a new gated residential community.

Building 10, which had once been one of the more appealing units at the cottages, was in a terrible state. The floors had been ripped up and most of the ceiling had been removed. The chapel and the old pharmacy were not much better, although in these buildings the floorboards had been retained. In all of them paint was peeling from the walls.

David did not spend more than ten minutes at the site before taking his leave. As he drove away he pondered what Patty Rodgers, one of the first residents relocated from Kew Cottages into the community, had said earlier. When asked about Kew, Patty Rodgers replied: 'I don't like it here … I hate it'.[48] And while the feelings of all the authors were not quite so strong, we understood what Rodgers was talking about when she followed that with a more positive spin by saying, 'I am happy to be out of Kew'.

Epilogue:
Connecting Past and Present

It was perhaps symbolic that the Australian government ratified the United Nations Convention on the Rights of Persons with Disabilities in 2008, the year that Kew Cottages closed. By doing so, the government committed to ensuring people with disabilities had the right to choose where and with whom they lived, as well as preventing their isolation and segregation from the community. Did this mark the beginning of one more new era for people with intellectual disabilities or just another round of promises that would remain unfulfilled? The history of Kew Children's Cottages—the first and last large institution for people with intellectual disabilities in Victoria—provides a prism through which to view the way this group has been regarded by society. This epilogue reflects on over a century of change and continuity in the experiences of people with intellectual disabilities in Australia. It looks back on the long history of Kew Cottages and forward from their closure to the 2020s.

Change

In the nineteenth and twentieth centuries most children and adults with intellectual disabilities lived with their parents, as they do today. Only a small minority have ever lived in institutions like Kew Cottages, yet their history and eventual closure illustrate changing perspectives about the role of the state in providing services and support to such people and their families. When they were built, Kew Cottages provided the only alternative to family care. In the 1970s small group homes in ordinary communities were added, and in the 2000s individualised housing and support options further broadened the residential possibilities available to people with intellectual disabilities. The last residents of Kew were relocated to new group homes scattered across Victoria, with the exception of the hundred who moved into sparkling white homes clustered in a corner of the new housing estate on the former Kew Cottages site.

Several decades of reports and recorded experience leave little doubt that group homes offer their residents a much-improved quality of life compared to institutional living.[1] Certainly, the material conditions ex-Kew residents experienced in their new homes were far superior to those at Kew at any time in its history. Post-Kew residents lived with no more than five others, their homes had glass in the windows, sprinklers in the ceilings, heating and cooling. They had their own income, bedroom, clothes and a place at a day program.[2] However, group homes vary enormously, and there is considerable scope in many to further improve residents' quality of life, particularly in terms of community inclusion, choice and control, safety and wellbeing.[3]

Some observers and critics have argued that group homes simply replicate, on a smaller scale, the culture and closed environment of institutions like Kew Cottages.[4] Small size and community location of group homes are necessary but not sufficient conditions for a good life. Rather, it is the quality of staff practices that makes most difference and predicts the outcomes for residents.[5] Research has demonstrated that some of the ex-residents of Kew Cottages continued to be subjected to staff practices characteristic of institutions.[6] They experienced rigid routines, block treatment, depersonalisation and social distance from staff, albeit in qualitatively distinct and less harsh or restrictive ways than experienced by earlier generations of Kew residents. One might argue that, when Kew was closing, group homes had already been superseded by more individualised models offering greater potential for a good life, and that it was a mistake, driven by industrial muscle, to simply transfer staff from the institution to community homes. But, then again, the closure might never have happened if it had been based on ideals rather than pragmatics.

Public policy's perception of people with intellectual disabilities changed dramatically over the course of Kew Cottages' history. Attitudes cycled through regarding people with intellectual disabilities as: objects of pity in need of care; people who might contribute to society if only they were trained well; a menace to be feared from whom society should be protected; a vulnerable group in need of care; and, finally, equal citizens with rights to inclusion. Rights gained increasing prominence in Victorian and Commonwealth legislation after the 1970 United Nations Declaration on the Rights of the Mentally Retarded.

Yet, despite this and shifts in the understanding of disability from a medical to a social model, the general public's perceptions have remained remarkably similar. Most commonly, public interest in people with intellectual disabilities is piqued by intermittent media stories of neglect and scandal, and the response is outrage salved by offers of charitable donations. That the public's attitudes towards people with intellectual disabilities remains both stigmatising and paternalistic is indicative of the community's failure to recognise its own need to change in order to further rights and social inclusion for these people.

The voices of people with intellectual disabilities were rarely heard during much of Kew Cottages' history. Rather it was the views of medical men, politicians, the media and Kew ratepayers that held sway. Parents, social workers and other professionals entered the conversation in the 1950s, but it was not until the early 1980s that self-advocacy groups added the voices of people with intellectual disabilities to public debates. The balance continues to shift. After years of uncertain funding, self-advocacy is flourishing, and co-design has emerged as a way of doing business in the National Disability Insurance Scheme (NDIS). The 2019 Royal Commission into Violence, Abuse, Neglect and Exploitation of People with Disability has stated: 'the voices of people with disability are at the forefront of our work'.[7] The new question generated by these changes is whether the voices of people with intellectual disabilities are loud enough to be heard among those of others with disabilities. There are certainly indications that the NDIS, Australia's latest reform program, was not designed with people with intellectual disabilities in mind and that it continues to meet poorly the shared needs of this group.[8]

Issues of voice are allied with those of dedifferentiation: meaning the dissolution of categories and the inclusion of people with intellectual disabilities in the larger group of people with disabilities. Dedifferentiation waxed and waned during Kew Cottages' history and remains an unsettled issue. The establishment of Kew Cottages began a long and hesitant process of differentiating people with intellectual disabilities from those with mental illness, as well as from each other, through elaborate classification schemes based on the severity of impairment and educative potential. The high-water mark of this process of differentiation was the 1986 *Intellectually Disabled Person's Services Act*, the only piece of Victorian legislation dedicated solely to this group that was both passed and enacted.

A few years later, however, it was superseded by the largely dedifferentiated 2006 *Victorian Disability Act*. This move reflected the traction gained by the social model of disability, which draws attention away from the nature and severity of impairment to the common and discriminatory experiences of all people with disabilities.

In a curious juxtaposition of progressive and illiberal ideas, the growth of neo-liberalism during this period prioritised individualism rather than group membership. Together, these forces fuelled the dedifferentiation of people with intellectual disabilities, meaning they are less and less identified as a separate group in service systems and are simply seen as individuals or part of a larger group of people with disabilities. Diagnosis, for example, does not figure in eligibility for the NDIS, which is determined by functional capacity. Individualised funding packages are based on each individual's reasonable and necessary disability-related support needs. Those who argue in favour of dedifferentiation cite advantages in discarding the string of derogatory labels that have marked people with intellectual disabilities out as different, and have been used to justify their exclusion from society on the supposition that reason and rationality are prerequisites of citizenship.[9] Proponents of dedifferentiation also point to the strength of the collective voice of people with disabilities in leveraging social change, compared to the disparate and splintered group-specific claims of the past.[10]

There are, however, advantages in differentiation, which can identify shared as well as unique characteristics of individuals with intellectual disabilities. Social inclusion will only be achieved by understanding and dismantling the barriers particular to people with intellectual disabilities—lifts, ramps and guide dogs will not do the trick for this group. Rather, what they need are affirming expectations and public attitudes that accept their humanity and value their differences, adjustments to modes of communication and complex social processes, and skilled support to enable their engagement in meaningful activities and social relationships. Going forward, a less dichotomous critical realist approach may be preferable, whereby society treats people with intellectual disabilities as members of the broader disability group wherever possible but also protects and develops differentiated opportunities, adjustments and services whenever necessary.[11]

Continuity

Alongside change, significant continuities can be observed in the experiences of people with intellectual disabilities and societal responses to them. First, family members for people with intellectual disabilities continue to be their staunchest and most committed lifelong allies. The bonds of love are strong. Second, Australia continues to look internationally for policy ideas, following but lagging somewhat behind developments overseas. Often the lag is not sufficient to allow Australian policy makers to benefit fully from the implementation outcomes and experiences, and the identification of any unexpected or undesirable consequences of new policies. The third continuity, and one worthy of more discussion, is the abuse and neglect experienced by people with intellectual disabilities in services established to care for or educate them. The fourth and related continuity is ambitious but unfulfilled promises of successive governments to do better.

Abuse was a 'significant, if hidden, dimension of institutional life'.[12] Despite the paucity of documented instances in the archives of verbal or physical 'ill treatment' of residents, the history of Kew Children's Cottages reads as a litany of abuse and neglect of its residents. Extending far beyond individual incidents of harm, such abuse and neglect were systemic. Carelessness and callousness were evident in the overcrowding, insanitary conditions, inadequate heating, poor food, inadequate health care, and the shoddy and unsafe fabric of buildings. Added to this was, above all, the insufficient and poorly trained staff were inadequate to meet residents' basic personal care or developmental needs. That the standards of 'care' experienced by residents of Kew Cottages were unacceptable in terms of the prevailing community expectations at every point in its history is evident in the contemporaneous descriptions of journalists, parents, official visitors, and government enquiries. Demands for change by the authors of these exposés were consistently countered by promises from government of more money, new positions or departments, and public works. Most promises were never fulfilled.

People with intellectual disabilities continue to experience abuse and neglect well after the closure of Kew Cottages. This is on a scale sufficient to warrant more media attention and public enquiries. The latest investigation is the 2019 Royal Commission into Violence, Abuse, Neglect and Exploitation of People with Disability, chaired by Ronald Sackville. Its approach has been very different from the earlier Zox and Ellery royal commissions, as almost half of all public submissions have come from people with disabilities themselves.

For the first time, the abuse and neglect of people with disabilities is being methodically explored. The royal commission has been encouraged to expose 'the way it is enacted through a diverse range of incidents, consistently as part of everyday experiences and through the operations of family structures, relationships, institutions, service delivery and policy and legislative settings'.[13] To date, the findings only skim the surface but are shocking. People with disabilities experience much higher rates of abuse than those in the general community— 64 per cent of all people with disabilities over the age of fifteen report having experienced physical violence, sexual violence, intimate partner violence, emotional abuse and/or stalking, compared to 45 per cent of people without disability. The risks are heightened still further for women, young people and those with intellectual disabilities.

The vulnerability of people with intellectual disabilities to abuse and neglect is neither an inherent personal nor a situational characteristic. Rather, it is created through the failure of public policies to deliver quality and safe support services that, among other things, enable people to build diverse social connections to other community members and thus provide natural safeguards to wellbeing. This state of affairs is not the result of want of ambition. The history of Kew Cottages, and intellectual disability services more generally right up to the present time, is replete with ambitious plans for reform and government promises of greater resources. Yet, somehow, these promises remain unfulfilled; what is delivered always falls short of what has been promised.

Public outrage and professional passion have managed to get ideas about the types of lives that could be experienced by people with intellectual disabilities onto policy agendas. But there has been a continuing failure of implementation for reasons such as poorly drafted policies, insufficient resources, and lack of political will, to name but a few. A recent example of an unfulfilled promise closely linked to the closure of Kew Cottages was the private sale of the three remaining historic buildings on the site, which had been earmarked by the Bracks government as a community centre for new and old residents. Another was reneging on the agreement to relocate the hundred residents left on the site more evenly through the development once it was finished in order to avoid perpetuating the enclave, though this was a result of building delays that had been created in 2008.

Finally, other continuities are the disparities in life expectancy and health status of people with intellectual disabilities compared to the general population. As a group, they continue to experience higher rates of mortality, avoidable deaths and untreated health conditions.[14] Nevertheless, their longevity has increased dramatically since Kew Cottages was first established, at which time few children with intellectual disabilities made it into adulthood. Living longer lives is something to be celebrated but brings more jeopardies for people with intellectual disabilities than others experience. Who will 'care about' individuals once their parents die? And where should 'caring for' take place? Siblings, nieces, nephews or family friends usually take over the mantel of 'caring about' from parents. But in terms of 'caring for', there is a very real possibility that aging may result in relocation to institutions of another kind: residential aged care. And the evidence suggests that being classified as an older person may be even riskier in terms of abuse and neglect than being a person with intellectual disability. This is something to be avoided. The aged care sector has much to learn from the disability sector, at least in terms of articulating ambitions about rights.

Concluding Thoughts

Debates about the merits of Kew Cottages commenced almost as soon as the institution opened, along with frequent promises about its closure. The 'Not in My Back Yard' stance was quickly adopted by members of the local Kew Shire Council and ratepayers, who argued for closure as far back as 1905. A hundred years later these groups flipped, opposing closure and sale of the site to protect their open space. This time they argued alongside the Kew Cottages Parents' Association, which was seeking to protect people with intellectual disabilities from negative community attitudes by building a 'Centre of Excellence' on the site.

Australia has taken much longer than the Scandinavian countries to close large institutions for people with intellectual disabilities, and current NDIS funding rules obstruct their re-emergence. But creating smaller places where people with intellectual disabilities are clustered together remains contentious, and arguments about unwelcoming communities, or people preferring to live with peers as do other subgroups of the population, re-emerge from time to time. It remains to be seen whether, in the future, evidence about the negative impact of segregating people with intellectual disabilities from others, and congregating many of them together, will be trumped by the neo-liberal dictum of individual choice and control, which is now firmly embedded in disability policies.

In 2021, the maturing NDIS, the refreshed National Disability Strategy, and Australia's signature on the UN Convention on the Rights of Persons with Disabilities are all potential catalysts for turning ideas about rights into realities. The 2023 report of the Royal Commission into Violence, Abuse, Neglect and Exploitation of People with Disability is likely to provide further impetus. Breaking the pattern of the past poses major challenges for people with intellectual disabilities, who fit poorly into the mould of individualism, productivity and status that shapes current society. Strong and powerful long-term allies must also be found for this group of people, because people with intellectual disabilities and their families find advocating for themselves and their family members full of onerous, and sometimes insurmountable, challenges.

Appendix of Institutions in Victoria for those with Intellectual Disabilities

Listed in Order of their Establishment and their Name Changes

Yarra Bend Lunatic Asylum in Kew (1848–1925)
Later called Yarra Bend Hospital for the Insane.

Ararat Lunatic Asylum (1867–1993)
Later called: Ararat Hospital for the Insane; Ararat Mental Hospital; Aradale Training Centre.

Beechworth Lunatic Asylum (1867–1993/95)
Later called: Beechworth Hospital for the Insane; Beechworth Mental Hospital; Beechworth Psychiatric Hospital; May Day Hills Hospital; May Day Hills Training Centre.

Kew Lunatic Asylum (1872–1988)
Later called: Kew Hospital for the Insane; Kew Mental Hospital; Kew Psychiatric Hospital; Willsmere Hospital.

Ballarat Asylum (1877–1879)

Kew Idiot Asylum (1887–2008)
Later called: Children's Cottages; Kew Training Centre; Kew Cottages; Kew Residential Services.

Sunbury Lunatic Asylum (1879–1993)
Later called: Sunbury Hospital for the Insane; Sunbury Mental Hospital; Sunbury Mental Hospital/Training Centre; Caloola Training Centre.

APPENDIX

Ballarat Hospital for the Insane (1893–1990s)
Later called: Ballarat Mental Hospital; Lakeside Mental Hospital;
Lakeside Psychiatric Hospital.

Mont Park Mental Hospital in Bundoora (1912–1990s)
Later called: Mont Park Hospital for the Insane; Military Mental
Hospital; Mont Park Mental Hospital; Mont Park Psychiatric Hospital.

Travancore Special School in Flemington (1933—)
Later called: Travancore Developmental Centre; Travancore Psychiatric
Development Centre; Travancore Child and Family Centre; Travancore
School—Early Childhood Intervention Service.

Janefield Colony in Bundoora (1937–1996)
Later called Janefield Training Centre.

Pleasant Creek Special School in Stawell (1937–1998)
Later called Pleasant Creek Training Centre.

Larundel Mental Hospital in Bundoora (1953–1990s)
Later called Larundel Psychiatric Hospital.

Sandhurst Boys' Home in Bendigo (1956–2016)
Also known as: the Sandhurst Centre; the Bendigo Training Centre;
the Sandhurst Boys' Centre.

St Nicholas Hospital in Carlton (1963–1985)

Kingsbury Training Centre in Bundoora (1973–1996)

Colanda Centre in Colac (1976–2019)

Acknowledgments

The very many people who contributed to the research and writing of this book reflect the significant place Kew Cottages occupied both in the history of Victoria and in people's everyday lives.

This book is the final outcome of a project initiated by Alma Adams, manager of Kew Residential Services Redevelopment, to mark the closure of the cottages. As project officer, Kerrie Soraghan supported the research and writing in myriad ways, particularly in facilitating access to resident files and other restricted archival material.

A great many people from the cottages community contributed to the project in interviews and by donating photographs and documents, creating an extensive archive from which to draw. We owe particular thanks to Fran van Brummelen, who generously shared oral histories and other research from the Kew Cottages Historical Society, and to Louise Godwin, executive officer, Kew Cottages Parents' Association (KCPA), who took considerable interest in the research. Beryl Power, from the KCPA, volunteered important documents and several days of her time copying them for inclusion in the project archive. Astrid Judge, daughter of Dr Cliff Judge, shared her memories of growing up at Kew. Ted Rowe, a resident at Kew in the 1920s, also shared his memories.

Mrs Norma Sutherland and Mrs Brenda Lawton, descendants of the cottages' first head teacher, Theophilus Eastham, shared their family history research. Norma also allowed us to reproduce a number of photographs from her collection, including significant images taken of the cottages by notable Melbourne photographer Nicholas Caire, not previously published.

Historians depend on the work of archivists and librarians to write their histories. We would like to thank the staff of Public Record Office Victoria and the Department of Health and Human Services Archival Services, and, at the latter especially, Catherine Green and Istarlin Omar, who spent much time retrieving patient and other records. Thanks also to the staff

ACKNOWLEDGMENTS

at State Library Victoria, La Trobe University's Borchardt Library, the Mental Health Library at the Royal Melbourne Hospital's Health Sciences Library, the Wellcome Library in London, and Lancashire Records Office.

Dr Yvonne Ward made a significant contribution to the research for this book, particularly in her painstaking search of newspaper indexes and of patient admission warrants. Dr Anne Westmore, an expert in the history of psychiatry in Victoria, willingly shared her knowledge and research on several aspects of that history. Anne Pitkethly similarly shared her extensive research on Nicholas Caire.

The members of the Social History of Learning Disability Group at the Open University, Milton Keynes, were both welcoming and inspiring. The importance of the cottages' history was recognised by the award of an Australian Research Council Linkage Grant (LP0455016), jointly funded by the ARC, Industry (Linkage) partner Kew Residential Services/Department of Human Services and La Trobe University. Part Two of the book was completed by co-author David Henderson, whose contribution was made possible by the financial assistance for over a year of Christine Bigby and funds from her Living with Disability Research Centre, at La Trobe University. A grant from La Trobe University also funded the expert copy-editing by Judith Smart.

The chief investigators of the ARC grant, Professors Richard Broome, Christine Bigby and Katie Holmes, have overseen the project since its inception, including the writing of this book. They each read the draft chapters, offering insightful comments and editorial suggestions that helped sharpen the final result. In addition, Richard assumed responsibility for writing chapter 11 and managing the book to publication.

Without the support of family, friends and colleagues, books would never be written. David would particularly like to thank Christine Bigby, director of the Living with Disability Research Centre, who, in addition to funding his writing, read each of his chapters and provided considered commentary and feedback that helped him draw out the major themes at the heart of this book. David's thanks are also extended to Lee-Ann Monk—'to collaborate on such a challenging history at such a challenging time is no easy feat'. In addition he would like to thank his colleagues at the Living with Disability Research Centre, La Trobe University. David also thanks Mim Hayes, 'who has had to put up with me at work and at home for the last few years and our three beautiful children, Archie, Leo and Sunday, who always managed to elicit from me a pained groan at the dinner table whenever they enquired about the progress of this book'.

Lee-Ann especially thanks Professor Diane Kirkby for her sage advice and support. 'Both Diane and Associate Professor Emma Robertson very generously allowed time away from working on their projects to finish this book. Special thanks also to Richard Broome for agreeing to work closely with me in the final stages. The history of disability is not always easy to research and write, and there were other obstacles on the way. I thank especially my colleague on the project, Dr Corinne Manning, without whose support, encouragement and sense of humour the task would have been so much the harder. Thank you, my friend, for taking those calls from the archives on bad days. Yvonne Ward was great company in the archives. David Henderson, my co-author, became a welcome companion on the project and encouraged me in my writing, as well as literally helping with the heavy lifting. Special thanks to my friends and colleagues, especially Janet Butler, Liz Dimock and Fiona Paisley, who provided unfailing support and belief that I could get it done. Last, but never ever least, I thank my partner Ian McNaughton, who did everything possible to help me write this book, including taking photographs of the cottages' redevelopment. I thank him for all of it, including the illicit cake.'

Finally, we must thank Julia Carlomagno, publisher and director of Monash University Publishing, and her team, who recognised the importance of this book and its compelling story.

Project Outcomes
(2006–23)

In 2005 a group of researchers at La Trobe University in Melbourne, namely Christine Bigby, Richard Broome, Katie Holmes, Lee-Ann Monk, Corinne Manning, John Tebbutt and Christine Dew, began an Australian Research Council Linkage grant with Kew Residential Services to write a multi-outcome history of Kew Cottages. This institution was about to shut down, and Kew Residential Services, a part of the Department of Human Services in Victoria, wanted a history written to mark the closure of the cottages after 121 years.

The project's title was 'A Great and Crying Need: A History of Kew Residential Services, 1887–2007, through innovative textual, oral, aural and experiential media'. It aimed to do the following:

This original history of Kew Residential Services (KRS), formerly known as Kew Cottages, will trace the lives of its residents from 1887, analysing the changing discourses, policies and practices for people with intellectual disability. It will analyse the history of Kew Residential Services in terms of a modern society's shifting response to difference. The Project is internationally innovative researching with and for people with intellectual disability and giving voice to their experiences.

The project promised to produce two books—a history and an oral history—as well as an exhibition, a radio program, photographic research, non-verbal research with residents, a website and other academic articles.

During the project Cameron Rose replaced Christine Dew on the aural/experiential part of the project, and he produced further digital stories with non-verbal residents of Kew Cottages and an exhibition.

Also, David Henderson came on board (supported by funding from the director of the Living with Disability Research Centre at La Trobe University, Christine Bigby) to become co-author with Lee-Ann Monk of the history of Kew Cottages. Over a period of fifteen years, this project's outputs were mentored and steered by Chief Investigators Christine Bigby, Richard Broome and Katie Holmes.

Below are listed the nineteen publications and thirteen conference presentations deriving from this project.

Book Publications

Corinne Manning, *Bye-Bye Charlie: Stories from the Vanishing World of Kew Cottages* (Sydney: University of New South Wales Press, 2008).

Lee-Ann Monk & David Henderson with Christine Bigby, Richard Broome and Katie Holmes, *Failed Ambitions: Kew Cottages and Changing Ideas of Intellectual Disabilities* (Melbourne: Monash University Publishing, 2023).

Chapters and Articles

Lee-Ann Monk, '"Made enquires, can elicit no history of injury": Researching the History of Institutional Abuse in the Archives', *Provenance: The Journal of Public Record Office Victoria*, no. 6 (September 2007), https://prov.vic.gov.au/explore-collection/provenance-journal/provenance-2007/made-enquiries-can-elicit-no-history-injury.

Corinne Manning, 'Imprisoned in State Care: Life Inside Kew Cottages, 1925–2008', *Health and History*, 11, no. 1 (May 2009): 149-171.

Lee-Ann Monk, 'Exploiting Patient Labour at Kew Cottages, Australia, 1887–1950', *British Journal of Learning Disabilities Special Issue: Histories of Institutional Change, Choice and Money*, 38, no. 2 (June 2010): 86–94.

Corinne Manning, '"My memory's back!" Inclusive Learning Disability Research Using Ethics, Oral History and Digital Storytelling', *British Journal of Learning Disabilities*, 38, no. 3 (September 2010): 160–67.

Christine Bigby and Dorothy Atkinson, 'Written out of History: Invisible Women in Intellectual Disability Social Work', *Australian Social Work*, 63, no. 1 (2010): 4–17.

Corinne Manning, 'From Surrender to Activism: The Transformation of Disability and Mothering at Kew Cottages, Australia', in *Disability and Mothering: Liminal Spaces of Embodied Knowledge*, eds Cynthia Lewiecki-Wilson and Jen Cellio (Syracuse: Syracuse University Press, 2011), 183–202.

Lee-Ann Monk and Corinne Manning, 'Exploring Patient Experience in an Australian Institution for Children with Learning Disabilities, 1870–1933', in *Disabled Children: Contested Caring 1850–1979*, eds Anne Borsay and Pamela Dale (London and Brookfield, Vermont: Pickering & Chatto, 2012), 73–86.

Lee-Ann Monk, 'Intimacy and Oppression: A Historical Perspective', in *Sexuality and Relationships in the Lives of People with Intellectual Disabilities: Standing in My Shoes*, eds Rohhss Chapman, Sue Ledger, and Louise Townson, with Daniel Docherty (London: Jessica Kingsley Publishers, 2015), 46–64.

Lee-Ann Monk, 'Paradoxical Lives: Intellectual Disability Policy and Practice in Twentieth-Century Australia', in *Intellectual Disability in the Twentieth Century: Transnational Perspectives on People, Policy and Practice*, eds Jan Walmsley and Simon Jarrett (Bristol: Policy Press, 2019), 21–33.

Richard Broome, '"They had little chance"': The Kew Cottages Fire of 1996', *Victorian Historical Journal*, 91, no. 2 (December 2020): 245–66.

Exhibitions

Cameron Rose (designed and developed from an original concept by Chris Dew), *Kew Cottages Exhibition*, State Library Victoria, June 2008; Hawthorn Town Hall Gallery, November 2008.

Corinne Manning, 'Kew Cottages Digital Histories', Exhibitor Kew Festival, 2008.

Multimedia

Chris Dew, *A Great Big Bag*, short film, 2005.

Cameron Rose, *Three Short Films about Kew Cottages Residents*, DVD, La Trobe University, 2008.

John Tebbutt and Michelle Rayner, *A Great and Crying Need: A History of Kew Cottages*, ABC RN *Hindsight*, 24 August 2008, http://www.abc.net.au/rn/hindsight/stories/2008/2334093.htm.

Websites

Corinne Manning and Lee-Ann Monk (content development) 2008, Cameron Rose and Amber Benjafield (website development and design), *Kew Cottages: A History* www.kewcottageshistory.com.au, launched 2010 but now archived.

Corinne Manning and Lee-Ann Monk (content development) 2008 (website development and design), *Kew Cottages: A History*, second rebuilt edition, www.kewcottageshistory-latrobe.com.au.

Conferences and Symposiums

Corinne Manning, 'Violent Imaginings: Oral History and Abuse at Kew Cottages', Australian Historical Association Conference, Australian National University, Canberra, 2006.

Lee-Ann Monk, 'Researching and Writing the History of Institutional Abuse from Archival Sources, Kew Cottages, 1887–1908', Australian Historical Association Conference, Australian National University, Canberra, 2006.

Corinne Manning, 'Working with the "Children of the Darkness": Conducting Oral History with Intellectually Disabled Residents of Kew Cottages', Revising the Past and the Future: Current Research on Intellectual and Physical Disability, Faculty of Health Sciences, La Trobe University, Annual Conference, 2006.

Corinne Manning, '"We just wore ordinary clothes, like prison clothes": The Importance of Oral History in Understanding the World of Kew Cottages', Interdisciplinary Symposium, La Trobe University, 2007.

Corinne Manning, 'Imprisoned in State Care: Life Inside Kew Cottages 1925–2008', Public Seminar on the History of Mental Illness and Mental Hospitals in Australia, Museum of Brisbane and the Centre for Public Culture and Ideas, 2007.

Corinne Manning, 'Working with the "Children of the Darkness", 'Researching Institutional Histories', Social History of Learning Disability Research Group, International Seminar, The Open University, Milton Keynes, United Kingdom, 2007.

Corinne Manning and Lee-Ann Monk, '"Sexual vices are kept within a very limited compass": Sexual Understandings and Expression in Australia's Largest Institution for People with learning Disabilities, 1887–2006', 'Learning Disability, Relationships and Sexuality: Past and Present', Social History of Learning Disability Research Group Conference, The Open University, Milton Keynes, United Kingdom, 2007.

Lee-Ann Monk, '"On the same lines as those in England": British Influences on an Australian Institution for People with Learning Disabilities', 'Researching Institutional Histories', International Seminar, The Open University, Milton Keynes, United Kingdom, 2007.

Dorothy Atkinson & Alistair Thompson, Keynote Address, 'Life Stories, History and Intellectual Disability', Kew Project Conference, La Trobe University, 2007.

Corinne Manning, 'When State Care Turns Lethal: The 1996 Fire at Kew Cottages', Australian Historical Association Conference, University of Melbourne, 2008.

Lee-Ann Monk, '"Little better than chattel slaves": Inmate Labour in an Australian Institution for Learning Disability', 'Spending Time in Institutions', International Research Seminar, The Open University, Milton Keynes, United Kingdom, 2008.

Lee-Ann Monk, 'Changing Definitions of Difference: The Establishment of Kew Cottages', Constructing Intellectual Disability: A Symposium on the History of a Concept, sponsored by the Centre for Disability Studies, University of Sydney, 2009.

Lee-Ann Monk, 'Changing Definitions of Difference: The Establishment of Kew Cottages', Constructing Intellectual Disability: A Symposium on the History of a Concept, sponsored by Griffith Abilities Research Program in partnership with The Disability Studies Research Construction, School of Human Services and Social Work, Griffith University, Brisbane, 2009.

Notes

Foreword

1 Exhibit 3–24, Statement of Christine Bigby, 28 November 2019; Transcript, Christine Bigby, Public Hearing 3, 6 December 2019, pp. 398–419. Both Professor Bigby's statement and the transcript of her oral evidence are available on the Royal Commission's website: https://disability. royalcommission.gov.au/public-hearings/public-hearing-3. Two co-authors of the book have also contributed to the work of the royal commission. Dr Lee-Ann Monk's work was cited in the royal commission's *Interim Report*, October 2020, pp. 51, 72. An article co-authored by Dr David Henderson was admitted into evidence at Public Hearing 5 ('Experiences of People with Disability during the ongoing COVID-19 Pandemic'): Exhibit 5–29.19, EXP.0027.0001.1441.

2 The title of Chapter 6 of *Failed Ambitions*.

3 Elisabeth Bredberg, 'Writing Disability History: Problems, Perspectives and Sources', *Disability and Society*, 14, no. 2 (1999): 198, cited in Lorna Hallahan, *Disability in Australia: Shadows, Struggles and Successes: A Usable Socio-cultural History of Disability in Australia* (Canberra: Research Report, Royal Commission into Violence, Abuse, Neglect and Exploitation of People with Disability, 2021), 118 n. 30.

4 See Chapter 5 ('A New Deal for Mental Defectives' 1924–1939), referring to unsuccessful attempts in Victoria to enact legislation authorising the sterilisation of the 'mentally afflicted'.

5 See Chapter 12 ('Deinstitutionalisation').

Introduction

1 *Commonwealth Parliamentary Debates (CPD)*, House of Representatives, No. 17, 2012, 1378.

2 Leo Kanner, *A History of the Care and Study of the Mentally Retarded* (Springfield, Illinois: Charles C. Thomas, 1964); R.C. Scheerenberger, *A History of Mental Retardation* (Baltimore, MD: Paul H. Brookes, 1983).

3 Frances Koestler, *The Unseen Minority: A Social History of Blindness in the United States* (New York: David McKay and Co., 1976); Paul K. Longmore and Lauri Umansky (eds), *The New Disability History: American Perspectives* (New York and London: New York University Press, 2001).

4 Dorothy Atkinson, 'Research and Empowerment: Involving People with Learning Difficulties in Oral and Life History Research', *Disability and Society*, 19, no. 7 (2004): 691–702; Christine Bigby, Patsie Frawley and

NOTES

Paul Ramcharan, 'Conceptualizing Inclusive Research with People with Intellectual Disability', *Journal of Applied Research in Intellectual Disabilities*, 27, no. 1 (2014): 3–12; Jan Walmsley and Kelley Johnson, *Inclusive Research with People with Learning Disabilities: Past, Present and Futures* (London: Jessica Kingsley Publishers, 2003).

5   Tom Shakespeare, 'Rules of Engagement: Doing Disability Research', *Disability and Society*, 11, no. 1 (1996): 115–19; Kirsten Stalker, 'Some Ethical and Methodological Issues in Research with People with Learning Disabilities', *Disability and Society*, 13, no. 1 (1998): 5–19.

6   For example, Maggie Potts and Rebecca Fido, *'A Fit Person to be Removed': Personal Accounts of Life in a Mental Deficiency Institution* (Plymouth: Northcote House, 1991); 'Mabel Cooper's Life Story', in *Forgotten Lives: Exploring the History of Intellectual Disability*, eds Dorothy Atkinson, Mark Jackson and Jan Walmsley (Kidderminster: BILD Publications, 1997), 21–34.

7   Corinne Manning, *Bye-Bye Charlie: Stories from the Vanishing World of Kew Cottages* (Sydney: University of New South Wales Press, 2008), 23.

8   David Henderson & Christine Bigby, 'Whose Life Story Is It? Self-Reflexive Life Story Research with People with Intellectual Disabilities', *Oral History Review*, 44, no. 1 (2017): 39–55; David Henderson & Christine Bigby, 'We Were More Radical Back Then: Victoria's First Self-Advocacy Organisation for People with Intellectual Disability', *Health and History*, 18, no. 1 (2016): 42–66.

9   Charles Fox, '"Forehead Low, Aspect Idiotic": Intellectual Disability in Victorian Asylums, 1870–1887', in *'Madness' in Australia: Histories, Heritage and the Asylum*, eds Catharine Coleborne and Dolly MacKinnon (Brisbane: University of Queensland Press, 2003), 145–56, 153.

10 *Lunacy Statute 1867*, s.21; *Lunacy Act 1890*, s.31; *Lunacy Act 1903*, s.37.

11 Jonathan Andrews, 'Case Notes, Case Histories and the Patient's Experience of Insanity at Gartnavel Royal Asylum, Glasgow, in the Nineteenth Century', *Social History of Medicine*, 11, no. 2 (1998): 255–81, 264–6.

12 Geoffrey Reaume, '"Keep your labels off my mind!" Or "Now I am going to pretend I am craze but don't be a bit alarmed": Psychiatric History from the Patients' Perspectives', *Canadian Bulletin of the History of Medical History*, 11, no. 2 (1994): 397–424, at 401; Kelley Johnson, *Deinstitutionalising Women: An Ethnographic Study of Institutional Closure* (Cambridge: Cambridge University Press, 1998), 57.

13 Fox, 147.

14 Reaume, 399, 402.

15 Reaume, 397, 399.

16 Joanna Ryan, with Frank Thomas, *The Politics of Mental Handicap*, Revised Edition (London: Free Association Books, 1987).

17 Rannveig Traustadóttir and Kelley Johnson, 'Introduction: In and Out of Institutions', in *Deinstitutionalization and People with Intellectual Disabilities*, eds Rannveig Traustadóttir and Kelley Johnson (London: Jessica Kingsley Publishers, 2008), 13–29, 18–19.

NOTES

18   Dave Earl, 'Australian Histories of Intellectual Disabilities', in *The Routledge History of Disability*, eds Roy Hanes, Ivan Brown and Nancy E. Hansen (Oxford and New York: Routledge, 2018), 308; and Jan Walmsley and Simon Jarrett, 'Introduction', in *Intellectual Disability in the Twentieth Century: Transnational Perspectives on People, Policy and Practice*, eds Jan Walmsley and Simon Jarrett (Bristol: Policy Press, 2019), 5.

19   Earl, 309; James W. Trent, *Inventing the Feeble Mind: A History of Intellectual Disability in the United States*, Second Edition (New York: Oxford University Press, 2017), xix–xx.

20   Manning, 21.

Chapter 1: 'In the City of the Insane' 1867–87

1   'The Asylum for the Insane at the Yarra Bend', *Herald*, 17 October 1868, 3, and 23 October 1868, 3.

2   Lee-Ann Monk, *Attending Madness: At Work in the Australian Colonial Asylum* (Amsterdam and New York: Editions Rodopi B.V., 2008), 24–5.

3   Elizabeth Malcolm, 'Australian Asylum Architecture through German Eyes: Kew, Melbourne, 1867', *Health and History*, 11, no. 1 (2009): 47–9; C.R.D. Brothers, *Early Victorian Psychiatry, 1835–1905* (Melbourne: Government Printer, 1961), 19, 32.

4   VPRS 7400/P1, Unit 1, pp. 61, 189, 246, 292, 293, 318, 402, Public Record Office Victoria (PROV).

5   Report of the Board of Visitors, 12 December 1861, VPRS 1189/P, Unit 569, File 1861/S9716, PROV.

6   *Victorian Parliamentary Debates (VPD)*, Vol. VIII, 17 June 1862, 1340; 'Summary for Europe', *Argus*, 25 June 1862, 5.

7   Brothers, 66; Andrew Crowther, 'Administration and the Asylum in Victoria, 1860s – 1880s', in *'Madness' in Australia: Histories, Heritage and the Asylum*, eds Catharine Coleborne and Dolly MacKinnon (Brisbane: University of Queensland Press, 2003), 86; 'Yarra Bend in 1864', *Argus*, 1 July 1864, 7.

8   'The Yarra Bend Asylum, near Melbourne', *Journal of Mental Science*, 8, no. 44 (January 1863): 619; Malcolm, 59.

9   Brothers, 41, 64–5; Malcolm, 48–50.

10   Malcolm, 51; Cheryl Day, 'Magnificence, Misery and Madness: A History of Kew Asylum, 1872–1915' (PhD thesis, University of Melbourne, 1998), 31–4; 'The New Lunatic Asylum at Kew', *Argus*, 15 December 1871, 6.

11   Brothers, 84–90, 97–8.

12   *Report of the Inspector of Lunatic Asylums on the Hospitals for the Insane, for the Year 1870* (Melbourne: John Ferres, Government Printer, 1871), 13.

13   Brothers, 90, 97–8.

14   *Royal Commission on Asylums for the Insane and Inebriate, Report and Minutes of Evidence*, in *Victorian Parliamentary Papers*, 1886, Vol. II (Melbourne: John Ferres, Government Printer, 1886) (hereafter Royal Commission, 1884–86), Minutes of Evidence, Q.7567, 305.

15   Royal Commission, 1884–86, Minutes of Evidence, Q.10135, 426.

299

NOTES

16   Richard Broome, *The Victorians: Arriving* (Sydney: Fairfax, Syme & Weldon, 1984), 26.

17   *Report of the Inspector of Lunatic Asylums 1870*, 7–9.

18   Royal Commission, 1884–86, Minutes of Evidence, Q.8960–8695, 363–4, and Final Report, xxi; Brothers, 98, 109, 139, 168.

19   *Report of the Inspector of Lunatic Asylums 1870*, 9, 4.

20   *Report of the Inspector of Lunatic Asylums, 1870*, 4, 12–13, 20; *Report of the Inspector of Lunatic Asylums on the Hospitals for the Insane, for the Year 1868* (Melbourne: John Ferres, Government Printer, 1869), 5, 6.

21   *Report of the Inspector of Lunatic Asylums, 1870*, 11–12.

22   *Report of the Inspector of Lunatic Asylums, 1870*, 12, 13; *Report of the Inspector of Lunatic Asylums on the Hospitals for the Insane, for the Year 1872* (Melbourne: John Ferres, Government Printer, 1873), 9; *Report of the Inspector of Lunatic Asylums on the Hospitals for the Insane, for the Year 1876* (Melbourne: John Ferres, Government Printer, 1877), 10.

23   Charles Fox, "'Forehead Low, Aspect Idiotic": Intellectual Disability in Victorian Asylums, 1870–1887', in *'Madness' in Australia: Histories, Heritage and the Asylum*, eds Catharine Coleborne and Dolly MacKinnon (Brisbane: University of Queensland Press, 2003), 147; Anne Digby, 'Contexts and Perspectives', in *From Idiocy to Mental Deficiency: Historical Perspectives on People with Learning Disabilities*, eds David Wright & Anne Digby (London and New York: Routledge, 1996), 5.

24   David Wright, *Mental Disability in Victorian England: The Earlswood Asylum* (Oxford: Oxford University Press, 2001), 25–36, 137; David Gladstone, 'The Changing Dynamic of Institutional Care: The Western Counties Idiot Asylum, 1864–1914', in *From Idiocy to Mental Deficiency: Historical Perspectives on People with Learning Disabilities*, eds David Wright & Anne Digby (London and New York: Routledge, 1996), 138.

25   Gladstone, 137; Anne Borsay, *Disability and Social Policy in Britain since 1750* (Basingstoke: Palgrave Macmillan, 2005), 99.

26   Digby, 1–21; Gladstone, 137–8; Wright, 6, 41.

27   Wright, 41, 138, 144–9, 153; Gladstone, 151–4.

28   *Report of the Inspector of Lunatic Asylums, 1872*, 11.

29   *Report of the Inspector of Lunatic Asylums on the Hospitals for the Insane, for the Year 1875* (Melbourne: John Ferres, Government Printer, 1876), 11–12.

30   HRRA/31/4/3, Lancashire Record Office (LRO); Milton Lewis, *Managing Madness: Psychiatry and Society in Australia 1788–1980* (Canberra: Australian Government Publishing Service, 1988), 24–5; Norman Megahey, 'Living in Fremantle Asylum: The Colonial Experience of Intellectual Disability 1829–1900', in *Under Blue Skies: The Social Construction of Intellectual Disability in Western Australia*, eds Errol Cocks, Charlie Fox, Mark Brogan and Michael Lee (Perth: Centre for Disability Research and Development, Faculty of Health and Human Sciences, Edith Cowan University, 1996), 32–3, 47.

31   C.J. Cummins, *A History of Medical Administration in New South Wales*; HRRA/31/4/3, LRO; Ann K. Williams, 'Managing the "Feebleminded": Eugenics and the Institutionalisation of People with Intellectual Disabilities

NOTES

in New South Wales, 1900 to 1930' (PhD thesis, Department of History, University of Newcastle, 1998).

32 HRRA/31/4/3, LRO; *Report of the Inspector-General of the Insane, 1878–79*, quoted in G.A. Tucker, *Lunacy in Many Lands* (Sydney: Charles Potter, Government Printer, 1887), 646.

33 'A Visit to the Yarra Bend', *Age*, 13 February 1874, 3.

34 Vagabond, 'A Month in Kew Asylum and Yarra Bend', *Argus*, 29 July 1876, 4.

35 Vagabond, 'A Month in Kew Asylum and Yarra Bend', *Argus*, 26 August 1876, 9.

36 *Report of the Inspector of Lunatic Asylums on the Hospitals for the Insane, for the Year 1877* (Melbourne: John Ferres, Government Printer, 1878), 21; *Report of the Inspector of Lunatic Asylums on the Hospitals for the Insane, for the Year 1879* (Melbourne: John Ferres, Government Printer, 1880), 28–9; VPRS 3991/P, Box 957, File 77/M8433, PROV.

37 *Report of the Inspector of Lunatic Asylums, 1879*, 11.

38 *Report of the Inspector of Lunatic Asylums, 1879*, 11; *Report of the Inspector of Lunatic Asylums on the Hospitals for the Insane, for the Year 1880* (Melbourne: John Ferres, Government Printer, 1881), 11; *Report of the Inspector of Lunatic Asylums on the Hospitals for the Insane, for the Year 1881* (Melbourne: John Ferres, Government Printer, 1882), 5 and 28; VPRS 3991/P, Unit 1326, File 1882/ W4730, PROV.

39 VPRS 3993, Unit 45, Entry 83/Y7458, PROV; Richard Bonwick, 'The History of the Yarra Bend Lunatic Asylum, Melbourne' (Master of Medicine (Psychiatry) thesis, University of Melbourne, 1995), 57.

40 VPRS 3993, Unit 44, 1882, Entry X5619; Unit 45, 1883, Entry Y5691; Unit 46, Entry Z10536; VPRS 3994, Unit 2, 1884, Entry B1766; VPRS 3991, Unit 1406, File 83/Z3643, PROV.

41 Jill Giese, *The Maddest Place on Earth* (Melbourne: Australian Scholarly Publishing, 2018); Crowther, 93.

42 Lewis, 17; Brothers, 102, 129, 134.

43 Royal Commission, 1884–86, Miscellaneous, Victorian Branch, British Medical Association, Kew Lunatic Asylum, cxlii–iv, and Remarks of Dr Dick on the Report of the Victorian Branch of the British Medical Association, cxliv–vi; Brothers, 100–02.

44 *Argus*, 27 November 1879, 5; 'Kew Lunatic Asylum', *Argus*, 28 November 1879, 7; also 29 November 1879, 6; 17 January 1880, 9; 'Overcrowding of the Kew Lunatic Asylum', *Age*, 27 November 1879, 4, and 3 February 1880, 2.

45 *VPD*, Vol. 32, 17 December 1879, 2302; Vol. 35, 7 December 1880, 1075; 20 January 1881, 2339–40; 7 April 1881, 2026; Vol. 38, 12 December 1881, 1155–7; Vol. 42, 26 July 1883, 377; Vol. 44, 11 September 1883, 986–8, and 18 October 1883, 1520; Lewis, 17.

46 Royal Commission, 1884–86, Minutes of Evidence, Q.8677–80, 349; Q.9310–11, 390; Q.9383–6, 394; Q.9625, 405; Q.10322–5, 436; Q.11027–9, 477; Q.12345, 529; Q.12948–50, 550; Q.11424–7, 497.

47 Royal Commission, 1884–86, Minutes of Evidence, Q.9383, 394; Q.9180–3, 380; Q.9627–31, 405–06; Q.10323–7, 436; Q.12942–7, 550.

NOTES

48 Royal Commission, 1884–86, Minutes of Evidence, Q.9383, 394.

49 Royal Commission, 1884–86, Minutes of Evidence, Q.9625–31, 405–06.

50 Royal Commission, 1884–86, Minutes of Evidence, Q.9181–4, 380; Q.9384–5, 394; Q.9629–32, 406; Q.10323, 328; Q.12942–9, 550.

51 Royal Commission, 1884–86, Minutes of Evidence, Q.11022–6, 477.

52 Royal Commission, 1884–86, Minutes of Evidence, Q.12344, 529; Q.8560–4, 344.

53 Royal Commission, 1884–86, Report, xlii, xlv.

54 *Argus*, 9 October 1885, 4.

55 *Argus*, 5 January 1887, 4.

56 'A Necessary Reform', *Herald*, 27 January 1886, 2.

57 *Argus*, 9 October 1885, 5.

58 VPRS 3993, Unit 45, 1883, Entries 83/Y7458 and Z10536, PROV.

59 VPRS 981, Unit 14, 181, Contract 1876, PROV; 'Tenders', *Herald*, 5 November 1885, 3; Malcolm, 47.

60 Allan Willingham, 'A Permanent and Extensive Exhibition Building', in *Victorian Icon: The Royal Exhibition Building Melbourne*, ed. David Dunstan (Melbourne: The Exhibition Trustees, 1996), 52–8.

61 *Argus*, 30 August 1886, 4.

62 *Argus*, 5 January 1887, 4.

63 *Herald*, 27 January 1887, 3; 17 February 1887, 3; 24 March 1887, 3; *Age*, 5 February 1887, 15; 29 April 1887, 6.

64 *Report of the Inspector of Lunatic Asylums on the Hospitals for the Insane, for the Year 1886* (Melbourne: John Ferres, Government Printer, 1887), 18.

65 Brothers, 40; Day, 47–8.

66 'News of the Day', *Age*, 8 September 1886, 4.

67 'News of the Day', *Age*, 25 November 1886, 4; 13 September 1887, 4; 29 September 1887, 5.

68 *Argus*, 20 October 1887, 7.

Chapter 2: 'Always a Curious Boy' 1887–1908

1 E. Bishop to F. Longmore MLA, VPRS 3992, Box 676, File 1897/E7757, Public Record Office Victoria (PROV).

2 Analysis of 'Table: Showing the Manner in which Patients were Admitted', in Reports of the Inspector of Lunatic Asylums and Reports of the Inspector-General of the Insane, 1894–1907.

3 Dave Earl, 'Australian Histories of Intellectual Disabilities', in *The Routledge History of Disability*, eds Roy Hanes, Ivan Brown and Nancy E. Hansen (Oxford and New York: Routledge, 2018), 310; Jessa Chupik and David Wright, 'Treating the "Idiot" Child in early 20th-century Ontario', *Disability and Society*, 21, no. 1 (January 2006): 82.

4 David Wright, *Mental Disability in Victorian England: The Earlswood Asylum 1847–1901* (Oxford: Clarendon Press, 2001), chapters 3 and 4.

5 Milton Lewis, *Managing Madness: Psychiatry and Society in Australia, 1788–1980* (Canberra: AGPS, 1988), 22.

302

NOTES

6   *An Act to Consolidate and Amend the Law relating to Lunatics 1867* (Lunacy Statute 1867), Eleventh Schedule; *An Act to Amend the Law relating to Lunacy 1903* (Lunacy Act 1903), Schedule Four; David Wright, '"Childlike in his Innocence": Lay Attitudes to "Idiots" and "Imbeciles" in Victorian England', in *Idiocy to Mental Deficiency: Historical Perspectives on People with Learning Disabilities*, eds David Wright and Anne Digby (London and New York: Routledge, 1996), 118.

7   Lunacy Statute 1867, s. 11; Lunacy Act 1903, s. 26; Wright, '"Childlike in his Innocence"', 120.

8   Lunacy Statute 1867, s. 21; Lunacy Act 1903, s. 12 (1).

9   Earl, 'Australian Histories of Intellectual Disabilities', 309.

10   The following discussion is based on an analysis of admission documents in VPRS 7565/P1, Units 1–4, PROV.

11   Wright, *Mental Disability in Victorian England*, 53.

12   Compare Wright, *Mental Disability in Victorian England*, 51–2; David Wright, 'Familial Care of "Idiot" Children in Victorian England', in *The Locus of Care: Families, Communities and the Provision of Welfare since Antiquity*, eds Peregrine Holden and Richard Smith (London: Routledge, 1998), 182–3.

13   Wright, *Mental Disability in Victorian England*, 52.

14   Wright, *Mental Disability in Victorian England*, 52; VPRS 7565/P1, Unit 3, PROV.

15   Wright, *Mental Disability in Victorian England*, 60; 'Country Weddings', *Weekly Times*, 7 June 1902, 30.

16   *Kerang Times*, 20 October 1893.

17   David Wright, 'Family Strategies and the Institutional Confinement of "Idiot" Children in Victorian England', *Journal of Family History*, 23, no. 2 (April 1998): 197; 'A Husband's Extravagance', *Argus*, 2 May 1908, 9.

18   *Cf* Wright, 'Family Strategies', 195–6.

19   Mark Friedberger, 'The Decision to Institutionalize: Families with Exceptional Children in 1900', *Journal of Family History*, 6, no. 4 (Winter 1981): 399.

20   Based on an analysis of VPRS 7419/P1, Units 1–2, PROV.

21   David Wright, 'Getting Out of the Asylum: Understanding the Confinement of the Insane in the Nineteenth Century', *Social History of Medicine*, 10, no. 1 (April 1997): 151.

22   *Report of the Inspector of Lunatic Asylums on the Hospitals for the Insane, for the Year 1870* (Melbourne: John Ferres, Government Printer, 1871), 11–12; C.R.D. Brothers, *Early Victorian Psychiatry, 1835–1905* (Melbourne: Government Printer, 1961), 162–4; Richard Bonwick, 'The History of the Yarra Bend Lunatic Asylum, Melbourne' (Master of Medicine (Psychiatry) thesis, University of Melbourne, 1995), 98–102.

23   *Report of the Inspector of Lunatic Asylums, 1870*, 11.

24   Dave Earl, '"A Group of Parents Came Together": Parent Advocacy Groups for Children with Intellectual Disabilities in Post-World War II Australia', *Health and History*, 13, no. 2 (2011): 84–103.

NOTES

25 'Victorian Lunacy Laws', *Argus*, 14 February 1890, 11.

26 Shurlee Swain, 'Education Special', *eMelbourne*, https://www.emelbourne. net.au/biogs/EM00508b.htm.

27 Alice Henry, 'Brightening the Dull', *Argus*, 27 May 1899, 13; Brothers, 154–5; *Ovens and Murray Advertiser* (Beechworth), 22 July 1899, 1.

28 'Table: Showing the Manner in which Patients were Admitted', in Reports of the Inspector of Lunatic Asylums and Reports of the Inspector-General of the Insane 1887–1908.

29 Inspector of Asylums to Under Secretary, 17 August 1887, VPRS 3992/P, Unit 194, 87/H7259, PROV.

30 'Yarra Bend Asylum', *Argus*, 16 April 1886, 9; 'Gossip', *Sydney Mail and New South Wales Advertiser*, 25 December 1897, 1349.

31 'Treatment of Imbecile Children', *Age*, 30 December 1897, 6; 'Training of Idiot Children', *Leader*, 5 January 1895, 23.

32 VPRS 7419/P, Unit 1, pp. 170, 248, 274, 322, 171, 198, PROV.

33 'Clunes', *Ballarat Star*, 13 January 1897, 4.

34 Chief Secretary to Inspector, 15 February 1897, VPRS 3992, Unit 652, File 97/E1977, PROV.

35 Wright, *Mental Disability in Victorian England*, 66; Wright, 'Familial Care of "Idiot" Children', 187–8.

36 Friedberger, 400.

37 VPRS 7420/P, Unit 1, p. 227, PROV.

38 VPRS 3992/P0, Unit 996, File 1905/V4860, PROV.

39 VPRS 7420/P, Unit 1, p. 335, PROV.

40 Ellen Dwyer, 'The State and the Multiply Disadvantaged', in *Mental Retardation in America: A Historical Reader*, eds Steven Noll and James W. Trent (New York: New York University Press, 2004), 266, 269.

41 VPRS 7419/P1, Unit 1, pp. 326, 336, PROV.

42 VPRS 7419/P1, Unit 1, pp. 312, 193; and VPRS 7420/P1, Unit 1, pp. 93, 269, PROV.

43 VPRS 7420/P1, Unit 1, pp. 71, 213, 214, 241, 263, 345, PROV.

44 VPRS 7420/P1, Unit 1, 4 November 1906, p. 287 and Unit 2, 4 November 1906, p. 56, PROV; Inspector to Under Secretary, 17 March 1903, VPRS 3992/P0, Unit 915, File 1903/S1879, PROV.

45 VPRS 7419/P1, Unit 1, p. 216, PROV.

46 VPRS 7420/P1, Unit 2, p. 43, PROV.

47 VPRS 7419/P1, Unit 1, p. 314, PROV.

48 VPRS 7419/P1, Unit 1, p. 308, PROV.

Chapter 3: 'For the Care and Training of Feeble-minded Children' 1887–1907

1 VPRS 4527/P, Unit 30, p. 269; VPRS 7417, Unit 8, p. 56, Public Record Office Victoria (PROV).

2 VPRS 7420, Unit 1, PROV.

NOTES

3   Inspector to Under Secretary, 1 September 1886, VPRS 3992/P, File 87/
      J7408, PROV.
4   Inspector to Chief Secretary, 12 August 1887, VPRS 3992/P, Unit 194, File
      87/H7259, PROV; C.R.D. Brothers, *Early Victorian Psychiatry, 1835–1905*
      (Melbourne: Government Printer, 1961),153.
5   VPRS 7419, Unit 1, PROV.
6   *Report of the Inspector of Lunatic Asylums on the Hospitals for the Insane, for
      the Year 1887* (Melbourne: Robert S. Brain, Government Printer, 1888),
      Appendix C, 44.
7   Brothers, 167; 'From Leeches to the X-ray', *Herald*, 3 February 1928, 7.
8   Alice Henry, 'Teaching the Unteachable', *Argus*, 8 January 1898, 14.
9   Lee-Ann Monk, 'A Duty to Learn: Attendant Training in Victoria,
      Australia, 1880–1907', in *Mental Health Nursing: The Working Lives of Paid
      Carers in the Nineteenth and Twentieth Centuries*, eds Anne Borsay and Pamela
      Dale (Manchester: Manchester University Press, 2015), 54–74; Brothers,
      178; Ann Westmore and Bruce S. Singh, A Century of Psychiatry, Victoria,
      1900–2000, forthcoming.
10   'News of the Day', *Age*, 16 January 1899, 4.
11   James V. McCreery, 'Idiocy and Juvenile Insanity in Victoria', *Intercolonial
      Medical Congress of Australasia* (Sydney: Charles Potter, 1893), 665.
12   Eastham to Inspector Dick, 28 August 1886, VPRS 3992, Unit 194, File 87/
      J7408, PROV.
13   VPRS 3992, Unit 194, File 87/J7408, PROV.
14   McCreery to Inspector, 9 July 1888, VPRS 3992/P, Unit 341, File 90/P3520,
      PROV; Eastham to Reclassification Board, 9 March 1898, VPRS 3992/P,
      Unit 705, File 98/H2443, PROV.
15   Eastham to Reclassification Board, 9 March 1898, VPRS 3992/P, Unit 705,
      File 98/H2443, PROV.
16   McCreery, 'Idiocy and Juvenile Insanity', 667.
17   McCreery, 'Idiocy and Juvenile Insanity', 667.
18   Henry, 14.
19   *Report of the Inspector of Lunatic Asylums, 1887*, 15, 47; McCreery, 'Idiocy and
      Juvenile Insanity', 667.
20   Henry, 14.
21   Henry, 14; *Report of the Inspector of Lunatic Asylums, 1887*, 47.
22   McCreery, 'Idiocy and Juvenile Insanity', 667.
23   VPRS 7419 and VPRS 7420, PROV; Henry, 14.
24   Eastham to Reclassification Board, VPRS 3992/P, Unit 705, File 98/
      H2443, 9 March 1898, PROV; Joe Alston, Elizabeth Roberts and Otto
      Wangermann, *The Royal Albert: Chronicles of an Era* (Lancaster: Centre for
      North-West Regional Studies, University of Lancaster, 1992), 18.
25   *Hospitals for the Insane: Report of the Inspector of Lunatic Asylums for the Year
      Ended 31st December, 1892* (Melbourne: Robert S. Brain, Government Printer,
      1893), 14.
26   Henry, 14; D.G. Gray to Reclassification Board, 28 February 1898, VPRS
      3992/P, Unit 704, File 98/G1990, PROV.

305

Notes

27 'Holding High Holiday at the Kew Asylum', *Herald*, 21 January 1891, 4.

28 'The Training of Idiots', *Leader*, 5 January 1895, 23; 'Treatment of Imbecile Children', *Age*, 30 December 1897, 6; 'A Christmas Treat to Afflicted Children', *Age*, 31 December 1903, 6.

29 'Kew Asylum Christmas Tree', *Argus*, 14 December 1895, 11; 'Kew Asylum for Idiots', *Argus*, 10 December 1901, 7.

30 Henry, 14.

31 Henry, 14; Tony Dingle, *The Victorians: Settling* (Sydney: Fairfax, Syme & Weldon, 1984), 124; Geoffrey Blainey, *A History of Victoria* (Melbourne: Cambridge University Press, 2006), 144.

32 VPRS 3992, Unit 556, File 94/X6986, PROV; *Hospitals for the Insane: Report of the Inspector of Lunatic Asylums for the Year Ended 31st December, 1893* (Melbourne: Robert S. Brain, Government Printer, 1894), 12–13.

33 Analysis of 'Distribution of the Insane at 31st December', in Reports of the Inspector of Lunatic Asylums 1887–94; Inspector to Under Secretary, 30 January 1895, VPRS 3992/P, Unit 714, File 98/H4943, PROV.

34 Chief Secretary to Public Service Board, July 1893, VPRS 3992/P, Unit 515, File 93/W5581, PROV; Inspector to Under Secretary 27 June 1893, VPRS 3992/P, Unit 550, File 94/Y5379 and Inspector to Under Secretary, 30 July 1894, VPRS 3992/P, File 94/X5533, PROV; Inspector to Under Secretary, 5 November 1894, VPRS 3992/P, Unit 561, File 94/X8150, PROV; Inspector to Under Secretary, 26 and 27 February 1895, VPRS 3992/P, Unit 581, File 95/B3324, PROV; Inspector to Under Secretary, 26 April 1895, VPRS 3992/P, Unit 581, File 95/B3396, PROV.

35 *Hospitals for the Insane: Report of the Inspector of Lunatic Asylums for the Year Ended 31st December, 1891* (Melbourne: Robert S. Brain, Government Printer, 1892), 16; *Report of the Inspector of Lunatic Asylums 1892*, 15.

36 *Report of the Inspector of Lunatic Asylums 1891*, 3.

37 *Report of the Inspector of Lunatics Asylums 1891*, 15; *Report of the Inspector of Lunatic Asylums 1892*, 12; *Hospitals for the Insane: Report of the Inspector of Lunatic Asylums for the Year Ended 31st December, 1894* (Melbourne: Robert S. Brain, Government Printer, 1895), 13.

38 'Fire at Kew Asylum', *Argus*, 3 August 1895, 8.

39 'Fire at Kew Asylum', 8; Inspector to Under Secretary, 5 August 1895, VPRS 3992/P, Unit 591, File 1895/B5938, PROV.

40 VPRS 3992/P, Unit 592, File 1895/B6246, PROV.

41 'Fire at Kew Asylum', 8.

42 Inspector to Under Secretary, 24 May 1892, VPRS 3992/P, Unit 467, File 1892/U5603; Unit 505, File 1883/V3071; Unit 591, File 1895/B5938; Inspector to Under Secretary, 28 October 1895, Unit 599, File 1895/A7963, all in PROV.

43 *Hospitals for the Insane: Report of the Inspector of Lunatic Asylums for the Year Ended 31st December, 1895* (Melbourne: Robert S. Brain, Government Printer, 1896), 12; VPRS 3992/P, Unit 592, File 1895/A6189; Unit 917, File 1903/R2220, both in PROV.

44 *Argus*, 15 May 1896, 4; VPRS 3992/P, Unit 632, File 1896/C7220; Unit 646, File 1897/F95, both in PROV.

NOTES

45 VPRS 3992/P, Unit 636, File 1896/C8382, PROV.

46 Notes of an Interview with the Chief Secretary, 22 December 1897, VPRS 3992/P, Unit 697, File 1897/F12908, PROV.

47 Report of the Official Visitors, 26 April 1898, and McCreery to Under Secretary, 27 April 1898, VPRS 3992/P, Unit 709, File 1898/H3727, PROV.

48 Report of the Official Visitors, 27 October 1898, and McCreery to Under Secretary, 17 November 1898, VPRS 3992/P, Unit 732, File 1898/G9768, PROV; Report of the Official Visitors, 30 September 1902, Unit 900, File 1902/P9557, PROV.

49 *Hospitals for the Insane: Report of the Inspector of Lunatic Asylums for the Year Ended 31st December, 1898* (Melbourne: Robert S. Brain, Government Printer, 1899), 13; VPRS 7419/P1, Unit 1, p. 168, PROV.

50 Henry, 14.

51 Report of the Official Visitors, 4 January 1899, VPRS 3992/P, Unit 775, File 1899/K11022, PROV; *Report of the Inspector of Lunatic Asylums 1898*, 14.

52 *Hospitals for the Insane: Report of the Inspector of Lunatic Asylums for the Year Ended 31st December, 1899* (Melbourne: Robert S. Brain, Government Printer, 1900), 13.

53 *Hospitals for the Insane: Report of the Inspector of Lunatic Asylums for the Year Ended 31st December, 1900* (Melbourne: Robert S., Brain, Government Printer, 1901), 14.

54 *Hospitals for the Insane: Report of the Inspector of Lunatic Asylums for the Year Ended 31st December, 1896* (Melbourne: Robert S. Brain, Government Printer, 1897), 13; *Report of the Inspector of Lunatic Asylums 1899*, 15.

55 Official Visitors Quarterly Report, 7 August 1901, VPRS 3992/P, Unit 852, File 1901/O8677, PROV.

56 Brothers, 178–89; 'Our Lunatic Asylums', *Age*, 29 January 1898, 13; 2 June 1900, 9; 23 February 1903, 4.

57 F. Norton Manning, 'President's Address, Section of Psychological Medicine', *Intercolonial Medical Congress of Australasia: Transactions of the Second Session held in Melbourne, Victoria, January 1889* (Adelaide: Vardon and Pritchard, 1889), 824.

58 *Hospitals for the Insane: Report of the Inspector of Lunatic Asylums for the Year Ended 31st December, 1902* (Melbourne: Robert S. Brain, Government Printer, 1903), 15.

59 Benvolio, 'Melbourne Jottings', *Illustrated Sydney News*, 6 March 1890, 23; 'In the Strange Land of the Idiot Children', *Herald*, 31 December 1890, 2; 'The Training of Idiots', *Leader*, 5 January 1895, 23; 'Treatment of Imbecile Children', *Age*, 30 December 1897, 6; 'Lazarettes of Lunacy', *Truth* (Sydney), 30 November 1902, 5.

60 Alexander Sutherland, 'Reclaimed Human Waste', *Australasian*, 25 August 1900, 422.

61 Elizabeth O'Callaghan, *The Great Warrnambool Exhibition: The Story of the Warrnambool Industrial and Art Exhibition 1896–97* (Warrnambool: Warrnambool and District Historical Society, 2002), 56; 'Victorian Gold Jubilee Exhibition', Supplement to the *Bendigo Advertiser*, 28 November 1901, p. 1S.

NOTES

62 Henry, 14; E.L. Rossiter to Eastham, 12 May 1897, Letter Book of the Exhibition Secretary—Letter 86, Warrnambool Industrial and Art Exhibition, 1896–97 (held at Flagstaff Hill Museum Library Warrnambool).

63 Sutherland, 422.

64 Henry, 14.

65 Reports of the Inspector of Lunatic Asylums, 1887, 46; 1888, 49; 1889, 55; 1890, 54.

66 McCreery, 'Idiocy and Juvenile Insanity', 667.

67 VPRS 7420/P1, Unit 1, p. 11, PROV.

68 VPRS 7420/P1, Unit 1, p. 251, PROV.

69 VPRS 7420/P1, Unit 1, pp. 23, 53; 7419/P1, Unit 1, pp. 86, 226, 228, both in PROV.

70 McCreery, 'Idiocy and Juvenile Insanity', 666.

71 VPRS 7420/P1, Unit 1, p. 1, PROV.

72 VPRS 7419/P1, Unit 1, pp. 200, 110, PROV.

73 VPRS 7419/P1, Unit 1, p. 229, PROV; David Wright, *Mental Disability in Victorian England: The Earlswood Asylum* (Oxford: Oxford University Press, 2001), 97.

74 McCreery, 'Idiocy and Juvenile Insanity', 666.

75 Wright, 142–3.

76 McCreery, 'Idiocy and Juvenile Insanity', 667; McCreery to Inspector of Asylums, 20 March 1890, VPRS 3992/P, Box 341, File 90/P3520, PROV.

77 Sutherland, 422; Corinne Manning, *Bye-Bye Charlie: Stories from the Vanishing World of Kew Cottages* (Sydney: UNSW Press, 2008), 185, 193.

78 VPRS 7419/1, Unit 1, p. 42, PROV; VPRS 7420/1, Unit 1, pp. 168, 287, PROV.

79 Lee-Ann Monk, '"Made enquires, can elicit no history of injury": Researching the History of Institutional Abuse in the Archives', *Provenance*, 6 (September 2007), https://prov.vic.gov.au/explore-collection/provenance-journal/provenance-2007/made-enquiries-can-elicit-no-history-injury.

80 VPRS 3992/P, Unit 920, File 1903/R3064; Unit 924, File 1903/S4204, PROV.

81 Joanna Ryan, with Frank Thomas, *The Politics of Mental Handicap* (Harmondsworth: Penguin, 1980), 92–3; Anne Borsay, *Disability and Social Policy in Britain since 1750: A History of Exclusion* (Basingstoke: Palgrave Macmillan, 2005), 101.

82 McCreery, 'Idiocy and Juvenile Insanity', 666.

83 Sutherland, 422.

84 VPRS 3992/P, Unit 937, File 1903/S6965, notation 14 August 1903, PROV.

85 McCreery to Under Secretary, 26 February 1903 and 3 March 1903, VPRS 3992/P, Unit 928, File 1903/R4991, PROV.

86 Benvolio, 23.

87 VPRS 7420/P1, Units 1 and 2, and VPRS 7419/P1, Unit 1, PROV.

88 VPRS 7420/P1, Units 1 and 2, and VPRS 7419/P1, Unit 1, PROV.

89 For example, VPRS 7420/P1, Unit 1, pp. 75, 153, 229, PROV.

NOTES

90 VPRS 7405/P2, Unit 3, p. 68, and VPRS 8236/P1, Unit 3, PROV.
91 'A Christmas Treat to Afflicted Children', 6.

Chapter 4: 'Mental Defectives: A Serious Social Problem' 1907–24

1 VPRS 7419/P1, Unit 1, pp. 278, 342, Public Record Office Victoria (PROV).
2 *Hospitals for the Insane: Report of the Inspector-General of the Insane for the Year Ended 31st December 1907* (Melbourne: J. Kemp, Government Printer, 1908), 19–20, 31; 1908, 28; VPRS 3992, Unit 1065, File 1907/B7555, PROV.
3 *Report of the Inspector-General of the Insane 1907*, 21.
4 'Our Lunatic Asylums—A Serious Indictment', *Age*, 29 January 1898; 'The Insane and their Treatment', *Argus*, 27 February 1901, 6.
5 J.W. Springthorpe, 'Our Metropolitan Asylums', *Intercolonial Medical Journal of Australasia*, VIII, no. 3 (20 March 1903): 109–24.
6 'Lunacy Reform', *Age*, 15 July 1903, 5; 'Care of the Insane', *Argus*, 15 July 1903.
7 *Argus*, 17 July 1903, 4; 'Care of the Insane', *Argus*, 1 August 1903, 13.
8 C.R.D. Brothers, *Early Victorian Psychiatry, 1835–1905* (Melbourne: Government Printer, 1961), 178–91; Ruth J. Inall, *State Health Services in Victoria* (Sydney: Department of Government and Public Administration, 1971), 72–4.
9 *Victorian Parliamentary Debates* (*VPD*), Vol. 108, 7 September 1904, 1453–4; 'News of the Day', *Age*, 7 July 1904, 4; 'People We Know', *Punch*, 18 January 1917, 6.
10 S.G. Foster, 'Jones, William Ernest 1867–1957', *Australian Dictionary of Biography* (*ADB*), National Centre of Biography, ANU, http://adb.anu.edu.au/biography/jones-william-ernest-6882, accessed online 25 March 2019; 'People We Know', 6; *VPD*, Vol. 108, 7 September 1904, 1453–4. Thanks to Ann Westmore for sharing her research.
11 'Treatment of the Insane', *Age*, 15 February 1905, 5.
12 *Hospitals for the Insane: Report of the Inspector-General of the Insane for the Year Ended 31st December 1905* (Melbourne: J. Kemp, Acting Government Printer, 1906), 3.
13 *Report of the Inspector-General of the Insane 1905*, 16–17; W.Ernest Jones, 'Psychiatry: Past, Present and Future: A Retrospect', *Medical Journal of Australia*, 1, no. 7 (1939): 249–56.
14 *Report of the Inspector-General of the Insane 1905*, 32–3.
15 *Report of the Inspector-General of the Insane 1905*, 33; *VPD*, Vol. 110, 25 July 1905, 521.
16 VPRS 3992, Unit 1891, File 1930/X2992, PROV; 'Action by Kew Council', *Age*, 30 July 1903, 6; 'Lunacy Reform', *Age*, 21 August 1903, 5; 'Mr Murray and Lunacy Reform', *Age*, 25 August 1903, 5.
17 'Kew Asylum', *Argus*, 5 August 1905, 16; 'Kew Asylum Grounds', *Age*, 10 August 1905, 6.
18 'Kew Asylum Grounds', *Age*, 10 August 1905, 6; Deputation to the Premier, 9 August 1905, VPRS 3992, Unit 1891, File 1903/X2992, PROV.

NOTES

19   'Lunacy Reform', *Argus*, 12 August 1905, 16; VPRS 3992, Unit 1891, File 1903/X2992, PROV; Jones, 254.

20   *Report of the Inspector-General of the Insane 1905*, 32–3.

21   'New Lunatic Asylum', *Argus*, 21 March 1907, 9; *Hospitals for the Insane: Report of the Inspector-General of the Insane for the Year Ended 31st December 1909* (Melbourne: J. Kemp, Government Printer, 1910), 47; *Hospitals for the Insane: Report of the Inspector-General of the Insane for the Year Ended 31st December 1911* (Melbourne: Albert J. Mullett, Acting Government Printer, 1912), 46.

22   *Report of the Inspector-General of the Insane 1911*, 17, 48; *Hospitals for the Insane: Report of the Inspector-General of the Insane for the Year Ended 31st December 1912* (Melbourne: Albert J. Mullett, Government Printer, 1913), 43–4 ; *Hospitals for the Insane: Report of the Inspector-General of the Insane for the Year Ended 31st December 1914* (Melbourne: Albert J. Mullett, Government Printer, 1915), 62; *Hospitals for the Insane: Report of the Inspector-General of the Insane for the Year Ended 31st December 1915* (Melbourne: Albert J. Mullett, Government Printer, 1916), 37; Brothers, 197.

23   VPRS 7468/P1, Unit 1, Ernest Jones, 11 January 1909, np; Ernest Jones, 26 February 1909, np, PROV.

24   *Hospitals for the Insane: Report of the Inspector-General of the Insane for the Year Ended 31st December 1908* (Melbourne: J. Kemp, Government Printer, 1909), 21; Extract from Letter of the IGI, 24 June 1908, VPRS 892/P0, Unit 102, File 1196, PROV.

25   Jones to Tate, 10 June 1908, VPRS 892/P0, Unit 89, File 1113, PROV; Jones to Under Secretary, 30 October 1909, VPRS 892/P0, Unit 102, File 1196, PROV.

26   VPRS 7468/P1, Unit 1, 26 May 1909, np; 5 May 1909, np; 18 August 1909, np; 7 December 1910, np, PROV.

27   Appendix A, Draft of Suggested Recommendations for the Minister, 6 February 1911, VPRS 892/P, Unit 89, File 1113, PROV.

28   'Mental Defectives: A Serious Social Problem', *Age*, 14 January 1911, 17.

29   'Mental Defectives: A Serious Social Problem', 17.

30   James W. Trent, *Inventing the Feeble Mind: A History of Mental Retardation in the United States* (Berkley, California: University of California Press, 1994), 141, 160–5, 178; Mary Dendy, *The Importance of Permanence in the Care of the Feeble-Minded* (Manchester: pamphlet (1901), originally published 1899, in the *Education Review*), 2, quoted in Mark Jackson, 'Institutional Provision for the Feeble-minded in Edwardian England: Sandlebridge and the Scientific Morality of Permanent Care', in *From Idiocy to Mental Deficiency: Historical Perspectives on People with Learning Disabilities*, eds David Wright & Anne Digby (London and New York: Routledge, 1996), 169.

31   Mathew Thomson, 'Disability, Psychiatry and Eugenics', in *The Oxford Handbook of the History of Eugenics*, eds Alison Bashford and Philippa Levine (Oxford and New York: Oxford University Press, 2010), 119.

32   Harvey G. Simmons, 'Explaining Social Policy: The English Mental Deficiency Act of 1913', *Journal of Social History*, 11, no. 3 (Spring 1978): 394–5; Jackson, 'Institutional Provision for the Feeble-minded 1996', p. 172.

NOTES

33   *Royal Commission on Asylums for the Insane and Inebriate, Report* (Melbourne: John Ferres, Government Printer, 1886) (hereafter Royal Commission, 1884–86), Minutes of Evidence, Q.9625–31, 405–06; J.W.Y. Fishbourne, 'The Segregation of the Epileptic and Feeble-minded', Australasian Medical Congress, *Transactions of the Ninth Session Held in Sydney, New South Wales, September 1911*, Vol. II (Sydney: William Applegate Gullick, Government Printer, 1913) (hereafter *Transactions of the Ninth Session*), 889–90.

34   Harvey Sutton, 'The Feeble-Minded—Their Classification and Importance', *Transactions of the Ninth Session*, 894–905.

35   E.M. Steven, 'The Treatment of Mentally Deficient Children from a National Standpoint', *Transactions of the Ninth Session*, 891–3.

36   *Transactions of the Ninth Session*, 908; 'Feeble-Minded Children', *Argus*, 16 May 1912, 6; 'Mental Defectives', *Age*, 12 March 1913, 13.

37   'Care of the Feeble-minded in Australasia', Australasian Medical Congress, *Transactions of the Tenth Session held in Auckland, New Zealand, February 1914* (Wellington: John Mackay, Government Printer, 1916) (hereafter *Transactions of the Tenth Session*), 711; 'News of the Day', *Age*, 23 April 1912, 6; 'Science and Citizenship', *Age*, 1 August 1912, 8; 'The Eugenic Standpoint', *Age*, 30 April 1913, 11.

38   For example, Mary Booth, 'Report of Central Committee of the Australian Medical Congress on the Care and Control of the Feeble-Minded', *Australian Medical Journal (AMJ)*, 1 March 1913, 929; Harvey Sutton, 'Education of the Feeble-Minded in Victoria', *AMJ*, 8 March 1913, 936; 'Report of the South Australian Committee for the Feeble-Minded', *AMJ*, 19 April 1913, 1000–01.

39   *Transactions of the Tenth Session*, 711; 'The Mentally Infirm', *Argus*, 12 March 1913, 12.

40   *Age*, 1 June 1911, 7; 23 June 1911, 6; 9 September 1911, 12; 28 December 1911, 4; 11 June 1912, 6; 25 June 1912, 6; 29 July 1912, 6; 21 December 1912, 16; 10 February 1913, 8.

41   Ross Jones, 'Skeletons in Toorak and Collingwood Cupboards: Eugenics in Educational and Health Policy in Victoria, 1919 to 1929' (PhD thesis, Monash University, 2000), 53–4; *Report of the Inspector-General of the Insane 1905*; *Report of the Inspector-General of the Insane 1909*; *Report of the Inspector-General of the Insane 1911*.

42   *Transactions of the Ninth Session*, 908; *Transactions of the Tenth Session*, 711. For example, W.E. Jones, 'Eugenics in Relation to the Feeble-Minded Question', *AMJ*, 8 March 1913, 935.

43   Ross Jones, 'The Master Potter and the Rejected Pots: Eugenic Legislation in Victoria, 1918–1939', *Australian Historical Studies*, 29, no. 113 (1999): 319–42; Ross Jones, 'Removing Some of the Dust from the Wheels of Civilization: William Ernest Jones and the 1928 Commonwealth Survey of Mental Deficiency', *Australian Historical Studies*, 40, no. 1 (2009): 63–78.

44   Mark Jackson, *The Borderland of Imbecility: Medicine, Society and the Fabrication of the Feeble Mind in late Victorian and Edwardian England* (Manchester: Manchester University Press, 2000), 28–33, 219.

Notes

45 'Mental Defectives', *Age*, 12 March 1913, 13; 'The Mentally Infirm', *Argus*, 12 March 1913, 12; *Transactions of the Tenth Session*, 709–10.

46 Deputation from the Medical Profession, 4 April 1913, VPRS 892/P/0, Unit 102, File 1196, PROV; 'Feebleminded Children', *Argus*, 5 April 1913, 9; John Lewis, 'Removing the Grit: The Development of Special Education in Victoria, 1887–1947' (PhD thesis, Latrobe University, 1989), 112.

47 Deputation from the Medical Profession, 4 April 1913, VPRS 892/P/0, Unit 102, File 1196, PROV.

48 *Hospitals for the Insane: Report of the Inspector-General of the Insane for the Year Ended 31st December 1913* (Melbourne: Albert J. Mullett, Government Printer, 1914), 61; 'News of the Day', *Age*, 8 July 1913, 6; 23 July 1913, 8; 4 November 1913, 10.

49 'News of the Day', *Age*, 8 July 1913, 6; 'The Increase of Insanity', *Age*, 1 October 1913, 10; 'News of the Day', *Age*, 14 November 1913, 10.

50 *Report of the Inspector General of the Insane 1914*, 60.

51 *Report of the Inspector-General of the Insane 1912*, 61.

52 Jones to Chief Secretary, 23 October 1911, VPRS 892/P0, Unit 102, File 1196, PROV; IGI to Under Secretary, 25 February 1915, VPRS 3992, Unit 1369, File 1915/S1797, PROV.

53 IGI to Under Secretary, 15 July 1916, VPRS 892/P/0 Unit 102, File 1196, PROV.

54 'Mental Defectives', *Age*, 17 January 1911, 8; Lewis, 85.

55 Lewis, 89–91; VPRS 892/P/0, Unit 89, File 1113, PROV.

56 VPRS 892/P/0, Unit 102, File 1196, PROV.

57 *Report of the Inspector-General of the Insane 1914*, 32, 61; *Report of the Inspector-General of the Insane 1915*, 36; *Hospitals for the Insane: Report of the Inspector-General of the Insane for the Year Ended 31st December 1917* (Melbourne: Albert J. Mullett, Government Printer, 1918), 22; *Hospitals for the Insane: Report of the Inspector-General of the Insane for the Year Ended 31st December 1918* (Melbourne: Albert J. Mullett, Government Printer, 1919), 18; *Hospitals for the Insane: Report of the Inspector-General of the Insane for the Year Ended 31st December 1919* (Melbourne: Albert J. Mullett, Government Printer, 1920), 19; *Hospitals for the Insane: Report of the Inspector-General of the Insane for the Year Ended 31st December 1920* (Melbourne: Albert J. Mullett, Government Printer, 1921), 16; *Hospitals for the Insane: Report of the Inspector-General of the Insane for the Year Ended 31st December 1921* (Melbourne: Albert J. Mullett, Government Printer, 1922), 13; *Hospitals for the Insane: Report of the Inspector-General of the Insane for the Year Ended 31st December 1922* (Melbourne: Albert J. Mullett, Government Printer, 1923), 16; *Hospitals for the Insane: Report of the Inspector-General of the Insane for the Year Ended 31st December 1923* (Melbourne: H.J. Green, Government Printer, 1924), 15, 27.

58 'Lunatic Asylums: Shocking Neglect', *Argus*, 7 February 1922, 7.

59 Notes of an interview by Messrs. McPherson and Merrett, 7 June 1916, VPRS 4723/P, Unit 502, File 1917/W9909, PROV.

60 *Report of the Inspector-General of the Insane 1915*, 36–7; *Hospitals for the Insane: Report of the Inspector-General of the Insane for the Year Ended 31st December*

Notes

1916 (Melbourne: Albert J. Mullett, Government Printer, 1917), 38; *Report of the Inspector-General of the Insane 1917*, 39.

61 'Kew Asylum Buildings: To the Editor of the *Argus*', *Argus*, 11 February 1922, 21.

62 Visitors Book 17 and 29 March 1922, VPRS 7468/P1, Unit 2, pp. 84–5, PROV.

63 Visitors Book, 26 March 1923, VPRS 7468/P1, Unit 2, p. 97, PROV.

64 Visitors Book, 31 October 1922, VPRS 7468/P1, Unit 2, pp. 91–2, PROV.

65 Transcript of Evidence given before the Royal Commission of Inquiry, pp. 640–1, VPRS 7526/P1, Unit 1, PROV; Robert M. Kaplan, 'The First Psychiatric Royal Commission: Reg Ellery and the Attendants at Kew Hospital', *Health and History*, 16, no. 1 (2015): 47.

66 Jones to Chief Secretary, 23 August 1924, VPRS 7526/P1, Unit 1, PROV.

67 'Charges of Cruelty', *Age*, 3 October 1924, 11; 'Doctor's Accusers', *Herald*, 3 October 1924, 1; 'Kew Asylum Charges', *Age*, 4 October 1924, 17.

68 'Kew Asylum in Ferment', *Smith's Weekly* (Sydney), 4 October 1924, 1; 'Kew Asylum Scandal', *Truth*, 4 October 1924, 7, 10.

69 'Is it True or is it False? Victoria Uneasy about Kew Asylum', *Smith's Weekly* (Sydney), 11 October 1924, 1-2; 'Amazing Allegations at Kew', *Truth*, 11 October 1924, 1.

70 'Kew Asylum, Second Inquiry Not Proposed', *Herald*, 14 October 1924, 18; '"Smith's" Forces Asylum Inquiry', *Smith's Weekly* (Sydney), 25 October 1924, 11.

71 '"Smith's" Forces Asylum Inquiry', 11; 'Kew Asylum Scandal', *Truth*, 4 October 1924, 7, 10.

72 'Kew Asylum', *Herald*, 16 October 1924, 5; 'Kew Asylum Management', *Age*, 17 October 1924, 10; 'Kew Asylum', *Argus*, 17 October 1924, 8.

73 Laurence W. Maher, 'Menzies, Frank Gladstone (1892–1978)', *ADB*, National Centre of Biography, Australian National University, https://adb.anu.edu.au/biography/menzies-frank-gladstone-11110/text19781, published first in hardcopy 2000, accessed online 15 July 2019; A.W. Martin, 'Menzies, Sir Robert Gordon (Bob) (1894–1978)', *ADB*, National Centre of Biography, Australian National University, http://adb.anu.edu.au/biography/menzies-sir-robert-gordon-bob-11111/text19783, published first in hardcopy 2000, accessed online 15 July 2019.

74 Stephen Garton, *Medicine and Madness: A Social History of Insanity in New South Wales 1880–1940* (Sydney: New South Wales University Press, 1988), 170.

75 Kevin Ryan, 'Brennan, Francis (Frank) (1873–1950)', *ADB*, National Centre of Biography, ANU http://adb.anu.edu.au/biography/brennan-francis-frank-5347/text9041, published first in hardcopy 1979, accessed online 15 July 2019; Kevin Ryan, 'Frank Brennan: A Political Biography' (MA thesis, La Trobe University, 1978), ix, 141–2, 186, 272.

76 'News of the Day', *Age*, 6 November 1924, 8.

77 A.A. Kelley, *Hospital for the Insane, Kew: Report of Commission* (Melbourne: La Trobe University, 1982), 14, 15, 21–3.

NOTES

78 Kelley, *Report of Commission*, 19–20; Hollow, Memo, 14 August 1924, and A29 List of Administrative Acts, Ellery, VPRS 4723, Unit 517, Kew Royal Commission Certain Exhibits, PROV.

79 Kelley, *Report of Commission*, 19–20; Ellery [Statement], 2, VPRS 7526/P1, Unit 1, PROV.

80 Kelley, *Report of Commission*, 20.

81 Kelley, *Report of Commission*, 9–10.

82 Jones to Chief Secretary, 23 August 1924, VPRS 7526/P1, Unit 1, PROV; Kelley, *Report of Commission*, 9.

83 Transcript of Evidence given before the Royal Commission of Inquiry, 14.

84 Lee-Ann Monk, 'A Duty to Learn: Attendant Training in Victoria, Australia, 1880–1907', in *Mental Health Nursing: The Working Lives of Paid Carers in the Nineteenth and Twentieth Centuries*, eds Anne Borsay and Pamela Dale (Manchester: Manchester University Press, 2015), 54–74; *Report of the Inspector-General of the Insane 1916*, 14.

85 *Report of the Inspector-General of the Insane 1912*, 30.

86 'In Kew Asylum', *Age*, 19 November 1924, 11.

87 Evidence, 27A–27B, 21–22, 553–5, 571a–571b, 684–5, 727, 773, 775.

88 Evidence, 26, 584–5, 711, 774, 837–8, 841.

89 Evidence, 770; see also 21, 684–6.

90 Evidence, 708–09, 586.

91 Evidence, 872–4; Kelley, *Report of Commission*, 22.

92 Evidence, 17, 570–1a, 684–6, 771–3.

93 Evidence, 570, 685, 770–4.

94 Evidence, 553–4, 684–5, 772.

95 Evidence, 772–3.

96 Evidence, 685.

97 Evidence, 30, 569; see also 564. Note, however, that Jones seemed to disagree on this point and that Hollow had been negligent in his oversight of Ellery, 682.

98 Evidence, 837–8; 27B, 30.

99 VPRS 3992/P, Unit 1105, File 1908/D8867, and Unit 1464, 1918/X8341, PROV; *Report of the Inspector-General of the Insane 1917*, 39; *Report of the Inspector-General of the Insane 1921*, 24–5; Evidence, 456, 459.

100 Evidence, 592–5.

101 Evidence, 456–8; Kelley, *Report of Commission*, 9.

102 For example, Evidence, 40–46 and 875–6, 879–83.

103 Evidence, 532, 650–1.

104 Evidence, 22, 556–7, 649–50, 801–06; Kelley, *Report of Commission*, 11.

105 Evidence, 871, 133, 587.

106 'Kew Asylum Administration', *Argus*, 19 November 1924, 7.

107 Evidence, 133–4, see also 590–1.

108 VPRS 4723/P, Unit 493, 1917/W4997, PROV.

109 Kelley, *Report of Commission*, 23, 13.

110 Kelley, *Report of Commission*, 25.

NOTES

111 *Hospitals for the Insane: Report of the Inspector-General of the Insane for the Year Ended 31st December 1924* (Melbourne: H.J. Green, Government Printer, 1925), 35.

112 R.S. Ellery, *The Cow Jumped over the Moon: Private Papers of a Psychiatrist* (Melbourne: F.W. Cheshire, 1956), 143.

113 No title, *Age*, 27 November 1924, 8; 'The Scandal of Kew Asylum', *Herald*, 27 November 1924, 8; No title, *Age*, 1 December 1924, 8.

114 Kaplan, 61, 63; Joy Damousi, '"Eyes Left": Psychiatrist Reginald Ellery and the Soviet Dream', in *Political Tourists: Travellers from Australia to the Soviet Union in the 1920s – 1940s*, eds Sheila Fitzpatrick and Carolyn Rasmussen (Melbourne: Melbourne University Press, 2008), 173.

115 *Report of the Inspector-General of the Insane 1924*, 34; *VPD*, 18 December 1924, 2097–115.

Chapter 5: 'A New Deal for Mental Defectives' 1924–39

1 'Menace of Degeneracy', *Herald*, 29 April 1924, 9.

2 Notes of a Deputation from the Association to Combat the Social Evil, 25 June 1918, VPRS 892/P/0, Unit 102, File 1196. Public Record Office Victoria (PROV); John Lewis, 'Removing the Grit: The Development of Special Education in Victoria 1887–1947' (PhD thesis, Latrobe University, 1989), 202–04.

3 Lewis, 209, 220–1; Ross Jones, 'Skeletons in Toorak and Collingwood Cupboards: Eugenics in Educational and Health Policy in Victoria, 1919 to 1929' (PhD thesis, Monash University, 2000), 50–1, 125–7.

4 'The Feeble-Minded', *Age*, 14 June 1921, 9.

5 Margaret Pawsey to Frank Tate, 27 October 1924, VPRS 982/P/0, Unit 102, File 1196, PROV.

6 'Mental Defectives', *Age*, 5 July 1923, 11; 'Cradling Crime', *Herald*, 4 July 1923, 9.

7 Notes of a Deputation from the Association to Combat the Social Evil, 25 June 1918; 'Cradling Crime', *Herald*, 4 July 1923, 9.

8 Don Garden, *Victoria: A History* (Melbourne: Nelson, 1984), 356–61; Geoffrey Blainey, *A History of Victoria*, Second Edition (Melbourne: Cambridge University Press, 2013), 204–05.

9 William Henderson to Acting Director of Education Department, 24 March 1923, file note 5 April 1923, VPRS 892/P/0, Unit 102, File 1196, PROV; Garden, 349–50.

10 Lewis, 205, 215–23, 243–4, 267; see, for example, Report on the Subject of Feeble-Minded Children by the Committee, 1922, VPRS 892/P, Unit 102, File 1196, PROV.

11 'Defective Children', *Herald*, 6 August 1924, 10; 'Mental Deficients', *Herald*, 14 August 1924, 8; Editorial, *Age*, 25 January 1925, 14.

12 'Dull Children', *Weekly Times*, 12 June 1926, 71.

13 *Hospitals for the Insane: Report of the Inspector-General of the Insane for the Year Ended 31st December 1926* (Melbourne: H.J. Green, Government Printer, 1927), 9; '1d. in £1 State Income Tax Increase', *Herald*, 22 October 1925, 1.

14 'Mental Defectives', *Age*, 2 September 1924, 10.

NOTES

15 Deputation, 24 June 1926, VPRS 3992/P, Unit 1745, File 1926/Q8938, PROV; 'Travancore Home', *Herald*, 24 June 1926, 4.

16 'Mental Defectives', *Age*, 2 September 1924, 10; 'Travancore Home', *Herald*, 24 June 1926, 4; VPRS 3992/P, Unit 1758, File 1926/Q13178, PROV.

17 'Coming State Session', *Geelong Advertiser*, 25 June 1926, 1; 'State Government's Policy', *Age*, 25 June 1926, 9.

18 *Victorian Parliamentary Debates (VPD)*, Legislative Assembly, 13 August 1926, 1851, 800; *Report of the Inspector-General of the Insane 1926*, 39.

19 Ross Jones, 'The Master Potter and the Rejected Pots: Eugenic Legislation in Victoria, 1918–1939', *Australian Historical Studies*, 29, no. 113 (1999): 325–6.

20 *VPD*, Legislative Assembly, 13 August 1929, 803–05.

21 *VPD*, Legislative Assembly, 13 August 1929, 805, 811, 816; 8 October 1929, 2105.

22 Bills Introduced in the Legislative Assembly and Proceedings Thereon during Session 1929, ss. 14, 17, 43; *VPD*, Legislative Assembly, 13 August 1929, 816.

23 *VPD*, Legislative Assembly, 13 August 1929, 807–08.

24 'Mental Deficiency Bill Diagram A, to show how Mentally Defective Persons will be classified under the Act', VRPS 4723/P, Unit 513, File Mental Defectives Bill, PROV.

25 *VPD*, Legislative Assembly, 17 September 1929, 1655–6.

26 *VPD*, Legislative Assembly, 17 September 1929, 1665–9; 18 September 1929, 1708.

27 'Mental Deficiency', *Age*, 9 October 1929, 13; 'Premier's Policy Speech', *Herald*, 2 November 1929, 4; Garden, 360–1.

28 *VPD*, Legislative Council, 29 December 1933, 2930–1.

29 Lee-Ann Monk, 'Intimacy and Oppression: A Historical Perspective', in *Sexuality and Relationships in the Lives of People with Intellectual Disabilities: Standing in My Shoes*, eds Rohhss Chapman, Sue Ledger, and Louise Townson with Daniel Docherty (London: Jessica Kingsley Publishers, 2015), 50; *VPD*, Legislative Council, 29 December 1933, 2932.

30 See Marian Quartly and Judith Smart, *Respectable Radicals: A History of the National Council of Women of Australia 1896–2006* (Melbourne: Monash University Publishing in conjunction with the NCWA, 2015), 174–7.

31 Jones, 'Master Potter', 328–30; 'Mentally Unfit', *Argus*, 10 April 1934, 11.

32 *VPD*, Legislative Council, 12 September 1934, 1753.

33 'Mental Defectives', *Age*, 26 February 1935, 13; 'Mental Disorders', *Argus*, 7 March 1934, 7; Dr Paul G. Dane, 'Eugenics or Economics?', *Argus*, 20 January 1934, 20.

34 'Travancore School', *Argus*, 22 March 1932, 7.

35 VPRS 7565/P1, Unit 7; Report of the Inspector-General of the Insane, 1925, 17, PROV.

36 'Items of Interest: Kew Idiot Asylum Improvements', *Argus*, 17 December 1924, 22.

37 *Hospitals for the Insane: Report of the Inspector-General of the Insane for the Year Ended 31st December 1928* (Melbourne: H.J. Green, Government Printer,

NOTES

1930), 23; *Hospitals for the Insane: Report of the Inspector-General of the Insane for the Year Ended 31st December 1932* (Melbourne: H.J. Green, Government Printer, 1933), 25.

38 Official Visitors' Book, VPRS 7468/P1, Unit 2, pp. 152–3, PROV.

39 Edward Rowe, Interview with Corinne Manning, 20 April 2006, Kew Cottages History Project Archive, Melbourne, La Trobe University. All subsequent quotes from Edward 'Ted' Rowe are from this interview.

40 29 September 1926, 139, VPRS 7468/P1, Unit 2, PROV.

41 VPRS 7468/P1, Unit 2, pp. 123, 187, PROV.

42 R.S. Ellery, *The Cow Jumped over the Moon: Private Papers of a Psychiatrist* (Melbourne: F.W. Cheshire, 1956), 136.

43 Quoted in Cliff Judge and Fran van Brummelen, *Kew Cottages: The World of Dolly Stainer* (Melbourne: Spectrum Publications, 2002), 115–17.

44 'Child-Woman Has Hand Mangled in Mental Home', *Truth*, 27 February 1937, 12.

45 'Two Living Tragedies at Kew', *Truth*, 26 June 1937, 1.

46 Hollow to Director of Mental Hygiene, 8 March 1937, VPRS 3992/P, Unit 2503, File 1937/N1741, PROV.

47 Ellery, 136; VPRS 7420, Units 1–3, PROV; VPRS 7449, Unit 1, PROV; Acc 92/184, Units 1–4, DHS Victoria Archives.

48 Jones to Under Secretary, 10 March 1937, and J. Hollow to Director, 8 March 1937, VPRS 3992/P, Unit 2053, File 1937/N1741, PROV; *Department of Mental Hygiene: Report of the Director of Mental Hygiene for the Year Ended 31st December 1937* (Melbourne: H.J. Green, Government Printer, 1938), 4.

49 Maggie Potts and Rebecca Fido, *'A Fit Person to be Removed': Personal Accounts of Life in a Mental Deficiency Institution* (Plymouth: Northcote House, 1991), 107; Manning, 159–60.

50 We would like to acknowledge Ms Kerrie Soraghan for first suggesting this to us.

51 Stanley D. Porteus, *A Psychologist of Sorts: The Autobiography and Publications of the Inventor of the Porteus Maze Tests* (Palo Alto, California: Pacific Books, 1969), 37–8.

52 VPRS 7420/P1, Unit 3, p. 36, PROV.

53 'Allegations of Shocking Neglect of Scalded Child', *Truth*, 3 October 1935, 1.

54 Transcript of Evidence given before the Royal Commission of Inquiry (hereafter Evidence), 640–1, VPRS 7526/P1, Unit 1, 919, 924–5, PROV; VRPS 4723, Unit 517, File 'Kew Royal Commission Certain Exhibits', 24, PROV.

55 Lunacy Acts 1903 s. 73; 1928 s. 73.

56 Evidence, 925.

57 VPRS 7420/P1, Unit 3, 98, PROV.

58 For example, VPRS 7420/P1, Unit 3, 22, 48, 50, 96, PROV.

59 VPRS 7448, Unit 1, 84; also 46, PROV.

60 VPRS 7419, Unit 2, 26, PROV.

61 For example, *Hospitals for the Insane: Report of the Inspector-General of the Insane for the Year Ended 31st December 1921* (Melbourne: Albert J. Mullett,

NOTES

Government Printer, 1922), 14; *Hospitals for the Insane: Report of the Inspector-General of the Insane for the Year Ended 31st December 1922* (Melbourne: Albert J. Mullett, Government Printer, 1923), 16, 27; *Hospitals for the Insane: Report of the Inspector-General of the Insane for the Year Ended 31st December 1925* (Melbourne: H.J. Green, Government Printer, 1926), 17; *Hospitals for the Insane: Report of the Inspector-General of the Insane for the Year Ended 31st December 1927* (Melbourne: H.J. Green, Government Printer, 1928), 42.

62   *Report of the Inspector-General of the Insane 1927*, 42; Jones to Under Secretary, 15 October 1928, VPRS 3992/P, Unit 1916, File Y10455, PROV.

63   Lewis, 309; VPRS 3992/P, Unit 1916, File Y10455, PROV; L.J. Blake, *Vision and Realisation: A Centenary History of State Education in Victoria*, Vol. 3 (Melbourne: Education Department of Victoria, 1973).

64   VPRS 7468/P1, Unit 2, 185, PROV.

65   'The Backward Child', *Age*, 27 November 1929, 16.

66   DHS 92/184/4, Department of Human Services Archival Services.

67   Lewis, 310.

68   VPRS 7468, Unit 3, 68, PROV.

69   VPRS 3992/P, Unit 1891, File 1930/X3006, PROV.

70   Lee-Ann Monk, 'Paradoxical Lives: Intellectual Disability Policy and Practice in Twentieth-Century Australia', in *Intellectual Disability in the Twentieth Century: Transnational Perspectives on People, Policy and Practice*, eds Jan Walmsley and Simon Jarrett (Bristol: Policy Press, 2019), 21–5.

71   'Removing Kew Asylum', *Argus*, 10 May 1929, np, in VPRS 3992, Unit 1891, File 1930/X2992, PROV.

72   *Report of the Inspector-General of the Insane 1925*, 14.

73   'Kew Asylum', *Argus*, 3 May 1928, 20; 'Real Estate and Building', *Argus*, 8 May 1928, 6.

74   Town Clerk to Chief Secretary, 7 May 1928, VPRS 3992, Unit 1891, File 1930/X2992, PROV.

75   *VPD*, Legislative Assembly, 30 October 1928, 2563.

76   Memorandum, 12 April 1928, VPRS 3992, Unit 1891, File 1930/X2992, PROV; *Report of the Inspector-General of the Insane 1927*, 40–1.

77   Under Secretary to W.S. Kent Hughes, 19 April 1928, and Under Secretary to Town Clerk, 14 May 1928, VPRS 3992, Box 1891, File 1930/X2992, PROV.

78   W.D. Vaughan, *Kew's Civic Century* (Melbourne: D Vaughan, 1960), 79.

79   'Moving Kew Asylum', *Age*, 22 January 1929, 9; 'Kew Suggestions for Cabinet?', *Sun*, 22 January 1929, 5.

80   'Kew Asylum', *Age*, 4 May 1929, 20; 'Removal of Kew Asylum', *Age*, 9 May 1929, 8.

81   'Removing Kew Asylum', *Argus*, 10 May 1929, np, in VPRS 3992, Unit 1891, File 1930/X2992, PROV.

82   'Mentally Afflicted', *Argus*, 19 January 1929, 22. On its activities, see for example, *Argus*, 1 May 1930, 5; 23 March 1931, 15; 20 December 1934, 17.

83   'Removing Kew Asylum', *Argus*, 10 May 1929, np, in VPRS 3992, Unit 1891, File 1930/X2992, PROV; 'Kew Asylum', *Age*, 10 May 1929, 10.

NOTES

84 'Removing Kew Asylum', *Argus*, 15 May 1929, 10.

85 'Deputation Wants Kew Asylum Moved', *Herald*, 18 June 1929, 4.

86 'Kew Asylum', *Age*, 6 August 1929, 10; 'Transfer of Kew Asylum', *Argus*, 14 September 1929, 10.

87 'Kew Asylum', *Argus*, 8 July 1930, 12; 'News of the Day', *Age*, 8 July 1930, 8.

88 'Overcrowded Mental Hospitals', *Argus*, 22 August 1933, 6.

89 'Crowding at Asylum', *Herald*, 22 August 1933, 4.

90 'Kew Asylum', *Age*, 23 August 1933, 9; 'Mental Hospitals', *Argus*, 23 August 1933, 8.

91 'State Mental Institutions', *Argus*, 3 October 1933, 9; 'Overcrowded Mental Hospitals', *Argus*, 22 August 1933, 6.

92 'State Offices: Remodelling to Cost £40,000', *Argus*, 22 August 1933, 6.

93 *Report of the Inspector-General of the Insane 1932*, 25.

94 'Kew Asylum', *Argus*, 7 October 1932, 8; 'Hospital for the Insane', *Argus*, 22 September 1932, 5.

95 Garden, 368–76; Geoff Browne, 'Stanley Argyle: The Incidental Premier', in *The Victorian Premiers 1856–2000*, eds Paul Strangio and Brian J. Costar (Sydney: Federation Press, 2006), 208–10.

96 'Kew Asylum', *Age*, 1 November 1933, 10; *Report of the Inspector-General of the Insane 1932*, 26.

97 'Old Buildings', *Argus*, 9 May 1935, 12.

98 'Mental Hygiene', *Age*, 10 April 1935, 12; 28 November 1935, 12; 29 November 1935, 16.

99 'Kew Asylum to be Closed', *Argus*, 29 April 1936, 7; 'Kew Asylum to Go', *Age*, 29 April 1936, 11.

100 'Kew Asylum to be Closed', *Argus*, 29 April 1936, 7; 'Kew Asylum to Go', *Age*, 29 April 1936, 11.

101 'Better Care for the Mentally Sick', *Herald*, 29 April 1936, 6; 'The Mental Hospital Scheme', *Age*, 30 April 1936, 8.

102 Vaughan, 83.

103 *Department of Mental Hygiene: Report of the Director of Mental Hygiene for the Year Ended 31st December 1935* (Melbourne: H.J. Green, Government Printer, 1936), 26.

104 'More Mental Deficients in Victoria', *Argus*, 6 November 1936, 11.

105 *Department of Mental Hygiene: Report of the Director of Mental Hygiene for the Year Ended 31st December 1936* (Melbourne: H.J. Green, Government Printer, 1937), 14.

106 'Mentally Deficient Children', *Age*, 4 June 1931, 10; 'Travancore Auxiliary', *Age*, 28 March 1933, 5; 'Travancore School', *Age*, 19 March 1935, 7.

107 'Problem of Mental Deficiency', *Herald*, 17 June 1937, 28; 'Problem of Mental Deficiency', *Age*, 4 June 1938, 15.

108 'Mental Children Problem', *Herald*, 28 November 1933, 1; 'Mental System Attack', *Herald*, 25 February 1935, 1; 'Problem of Mental Deficiency', *Herald*, 17 June 1937, 28.

109 Report by the Director of Mental Hygiene, DHS 98/349s, Box 13, 5, DHS Archival Services.

NOTES

110 'Money for Asylum Buildings', *Argus*, 4 July 1935, 9; 'Mental Hospitals', *Age*, 4 July 1935, 7.
111 *Report of the Director of Mental Hygiene 1935*, 27.
112 Lewis, 311–12.
113 *VPD*, Legislative Assembly, 12 October 1939, 1552, 1555.
114 *VPD*, Legislative Assembly, 12 October 1939, 1552–62.
115 'Praise for Bill', *Herald*, 11 December 1939, 8; 'Assembly Amity', *Age*, 1 December 1939, 10.
116 'News of the Day: Mental Deficiency Bill', *Age*, 13 October 1939, 8.
117 'Mental Defectives', *Age*, 26 February 1935, 13; *VPD*, 31 October 1939, 1853, 1838; 22 November 1939, 2215.
118 *VPD*, Legislative Assembly, 12 October 1939, 1557; 31 October 1939, 1839; *Report of the Director of Mental Hygiene 1936*, 3, 29; *Report of the Director of Mental Hygiene 1937*, 17.
119 *VPD*, Legislative Assembly, 12 October 1939, 1558; 22 November 1939, 2217; 'New Deal for Delinquents', *Herald*, 21 July 1938, 3.
120 *VPD*, Legislative Assembly, 30 November 1939, 2364.

Chapter 6: 'A Hillside of Sadness' 1939–50

1 V. Jarvie to H.S. Bailey, 10 March 1938, VPRS 3992/P/0, Unit 2095, File 1938/Q2271, Public Record Office Victoria (PROV).
2 *Department of Mental Hygiene: Report of the Director of Mental Hygiene for the Year Ended 31st December 1937* (Melbourne: H.J. Green, Government Printer, 1938), 18; *Department of Mental Hygiene: Report of the Director of Mental Hygiene for the Year Ended 31st December 1938* (Melbourne: T. Rider, Government Printer, 1939), 14.
3 *Department of Mental Hygiene: Report of the Director of Mental Hygiene for the Year Ended 31st December 1935* (Melbourne: H.J. Green, Government Printer, 1936), 27; 'Money for Asylum Buildings', *Argus*, 4 July 1935, 9.
4 Jarvie to Bailey.
5 Catarinich to Under Secretary, 15 March 1938, VPRS 3992/P/0, Unit 2095, File 1938/Q2271, PROV.
6 Mrs M. Thomas to Chief Secretary, 25 April 1938, VPRS 3992/P/0, Unit 2098, File Q3613, PROV.
7 Mrs E. Thomas, 12 April 1938, VPRS 3992/P/0, Unit 2097, File 1938/ P3198, PROV; Mr F. Forster to Chief Secretary, 5 May 1938, Unit 2098, File 1938/Q3793, PROV.
8 For example, 'Case Against Removal', *Argus*, 4 July 1935, 9; 'New Mental Home', *Argus*, 2 March 1938, 10; 'Seeks Royal Commission', n.d., MS PA89/140, Box 13, Folder News Clippings, State Library Victoria (SLV).
9 For example, Under Secretary to Mrs Jarvie, 22 March 1938, VPRS 3992/P/0, Unit 2095, File Q2271, PROV.
10 Director of MH to Under Secretary, 8 March 1939, VPRS 3992, Unit 2166, File 1940/U1127, PROV.
11 *Report of the Director of Mental Hygiene 1938*, 4, 14.

NOTES

12 VPRS 3992, Unit 2166, File 1940/U1127, PROV.

13 *Report of the Director of Mental Hygiene 1938*, 14; *Department of Mental Hygiene: Report of the Director of Mental Hygiene for the Year Ended 31st December 1939* (Melbourne: H.E. Daw, Acting Government Printer, 1940), 13.

14 *Report of the Director of Mental Hygiene1938*, 14; *Report of the Director of Mental Hygiene1939*, 13.

15 Director to Under Secretary, VPRS 3992, Unit 2217, File 1941/V3258, PROV.

16 Director to Under Secretary, VPRS 3992, Unit 2217, File 1941/V3258, PROV; Reports of the Director of Mental Hygiene 1938–1941.

17 VPRS 3992, Unit 2217, File 1941/V3258, PROV.

18 Mental Hospital Auxiliaries of Victoria, MS PA 89/140, SLV; Belinda Robson, '"He made us feel special": Eric Cunningham Dax, Edith Pardy and the Reform of Mental Health Services in Victoria, 1950s and 1960s', *Australian Historical Studies*, 34, no. 122 (2003): 270–89.

19 'Mental Hospital Cottages', *Argus*, 14 February 1941, 10; also 'Children's Cottages at Kew', *Age*, 11 February 1941, 3.

20 VPRS 3992, Unit 2217, File 1941/3258, PROV.

21 *Department of Mental Hygiene: Report of the Director of Mental Hygiene for the Year Ended 31st December 1940* (Melbourne: H.E. Daw, Government Printer, 1941), 30; *Department of Mental Hygiene: Report of the Director of Mental Hygiene for the Year Ended 31st December 1941* (Melbourne: H.E. Daw, Government Printer, 1942), 25; Don Garden, *Victoria: A History* (Melbourne: Nelson, 1984), 385–7.

22 'Mental Hospital Cottages', *Argus*, 14 February 1941, 10; also 'Children's Cottages at Kew', *Age*, 11 February 1941, 3.

23 AS 1992/184, Male Folio Patient Files, Units 1–4, Department of Human Services Archive Services.

24 'Jacqueline Gore Answers Inquiries', *Weekly Times*, 15 December 1934, 19.

25 'Intelligent Care for Subnormal Children', *Argus Weekend Magazine*, 6 March 1946, 9; 'Mental Defectives', *Age*, 11 February 1934, 15; 'Auxiliary to Travancore', *Argus*, 4 June 1931, 3.

26 Emily K. Abel, *Hearts of Wisdom: American Women Caring for Kin, 1850–1940* (Cambridge, Mass: Harvard University Press, 2000), chapter 8.

27 VPRS 7468/P1, Unit 2, 152–3, PROV.

28 'Mental Homes', *Herald*, 29 December 1945, 7.

29 *Herald*, 8 January 1946, 7; 4 January 1946, 7.

30 I. Booth, 'Mental Homes', *Herald*, 1 January 1946, 7.

31 'Staff Short in Mental Hospitals', *Herald*, 2 January 1946, 6.

32 'Appalling Conditions', *Herald*, 7 January 1946, 8.

33 Booth, 'Mental Homes', 7.

34 'Mental Homes', *Herald*, 14 January 1946, 8.

35 'Mental Homes', *Herald*, 4 January 1946, 7.

36 VPRS 6345/P1, Unit 20, File 651, PROV; *Department of Mental Hygiene: Report of the Director of Mental Hygiene for the Year Ended 31st December 1942* (Melbourne: H.E. Daw, Government Printer, 1943); *Department of*

Notes

Mental Hygiene: Report of the Director of Mental Hygiene for the Year Ended 31st December 1943 (Melbourne: H.E. Daw, Government Printer, 1944); *Department of Mental Hygiene: Report of the Director of Mental Hygiene for the Year Ended 31st December 1944* (Melbourne: J.J. Gourley, Government Printer, 1945); *Department of Mental Hygiene: Report of the Director of Mental Hygiene for the Year Ended 31st December 1945* (Melbourne: J.J. Gourley, Government Printer, 1946).

37 'Mental Homes', *Herald*, 8 January 1945, 7.

38 'Accommodation Sought for Mental Patients', *Herald*, 14 January 1946, 7; 'New Buildings for Kew Hospital', *Herald*, 15 January 1946, 6; 'Mental Hospital Moves', *Age*, 16 January 1946, 3.

39 'Treating Mental Ills', *Age*, 4 December 1947, 3; 'Sad Story of Kew Asylum', *Herald*, 19 January 1949, 8.

40 Garden, 392–3; *Report of the Director of Mental Hygiene 1945*; *Department of Mental Hygiene: Report of the Director of Mental Hygiene for the Year Ended 31st December 1947* (Melbourne: J.J. Gourley, Government Printer, 1948); *Department of Mental Hygiene: Report of the Director of Mental Hygiene for the Year Ended 31st December 1948* (Melbourne: J.J. Gourley, Government Printer, 1949).

41 K.S. Inglis, 'Rivett, Rohan Deakin (1917–1977)', *Australian Dictionary of Biography*, National Centre of Biography, Australian National University, https://adb.anu.edu.au/biography/rivett-rohan-deakin-11533/text20575, published first in hardcopy 2002, accessed online 20 August 2021; 'Rohan Rivett: Journalist, Author and Fighter', *Canberra Times*, 7 October 1977, 2. Rivett was also a grandson of Alfred Deakin.

42 Rohan Rivett, 'A Hillside of Sadness', *Herald*, 28 September 1948, 5.

43 'Letter from a Mother to the Editor', *Herald*, 5 October 1948, 4.

44 *Herald*, 9 October 1948, 1; 11 October 1948, 1; 14 October 1948, 1.

45 'Joy Comes to "Hillside of Sadness"', *Herald*, 15 October 1948, 1; 'Toys make Kew Children Happy', *Herald*, 30 October 1948, 2.

46 'Toy SOS Brings Fine Response', *Herald*, 12 October 1948, 5.

47 Mark Jackson, '"Grown-Up Children": Understandings of Health and Mental Deficiency in Edwardian England', in *Cultures of Child-Health in Britain and the Netherlands in the Twentieth Century*, eds Marijka Gijswijt-Hofstra and Hilary Marland (Amsterdam and New York: Rodopi, 2003), 151–4; Janice Brockley, 'Rearing the Child Who Never Grew' (PhD thesis, Rutgers University, 2001), 153–4; H.H. Goddard, *Feeble-Mindedness: Its Causes and Consequences* (New York, Macmillan, 1914), quoted in Brockley, 40.

48 Dave Earl, 'Help for Children and their Families: Presenting "Subnormal" and "Spastic" Children to the Public in 1950s New South Wales', *Antithesis*, 19 (March 2009): 154–65.

49 Denis Warner, 'Kew Conditions "Horrifying"', *Herald*, 14 December 1946, 4.

50 'Minister's Reply to Asylum Charges', *Herald*, 21 December 1946, 5; *Victorian Parliamentary Debates* (*VPD*), Legislative Assembly, 20 December 1946, 4608–11.

51 'Alienists Urge Overhaul of Mental Hygiene', *Herald*, 4 January 1947, 5.

NOTES

52 'Mental Hospital Review', *Age*, 13 May 1947, 5; 'Churches to Investigate Mental Homes', *Argus*, 14 June 1947, 6; 'Report on Mental Hygiene', *Herald*, 6 January 1947, 3.

53 'Giving Youth Its Chance', *Herald*, 17 July 1947, 4; National Council of Women of Victoria, *Annual Reports 1947 & 1948*, 6; 'Editorial: A Mixed Committee, Indeed', *Sun*, 17 July 1947, 6.

54 *Report of the Mental Hospitals Inquiry Committee on the Department of Mental Hygiene, Its Hospitals and Its Administration* (Melbourne: J.J. Gourley, Government Printer, 1948), 3.

55 'Mental Hygiene Advice from UK Proposed', *Sun*, 26 March 1949, 13; 'British Expert to Advise on Mental Hygiene', *Argus*, 20 April 1949, 8.

56 Alexander Kennedy, *Report to the Minister for Health on Mental Health and Mental Hygiene Services in the State of Victoria* (Melbourne: J.J. Gourley, Government Printer, 1950), 10.

57 Kennedy, 4, 11–12.

58 Kennedy, 4, 11–12.

59 Kennedy, 4, 11–12.

60 *Report of the Mental Hospitals Inquiry Committee*, 1948, 7.

61 Kennedy, 8; 'Minister Plans Mental Reform', *Argus*, 9 March 1950, 3.

Chapter 7: Eric Cunningham Dax and the Reform of the Kew Children's Cottages 1951–60

1 *Victorian Parliamentary Debates (VPD)*, Legislative Assembly, 31 October 1950, 1736.

2 *VPD*, Legislative Assembly, 1 November 1950, 1808.

3 Alexander Kennedy, *Report to the Minister for Health on Mental Health and Mental Hygiene Services in the State of Victoria* (Melbourne: J.J. Gourley, Government Printer, 1950), 45.

4 *Argus*, 26 June 1951, 3.

5 *Advocate*, 26 June 1951, 2.

6 *Argus*, 28 June 1951, 6.

7 *Argus*, 29 August 1951, 6.

8 *Argus*, 28 June 1951, 5.

9 *Argus*, 20 July 1951, 2.

10 Belinda Robson, 'The Making of a Distinguished English Psychiatrist: Eric Cunningham Dax and the Mythology of Heroism in Psychiatry 1951 to 1969' (PhD thesis, University of Melbourne, 2000), 71.

11 Robson, 73.

12 John Worthen, *D.H. Lawrence: The Early Years 1885*–*1912* (Cambridge: Cambridge University Press, 1991), 246.

13 Robson, 105.

14 Robson, 109.

15 Eric Cunningham Dax, 'The Evolution of Modern Psychiatry: A Personal History', unpublished manuscript, 25, cited in Robson, 127.

NOTES

16   Dax, 'The Evolution of Modern Psychiatry', 26.

17   Ritchie Calder, 'Private Worlds', *New Statesman and Nation*, 28 May 1949, 550–1, cited in Robson, 134.

18   J.K. Wing and G.W. Brown, *Institutionalism and Schizophrenia: A Comparative Study of Three Mental Hospitals 1960–1968* (Cambridge: Cambridge University Press, 1970), 60.

19   Sidney Bloch, 'An Interview with Eric Cunningham Dax', *Australasian Psychiatry*, 4, no. 3 (1996): 130.

20   Robson, 181.

21   *Argus*, 29 December 1951, 4.

22   Robson, 26.

23   *Herald*, 28 August 1951, 4.

24   *Herald*, 28 August 1951, 4.

25   *Herald*, 28 August 1951, 4.

26   Richard Trembath, 'White, Osmar Egmont (1909–1991)', *Australian Dictionary of Biography*, National Centre of Biography, Australian National University, http://adb.anu.edu.au/biography/white-osmar-egmont-27040/text34513, published online 2018, accessed online 18 December 2019.

27   Cecil Edwards, *The Editor Regrets* (Melbourne: Hill of Content, 1972), 128.

28   *Herald*, 31 August 1951, 4.

29   *Herald*, 4 September 1951, 9.

30   *Department of Mental Hygiene: Report of the Director of Mental Hygiene for the Year Ended 31st December 1950* (Melbourne: J.J. Gourley, Government Printer, 1951), 44.

31   *Argus*, 20 July 1951, 2.

32   Interview, Eric Cunningham Dax and Corinne Manning, 23 January 2006.

33   Robson, 226.

34   Robson, 47.

35   Interview, Dax and Manning, 23 January 2006.

36   *Mental Hygiene Authority Act 1950*, 5.

37   *Report of the Mental Hygiene Authority for the Year Ended 30th June, 1952* (Melbourne: W.M. Houston, Government Printer, 1952–53), 5.

38   Interview, Dax and Manning, 9 January 2006.

39   All figures from *Report of the Mental Hygiene Authority for the Year Ended 30th June, 1952*.

40   E. Cunningham Dax, *Asylum to Community: The Development of the Mental Hygiene Service in Victoria, Australia* (Melbourne: F.W. Cheshire, for the World Federation for Mental Health, 1961), 118.

41   Interview, Dax and Manning, 9 January 2006.

42   Minutes, 18 January 1952, Mental Hygiene Authority: 1952–1962, VA2838, VPRS 18227, Public Record Office Victoria (PROV).

43   Interview, Dax and Manning, 9 January 2006.

44   *Age*, 12 June 1952, 4.

45   Interview, Dax and Manning, 9 January 2006.

46   *Report of the Mental Hygiene Authority for the Year Ended 30th June, 1952*, 48.

NOTES

47   Minutes, 18 January 1952, 25 February 1952, Mental Hygiene Authority: 1952–1962.
48   Interview, Dax and Manning, 9 January 2006.
49   *Age*, 27 November 1952, 2.
50   *Warwick Daily News* (Qld), 30 June 1952, 2.
51   *Report of the Mental Hygiene Authority for the Year Ended 30 June, 1953* (Melbourne: W.M. Houston, Government Printer, 1954), 10.
52   *Report of the Mental Hygiene Authority for the Year Ended 30th June, 1953*, 10.

Chapter 8: The Tipping Campaign and Public Support 1961–65

1   *Report of the Mental Hygiene Authority for the Year Ended 30th June, 1953* (Melbourne: W.M. Houston, Government Printer, 1954), 23.
2   Minutes, Mental Hygiene Branch, 18 January 1952 – 16 June 1954, VPRS 18225/P0001, and Minutes, Mental Hygiene Authority: 1952–1962, VA2838, VPRS 18227, Public Record Office Victoria (PROV).
3   Mental Hygiene Authority meeting, 4 September 1952, Minutes, Mental Hygiene Branch, 18 January 1952 – 16 June 1954.
4   Interview, Eric Cunningham Dax and Belinda Robson, 24 April 1996, in Belinda Robson, 'The Making of a Distinguished English Psychiatrist: Eric Cunningham Dax and the Mythology of Heroism in Psychiatry 1951 to 1969' (PhD thesis, University of Melbourne, 2000), 276.
5   All figures from annual reports, 1952–54.
6   *Report of the Mental Hygiene Authority for the Year Ended 30th June, 1953*, 11.
7   Interview, Eric Cunningham Dax and Corinne Manning, 9 January 2006.
8   Robson, 20.
9   Interview, Dax and Manning, 23 January 2006.
10   *Argus*, 30 August 1886, 4.
11   Interview, Alma Adams and Corinne Manning, 14 August 2006.
12   Mental Hygiene Authority meeting, 5 February 1952, Minutes, Mental Hygiene Branch, 18 January 1952 – 16 June 1954.
13   *Argus*, 14 May 1952, 1; 15 May 1952, 2; 16 May 1952, 5; 17 May 1952, 7.
14   *Herald*, 27 July 1963, 5.
15   Paul Tipping, *Independence, Choice and Community for All: A History of the First 40 Years of the E.W. Tipping Foundation* (Melbourne: E.W. Tipping Foundation, 2010).
16   Graeme Davison, 'Tipping, Edmond William (Bill) (1915–1970)', *Australian Dictionary of Biography*, Australian National University, http://adb.anu.edu.au/biography/tipping-edmond-william-bill-11868/text21249, first published in hardcopy in 2002, accessed online 18 December 2019.
17   *Sun*, 1 May 1970, 5.
18   *Herald*, 29 April 1970, 3.
19   Interview, Irene Higgins and Christine Bigby, 28 July 2005.
20   Cecil Edwards, *The Editor Regrets* (Melbourne: Hill of Content, 1972), 127.
21   Edwards, 127.

325

NOTES

22 Edwards, 127.

23 Edwards, 125.

24 Edwards, 127.

25 Tipping, 3.

26 *Herald*, 6 April 1953, 4.

27 *Herald*, 7 April 1953, 4.

28 Edwards, 5.

29 *Herald*, 10 April 1953, 5.

30 *Herald*, 8 April 1953, 5.

31 *Herald*, 14 April 1953, 3.

32 *Report of the Mental Hygiene Authority for the Year Ended 30th June, 1954* (Melbourne: W.M. Houston, Government Printer, 1955), 33.

33 Katie Holmes, 'Talking About Mental Illness: Life Histories and Mental Health in Modern Australia', *Australian Historical Studies*, 41, no. 1 (2016): 26.

34 Figures from Arthur Lloyd, *Payment by Results: Kew Cottages First 100 Years 1887–1987* (Melbourne: Kew Cottagers and St. Nicholas Parents' Association, 1987), 113.

35 Tipping, 5.

36 Corinne Manning, *Bye-Bye Charlie: Stories from the Vanishing World of Kew Cottages* (Sydney: University of New South Wales Press, 2008), 181.

37 *Report of the Mental Hygiene Authority for the Year Ended 30th June, 1954*, 33.

38 *Report of the Mental Hygiene Authority for the Year Ended 30th June, 1954*, 14–15.

39 5 April 1954, Minutes, Mental Hygiene Authority: 1952–1962.

40 *Herald*, 2 October 1954, 4.

41 *Report of the Mental Hygiene Authority for the Year Ended 30th June, 1955* (Melbourne: W.M. Houston, Government Printer, 1955–56), 57.

42 *Report of the Mental Hygiene Authority for the Year Ended 31st December, 1958* (Melbourne: A.C. Brooks, Government Printer, 1959–60), 78.

43 *Report of the Mental Hygiene Authority for the Year Ended 31st December, 1959* (Melbourne: A.C. Brooks, Government Printer, 1960–61), 81.

44 *Report of the Mental Hygiene Authority for the Year Ended 31st December, 1960* (Melbourne: A.C. Brooks, Government Printer, 1961–62), 8.

45 Typed list of waiting list numbers, in Higgins Papers, original copy with author.

46 Alexander Kennedy, *Report to the Minister for Health on Mental Health and Mental Hygiene Services in the State of Victoria* (Melbourne: J.J. Gourley, Government Printer, 1950), 4.

47 *Report of the Mental Hygiene Authority for the Year Ended 31st December, 1960*, 8.

Chapter 9: The Kew Cottages Parents' Association 1958–70

1 *Newsletter of the Kew Cottages and St. Nicholas Parents' Association*, November 1975, 1.

2 Astrid Judge, 'Growing up at Kew Cottages', *Health and History*, 9, no. 1 (2007): 131.

NOTES

3   Interview, Irene Higgins and Christine Bigby, 28 July 2005.

4   Irene Higgins, 'The Formation and Development of the Kew Cottages Parents' Association', paper presented at 2nd Annual Conference on Mental Retardation, New South Wales, 1960, Higgins Papers—Miscellaneous, copy with author.

5   *Newsletter of the Kew Cottages and St. Nicholas Parents' Association*, December 1997.

6   Higgins, 1.

7   Martin to Yeatman, 19 April 1956, VA 625, VPRO 6345/P1000, Unit 88, Public Record Office Victoria (PROV).

8   Higgins, 1.

9   Arthur Lloyd, *Payment by Results: Kew Cottages First 100 Years 1887–1987* (Melbourne: Kew Cottages and St. Nicholas Parents' Association, 1987), 106.

10 Higgins, 2.

11 June Epstein, *Image of the King: A Parent's Story of Mentally Handicapped Children* (Sydney: Ure Smith, 1970), 42.

12 Lloyd, 106.

13 Epstein, 40.

14 *Report of the Mental Hygiene Authority for the Year Ended 30 June, 1957* (Melbourne: A.C. Brooks, Government Printer, 1958), 71.

15 Epstein, 40.

16 Melanie Oppenheimer, 'Voluntary Action and Welfare in Post-1945 Australia: Preliminary Perspectives', *History Australia*, 2, no. 3 (2005): 106.

17 Dave Earl, '"A Group of Parents Came Together": Parent Advocacy Groups for Children with Intellectual Disability in Post-World War II Australia', *Health and History*, 13, no. 2 (2011): 96.

18 Jan Walmsley, Liz Tilley, Sue Dumbleton & Janet Bardsley, 'The Changing Face of Parent Advocacy: A Long View', *Disability and Society*, 32, no. 9 (2017): 1367.

19 Katherine Castles, '"Nice, Average Americans": Postwar Parents' Groups and the Defense of the Normal Family', in *Mental Retardation in America: A Historical Reader*, eds Steven Noll and James W. Trent Jr (New York: New York University Press, 2004), 358.

20 Ethel Temby, *Kew Cottages Parents' Association: A Brief Sketch* (Melbourne: Kew Cottages Parents' Association, 1970), 2, Higgins Papers—Miscellaneous.

21 Epstein, 44.

22 Constitution of the Kew Cottages Parents' Association, supplement in *Newsletter of the Kew Cottages Parents' Association*, April 1969.

23 Louise Godwin and Catherine Wade, *Kew Cottages Parents' Association: The First 50 Years 1957 to 2007* (Melbourne: Kew Cottages Parents' Association, 2007), 54.

24 Interview, Bill Westgarth and Corinne Manning, 19 January 2006.

25 Unsigned and undated letter to Irene Higgins, Higgins Papers—Personal, in author's possession.

26 Beryl Power, *Why I was Driven to be an Advocate/Activist with the Kew Cottages Parents' Association*, unpublished manuscript, in author's possession.

NOTES

27 Charles Wright Mills, *The Sociological Imagination* (Oxford: Oxford University Press, 1959), 10.

28 Corinne Manning, 'From Surrender to Activism: The Transformation of Disability and Mothering at Kew Cottages, Australia', in *Disability and Mothering: Liminal Spaces of Embodied Knowledge*, eds Cynthia Lewiecki-Wilson and Jen Cellio (Syracuse: Syracuse University Press, 2011), 192.

29 David Pitt, *For the Love of Children: My Life and Medical Career* (Melbourne: Pitt Publishing, 1999), 149.

30 Erving Goffman, *Asylums: Essays on the Social Situation of Mental Patients and Other Inmates* (Melbourne: Penguin Books, 1975, first published 1961), 20.

31 Goffman, 18.

32 Manning, 189.

33 Godwin and Wade, 4.

34 Godwin and Wade, 4.

35 Manning, 198.

36 Higgins, 2.

37 Power, 3.

38 *Newsletter of the Kew Cottages and St. Nicholas Parents' Association*, December 1964.

39 Godwin and Wade, 4.

40 *Newsletter of the Kew Cottages and St. Nicholas Parents' Association*, October 1974.

41 Godwin and Wade, 27.

42 For example. Kathleen Jones, 'Education for Children with Mental Retardation: Parent Activism, Public Policy, and Family Ideology in the 1950s', in *Mental Retardation in America: A Historical Reader*, eds Steven Noll and James W. Trent Jr (New York: New York University Press, 2004), 322–50; and Walmsley *et al.*, 1366–86.

43 Charter of the Information Committee, July 1962, Beryl Power Private Papers, copy in author's possession.

44 Godwin and Wade, 40.

45 Charter of the Information Committee, July 1962.

46 'About the Kew Cottages Parents Association', Supplement in *Newsletter of the Kew Cottages Parents' Association*, May 1963.

47 *How? Where? What? Why?*, leaflet, Kew Cottages Parents' Association, undated.

48 Interview, Bill Westgarth and Corinne Manning, 19 January 2006.

49 *What You Should Know about Mental Retardation*, leaflet, Kew Cottages Parents' Association, undated.

50 Castles, 358.

Chapter 10: Normalisation Emerges from 1970

1 *Newsletter of the Kew Cottages and St. Nicholas Parents' Association*, February 1974, 1.

2 Irene Higgins, 'Mental Retardation in Victoria: Historical Perspective', *Australian Children Limited*, October 1963, 3.

3 *Age*, 12 April 1969, 2; 8 September 1969, 6.

NOTES

4   *Report of the Mental Health Authority for the Year Ended 31st December, 1974* (Melbourne: C.H. Rixon, Government Printer, 1976), 24.

5   *Report of the Mental Hygiene Authority for the Year Ended 31st December, 1959* (Melbourne: A.C. Brooks, Government Printer, 1960–61), 7.

6   *Report of the Mental Health Authority for the Year Ended 31st December, 1962* (Melbourne: A.C. Brooks, Government Printer, 1963–64), 87.

7   *Mental Health Act 1959*, 541.

8   Unless otherwise specifically stated, statistics from the following overview of institutions in Victoria from *Report of the Mental Health Authority for the Year Ended 31st December, 1974.*

9   *Report of the Mental Hygiene Authority for the Year Ended 30th June, 1955* (Melbourne: W.M. Houston, Government Printer, 1955–56), 9, 62.

10   *Report of the Mental Health Authority for the Year Ended 31st December, 1974*, 117.

11   *Report of the Mental Health Authority for the Year Ended 31st December, 1974*, 107.

12   *Report of the Mental Health Authority for the Year Ended 31st December, 1974*, 104, 105, 125, 111, 119, 113.

13   *Report of the Mental Health Authority for the Year Ended 31st December, 1974*, 6.

14   Irene Higgins, 'Nursing of the Intellectually Handicapped is Nursing with a Difference', unpublished written observations, 1, Higgins Papers—Personal, in possession of author.

15   Higgins, 'Mental Retardation in Victoria', 3.

16   Maxwell Jones, *The Therapeutic Community: A New Treatment Method in Psychiatry* (New York: Basic Books, 1953), cited in Corinne Manning, *Bye-Bye Charlie: Stories from the Vanishing World of Kew Cottages* (Sydney: University of New South Wales Press, 2008), 147.

17   Higgins, 'Nursing of the Intellectually Handicapped'.

18   Manning, *Bye-Bye Charlie*, 85–6.

19   *Report of the Mental Health Authority for the Year Ended 31st December, 1962*, 87.

20   *Victorian Parliamentary Debates* (*VPD*), Legislative Assembly, 31 October 1939, 1839.

21   *VPD*, Legislative Assembly, 3 December 1959, 1923.

22   June Epstein, *Image of the King: A Parent's Story of Mentally Handicapped Children* (Sydney: Ure Smith, 1970), 114.

23   *Age*, 23 November 1969, 18.

24   Epstein, 116.

25   *Age*, 3 November 1972, 3.

26   *Age*, 6 May 1971, 5.

27   *Declaration on the Rights of Mentally Retarded Persons*, United Nations General Assembly Resolution 2856, adopted 20 December 1971.

28   Wolf Wolfensberger, *The Principle of Normalization in Human Services* (Toronto: National Institute on Mental Retardation, 1974), 13.

29   Niels Erik Bank-Mikkelsen, *Normalization: Letting the Mentally Retarded Obtain an Existence as Close to Normal as Possible* (Washington, DC: President's Committee on Mental Retardation, 1969). See also, Bengt Nirje, 'The Normalisation Principle and its Human Management Implications', in *Changing Patterns in Residential Services for the Mentally Retarded,*

329

NOTES

eds Robert B. Kugel and Wolf Wolfensberger (Washington D.C.: President's Committee on Mental Retardation, 1969), 181.

30 Peter Tyor & Leland Bell, *Caring for the Retarded in America: A History* (Westport, Connecticut: Greenwood Press, 1984), 148.

31 James Trent, *Inventing the Feeble Mind: A History of Intellectual Disability in the United* States (New York: Oxford University Press, 2017), 250.

32 Wolfensberger, 13, quoted in Trent, 249.

33 Wolfensberger, 13, quoted in Trent, 250.

34 Interview, Ethel Temby, 16 February 2009.

35 Interview, Brendan Lillywhite, 13 September 2009.

36 Irene Higgins, 'Introduction to the Children's Cottages Kew', unpublished manuscript, 3, Higgins Papers—Personal.

37 Jack L. Evans, 'Report of the Victorian Premier's Committee (on Mental Retardation): Blueprint for the 1980s', *Australian Journal of Mental Retardation*, 5, no. 6 (1979): 218.

38 Arthur Lloyd, *Payment by Results: Kew Cottages First 100 Years 1887–1987* (Melbourne: Kew Cottages and St. Nicholas Parents' Association, 1987), 38.

39 Interview, Temby; Interview, Gil Pierce, 3 October 2011.

40 Interview, Pierce.

41 *Report of the Mental Health Authority for the Year Ended 31st December, 1974*, 6.

42 *Report of the Mental Health Authority for the Year Ended 31st December, 1976* (Melbourne: F.D. Atkinson, Government Printer, 1976–77), 6.

43 *Report of the Mental Health Authority for the Year Ended 31st December, 1976*, 7.

44 *Report of the Mental Health Authority for the Year Ended 31st December, 1976*, 7.

45 Evans, 218.

46 Evans, 219.

47 *Intellectually Disabled Persons' Services Act 1986*, 743.

48 *Report of the Department of Community Services Victoria for the Year Ended 30 June 1987* (Melbourne: F.D. Atkinson, Government Printer, 1987), 12.

49 *Ten Year Plan for the Redevelopment of Intellectual Disability Services: Final Report* (Melbourne: Neilson Associates, August 1988), 19.

50 *Ten Year Plan for the Redevelopment of Intellectual Disability Services: Final Report*, 17.

51 *Ten Year Plan for the Redevelopment of Intellectual Disability Services: Final Report*, 17.

Chapter 11: A Disastrous Fire 1996

1 Chapter 11 is a version of an article by Richard Broome, '"They Had Little Chance": The Kew Cottages Fire of 0f 1996', *Victorian Historical Journal*, 91, no. 2 (December 2020): 245–66, and is published here with the permission of the Royal Historical Society of Victoria.

2 This account of the fire is from State Coroner Graeme Johnstone's report, *Inquest Findings, Comments and Recommendations into Fire and Nine Deaths at Kew Residential Services on 8 April 1996* (Melbourne: State Coroner's Office, 1997), 14–31.

330

NOTES

3   *Inquest Findings*, 24–5.

4   *Inquest Findings*, 14, 31–2.

5   *Inquest Findings*, 31.

6   *Inquest Findings*, 18.

7   *Age*, 2 July 1968.

8   *Herald Sun*, 10 April 1996.

9   Editorial and Paul Gray, 'When Care is a Slogan', *Herald Sun*, 10 April 1996.

10   *Australian*, 10 April 1996.

11   *Age*, 10 April 1996.

12   VALID, 'Media Release. Kew Cottage Tragedy', 15 April 1996, in the possession of Richard Broome.

13   Nikki Henningham, 'Hastings, Elizabeth', *The Encyclopedia of Women and Leadership in Twentieth-Century Australia*, http://www.womenaustralia.info/leaders/biogs/WLE0125b.htm.

14   Elizabeth Hastings, 'Pushing Open the Door of Disability', *Age*, 23 April 1996.

15   *Age*, 10 April 1996.

16   'The Forgotten People', *Age*, 13 May 1996.

17   'Kew Residents Barred from Community Life', *Age*, 13 May 1996.

18   *Age*, 9 April 1996.

19   Alan Jones, *Age*, 12 April 1996. See also Pauline Williams of Yarraville, *Age*, 11 April 1996, and Marie Nash, *Age*, 12 April 1996.

20   Vivien Millane, *Age*, 13 April 1996.

21   Anne McDonald, *Herald Sun*, 12 April 1996, and Rosemary Crossley, *Age*, 13 April 1996.

22   Vic Symons, *Age*, 12 April 1996.

23   David Green, *Age*, 13 April 1996.

24   John Hanrahan, *Age*, 13 April 1996. Hanrahan, a lecturer at RMIT and a poet, had an intellectually disabled daughter.

25   'Angry and Sad Mother', *Herald Sun*, 16 April 1996.

26   Rosalie Trower, *Age*, 24 April 1996.

27   Craig Binnie and Paul Dowsley, 'Pain and Anger Linger', *Herald Sun*, 11 April 1996.

28   'Ignored in Life ... Now Noticed in Death', *Age*, 13 April 1996.

29   Paul Dowsley, 'Family's Praise for Heroic Cottage Staff', *Herald Sun*, 11 April 1996.

30   Interview, Julie Carpenter and Corinne Manning, quoted in Corinne Manning, *Bye-Bye Charlie: Stories from the Vanishing World of Kew Cottages* (Sydney: University of New South Wales Press, 2008), 219.

31   Manning, 220.

32   On David Welchman, see Sandy Guy, '100 Year War', *Age*, 13 April 1996; John Dusink Jr, *Ringwood Mail*, 16 April 1996.

33   'For the Sake of a Son', *Progress Press*, 4 June 1996.

34   Nicole Brady & Sandra McKay, 'Don't Politicise Deaths: Kennett', *Age*, 10 April 1996.

35   Sandra McKay, 'Premier's Appeal Over Fire Leaves Mothers Incensed', *Age*, 12 April 1996; see also Sandy Guy, '100 Year War', *Age*, 13 April 1996.

Notes

36 Nancy Harper, 'Relief for Now, but the Fear Remains', *Progress Press*, 16 April 1996.

37 Editorial, *Age*, 11 April 1996.

38 Tim Pegler, 'Kew Fire Probe Rejected', *Age*, 21 May 1996.

39 Kendall Hill, 'Writ Alleges Cuts in Services', *Age*, 13 April 1996.

40 Letter to KPA parents from Valerie Yule (?), 21 April 1996, in possession of the Kew Cottages history project.

41 Russell Coulson, 'State Loss over Kew', *Herald Sun*, 22 August 1996.

42 Editorial, *Age*, 11 July 1996.

43 'Remembering a Sad Day at Kew', *Kew Cottages and St. Nicholas Parents' Association Newsletter*, April 1997, pp. 1-2.

44 Copies in possession of the project.

45 Irena Higgins to KPA, 21 April 1996, copy in possession of the project.

46 Patsy Morrison, Executive Director Victorian Council of Social Service to Geoff Welchman, KPA, 17 April 1996, copy in possession of the project.

47 'Address by Bishop James Grant, Dean of Melbourne, at the Memorial Service for the Victims of the Fire at Kew Cottages, 17 April 1996, 12 noon', copy in possession of the Kew Cottages history project.

48 Heather de-Pyper Bottomley-Tipping, *Age*, 24 April 1996.

49 June Guest, *Age*, 24 April 1996.

50 Rosalie Trower, *Age*, 24 April 1996.

51 Heather Kennedy, 'Kew Fire Reveals Mum's Agony', *Herald Sun*, 28 April 1996.

52 Don and Zoe Anderson to the Hon. Jeff Kennett, 30 April 1996, copy in possession of the Kew Cottages history project.

53 Mary Walsh to Bob, Rosalie, Geoff and Fellow Parents, 12 April 1996, copy in possession of the Kew Cottages history project.

54 Tim Pegler & Thom Cookes, 'Kew Fire: State was Warned', *Age*, 11 July 1996.

55 John Dubois, 'Kew Cottages "still in danger"', *Progress Press*, 16 July 1996.

56 Matt Deighton and John Dubois, 'Kew Parents Angry Again', *Progress Press*, 15 October 1996.

57 Michael Gleeson, 'Pain of Loss Lingers', *Herald Sun*, 12 October 1996.

58 Rosalie Trower, *Age*, 12 October 1996.

59 Des Crowther, executive Office PA, to members, 8 October 1996. Conversation between Geoff Welchman and Richard Broome, 12 August 2005.

60 'Conclusions to Findings, Comments, and Recommendations', *Inquest Findings*, 12.

61 Louise Godwin, email to Lee-Ann Monk, 16 August 2005, and to Richard Broome, 17 August 2005, in possession of Richard Broome.

Chapter 12: Deinstitutionalisation 1985–2008

1 *Australian*, 7 September 1999, 8.

2 Christine Bigby, Margarita Federico & Brian Cooper, *Not Just a Residential Move but Creating a Better Lifestyle for People with Intellectual Disabilities: Report of the Evaluation of the Kew Residential Services Community Relocation Project 1999* (Melbourne: DHS Disability Services Branch, 2004), 4.

NOTES

3   Community Services Victoria, *The St. Nicholas Report: The Evaluation of a Deinstitutionalisation Project in Victoria* (Melbourne: Jean Gordon, Government Printer, 1988), 6.

4   David Dunt & Robert A. Cummins, 'The Deinstitutionalisation of St. Nicholas Hospital: I Adaptive Behaviours and Physical Health', *Australia and New Zealand Journal of Developmental Disabilities*, 16, no. 1 (1990): 5–17.

5   Community Services Victoria, *The St. Nicholas Report*, xi.

6   Community Services Victoria, *The St. Nicholas Report*, 13.

7   See for example Charlie Fox, 'Debating Deinstitutionalisation: The Fire at Kew Cottages in 1996 and the Idea of Community', *Health and History*, 5, no. 2 (2003): 43.

8   Ilan Wiesel & Christine Bigby, 'Movement on Shifting Sands: Deinstitutionalisation and People with Intellectual Disability in Australia, 1974–2014', *Urban Policy and Research*, 33, no. 2 (2015): 179.

9   C. Picton, B. Cooper, L. Owen & R. Chanty, *Evaluation of the Relocation of Caloola Clients Project: A Three Year Follow-up of Former Caloola Training Centre Clients* (Melbourne: La Trobe University, 1995), 34.

10   *Herald Sun*, 5 May 2001, 7.

11   Interview, Manning and Adams, 14 August 2006, 2.

12   *KCPA Newsletter*, July 1977, 2. Quoted in Fox, 49.

13   *Age*, 5 May 2001, 3.

14   *KCPA Newsletter*, May 2001, 2.

15   *Australian*, 6 August 2003, 6.

16   *Age*, 3 September 2002, 8.

17   Fox, 51.

18   *Age*, 3 September 2002, 8.

19   *Herald Sun*, 17 September 2003, 17.

20   Fox, 48.

21   *Herald Sun*, 8 August 2003, 9.

22   *Australian*, 11 August 2003, 2.

23   Interview, Manning and Adams, 14 August 2006, 23.

24   Interview, Corinne Manning and Alma Adams, 30 July 2007, 4.

25   Eric Emerson and Chris Hatton, 'Deinstitutionalization in the UK and Ireland: Outcomes for Service Users', *Journal of intellectual and Developmental Disabilities*, 21, no. 1 (1996): 30.

26   Agnes Kozma, Jim Mansell and Julie Beadle-Brown, 'Outcomes in Different Residential Settings for People with Intellectual Disability: A Systematic Review', *American Journal on Intellectual and Developmental Disabilites*, 114, no. 3 (2009): 210.

27   Cliff Picton, Brian Cooper, and Lloyd Owen, *Evaluation of the Relocation of the Aradale and Mayday Hills Clients Project* (Melbourne: Human Resources Centre and Graduate School of Social Work, La Trobe University, 1997); Cliff Picton, Brian Cooper, and Lloyd Owen, *Evaluation of the Relocation of the Caloola Clients Project: A Three Year Follow-up of the Former Caloola Training Centre Clients* (Melbourne: Human Resources Centre and Graduate School of Social Work, La Trobe University, 1997).

NOTES

28   Jenny Miller, *Closure of Kew Residential Services: Media Review* (Melbourne: Office of the Public Advocate, September 2003), 2.

29   *Better Services for the Residents of Kew Residential Services: An Update* (Melbourne: DHS Victoria, July 2003), 3.

30   Intellectual Disability Review Panel, *A Right to be Heard: 20 Years of the Intellectual Disability Review Panel, 1987–2007* (Melbourne: DHS, Disability Services Division, 2007), 40.

31   Interview, Manning and Adams, 30 July 2007.

32   *Age*, 22 September 2002, 5.

33   *Age*, 22 September 2002, 5.

34   *Kew News*, June 2004, 2.

35   Gary Radler, *Initial Review of the Kew Residential Services Redevelopment: Preliminary Report* (Melbourne: DHS, Disability Services Division, 2003), 2.

36   Interview, Corinne Manning and Alma Adams, 1 August 2007, 12.

37   *Age*, 11 March 2005, 6.

38   *Kew News*, July 2005, 2.

39   *Kew News*, April 2006, 2.

40   *Kew News*, April 2008, 3.

41   *Kew News*, April 2008, 3.

42   *Age*, 13 December 2008, 4.

43   Kozma, *et al.*, 210.

44   Christine Bigby, Brian K. Cooper & Kate Reid, *Making Life Good in the Community: Measures of Resident Outcomes and Staff Perceptions of the Move from an Institution* (Melbourne: DHS Victoria, Disability Services, 2012), 2–3.

45   *Age*, 18 March 2017, 8.

46   *Progress Leader*, 16 September 2008, 7.

47   Corinne Manning, *Bye-Bye Charlie: Stories from the Vanishing World of Kew Cottages* (Sydney: University of New South Wales Press, 2008), 238.

48   Manning, *Bye Bye Charlie*, 238.

Epilogue: Connecting Past and Present Experiences of People with Intellectual Disabilities

1   Agnes Kozma, Jim Mansell and Julie Beadle-Brown, 'Outcomes in Different Residential Settings for People with Intellectual Disability: A Systematic Review', *American Journal on Intellectual and Developmental Disabilites*, 114, no. 3 (2009): 193–222; Mary McCarron, Richard Lombard-Vance, Esther Murphy, Peter May, Naoise Webb, Greg Sheaf, Philip McCallion, Roger Stancliffe, Charles Normand, Valerie Smith, and Mary-Ann O'Donovan, 'Effect of Deinstitutionalisation on Quality of Life for Adults with Intellectual Disabilities: A Systematic Review', *BMJ Open*, 9, no. 4 (2019).

2   Christine Bigby, Brian K. Cooper & Kate Reid, *Making Life Good in the Community: Measures of Resident Outcomes and Staff Perceptions of the Move from an Institution* (Melbourne: DHS Victoria, Disability Services, 2012); Tim Clement & Christine Bigby, *Group Homes for People with Intellectual*

NOTES

Disabilities: Encouraging Inclusion and Participation (London: Jessica Kingsley Publishers, 2009).

3   Jim Mansell., Julie Beadle-Brown & Christine Bigby, 'Implementation of Active Support in Victoria: An Exploratory Study', *Journal of Intellectual and Developmental Disabilities*, 38, no. 1 (2013): 48–58.

4   Claire Spivakovsky, 'Governing Freedom through Risk: Locating the Group Home in the Archipelago of Confinement and Control', *Punishment and Society*, 19, no. 3 (2017): 366–83; Janice C. Sinson, 'Micro-Institutionalisation? Environmental and Managerial Influence in Ten Living Units for People with Mental Handicap', *British Journal of Mental Subnormality*, 36, no. 71 (1990): 77–86.

5   Christine Bigby & Julie Beadle-Brown, 'Improving Quality of Life Outcomes in Supported Accommodation for People with Intellectual Disability: What Makes a Difference?', *Journal of Applied Research in Intellectual Disabilities*, 31, no. 2 (2018): e182–e200.

6   Erving Goffman, *Asylum: Essays on the Social Situation of Mental Patients and Other Inmates* (Harmondsworth: Penguin Books, 1961); Bigby, Cooper & Reid, *Making Life Good in the Community*.

7   *Royal Commission into Violence, Abuse, Neglect and Exploitation of People with Disability*, Interim Report (Canberra: Attorney-General's Department, Commonwealth of Australia, 2020), ix.

8   Christine Bigby, 'Dedifferentiation and People with Intellectual Disabilities in the Australian National Disability Insurance Scheme: Bringing Research, Politics and Policy Together', *Journal of Intellectual & Developmental Disability*, 45, no. 4 (2020): 309–19.

9   Jennifer Clegg, & Christine Bigby, 'Debates about Dedifferentiation: Twenty-first Century Thinking about People with Intellectual Disabilities as Distinct Members of the Disability Group, *Research and Practice in Intellectual and Developmental Disabilities*, 4, no. 1 (2017): 80–97.

10   Clegg & Bigby, 'Debates about Dedifferentiation'.

11   Christine Bigby & Jennifer Clegg, 'Commentary on ASID Position Statement: Addressing the Shortcomings of Dedifferentiation: Introduction and Summary', *Research and Practice in Intellectual and Developmental Disabilities*, 5, no. 1 (2018): 1–7.

12   Lee-Ann Monk, '"Made enquiries, can elicit no history of injury": Researching the History of Institutional Abuse in the Archives', *Provenance: The Journal of Public Record Office Victoria*, no. 6 (September 2007).

13   Centre of Research Excellence in Disability and Health, *Research Report: Nature and Extent of Violence, Abuse, Neglect, and Exploitation against People with Disability in Australia* (Melbourne: Royal Commission into Violence, Abuse, Neglect and Exploitation of People with Disabilities, 2021), 6.

14   Carmela Salomon & Julian Trollor, 'A Scoping Review of Causes and Contributors to Deaths of People with Disability in Australia: Findings (2013–2019)', presented to National Disability Insurance Scheme's (NDIS) Quality and Safety Commission, 2019.

Select Bibliography

Primary Sources

Many of the surviving sources for Kew Cottages are held by Public Record Office Victoria (PROV). Most are medical records, including documents related to the admission and discharge of patients and the case books, which record individual patient histories. Of these, records created during the first three decades of the cottages' history are open to the public. Some of the records related to admission and discharge are now open to 1922–30 but the case books are still closed after 1912. Later records remain restricted to protect the privacy of residents. Information about accessing closed records is available from PROV https://prov.vic.gov.au/closed-records.

Few administrative records from the cottages survive. The books in which the official visitors recorded their observations are in the records of the Kew Mental Hospital. Correspondence between the cottages' superintendents and head of the department (variously the inspector or inspector-general of the insane, later director of mental hygiene) and between the department heads and the government minister, are in Chief Secretary's Correspondence at PROV. The few surviving letters from families can also be found in this correspondence.

In 1944 the Health Department assumed responsibility for mental health. After that date, material on intellectual disabilities was filed in the general correspondence of the Health Commission and Mental Health Authority. The Department of Health and Human Services holds administrative records for the cottages' later history; these too are closed to the public.

Departmental annual reports were published in *Victorian Parliamentary Papers*, usually in the year following the year of the report, though occasionally later. Reports and evidence from royal commissions were also published in parliamentary papers. One significant exception is the 1924 Ellery royal commission. Its minutes of evidence are held by PROV. A copy of Commissioner A.A. Kelley's report is available in the Borchardt Library, La Trobe University.

Many of the newspaper articles cited are available via the National Library of Australia's TROVE database or in State Library Victoria's extensive newspaper collection.

The records of the Kew Cottages Parents' Association are held by State Library Victoria.

The recordings and transcripts of the interviews conducted for this project are to be found in the La Trobe University Records Services.

Books, Book Chapters and Journal Articles Cited

Abel, Emily K., *Hearts of Wisdom: American Women Caring for Kin 1850–1940* (Cambridge, MA: Harvard University Press, 2000).

Bigby, Christine, Cooper, Brian, & Reid, Kate, *Making Life Good in the Community: Measures of Resident Outcomes and Staff Perceptions of the Move from an Institution* (Melbourne: Disability Services Division, DHS Victoria, 2012).

Bigby, Christine, & Beadle-Brown, Julie, 'Improving Quality of Life Outcomes in Supported Accommodation for People with Intellectual Disability: What Makes a Difference?', *Journal of Applied Research in Intellectual Disabilities*, 31, no. 2 (2016): e182–e200.

Bigby, Christine, & Clegg, Jennifer, 'Commentary on ASID Position Statement: Addressing the Shortcomings of Dedifferentiation: Introduction and Summary', *Research and Practice in Intellectual and Developmental Disabilities*, 5, no. 1 (2018): 1–7.

Bigby, Christine, 'Dedifferentiation and People with Intellectual Disabilities in the Australian National Disability Insurance Scheme: Bringing Research, Politics and Policy Together', *Journal of Intellectual & Developmental Disability*, 45, no. 4 (2020): 309–19.

Borsay, Anne, *Disability and Social Policy in Britain since 1750* (Basingstoke: Palgrave Macmillan, 2005).

Broome, Richard, 'They Had Little Chance'. The Kew Cottages Fire of 1996', *Victorian Historical Journal*, 91, no. 2 (December 2020): 245–66.

Brothers, C.R.D., *Early Victorian Psychiatry, 1835–1905* (Melbourne: A.C. Brooks, Government Printer, 1961).

Castles, Katherine, '"Nice, Average Americans": Postwar Parents' Groups and the Defense of the Normal Family', in *Mental Retardation in America: A Historical*

Reader, eds Steven Noll and James W. Trent Jr (New York: New York University Press, 2004), 351–70.

Centre for Research Excellence in Disability and Health, *Nature and Extent of Violence, Abuse, Neglect, and Exploitation against People with Disability in Australia* (Melbourne: Royal Commission into Violence, Abuse, Neglect and Exploitation of People with Disabilities, 2021).

Chupik, Jessa, & Wright, David, 'Treating the "Idiot" Child in early 20th Century Ontario', *Disability and Society*, 21, no. 1 (January 2006): 77–90.

Clegg, Jennifer, & Bigby, Christine, 'Debates about Dedifferentiation: Twenty-first Century Thinking about People with Intellectual Disabilities as Distinct Members of the Disability Group', *Research and Practice in Intellectual and Developmental Disabilities*, 4, no. 1 (2017): 80–97.

Clement, Timothy, & Bigby, Christine, *Group Homes for People with Intellectual Disabilities: Encouraging Inclusion and Participation* (London: Jessica Kingsley Publishers, 2009).

Crowther, Andrew, 'Administration and the Asylum in Victoria, 1860s–1880s', in *'Madness' in Australia: Histories, Heritage and the Asylum*, eds Catharine Coleborne and Dolly MacKinnon (Brisbane: University of Queensland Press, 2003), 85–95.

Digby, Anne, 'Contexts and Perspectives', in *From Idiocy to Mental Deficiency: Historical Perspectives on People with Learning Disabilities*, eds David Wright & Anne Digby (London and New York: Routledge, 1996), 1–21.

Dunt, David, & Cummins, Robert A., 'The Deinstitutionalisation of St. Nicholas Hospital: I Adaptive Behaviours and Physical Health', *Australia and New Zealand Journal of Developmental Disabilities*, 16, no. 1 (1990): 5–17.

Dwyer, Ellen, 'The State and the Multiply Disadvantaged: The Case of Epilepsy', in *Mental Retardation in America: A Historical Reader*, eds Steven Noll and James W. Trent Jr (New York: New York University Press, 2004), 258–80.

Earl, Dave, 'Help for Children and their Families: Presenting "Subnormal" and "Spastic" Children to the Public in 1950s New South Wales', *Antithesis*, 19 (March 2009): 154–65.

Earl, Dave, '"A Group of Parents Came Together": Parent Advocacy Groups for Children with Intellectual Disabilities in Post-World War II Australia', *Health and History*, 13, no. 2 (2011): 84–103.

Earl, Dave, 'Australian Histories of Intellectual Disabilities', in *The Routledge History of Disability*, eds Roy Hanes, Ivan Brown and Nancy E. Hansen (Oxford and New York: Routledge, 2018): 308–19.

Ellery, R.S., *The Cow Jumped over the Moon: Private Papers of a Psychiatrist* (Melbourne: F.W. Cheshire, 1956).

Emerson, Eric, & Hatton, Chris, 'Deinstitutionalization in the UK and Ireland: Outcomes for Services Users', *Journal of Intellectual and Developmental Disabilities*, 21, no. 1 (1996): 17–37.

Epstein, June, *Image of the King: A Parent's Story of Mentally Handicapped Children* (Sydney: Ure Smith, 1970).

Evans, Jack, 'Report of the Victorian Premier's Committee: Blueprint for the 1980's', *Australian Journal of Mental Retardation*, 5, no. 6 (1979): 218–23.

SELECT BIBLIOGRAPHY

Fox, Charles, "'Forehead Low, Aspect Idiotic": Intellectual Disability in Victorian Asylums, 1870–1887', in *'Madness' in Australia: Histories, Heritage and the Asylum*, eds Catharine Coleborne and Dolly MacKinnon, (Brisbane, University of Queensland Press, 2003), 144–56.

Fox, Charles, 'Debating Deinstitutionalisation: The Fire at Kew Cottages in 1996 and the Idea of Community', *Health and History*, 5, no. 2 (2003): 37–59.

Friedberger, Mark, 'The Decision to Institutionalize: Families with Exceptional Children in 1900', *Journal of Family History*, 6, no. 4 (Winter 1981): 396–409.

Garton, Stephen, *Medicine and Madness: A Social History of Insanity in New South Wales 1880–1940* (Sydney: New South Wales University Press, 1988).

Giese, Jill, *The Maddest Place on Earth* (Melbourne: Australian Scholarly Publishing, 2018).

Gladstone, David, 'The Changing Dynamic of Institutional Care: The Western Counties Idiot Asylum, 1864–1914', in *From Idiocy to Mental Deficiency: Historical Perspectives on People with Learning Disabilities*, eds David Wright & Anne Digby (London and New York: Routledge, 1996), 134–60.

Godwin, Louise and Wade, Catherine, *Kew Cottages Parents' Association: The First 50 Years 1957 to 2007* (Melbourne: Kew Cottages Parents' Association, 2007).

Holmes, Katie, 'Talking about Mental Illness: Life Histories and Mental Health in Modern Australia', *Australian Historical Studies*, 41, no. 1 (2016): 25–40.

Jackson, Mark, *The Borderland of Imbecility: Medicine, Society and the Fabrication of the Feeble Mind in Late Victorian and Edwardian England* (Manchester: Manchester University Press, 2000).

Jackson, Mark, 'Institutional Provision for the Feeble-minded in Edwardian England: Sandlebridge and the Scientific Morality of Permanent Care', in *From Idiocy to Mental Deficiency: Historical Perspectives on People with Learning Disabilities*, eds David Wright & Anne Digby (London and New York: Routledge, 1996), 161–83.

Jackson, Mark, "'Grown-Up Children": Understandings of Health and Mental Deficiency in Edwardian England', in *Cultures of Child-Health in Britain and the Netherlands in the Twentieth Century*, eds Marijka Gijswijt-Hofstra and Hilary Marland (Amsterdam and New York: Rodopi, 2003), 141–60.

Jones, Kathleen, 'Education for Children with Mental Retardation: Parent Activism, Public Policy, and Family Ideology in the 1950s', in *Mental Retardation in America: A Historical Reader*, eds Steven Noll and James W. Trent Jr (New York: New York University Press, 2004), 322–50.

Jones, Ross, 'The Master Potter and the Rejected Pots: Eugenic Legislation in Victoria, 1918–1939', *Australian Historical Studies*, 29, no. 113 (1999): 319–42.

Jones, Ross, 'Removing some of the Dust from the Wheels of Civilization: William Ernest Jones and the 1928 Commonwealth Survey of Mental Deficiency', *Australian Historical Studies*, 40, no. 1 (2009): 63–78.

Judge, Cliff, and van Brummelen, Fran, *Kew Cottages: The World of Dolly Stainer* (Melbourne: Spectrum Publications, 2002).

Kaplan, Robert M., 'The First Psychiatric Royal Commission: Reg Ellery and the Attendants at Kew Hospital', *Health and History*, 16, no. 1 (2015): 45–65.

SELECT BIBLIOGRAPHY

Kozma, Agnes, Mansell, Jim, & Beadle-Brown, Julie, 'Outcomes in Different Residential Settings for People with Intellectual Disability: A Systematic Review', *American Journal on Intellectual and Developmental Disabilities*, 114, no. 3 (May 2009): 193–222.

Lewis, Milton, *Managing Madness: Psychiatry and Society in Australia, 1788–1980* (Canberra: AGPS, 1988).

Lloyd, Arthur, *Payment by Results: Kew Cottages First 100 Years 1887–1987* (Melbourne: Kew Cottages and St. Nicholas Parents' Association, 1987).

McCreery, James V., 'Idiocy and Juvenile Insanity in Victoria', *Intercolonial Medical Congress of Australasia* (Sydney: Charles Potter, 1893), 665–8.

Malcolm, Elizabeth, 'Australian Asylum Architecture through German Eyes: Kew, Melbourne, 1867', *Health and History*, 11, no. 1 (2009): 46–64.

Manning, Corinne, *Bye-Bye Charlie: Stories from the Vanishing World of Kew Cottages* (Sydney: University of New South Wales Press, 2008).

Manning, Corinne, 'From Surrender to Activism: The Transformation of Disability and Mothering at Kew Cottages, Australia', in *Disability and Mothering: Liminal Spaces of Embodied Knowledge*, eds Cynthia Lewiecki-Wilson and Jen Cellio (Syracuse: Syracuse University Press, 2011), 183–202.

Mansell, Jim, Beadle-Brown, Julie, & Bigby, Christine, 'Implementation of Active Support in Victoria: An Exploratory Study', *Journal of Intellectual & Developmental Disabilities*, 38, no. 1 (2013): 48–58.

Megahey, Norman, 'Living in Fremantle Asylum: The Colonial Experience of Intellectual Disability 1829–1900', in *Under Blue Skies: The Social Construction of Intellectual Disability in Western Australia*, eds Errol Cocks, Charlie Fox, Mark Brogan and Michael Lee (Perth: Centre for Disability Research and Development, Faculty of Health and Human Sciences, Edith Cowan University, 1996), 13–52.

Monk, Lee-Ann, *Attending Madness: At Work in the Australian Colonial Asylum* (Amsterdam and New York: Rodopi, 2008).

Monk, Lee-Ann, 'Intimacy and Oppression: A Historical Perspective', in *Sexuality and Relationships in the Lives of People with Intellectual Disabilities: Standing in My Shoes*, eds Rohhss Chapman, Sue Ledger, and Louise Townson, with Daniel Docherty (London: Jessica Kingsley Publishers, 2015), 46–64.

Monk, Lee-Ann, 'A Duty to Learn: Attendant Training in Victoria, Australia, 1880–1907', in *Mental Health Nursing: The Working Lives of Paid Carers in the Nineteenth and Twentieth Centuries*, eds Anne Borsay and Pamela Dale (Manchester: Manchester University Press, 2015), 54–74.

Monk, Lee-Ann, '"Made enquires, can elicit no history of injury": Researching the History of Institutional Abuse in the Archives', *Provenance: The Journal of Public Record Office Victoria*, no. 6 (September 2007), https://prov. vic.gov.au/explore-collection/provenance-journal/provenance-2007/ made-enquiries-can-elicit-no-history-injury.

Monk, Lee-Ann, 'Paradoxical Lives: Intellectual Disability Policy and Practice in Twentieth-Century Australia', in *Intellectual Disability in the Twentieth Century: Transnational Perspectives on People, Policy and Practice*, eds Jan Walmsley and Simon Jarrett (Bristol: Policy Press, 2019), 21–33.

SELECT BIBLIOGRAPHY

Nirje, Bengt, 'The Normalisation Principle and its Human Management Implications', in *Changing Patterns in Residential Services for the Mentally Retarded*, Robert B. Kugel and Wolf Wolfensberger, eds (Washington D.C.: President's Committee on Mental Retardation, 1969), 179–95.

Oppenheimer, Melanie, 'Voluntary Action and Welfare in Post-1945 Australia: Preliminary Perspectives', *History Australia*, 2, no. 3 (2005): 82.1–82.16.

Picton, C., Cooper, B., Owen, L., & Chanty, R., *Evaluation of the Relocation of Caloola Clients Project: A Three Year Follow-up of Former Caloola Training Centre Clients* (Melbourne: La Trobe University, 1995).

Pitt, David, *For the Love of Children: My Life and Medical Career* (Melbourne: Pitt Publishing, 1999).

Porteus, Stanley D., *A Psychologist of Sorts: The Autobiography and Publications of the Inventor of the Porteus Maze Tests* (Palo Alto, California: Pacific Books, 1969).

Potts, Maggie, & Fido, Rebecca, *'A Fit Person to be Removed': Personal Accounts of Life in a Mental Deficiency Institution* (Plymouth: Northcote House, 1991).

Radler, Gary, *Initial Review of the Kew Residential Services Redevelopment: Preliminary Report* (Melbourne: DHS, Disability Services Division, 2003).

Robson, Belinda, '"He made us feel special": Eric Cunningham Dax, Edith Pardy and the Reform of Mental Health Services in Victoria, 1950s and 1960s', *Australian Historical Studies*, 34, no. 122 (2003): 270–89.

Ryan, Joanna, with Frank Thomas, *The Politics of Mental Handicap* (Harmondsworth: Penguin, 1980).

Ryan, Joanna, with Frank Thomas, *The Politics of Mental Handicap*, Revised Edition (London: Free Association Books, 1987).

Simmons, Harvey G., 'Explaining Social Policy: The English Mental Deficiency Act of 1913', *Journal of Social History*, 11, no. 3 (Spring 1978): 387–403.

Sinson, Janice C., 'Micro-Institutionalisation? Environmental and Managerial Influence in Ten Living Units for People with Mental Handicap', *British Journal of Mental Subnormality*, 36, no. 71 (1990): 77–86.

Spivakovsky, Claire, 'Governing Freedom through Risk: Locating the Group Home in the Archipelago of Confinement and Control', *Punishment and Society*, 19, no. 3 (2017): 366–83.

Temby, Ethel, *Kew Cottages Parents' Association: A Brief Sketch* (Melbourne: Kew Cottages Parents' Association, 1970).

Thomson, Mathew, 'Disability, Psychiatry and Eugenics', in *The Oxford Handbook of the History of Eugenics*, eds Alison Bashford and Philippa Levine (Oxford and New York: Oxford University Press, 2010), 116–33.

Tipping, Paul, *Independence, Choice and Community for All: A History of the First 40 Years of the E.W. Tipping Foundation* (Melbourne: E.W. Tipping Foundation, 2010).

Trent, James W., *Inventing the Feeble Mind: A History of Mental Retardation in the United States* (Berkley, California: University of California Press, 1994).

Trent, James W., *Inventing the Feeble Mind: A History of Mental Retardation in the United States*, Second Edition (New York: Oxford University Press, 2017).

Tucker, G.A., *Lunacy in Many Lands* (Sydney: Charles Potter, Government Printer, 1887).

SELECT BIBLIOGRAPHY

'The Yarra Bend Asylum, near Melbourne', *Journal of Mental Science*, 8, no. 44 (January 1863): 614–19.

Tyor, Peter, & Bell, Leland, *Caring for the Retarded in America: A History* (Westport, Connecticut: Greenwood Press, 1984).

Walmsley, Jan, Tilley, Liz, Dumbleton, Sue, & Bardsley, Janet, 'The Changing Face of Parent Advocacy: A Long View', *Disability and Society*, 32, no. 9 (2017): 1366–86.

Wiesel, Ilan, & Bigby, Christine, 'Movement on Shifting Sands: Deinstitutionalisation and People with Intellectual Disability in Australia, 1974–2014'. *Urban Policy and Research*, 33, no. 2 (2015): 178–94.

Wing, J.K., & Brown, G.W., *Institutionalism and Schizophrenia: A Comparative Study of Three Mental Hospitals 1960–1968* (Cambridge: Cambridge University Press, 1970).

Wolfensberger, Wolf, *The Principle of Normalization in Human Services* (Toronto: National Institute on Mental Retardation, 1974).

Wright, David, '"Childlike in his Innocence": Lay Attitudes to "Idiots" and "Imbeciles" in Victorian England', in *Idiocy to Mental Deficiency: Historical Perspectives on People with Learning Disabilities*, eds David Wright & Anne Digby (London and New York: Routledge, 1996), 118–33.

Wright, David, 'Getting Out of the Asylum: Understanding the Confinement of the Insane in the Nineteenth Century', *Social History of Medicine*, 10, no. 1 (April 1997): 137–55.

Wright, David, 'Family Strategies and the Institutional Confinement of "Idiot" Children in Victorian England', *Journal of Family History*, 23, no. 2 (April 1998): 190–208.

Wright, David, 'Familial Care of "Idiot" Children in Victorian England', in *The Locus of Care: Families, Communities and the Provision of Welfare since Antiquity*, eds Peregrine Holden and Richard Smith (London: Routledge, 1998), 176–97.

Wright, David, *Mental Disability in Victorian England: The Earlswood Asylum* (Oxford: Oxford University Press, 2001).

Reports to Government

Bigby, Christine, Federico, Margarita, & Cooper, Brian, *Not Just a Residential Move but Creating a Better Lifestyle for People with Intellectual Disabilities: Report of the Evaluation of the Kew Residential Services Community Relocation Project 1999* (Melbourne: DHS Disability Services Branch, 2004).

Bigby, Christine, Cooper, Brian K., & Reid, Kate, *Making Life Good in the Community: Measures of Resident Outcomes and Staff Perceptions of the Move from an Institution* (Melbourne: DHS Victoria, Disability Services, 2012).

Community Services Victoria, *The St. Nicholas Report: The Evaluation of a Deinstitutionalisation Project in Victoria* (Melbourne: Jean Gordon, Government Printer, 1988).

Intellectual Disability Review Panel, *A Right to be Heard: 20 years of the Intellectual Disability Review Panel, 1987–2007* (Melbourne: DHS, Disability Services Division, 2007).

Johnstone, Graeme, *Inquest Findings, Comments and Recommendations into Fire and Nine Deaths at Kew Residential Services on 8 April 1996* (Melbourne: State Coroner's Office, 1997).

Kelley, A.A., *Hospital for the Insane, Kew: Report of Commission* (Melbourne: La Trobe University, 1982). Also: Transcript of Evidence given before the Royal Commission of Inquiry, VPRS 7526/P1, Unit 1, Public Record Office Victoria.

Kennedy, Alexander, *Report to the Minister for Health on Mental Health and Mental Hygiene Services in the State of Victoria* (Melbourne: J.J. Gourley, Government Printer, 1950).

McCarron, Mary, Lombard-Vance, Richard, Murphy, Esther, May, Peter, Webb, Naoise, Sheaf, Greg, McCallion, Philip, Stancliffe, Roger, Normand, Charles, Smith, Valerie and Mary-Ann O'Donovan, 'Effect of Deinstitutionalisation on Quality of Life for Adults with Intellectual Disabilities: A Systematic Review', *BMJ Open*, 9, no. 4 (2019).

Miller, Jenny, *Closure of Kew Residential Services: Media Review* (Melbourne: Office of the Public Advocate, September 2003).

Report of the Mental Hospitals Inquiry Committee on the Department of Mental Hygiene, Its Hospitals and Its Administration (Melbourne: J.J. Gourley, Government Printer, 1948).

Royal Commission on Asylums for the Insane and Inebriate, Report and Minutes of Evidence, in *Victorian Parliamentary Papers*, 1886, Vol. II (Melbourne: John Ferres, Government Printer, 1886).

Royal Commission into Violence, Abuse, Neglect and Exploitation of People with Disabilities. Appointed 4 April 2019, still in session in March 2023, https://disability.royalcommission.gov.au/rounds/public-hearing-23-preventing-and-responding-violence-abuse-neglect-and-exploitation-disability-services-case-study.

Salomon, Carmela, & Trollor, Julian, 'A Scoping Review of Causes and Contributors to Deaths of People with Disability in Australia: Findings (2013–2019)', presented to National Disability Insurance Scheme's (NDIS) Quality and Safety Commission, 2019.

Ten Year Plan for the Redevelopment of Intellectual Disability Services: Final Report (Melbourne: Nielson Associates, August 1988).

Theses

Bonwick, Richard, 'The History of the Yarra Bend Lunatic Asylum, Melbourne' (Master of Medicine (Psychiatry) thesis, University of Melbourne, 1995).

Brockley, Janice A., 'Rearing the Child Who Never Grew: Parents, Professionals, and Children with Intellectual Disabilities, 1910–1965' (PhD thesis, Rutgers University, 2001).

Day, Cheryl, 'Magnificence, Misery and Madness: A History of Kew Asylum, 1872–1915' (PhD thesis, University of Melbourne, 1998).

Jones, Ross, 'Skeletons in Toorak and Collingwood Cupboards: Eugenics in Educational and Health Policy in Victoria, 1919 to 1929' (PhD thesis, Monash University, 2000).

SELECT BIBLIOGRAPHY

Lewis, John, 'Removing the Grit: The Development of Special Education in Victoria, 1887–1947' (PhD thesis, Latrobe University, 1989).

Williams, Ann K., 'Managing the "Feebleminded": Eugenics and the Institutionalisation of People with Intellectual Disabilities in New South Wales, 1900 to 1930' (PhD thesis, University of Newcastle, 1998).

Index

(Note: Illustrations are denoted by page number followed by '*i*')

Adams, Alma, 258, 258*i*, 259, 260, 262, 263, 264, 265, 265*i*, 271–2, 275
Adey, John, 84
Age (newspaper)
    call for judicial inquiry into Kew Cottages fire, 244
    coverage of fire at Kew Cottages, 237–8
    investigation into 'Victoria's Forgotten People', 239–40
    Minus Children Appeal, 221–2
Aldridge, Peter, 248
Aldridge, Ronald, 235, 248
Allan–Peacock government, 89, 90
Allison, Lyn, 244
Anderson, Bruce, 242, 247
Anderson, Don, 242, 243, 247
Anderson, Zoe, 242, 243, 247
Appleton, Mrs, 29
Aradale Training Centre, Ararat, 255
Ararat Hospital for the Insane, 59, 114
Ararat Lunatic Asylum, 6, 287
Ararat Training Centre, 209
Argyle, Stanley (Dr), 90, 91, 104, 106, 107, 111, 214
Argyle government, 106, 107–8
Argyle–Alan government, 93
Armstrong, Morgan, 30
Armstrong, Mrs, 30
Armstrong, Thomas, 30
Ashburner, J.V. (Dr), 155, 156, 157, 170, 173, 177, 187
Association of Friends and Relatives of the Mentally Ill, 126
Association to Combat the Social Evil, 87–8
asylum attendants, training, 76–7

Asylum for Imbeciles and Idiots, Newcastle, 12, 13
Australasian Medical Congress, Sydney 1911, 63–4
Australian (newspaper), 236–7
Australian Council for Mental Retardation, 190
Australian Natives Association, 88

Badenhope, Fred, 200
Bailey, Henry, 111, 115, 117
Baker, Henry, 266
Ballarat Asylum, 13, 287
Ballarat Hospital for the Insane, 59
Ballarat Mental Hospital, 146
Ballinger, James, 242
Bank-Mikkelson, Niels Erik, 217–18, 227
Barker, Walter, 54
Barnes, Allan, 100
Barr, Martin (Dr), 63
Barry, William 'Bill,' 121, 126, 169–70
Beechworth Hospital for the Insane, 59, 94, 114
Beechworth Lunatic Asylum, 6, 287
Beechworth Mental Hospital, 146, 151
Beechworth Training Centre, 209
Bell Street Special School, Fitzroy, 68, 87, 88–9
Bent government, 56, 59
Bernard, Peter Arthur, 235
Berry, Graham, 7–8, 14
Berry, Richard (Dr), 89
Berry government, 13
Berry Street Foundling Home, 109
Blackburn, Maurice, 93
Bodna, Ben, 239

INDEX

Bolte government, 175
Bomford, John (Dr), 208
Booroondara Council, 269
Booth, Angela, 87–8
Bourchier, Murray, 107
Bower, Herbert, 144
Bowie, Robert (Dr), 5
Bowser, John, 87
Boys Depot, Parkville, 34
Bracks, Steve, 257, 269
Bracks government, redevelopment of Kew Cottages site, 257–8, 260, 263, 270
Brady, Wilfred (Dr), 173, 178–9, 186, 187, 187*i*, 188, 207, 212
Brecon and Radnor County Asylum, Wales, 58
Brennan, Frank, 73*i*, 73–4, 76, 77, 78–9, 81–2
Brennan, Mary, 74
Brink, Denys Berrange (Dr), 209
British Medical Association, Victorian Branch, 14, 25, 64
Brotherhood of St Laurence, 244
Brothers, Charles R.D. (Dr), 134–5, 145, 151, 158
Brown, Violet, 31
Brumby, John, 246
Buck v. Bell 1927, 94
Bundoora, 89
Bundoora Mental Hospital, 146
'Bundoora Park,' 89, 90
Burrell, Amelia, 21
Byrnes, Percy, 142

Cain, John (Jnr), 226, 238
Cain, John (Snr), 170, 179
Cain (Snr) government (1945–47), 121, 126–7, 175
Cain (Jnr) government (1982–90), 226
Caloola Training Centre, Sunbury, 25, 256, 258
Campbell, Annie, 31
Campbell, Christine, 257
Campbell, Kirsten, 266
Carpenter, Julie, 242

Carroll, Mrs, 23–4
Catarinich, Dr, 129, 139, 142–3, 145–6, 150
Chea Earpeng (Peng), 242
Childers, Hugh, 5
children with intellectual disabilities, 21–9
    calls for specialised institutions for, 11–13, 14–15
    day centres, 154
    educability of, 4–5, 11–13, 26–7
    exemption from compulsory education, 25
    institutional segregation, 87–8
    negative assumptions about, 52–3
    parents' organisations, 189–91
    as problematic patients in hospitals and asylums for the 'insane,' 9–11
    special education and training system, 47
    at Yarra Bend Asylum, 4–5
    See also families of children with intellectual disabilities
Children's Cottages (formerly Kew Idiot Asylum; later Kew Cottages)
    admissions from other institutions, 95
    allegations of cruelty and maladministration, 71–2
    conditions, 68, 69–70, 74–5, 96, 97, 116, 117, 121, 129, 140–1
    confinement of residents as punishment, 99–100
    everyday life 1925–1933, 95–103
    government neglect, 83–4, 121, 141
    improvements and additions, 96, 97*i*
    local protests against existence of, 69
    location, 108*i*
    management, 72, 75
    medical procedures and patients' rights, 77–81
    notoriety, 133
    overcrowding, 74–5, 108–9, 115–16
    patients confined in wire enclosure, 122, 122*i*
    plans for closure, 87, 113, 114

346

INDEX

punishment of escapees, 100
regimentation, 97
relationships between residents,
101–2
resident numbers, 108, 115
royal commission into staff
complaints, 72–84, 86
special school, 102–3
staff numbers, 115–16, 120–1
staff-patient ratios, 121
toys from *Herald* appeal, 123–4, 124*i*
transfers to other institutions,
114–15
typhoid epidemic, 70
unpaid labour by residents, 98–9
Children's Depot, Royal Park, 95
Children's Welfare Department, 95,
109, 110
civic and community organisations, 190
Caire, Nicholas, 48
Clarke, James, 27
Clarke, William, 27
classification
early 20th century categories of
'mental deficiency', 64–65
clinic to identify and classify
children's degree of 'mental
deficiency,' 89, 111–12
'imbecile class,' 8–11
Mental Deficiency Act 1939, 111–12
Mental Health Act 1959, 92*i*
Mental Deficiency Bill 1929,
91–92, 92*i*
closure and redevelopment of Kew
Cottages site
Bracks government redevelopment
plan, 257–9, 268
closure process and relocation of
residents, 264–8
complaints by new homebuyers
about former Kew Cottages
residents, 256–7
development battle, 268, 269–72
evaluations of closure, 273–4
heritage listed buildings, 269–70,
275–6

local opposition to, 262
new homes for former residents, 271
opposition by Kew Coalition, 269
original cottages, 276, 276*i*
Kew Parents' Association
opposition to government plan,
259–61, 269
plans for redevelopment, 270–1
problems with, 274
public debate over, 259, 262–3
redeployment of former Kew
Cottages staff into community
homes, 266–7
Cody, Robert, 266
Colanda Centre, Colac, 228
Colville, Ernest, 52
community residential units, 252, 253
Community Services, Department of,
255
Conolly, John (Dr), 5
Corry, Annie, 100–1
Coutts, Bev, 180
Coutts, Robin, 199–200, 204
Coyle, Ernest, 112
Craig, Mary, 32
Crossley, Rosemary, 241, 252

Dale, Frank, 192
Davidson, Kenneth, 262
Dawson, Frank, 82
Dawson, Ralph, 275
Dax (nee Mills), Alice, 136, 144
Dax, Eric Cunningham, 140*i*
achievements in Victoria, 179, 204–5
appointment as chair of Mental
Hygiene Authority Board, 134,
135, 139, 143
arrival in Melbourne, 143–4
background, 135–8
character and charm, 160
fighting red tape, 156–9, 177
on *Herald* Appeal for Kew
Cottages, 168–9, 170
public relations skills, 158–60
reform plans for Victoria, 143,
153–4, 164

347

INDEX

relations with the press, 143–4, 157–8, 159
reputation, 135
on Sandhurst Boys' Centre, 208
and story of 'Michael,' 162
tour of mental institutions, 146–7
untangling mental illness from intellectual disability, 151–4, 185, 206–7
vision for Janefield, 209
on voluntary groups, 190
Dax, Henry, 135–6, 144
Dax, Richard, 159
Dax, Sussanah, 144
Deakin, Alfred, 17–18, 37
Defence, Department of, 61
deinstitutionalisation, 251, 253–4, 256, 272, 275
Dendy, Mary, 62–3
dental hygiene, 80–1
de-Pyper Bottomley-Tipping, Bruce, 246–7
de-Pyper Bottomley-Tipping, Heather, 246–7
Dick, Thomas, 17, 37
disability services, Ten-Year Plan, 227–8, 255
Disney, James, 93–4
'Distracted Mother' (*Herald*, letter to editor), 118–20, 119*i*
Dunstan, Albert, 107, 121
Dunstan, Keith, 165
Dunstan government, 107, 110
Dusink, Anne, 243
Dusink, John, 243

Eames J, Geoff, 245
Earlswood Asylum, England, 11, 12, 26–7
East Kew Women's Community Club, 126
Eastham, Theophilus, 36*i*, 36–7, 47, 54
Ebbs, Eric, 134, 135, 145, 150, 151, 158
Edmunds, Adrian, 234–5
Education, Department of, 61, 68, 102, 210

Edwards, Cecil, 141–2, 162–4, 168
Ellery, Reginald (Dr), 71–2, 75, 77–8, 79–81, 98, 99, 138
Epstein, Carey, 189
Epstein, Julius, 189
Epstein, June, 188, 189, 191, 192, 196, 201–2, 215–16
eugenics movement, 55, 56, 62–70, 153, 214
Evans, Jack, 222, 223
Evans Report, 225, 251
Everard, William, 89

Fairy, Mrs, 52
families of children with intellectual disabilities
advocacy for better conditions for their children, 115
caring for children, 21–9
continuities over time, 282
maintaining relationships with institutionalised children, 29–32, 113–14, 173
opposition to deinstitutionalisation, 260–1
organisations for, 189–91
pain of having children confined in dreadful conditions, 117–20, 123
parent advocacy, 194
stigma and social isolation, 202–3, 215
Fels, Alan, 262
Fewster, George, 134
Finlayson, John, 21
fire at Kew Cottages
bravery of firefighters and staff, 232, 234, 242
cause, 234
condolences, 245–6
Coronial Inquest, 234, 248–50
evacuation of residents, 232, 234
fatalities, 234–5
government funding cuts blamed, 236–8, 240–1, 244
inferno in Building 37, 230–4
interior of Unit 31 after fire, 233*i*

348

INDEX

memorial services and funerals, 245, 246
point of origin, 249*i*
press coverage, 235–7
Fishbourne, John (Dr), 14, 25, 63
Foley, Michael, 51
Forster, Ebenezer, 115
Forster, Mr, 115
Frlan, Bartful, 242
Fulton, Bill, 142, 143, 144, 149, 215

The Gables, Kew, 144
Gamble, Morris (Dr), 70, 100
Gardner, Julian, 270
Garrett, Mary Ellen, 32
Gartside, Charles, 127, 129
Gately, Annie, 50
Germany, eugenicist practices, 94, 214
Gilbert, Rosa, 126
Gillies government, 84
Glendenning, Miss, 87
Goddard, Henry H., 125
Godwin, Louise, 250
Goffman, Erving, 219
Goh, Victor, 266–7
Goldby, Alison, 30
Goldby, Margaret, 30
Govett, Mr, 80
Grant, Clarence, 31
Grant, Edward, 31
Grant, James, 13
Grant, James (Bishop), 246
Grant, Mary J., 77
Grant, Thomas Patrick, 235
Grant, William, 31, 51
Gray, David, 44
Gray, Paul, 236–7
Great Depression, 86, 106–7
Green, David, 241
Gregory, Mrs, 21
group homes, 252, 279

Haines, Ron, 237
Hamer, Rupert, 221
Hanrahan, John, 241
Harris, Matron, 124*i*

Harrison, Minnie, 22
Harrison, Walter, 22
Hastings, Elizabeth, 238–9
Hauser, Arthur, 61–2, 67
Haw, Bruce Mark, 235
Health, Department of, 255
Health and Community Services, Department of, 239, 240
Henderson, David, 275, 276–7
Henry, Alice, 35, 38–40, 43, 45, 48, 52
Herald (newspaper)
campaign to drive reform of mental hospitals, 125–6, 141–2, 163
'Distracted Mother' (letter to editor), 118–20, 119*i*
exposés of mental hospitals, 125–6, 139–41
toy appeal for Children's Cottages, 123–4, 124*i*
Herald Sun (newspaper), coverage of fire at Kew Cottages, 235–7
Heritage Victoria, 269
Hickford, Betty-Joy, 266
Higgins, Irene, 162, 182–8, 183*i*, 198, 204, 210–12, 221, 245–6
Higgs, W.G., 105, 106, 115
Hilgendorf, Johanna, 244
Hilgendorf, Myra, 244
Hockey, Athel (Dr), 215–16
Hogan, Edmond, 107
Hogan government, 104, 107
Hogg, Caroline, 227
Hollow, Joseph, 72, 76, 77–8, 79–81, 82
Hollway, Thomas, 127
Homes, Miss (Matron), 140*i*
Hook, Catherine, 50
Hospital Employees Federation, 126
Human Services, Department of, 250, 264, 266
Hutton, Geoffrey, 143

Iffla, Solomon (Dr), 14
insanity, legal definition, 7–8
institutions for those with intellectual disabilities: UK, 11, 12

349

institutions for those with intellectual disabilities: Victoria, 3–6, 59, 287–8
  closures under Kennett government, 255–6, 257
  day centres, 210
  deinstitutionalisation, 251, 256
  distinguishing between intellectual disability and mental illness, 151–4, 206–7
  downsizing, 255
  first steps towards, 9–11
  refurbishment by 1974, 205
  residential training centres, 206–12
  See also specific institutions
intellectual disability
  eugenics discourse on, 62–70, 90–1, 153
  human rights and, 216–17
  media role in shaping public perceptions, 158, 235
  normalisation, 217–21, 224–5, 226
  shift from medical to social model, 279–80
  untangling from mental illness, 151–4, 206–7
  See also children with intellectual disabilities; people with intellectual disabilities
Intellectually Disabled Persons' Services Act 1986, 225–9, 239, 245, 281

Janefield Colony, Bundoora, 146
  administration, 111
  classification and segregation, 112
  establishment, 110
  expansion, 175
  purchase of 'Bundoora Park', 89
  staff-patient ratios, 121
Janefield Training Centre, Bundoora, 208, 209, 228, 255, 258, 259–60
Jarvie, Laurel, 113, 114
Jarvie, Mr, 113, 114
Jarvie, Mrs, 113, 114
Johnstone, Graeme, 234, 249, 250
Johnstone, Neville, 169
Jones, Alan, 240–1

Jones, Maxwell, 211
Jones, Ruby, 101–2
Jones, William Ernest (Dr)
  appointment as inspector-general of the insane, 58–9
  as chair of Mental Hospitals Inquiry Committee, 126–7
  on education at Kew Idiot Asylum, 67–8, 102
  investigation of complaints against Ellery, 71
  on needs of asylums, 59, 60–1
  on neglect of Kew Idiot Asylum, 83
  support for eugenic control of mental deficiency, 64, 65–6, 89, 110
  on training institutions, 66–7
Judge, Astrid, 181, 182

Kelley, A.A., 72–3, 75, 76, 83
Kennedy, Alexander, 127–9, 179
Kennedy report, 127–9, 133, 134, 143, 145, 179
Kennett, Jeff, 237, 244, 246, 251, 257
Kennett government
  accused of breach of *Intellectually Disabled Persons' Services Act*, 244–5
  blamed for fire at Kew Cottages, 236–8, 240–1, 244
  closure of institutions for people with intellectual disabilities, 255–6
  cuts to community services, 236–7, 238
  neo-liberal agenda, 238, 255
  refusal to hold judicial inquiry Kew Cottages fire, 244
  rejection of cluster housing at Kew, 260
Kent Hughes, Wilfred, 104, 105
Kew (locality)
  concern over redevelopment of Kew Cottages site, 260, 262, 285
  local opposition to presence of asylum, 59–60, 285
  See also Kew Shire Council

INDEX

Kew Cottages and St Nicholas Parents'
Association, 237
Kew Cottages (formerly Children's
Cottages)
abuse and neglect of residents, 283
administrative separation from Kew
Mental Hospital, 185
admission of 'Michael,' 164, 166–7,
174
annual fete, 180–2, 181*i*, 200
building program, 175, 177–8
circa 1900, 269*i*
closure and redevelopment of site.
See closure and redevelopment of
Kew Cottages site
closure plans, 229, 230, 246–7, 248,
251
conditions, 146–7, 147*i*, 148*i*, 158,
164*i*, 165–6, 167, 168, 179, 194–5,
240, 257
consultation between mother and
nurse, 172*i*
education and training, 211–12,
218*i*
fire. *See* fire at Kew Cottages
funding, 150
Herald appeal to raise funds,
168–70, 177
improvements and additions, 148–9,
150*i*
normalisation efforts, 230–1
notoriety, 204
nurses attending residents, 149*i*
outings for residents, 212, 213*i*
overcrowding, 178, 210
patient/resident numbers, 171–2,
210, 250
personal stories of residents, 171–5
public perceptions of, 167*i*, 179
relationship between staff and
parents, 184–5, 198–9
renovation after fire, 247–8
residents at play, 176*i*, 197*i*, 222*i*
social worker appointed, 183–4
staff composition, 211, 212
waiting list, 179

Kew Cottages Parents' Association
advocacy, 200–3, 215
call for judicial inquiry into fire, 244
cluster housing proposal, 260
early days, 188–94
Finance Committee, 192
fostering sense of community,
198–9, 200
fundraising, 196, 200
improving conditions, 194–6,
199–200
inaugural meeting, 186–8
Information Committee, 201, 202
Liaison Committee, 199
on normalisation and
deinstitutionalisation, 259
objectives, 191–2
origins, 182–8
Publicity (later Information)
Committee, 192
on redevelopment of Kew Cottages
site, 258–9, 260
regional branches, 200
rejection of calls for closure of Kew
Cottages, 247
service for fire victims at St Paul's
Cathedral, 246
vigil at Coronial Inquest into fire, 249
writ against Victorian government,
244–5, 248, 250
Kew Hospital for the Insane
conditions, 106, 107
debate over future of, 106–7
local demands for removal, 103–5
location, 108*i*
overcrowding, 106
plans for closure, 60–1, 87, 103
Kew Idiot Asylum (later Children's
Cottages; Kew Cottages)
abuse of patients, 51–2
achievements, 47–53
admissions against parent's wishes, 27
admissions from other institutions,
25–6
arrival of first patients, 34
case notes of patients, 30, 51–2

351

Index

communal dining room, 28*i*
conditions, 57, 59, 61–2, 67
design and construction, 13, 15,
 16*i*, 17, 28*i*, 34, 68, 69*i*
entertainments and special events,
 42–3, 47*i*
establishment, 34, 57
exhibitions, 48
expansion, 43–4, 45–6
family-initiated admissions, 19,
 21–7, 29
fire, 44–5
funding, 43–6, 53–4, 59–60
industrial training, 39–40, 41–2*i*
legal requirements for admission, 20
MacFarlane, A.A. Dr, 51
male dormitory, 28*i*
management, 35–6
mission, 36, 53, 55, 98
moral training, 38, 51
neglect by government, 57, 61–2
overcrowding, 43–4, 45, 59
patient numbers, 34, 43–4, 55
patients who returned to the
 community, 54–5
photographs of patients, 32, 33*i*
physical training, 39, 40*i*
plans for closure, 56–7, 60–1
regimentation, 51
royal commission into, 57
sanitation, 45
schooling, 38*i*, 38–9
surveillance of residents, 51
suspension of schooling, 61–2, 67–8
transfers to public lunatic asylums,
 50, 54
typhoid epidemic, 56, 61
unpaid labour by residents, 42
Kew Lunatic Asylum
buildings, 6, 16*i*
children with intellectual
 disabilities, 14, 15
location, 6, 7*i*, 8, 8*i*
maintenance, 14
management, 35
Kew Mental Hospital

administrative separation from Kew
 Cottages, 185
conditions, 127–8
fatalities from fire, 235, 237
first visit by Dax, 146
management, 155, 156
neglect by government, 155
resident population, 151–2
social worker appointed, 182, 183–4
Kew News (newsletter), 266, 267
Kew Progress Association, 105
Kew Residential Services (formerly
 Kew Cottages), 239, 246
Kew Shire Council, opposition to
 presence of asylum, 17–18, 103–5,
 108, 285
Kew Training Centre (formerly
 Children's Cottages), 207, 210
Kilby, Mrs, 23
Kindloin Group, Balnarring, 243
Kingsbury Training Centre, Bundoora,
 210, 228, 255, 258, 259–60
Kirby, Harry, 200
Kirner government, 237–8
Knight, Mark, 235

Larundel Mental Hospital, Bundoora,
 121, 140
Lawson, H.S.W., 68
Lawson government, 88
Legge, Edmund, 34, 49, 52, 54, 55
Leonard, T.J., 207–8
Letherland, John, 265*i*
Lillywhite, Brendan, 221
Lindemann, Richard, 266
Logan, Andrew, 244
Logan, Hilda, 244
Loughnan, C.A., 105
Lucy, Michael, 169
Lunacy Act 1903 (Vic), 58, 66, 77, 91,
 92, 109, 110
Lunacy Commission (UK), 5
Lunacy Department, 35, 58, 70
Lunacy Statute 1867 (Vic), 8, 58
lunatic, legal definition, 66
Lyons, Gerald, 162

INDEX

Macfarlan, Albert, 94
MacFarlane, A.A., (Dr), 30, 31, 32, 51–2
Machin, Buckley, 214–15
Maddern, Frank, 60
Maltby, Thomas, 133–4
Manger, Mary, 21, 23
Manning, Corinne, 95, 98*i*
Manning, Frederick Norton (Dr), 12, 47
Mansfield, Bruce, 181
Martin, H.J., 185
Matthews, Rachael, 50
Matthews, Stanley, 235
Maudsley, H.F. (Dr), 126
Mayday Hills Training Centre, Beechworth, 255
Mays, Mrs, 24
McCarthy, Annie, 25–6
McCarthy, Rita, 25–6
McCreery, James (Dr), 30, 35–6, 37, 38, 45, 47, 49, 51–2, 53–5, 66
McDonald, Anne, 241
McDonald, William, 159
McGarvie, Richard, 246
McKell, William, 190
McLeod, Donald, 69
McNamara, Gregory, 266
McNeilly, Robert, 21, 22–3
McNeilly, Sarah, 21, 22
McNeilly, William, 22–3
McPherson, William, 69, 88, 105
McPherson government, 93, 104, 105
medical procedures and experimentation, and patients' rights, 77–81
Medical Society of Victoria, 57
Melbourne Fire Brigade (MFB), 232, 236
Mencap, UK, 191
men
    deaths in fire at Kew Cottages, 234–235
    domination of mental health services, 134, 184
    segregation from boys, 13

mental deficiency, legal definition and classification, 91–92, 111–12
Mental Deficiency Act 1939, 111–12, 128, 151, 152–3, 185, 214
mental deficiency bills
    1926, 90–3, 92*i*, 110
    1929, 110
    1939, 110–11, 112
Mental Health Act 1959, 206–7, 214, 226
Mental Health Authority
    and Department of Health, 226
    normalisation reforms, 224–5
mental health system
    decentralisation of services, 151
    untangling mental illness from intellectual disability, 151–4, 206–7
Mental Hospital Auxiliaries, 116–17
Mental Hospital Employees Association, 71–2, 75, 105
Mental Hospital Inquiries Committee, 126–7, 128
mental hygiene, Kennedy report, 127–9, 143, 145, 179
Mental Hygiene Act 1958, 185
Mental Hygiene Authority
    appointment of Eric Cunningham Dax, 134, 135, 138
    battles with Public Works Department, 156–7
    establishment, 129, 133
    function, 145
    headquarters, 139
    inaugural meeting, 148
    management, 134–5
    operating budget, 150, 156–7
    reform program, 153–4, 156
    social workers, 182, 183–4
    structure, 144–5
Mental Hygiene Authority Act 1950, 134
Mental Hygiene, Department of, 110, 117
    building program, 117, 121
    history and administration, 139, 142

353

INDEX

Mental Defectives Branch, 111, 151
Mental Hygiene Branch, 151
operating budget, 150
recommended reform, 129
mental illness, untangling from
intellectual disability, 151–4, 206–7
Mentally Retarded Children's
Education and Welfare Society, SA,
189–90
Menzies, Frank, 72, 82
Menzies, Robert, 72, 78, 80
Merrett, James, 69
Merrifield, Samuel, 178
'Michael' (boy tied to a stake) 162, 163,
164, 165–8, 171, 175
Middlesex Colony, England, 110, 112
Millane, Vivien, 241
Millar, Royce, 272–3
Miller, Violet, 56
Minus Children Appeal, 221–2
Molloy, Matron, 77
Mont Park Hospital for the Insane,
60–1, 89–90
Mont Park Mental Hospital, 146
Montague Special School, South
Melbourne, 87, 88–9
Morris, Ian, 234
Morrison, Patsy, 246
Muller, Noel, 102
Mulvaney, Barry (Dr), 159
Murray, John, 53, 57, 58, 65–6

National Association of Parents
and Friends of Mentally Retarded
Children, USA, 191
National Council of Women, 94, 127,
134
National Disability Strategy, 285
National Disability Insurance Scheme
(NDIS), 280, 285
Neglected Children, Department for,
24, 34, 66
Neglected Children's Depot, 67
Negri, Alan, 234
Neilson, Annie, 22, 29
Neilson, Elsie, 22, 25, 29

neo-liberalism, 238, 255, 281, 285
Netherne Hospital, Surrey, 136–8, 139
New Jersey Parent's Group for
Retarded Children, USA, 191
New Norfolk Asylum, 12
Newman, Shayne, 235
Nirje, Bengt, 217–18, 227
North Kew Progress Association, 103–4
Nyeman, Mark, 24

Oakleigh Centre, 243
Office of Intellectual Disability
Services, 227
Office of Mental Retardation, 225–6
O'Shanassy government, 5
Otis, Paul, 242
Otis, Peter, 242

Paley, Edward (Dr), 5–6, 7, 8–12 13, 25
Papadopoulos, Angelo, 265*i*
Pardy, Edith, 116–17
patients' rights, medical procedures and
experimentation, 77–81
Peacock, Alexander, 65
Peacock family, 19
people with intellectual disabilities
abuse and neglect of, 282–4, 285
changes in public policy
perceptions, 279–80
critical realist approach to, 282
dedifferentiation, 280
deinstitutionalisation, 251, 253–4,
256, 272, 273–4
differentiation, 280, 281
equality before the law, 238–9
expansion of services, 205–14
group homes, 252, 279
health status and life expectancy,
284–5
implementation of policy agendas
for, 284
institutional segregation, 65–6,
87–8
medical procedures and
experimentation on, 77–81
in mental hospitals, 152

Index

nomenclature, 64–5, 89, 111–12, 112*i*, 207
number in institutions before deinstitutionalisation, 257
as 'perpetual children,' 124–5
public attitudes towards, 27, 29, 74, 124–5, 212, 214–17, 280, 282
as residents in aged care, 285
rights protection, 226–7
royal commission into violence, abuse, neglect and exploitation of, 280
self-advocacy, 280
social inclusion, 282
sterilisation, 64, 65, 93–4
as witnesses, 81–2
See also children with intellectual disabilities; families of children with intellectual disabilities
Pickells, W.E., 42
Pierce, Gil, 222–3
Pike, Bronwyn, 260
Pittock, David, 44
Pleasant Creek Special School, Stawell, 110, 111, 116, 146, 175
Pleasant Creek Training Centre, Stawell, 208, 210, 228, 255
Plenty Residential Services, 260
Porteus, Stanley, 100
Posner, Joseph, 21
Posner, Rachel, 21
Power, Beryl, 194, 198–9
Prendergast government, 89
Pruer, Miss (Matron), 140*i*
Psychological Society of Melbourne, 47–8
Public Service Act, 145
Public Works Act, 145, 156
Public Works Department, 13, 17, 45, 117, 142, 154, 156–7, 164, 177

Quinton, F.R., 109

Radler, Gary, 273
Raymond, Joseph, 234
Regan, John, 44

Returned Services League, 126
Richardson, Frank, 169
Richmond, Joseph, 242
Riddiford, Robert F., 240
Rimmer, John, 226
Rimmer Report, 226
Rivett, Rohan, 121–2
Rodgers, Patty, 277
Rowe, Edward 'Ted,' 86, 95–103, 96*i*, 98*i*, 115
royal commissions
into asylums, 14–15, 57
Ellery royal commission, 72–84, 86, 88, 283
into violence, abuse, neglect and exploitation of people with disability, 280, 283–4, 286
Zox royal commission, 14–15, 57, 283
Royal Albert Asylum for Idiots and Imbeciles, Lancashire, 12, 37
Royal Park Children's Depot, 95
Ryan, Dr, 90–1

Sackville, Ronald, 283
Salt, Donald John Herbert, 171, 172–5
Salt, Elizabeth, 171, 173
Sandhurst Boys' Home, Bendigo, 208–9, 228
Schmidt, Karl, 31, 32
Schmidt, Mary, 31
sexual segregation, 101
sexuality
relationships between residents, 101
surveillance of residents to control 'sexual vices,' 38, 51
sexually transmitted diseases, 87
Shuttleworth, George (Dr), 37
Silke, Elizabeth, 242
Slow Learning Children's Group, WA, 190
Society for Mental Defectives Colony Association, 88
Society for the Welfare of the Mentally Afflicted, 115
Spicer, P.O., 182

INDEX

Springthorpe, J.W. (Dr), 6–7, 57, 70, 103, 118
St Aiden's school, Moonee Ponds, 25
St Gabriel's Training Centre, Balwyn, 228
St Nicholas Hospital, Carlton, 210, 225, 241, 251–4
Stanford, Henry, 49
STAR Victoria, 220
Steven, E.M. (Dr), 64
Stoller, Alan (Dr), 210, 223
Stone, Kevin, 237–8
Stott, Joseph, 23
Sullivan, Annie, 21
Sunbury Hospital for the Insane, 59, 84
Sunbury Lunatic Asylum, 6, 54, 287
Sunbury Mental Hospital, 146, 151, 228
Sunbury Mental Hospital/Training Centre, 207–8, 228–9
Sutherland, Alexander, 48, 51, 53
Sutton, Harvey, 63–4
Symons, Vic, 241

Tate, Frank, 67, 89
Temby, Allan, 201
Temby, Ethel, 191–2, 201, 202, 220–1, 222, 223
Thomas, Donald, 115
Thomas, Julian (the Vagabond), 12–13
Thomas, Mrs M., 115
Thompson, Mrs, 29–30
Thompson, William, 29–30
Thomson, Catherine Hay, 26–7
Thomson, Louisa, 101
Tipping, Edmond William (Bill), 161*i*
   admission of son to Kew Cottages, 174
   article on renovations at Kew Cottages, 177–8
   background, 160–2
   friendship with Dax, 160
   on *Herald* Appeal for Kew Cottages, 170
   story of 'Michael,' 162, 163, 165–8, 171

Tipping, Marjorie, 160, 174
Tipping, Peter, 174
Tipping Appeal, 162, 168–70, 177
Trainor, Mrs, 24
Travancore Clinic, Flemington, 111–12, 206
Travancore Special School, Flemington
   administration, 111
   capacity, 108
   conditions, 146
   diagnostic clinic, 205–6
   establishment, 89
   expansion, 110, 175
   local opposition to, 90
   modernisation, 116
   opening of, 95, 103
   overcrowding, 109
   purpose, 90, 205–6
   resident numbers, 206
Travers, Frank, 23
Trescowthick, Don, 222
Trower, Eric, 243
Trower, Rosalie, 241–2, 243, 244, 247, 248–9, 259
Trower, Steven, 243
Tunnecliffe, Thomas, 72, 90, 93

United Kingdom, institutions to care and train children with intellectual disabilities, 11, 26–7, 32
United Nations Convention on the Rights of Persons with Disabilities, 286
United Nations Declaration of the Rights of the Child, 201
United Nations Declaration on the Rights of Mentally Retarded Persons, 217, 280
United States, involuntary sterilisation, 94

Victoria
   campaigns to control 'mentally defective' during interwar years, 87–95, 109–10

institutions for people with intellectual disabilities. *See* institutions for those with intellectual disabilities: Victoria

political instability during interwar years, 86, 88–9, 94

prevalence of insanity late nineteenth century, 6–8

prevalence of mental deficiency in 1913, 64–5

public health facilities 1952–1962, 175

Victorian Advocacy League for Individuals with Disability (VALID), 237, 239

Victorian Committee on Mental Retardation, 220–5

Victorian Council of Social Services, 246

Victorian Disability Act 2006, 281

Victorian Farmers Union, Women's Section, 88

Victorian Federation of Mothers Clubs, 94, 109

Victorian Golden Jubilee Exhibition, Bendigo, 48

Vigor, Mrs, 24

Wade, Jan, 246

Walker, Lang, 274, 275

Walker Corporation, 270

Wallace, Jude, 239

Walters, Alfred, 49–50

Warner, Denis, 125–6, 141

Warrnambool Industrial Art Exhibition, 48

Warrnambool Training Centre, 209

Welchman, David, 242–3

Welchman, Elsie, 242–3

Welchman, Geoff, 237, 242–3, 245, 247, 248, 249

Westgarth, Bill, 202–3

Westgarth, Joan, 180

White, Osmar, 139–41, 168

William Booth Men's Home, Melbourne, 235

Williams, John F., 126

Willsmere Hospital (formerly Kew Mental Hospital), 254

Wilson, Helen, 242

Wilson, Myrtle, 21

Wolfensberger, Wolf, 219

women

as carers for family members with disabilities, 22–23

confined at Kew Cottages, 122, 122*i*

distress at confinement seen as sign of mental disorder, 5

exclusion from committee of inquiry, 127

exclusion from positions of power in mental health services, 134

Women Citizens' Movement, 94

Woolley, Mrs, 22

World War I, 61

World War II, 113, 117, 120

Yarra Bend Asylum

children with intellectual disabilities, 4–5, 12–13, 26–7

establishment, 3

location, 4*i*, 8*i*

management, 5–6

overcrowding, 5, 6

patient numbers, 3–4

Yarra Bend Hospital for the Insane, 59

closure, 103

patient numbers, 61

plans for closure, 60–1

Yorath, Edith, 51

Zox, Ephraim, 6, 14

Zox royal commission into asylums, 14–15, 57, 238

Zwar, Albert, 94

About the Authors

Dr Lee-Ann Monk is a historian and researcher with interests in the histories of mental health, disability and work. Her research into the history of intellectual disabilities has been published in articles and book chapters internationally. She is Adjunct Research Fellow in the Department of Archaeology and History at La Trobe University.

Dr David Henderson is a historian who was a researcher in the Living with Disability Research Centre at La Trobe University for eight years. He now works as a researcher in the disability area of the Victorian Department of Families, Fairness and Housing.

Christine Bigby is Professor and Director of Postgraduate Programs in the School of Social Work and Social Policy at La Trobe University.

Richard Broome, AM, FAHA is an Australian historian, academic and Emeritus Professor of History at La Trobe.

Katie Holmes FASSA is Professor of History at La Trobe University.

CPSIA information can be obtained
at www.ICGtesting.com
Printed in the USA
JSHW041922240523
42205JS00001B/10